The Anti-King(dom)

Not Just a King, But a Kingdom

THE ANTI-KING(DOM)
by D. E. Isom
First Edition, November 2017

Walk with the Word
P.O. Box 9265
Redlands, CA 92375
Website: WalkWithTheWord.org
Email: Servant@WalkWithTheWord.org

Other books by the author:
And THEN The End Will Come
Elijah to Come
The Walk with the Word Ecclesiastes Study Guide
The Walk with the Word Psalm 119 Study Guide

ISBN-13: 978-1979724005
ISBN-10: 1979724008

Table of Contents

Preface i

Introduction v
The Original Precedent vi
A New Testament Affirmation viii
The Foundation of the Word ix
Not Just Theology, But Eschatology xi

Part One: The Old Testament Foundation 1

1 • Daniel 2: The Ten Toes 3
The Context in Daniel 5
The Plain Meaning 6
The Final Kingdom 10

2 • Daniel 7: The Fourth Kingdom ... 13
The First Vision 14
The Fourth Beast 18
The Divine Kingdom 23
Many Parallels Already 25

3 • Daniel 8: The Small Horn 27
The Vision Explained 29
"The Indignation" 29
The Ram 31
The Goat 32
The Small Horn 33
More for Our Checklist 40

4 • Daniel 9: The Weeks of Years 43
Prayer & Eschatology 44
A Personal Agenda 49
The Timing of the King & Anti-King ... 51
A Final Caveat 61
In Conclusion 64

5 • Daniel 10-12: The Latter Days Milieu 67
Not the Same as Previous Experiences 69
The Sequence of the End 74

6 • Daniel 10-12: The Latter Days Forerunner 81
Lessons from Epiphanes 85
The Example of Epiphanes 91

7 • Daniel 10-12: The Latter Days Final Figure 93
A Time Limit 93
The Final Anti-King to Come 100
The Final Anti-Kingdom to Come 101

8 • Daniel 10-12: The Latter Days Focus 105
The Final Stretch 109
A Personal Commentary 113

9 • The Early Portrait 117
1st Century Understanding 117
The Historical Record 120
The Scriptural Portrait of the Anti-King 121
The Scriptural Portrait of the Anti-Kingdom 125
To Sum Up 125

Part Two: The New Testament Continuation 127

10 • The Early Church's Understanding 129
The Earliest Eschatology 131
The Olivet Discourse & the Book of Daniel 134
The Standard in the First Coming 138

11 • Paul & the Thessalonians 141
The Thessalonian Problem 141
A Dual Working 142
The Day of the Lord 144
A Reversal of the Order 145
A Confirmation of Attributes 147
Yet Another Parallel 148

The Didache....................................148

12 • John & the Early Church........151
Many Antichrists Already................151
"Lawlessness" & "Perdition" 152
It is the Last Hour............................154
An Important Type...........................155
The Spirit of Antichrist....................156
The Error of the Literal 158
A Change in Perspective 158
The New Testament Before Revelation..................................159

13 • The Last Vision......................161
The Combined, Global View 162
The Same Focused View 163
The Same Kind of Beginning............167

14 • The Three Woes 169
The Preface of the Seals 169
The First Four Trumpets..................171
What is a "Woe"? 172
Three Milestones.............................173

15 • Revelation 12: The Dragon 177
The Satanic Resume.........................178
Lessons from the Red Dragon..........182
The Satanic Agenda 191

16 • Revelation 13: The Beast from the Sea 193
The Beast from the Sea 196
Characteristics of the First Beast 202

17 • Revelation 13: The Beast from the Land 205
An Exclusive Agent...........................206
A Master Manipulator 207
A Supernatural Image of Worship ...208
The Mark 209
Summary 212

18 • Revelation 17: Babylon the Great.......................................215
Choosing Whom to Worship............215
The Importance of Babylon 218
The Mother of Harlots.....................219
The Beast Revisited.........................220
"Those Who Dwell on the Earth" 224
"The Great Harlot" 225
A Final Treachery 227

19 • Revelation 18: "Fallen, Fallen is Babylon the Great!" 229
Who is the Woman?........................232
Sins as High as Heaven 233
The Laments of the Kings & the Merchants of the Earth..............235
The Angel & the Stone.....................238
Summary 241

20 • The Total Scriptural Picture ...245
Different Aspects of the Same Thing..246
The Primary New Testament Anti-King 249
The Primary New Testament Anti-Kingdom.............................250
Other Types to Study 253
The Anti-King 254
The Second Beast: The False Prophet......................................259
The Anti-Kingdom 259
Babylon the Great............................261
A Closing Thought............................262

21 • Roles & Goals........................265

Appendix A: When Change Is Expressly Forbidden.............273
A Cut-and-Paste Hermeneutic 274
When It Becomes a Double Switch-A-Roo 276
Promoting a Single Eschatology.......277
The Sequence Becomes the Issue ...279
A Switch-A-Roo within a Switch-A-Roo 280
Historical Proof-Texting....................281
Not Just the English, But the Greek 282
Different Individuals but a Common Goal 284

Index 287

Preface

By no means can this book in the least be considered a completely original work. There will be unavoidable, and even purposeful, reuse of material presented in *Shadows of the Beast* by Jacob Prasch of Moriel Ministries. (www.Moriel.org) I cannot overstate my recommendation that his book be added to every Christian's personal library and designated essential reading.

This is unavoidable because I worked hand-in-hand with Jacob over the course of just over three years to produce that book. The process consisted of Jacob dictating every word to me from beginning to end, after which I would copy-edit the material and provide research as needed as issues arose from each session. Although not previously presented in such an organized format, the book drew heavily on nearly two dozen sermons Jacob repeatedly taught over the previous twenty or so years, all of which I also transcribed in preparation for the book. So I hope this explains the borderline plagiarism at times, but with all due acknowledgment of Jacob's work, it is impossible for me to talk or write on this subject, even in the most casual of settings, without drawing on *Shadows of the Beast*. If imitation is the sincerest form of flattery, then I may have finally made Jacob blush.

While revisiting that book in detail in preparation for the possibility of producing an updated second edition, in tandem with my continued personal study of the topic of the Antichrist, something happened again which I've experienced from time to time in my Christian life. In spite of a lifelong study of God's Word, in spite of an above average interest in all things eschatological, and in spite of the years of typing, re-typing and providing research and feedback for Jacob's book, I once again found myself staring at something in Scripture which I've obviously read countless times but suddenly grabbed my attention to the point of obsession. I would like to think that this takes place from time to time according to the timing and guidance of the Holy Spirit, but it seems unavoidable to feel more than a bit humbled, if not a little foolish, to read something which has been there all along without previously realizing its full importance.

We are all familiar with Revelation 13:18. Actually, it is one of the snippets of Scripture which not only the whole world is keenly aware, but even the Hollywood movie and television machine:

> ***<u>Here is wisdom</u>****. Let him who has understanding calculate the number of the beast, for the number is that of a man; and his number is six hundred and sixty-six.*
> — Revelation 13:18

Jacob does an excellent job of explaining that, biblically speaking, ***Christ*** is our wisdom (1 Co. 1:30; Col. 3:16), and this is addressing the fact that this man's identity cannot be discerned apart from Christ. (This explains a great deal as to why unbelievers will follow him even in spite of the world's common knowledge of "666".)

As a Bible teacher, I learned a long time ago that there is a difference between ***reading*** Scripture and ***studying*** Scripture, and it is when I engage in the latter when such epiphanies have occurred. When you undertake the process of writing about that which you're studying, it brings into play a scrutinization of Scripture which simply does not take place when just reviewing it. And so while engaging in a detailed, written study of the topic of Babylon, I was transfixed on the similarity to Revelation 13:18 above with that which is recorded in Revelation 17:

> *9"**Here is the mind which has wisdom**. The seven heads are seven mountains on which the woman sits, 10and they are seven kings; five have fallen, one is, the other has not yet come; and when he comes, he must remain a little while. 11The beast which was and is not, is himself also an eighth and is one of the seven, and he goes to destruction.*
>
> — Revelation 17:9-11

Yes, it is still talking about a man whom Scripture often calls "*the beast*", but in the overall context of Revelation 17-18, and all the supporting Scriptures referencing "*mountains*", it became clear that this and many more supporting passages *also* describe the Antichrist as a ***kingdom***. The wisdom of Christ necessary to discern him as an individual king is equally necessary in order to recognize his identity as a kingdom. We regularly engage in study and discussions of this figure as some kind of ruler, but rarely as the embodiment of an empire. We tend to discuss his kingdom as something detached and separate from him, when in fact every kingdom and empire in history is a direct reflection of their ruler(s).

If we consider this concept in its scriptural context, we will come to understand how this is actually the ultimate and total counterfeit of Christ. If we study the definition Jesus Himself taught as the meaning of a kingdom, especially examining what are popularly called "The Kingdom Parables" in Matthew 13, it does not take long to understand that He uses "kingdom" to mean something composed of people. Christ is the Head, and both as individual members, and collectively as a whole, we are changing into the image and likeness of Him. His kingdom is comprised of those who both on their own, and as part of the whole, reflect His character, qualities and behavior. Like a life-long married couple, in the end they begin to look like each other.

The Antichrist, in an obsessive pursuit of being the ultimate counterfeit of all things Christ, is likewise reflected in the membership of his kingdom, albeit to the opposite extreme. Just as the Church is the reflection of Christ the Lamb, Babylon the Great is a satanic mirror of the Beast. This is particularly apparent in the Greek Septuagint as a clean animal suitable for lawful sacrifices such as a lamb is identified as "*zoa*", (Strong's #2226) but an unclean animal and the term "*beast*" itself is "*therion*". (Strong's #2342) One makes His kingdom suitable for eternity with the Godhead, the other a kingdom destined for eternity in the Lake of Fire, each eventually looking respectively like each other.

The bottom line where this book is concerned is that I've come to realize that focusing on just the "*son of perdition*" is only the scriptural beginning; it needs to be followed through with the rest of the picture provided concerning his kingdom's character which is inevitably leading all of its members to that same fate of destruction, providing a visible reflection of him. Antichrist is not just in the business of replacing Christ the Head, he desires to replace the whole Body as well.

Just as there has been near endless speculation, not just today but for the entire history of the Church, as to the identity of this figure as a man, there has only been casual discussion of his respective kingdom and its working. At present we mostly seem to be laboring under the notion that it is some variation of the literal European Union due to that being presented in Hal Lindsey's seminal work, *The Late, Great Planet Earth* and carried forth in many variations to the present. Just as all the biblical and historical examples of Antichrist the man are required for us to even begin to form a proper silhouette of the final figure, so an equal effort needs to be put into the kingdoms associated with each. There is actually a scriptural mandate that through Christ we understand ***both***.

At present, we are not just witnessing the formation of a worldwide environment preparing for the public rise of the ultimate *therion*, but the final kingdom by which its citizens reflect everything about him. And just as John the Baptist initiated the preparation of God's people for the kingdom corresponding to the imminent arrival of the Messiah, so a satanic counterfeit is not just predicted in Scripture, but taking place in the presence of our present generation. We need the wisdom of Christ to not simply recognize both the man and his kingdom, but to know what to do about it, not just when it arrives, but as it was in the First Coming, taking the proper steps of spiritual preparation as soon as possible.

Introduction

*[18]**Here is wisdom**. Let him who has understanding calculate the number of the beast, for the number is that of a man; and his number is six hundred and sixty-six.*
— Revelation 13:18

*[24]but to those who are the called, both Jews and Greeks, **Christ** the power of God and **the wisdom of God**...[30]But by His doing you are in Christ Jesus, **who became to us wisdom from God**, and righteousness and sanctification, and redemption,*
— 1 Corinthians 1:24, 30

The best interpreter of Scripture is Scripture because, among other things, God's definition and meaning of words is contrary to those of the world's. When we became born again, Holy Spirit-filled believers in Christ, the role of God's Word became critical as a tool of re-education. That which the world calls "love" or "faith" or even "good" is misleading in contrast to God's intended meaning. The god of this world has put enormous effort into perverting the vocabulary of every language so that it either subtly alters, or outright replaces, the actual substance as employed in God's Word.

So when the world reads Revelation 13:18, they think "*wisdom*" is brain power or perhaps cleverness bordering on the genius, something achievable by human intellect or willpower. In scriptural terms, however, biblical "*wisdom*" is not possible apart from Christ. Paul explains in 1 Corinthians 1:18-29 that "*the word of the cross is foolishness to those who are perishing*", and that according to their standards, "*God has chosen the foolish things of the world to shame the things which are strong...so that no man may boast before God.*" The fact that just as Christ Himself is the whole Word of God (Jn. 1:1), He is the only source of Wisdom by which it can be truly and clearly understood.

While this is true for the whole of God's Word for every aspect of doctrine and theology, there is no exception when it comes to eschatology. In spite of all the book, television and movie plots attempting to exploit the mark of the beast, in spite of instilling in advance a fear of the consequences of bearing that brand, hundreds of millions, if not billions, will take it anyway. Without Christ, whatever wisdom endowed by the world will ultimately work for its foolishness.

The Original Precedent

A stunning example of this is provided in the very first vision in the opening chapters of Daniel, a foundational beginning for all things eschatological. When Jesus references him in the Olivet Discourse, He provides the caveat, "*Let the **reader** understand*". (Mt. 24:15) Not "the listener", but "*the **reader***". It is a personal appeal from Christ to study the whole of Daniel. And in the first vision given to the most powerful earthly king at the time, there is a very important lesson established from the outset concerning the requirement that it is only the wisdom of Christ which can explain such things.

> [1]*Now in the second year of the reign of Nebuchadnezzar, Nebuchadnezzar had dreams; and his spirit was troubled and his sleep left him.* [2]*Then the king gave orders to call in the magicians, the conjurers, the sorcerers and the Chaldeans to tell the king his dreams. So they came in and stood before the king.* [3]*The king said to them, "**I had a dream and my spirit is anxious to understand the dream.**"*
> — Daniel 2:1-3

Nebuchadnezzar has seen and yet does not understand. Just like all unbelievers who attempt to process God's Word, they will never know what it actually means. It always requires illumination from God.

> [4]*Then the Chaldeans spoke to the king in Aramaic: "O king, live forever! Tell the dream to your servants, and we will declare the interpretation."*
> [5]*The king replied to the Chaldeans, "The command from me is firm: if you do not make known to me the dream and its interpretation, you will be torn limb from limb and your houses will be made a rubbish heap.* [6]*But if you declare the dream and its interpretation, you will receive from me gifts and a reward and great honor; therefore declare to me the dream and its interpretation."*
> [7]*They answered a second time and said, "Let the king tell the dream to his servants, and we will declare the interpretation."*
> [8]*The king replied, "I know for certain that you are bargaining for time, inasmuch as you have seen that the command from me is firm,* [9]*that if you do not make the dream known to me, there is only one decree for you. For you have agreed together to speak lying and corrupt words before me until the situation is changed; therefore tell me the dream, that I may know that you can declare to me its interpretation."*
> [10]*The Chaldeans answered the king and said, "There is not a man on earth who could declare the matter for the king, inasmuch as no great king or ruler has ever asked anything like this of any magician, conjurer or Chaldean.* [11]*Moreover, the thing which the king demands is difficult, and **there is no one else who could declare it to the king except gods, whose dwelling place is not with mortal flesh**."*
> — Daniel 2:4-11

There is something extraordinary in Nebuchadnezzar's character in that he seems to know the true nature of "*the magicians, the conjurers, the sorcerers and the Chaldeans*". (Much like today, when non-believers easily see through the televangelists, but too many believers do not.) More remarkable still is that they actually know the truth that such could only be accomplished by "*gods, whose dwelling place is not with mortal flesh*" and that "*not a man on earth*" possesses this ability. They confirm what the king knew to be true, that earthly wisdom alone was incapable of providing the answer.

> *[12]Because of this the king became indignant and very furious and gave orders to destroy all the wise men of Babylon. [13]So the decree went forth that the wise men should be slain; and they looked for Daniel and his friends to kill them.*
> *[14]Then Daniel replied with discretion and discernment to Arioch, the captain of the king's bodyguard, who had gone forth to slay the wise men of Babylon; [15]he said to Arioch, the king's commander, "For what reason is the decree from the king so urgent?" Then Arioch informed Daniel about the matter. [16]So Daniel went in and requested of the king that he would give him time, in order that he might declare the interpretation to the king.*
> — Daniel 2:12-16

The fact that Daniel did not immediately have the answer either cannot be overstated. It is crucial for us to understand what Daniel did to obtain the answer in stark contrast to all those who could not. The unbelievers had no source to go to; the believers had ***the*** Source.

> *[17]Then Daniel went to his house and informed his friends, Hananiah, Mishael and Azariah, about the matter, [18]so* ***that they might request compassion from the God of heaven concerning this mystery****, so that Daniel and his friends would not be destroyed with the rest of the wise men of Babylon. [19]Then the mystery was revealed to Daniel in a night vision.*
> — Daniel 2:17-19a

The English word "*request*" used in verse 18 is not limited in meaning to "seek" or "ask", but is also found in Scripture as "pray" and "make petition". In other words, it describes someone not merely asking God for the answer, but having the kind of spiritual relationship wherein an attitude of prayerful submission takes place. This is evidenced by the verses following, where upon being given the answer, Daniel's first response is to praise and acknowledge God as the Source.

> *[20]Daniel said,*
> *"Let the name of God be blessed forever and ever,*
> *For* ***wisdom*** *and power* ***belong to Him****.*
> *[21]It is He who changes the times and the epochs;*
> *He removes kings and establishes kings;*
> ***He gives wisdom*** *to wise men*
> ***And knowledge*** *to men of understanding.*
> *[22]It is He who* ***reveals the profound and hidden things****;*
> *He* ***knows what is in the darkness,***
> *And* ***the light dwells with Him****.*
> *[23]To You, O God of my fathers, I give thanks and praise,*
> *For* ***You have given me wisdom*** *and power;*
> *Even now* ***You have made known to me*** *what we requested of You,*
> *For* ***You have made known to us*** *the king's matter."*
> — Daniel 2:20-23

Twice in these verses "*wisdom*" is attributed solely to the domain of God and supported with the attribution of "*wisdom to wise men*" and "*knowledge to men of understanding*", so that only He "*reveals the profound and hidden things*". Daniel categorically states, "*For You have made known to us the king's matter*". There is no getting around that only the Author of God's Word can provide the meaning of God's Word, and that biblical wisdom is impossible apart from a personal relationship with Him.

> [26]*The king said to Daniel, whose name was Belteshazzar, "Are you able to make known to me the dream which I have seen and its interpretation?"*
> [27]*Daniel answered before the king and said, "As for the mystery about which the king has inquired, neither wise men, conjurers, magicians nor diviners are able to declare it to the king.* [28]*However,* ***there is a God in heaven who reveals mysteries, and He has made known*** *to King Nebuchadnezzar* ***what will take place in the latter days****. This was your dream and the visions in your mind while on your bed.*
> [29]*"As for you, O king, while on your bed your thoughts turned to what would take place in the future; and* ***He who reveals mysteries has made known to you what will take place****.* [30]*But* ***as for me, this mystery has not been revealed to me for any wisdom residing in me more than in any other living man, but for the purpose of making the interpretation known to the king, and that you may understand the thoughts of your mind****.*
> — Daniel 2:26-30

Daniel actually confirms the opening assertion of the king's wise men that such a mystery can only be explained by divine intervention. But having experienced a direct revelation from God, Daniel also makes sure that Nebuchadnezzar knows "*this mystery has not been revealed to me for any wisdom residing in me*". The wisdom of God came about by His acting through those possessing a faith-based relationship with Him. The importance of this cannot be over-emphasized.

A New Testament Affirmation

Peter provides an additional affirmation that God's prophetic Word is most certainly within reach of the believer.

> [19]*So* ***we have the prophetic word made more sure****, to which you do well to pay attention as to* ***a lamp shining in a dark place****, until the day dawns and the morning star arises in your hearts.* [20]*But know this first of all, that no prophecy of Scripture is a matter of one's own interpretation,* [21]*for no prophecy was ever made by an act of human will, but men moved by the Holy Spirit spoke from God.*
> — 2 Peter 1:19-21

A common misconception, and in some cases presented as an outright lie, is the notion, "No one can know for sure". This is completely contrary to Peter's assertion that for New Testament believers, it is "*made* ***more*** *sure*".

This false assumption seems to have its root in the fact that there is one thing for which Christ inarguably states this is the case—the precise date of the Rapture of the Church, about which that single milestone of the End Times He plainly states, "*But of that day and hour no one knows*". (Mt. 24:36) It's almost as if, like pouting little toddlers, we stomp around our room whining, "Well, if we can't know ***that*** thing, then I guess we just can't know ***any*** of it!"

Never mind that in the parallel accounts of the Olivet Discourse in Matthew, Mark and Luke that Jesus is recorded fourteen times as warning to be alert, to not be deceived, and to recognize the fulfillment of all He has stipulated so as to be ready for that impossible-to-predict event. The willfully deceitful and woefully ignorant intone, "No one knows" so often that we begin to believe it, contrary to the plain teaching of Peter's statement and the rest of God's supporting Word.

As Peter points out, it is the Holy Spirit who spoke God's prophetic Word into existence, and it is only Holy Spirit-filled believers through whom the meaning is understood. Without faith in Christ through which the Holy Spirit is imparted, such things cannot be understood. But the notion that believers just cannot know ***any*** of it so it's all just a matter of opinion?

Daniel was a pretty smart cookie even by the world's standards, but it was not something he was born with or acquired by worldly means or experience along the way. Perhaps we need to remind ourselves that being "born again" so as to become a new creation in Christ means something has been imparted to us which we would otherwise have never obtained. This is why the Word was given so as to no longer "*be conformed to this world, but be transformed by the renewing of your mind*". (Rom. 12:2)

The Foundation of the Word

That which Daniel and his companions accomplished at this juncture was actually the result of what took place in the opening chapter of Daniel.

> [3]*Then the king ordered Ashpenaz, the chief of his officials, to bring in some of the sons of Israel, including some of the royal family and of the nobles, [4]youths in whom was no defect, who were good-looking, showing intelligence in every branch of wisdom, endowed with understanding and discerning knowledge, and who had ability for serving in the king's court; and he ordered him to teach them the literature and language of the Chaldeans...[6]Now among them from the sons of Judah were Daniel, Hananiah, Mishael and Azariah.*
> — Daniel 1:3-4, 6

Nebuchadnezzar valued not just raw "*intelligence*", but the ability to know what to do with it as here expounded by "*wisdom, endowed with understanding and discerning knowledge*". Not content with what in our time we might term "raw computing power", he desired the kind of software which made the most effective use of the data so as to properly interpret and apply it. Nebuchadnezzar was more interested in the practical results.

Daniel and his companions were among many who, from their worldly evaluation, met the minimum requirements. The text does not tell us the total number of qualified candidates, but it does reveal that which would distinguish them from all the others.

> [8]*But **Daniel made up his mind that he would not defile himself** with the king's choice food or with the wine which he drank; so he sought permission from the commander of the officials that he might not defile himself.*
> — Daniel 1:8

It really had nothing to do whatsoever with being smarter than the rest or more talented. The difference which became visibly evident to even outside observers which would elevate them to the top was their ***behavior***. Daniel maintained the greater spiritual priority "*that he might not defile himself*", and in this specific context of an Old Testament believer, recognized that this was not simply a dietary issue, but a test of whether or not they would continue to be obedient to God's Word above everything else. It had to do with not compromising his faith.

Throughout Scripture, food and eating are repeatedly used as metaphors for putting God's Word into practice. And in a spiritual twist on the worldly observation, "You are what you eat", our faith is defined by how we both handle and disseminate the Word.

> *[3]"He humbled you and let you be hungry, and fed you with manna which you did not know, nor did your fathers know, that He might make you understand that man does not live by bread alone, but man lives by everything that proceeds out of the mouth of the LORD.*
>
> — Deuteronomy 8:3

> *[45]"Who then is the faithful and sensible slave whom his master put in charge of his household to give them their food at the proper time? [46]Blessed is that slave whom his master finds so doing when he comes.*
>
> — Matthew 24:45-46

> *[15]"If you love Me, you will keep My commandments.*
>
> — John 14:15

> *[10]"If you keep My commandments, you will abide in My love; just as I have kept My Father's commandments and abide in His love.*
>
> — John 15:10

The issue came down to a test. For Daniel and company, it was most certainly a spiritual test where God's Word was concerned.

> *[12]"Please test your servants for ten days, and let us be given some vegetables to eat and water to drink. [13]Then let our appearance be observed in your presence and the appearance of the youths who are eating the king's choice food; and deal with your servants according to what you see."*
>
> *[14]So he listened to them in this matter and tested them for ten days. [15]At the end of ten days their appearance seemed better and they were fatter than all the youths who had been eating the king's choice food. [16]So the overseer continued to withhold their choice food and the wine they were to drink, and kept giving them vegetables.*
>
> — Daniel 1:12-16

According to the text these above average candidates met and even exceeded the worldly expectations of the king's staff, but the real story here is what resulted from their passing the test where God's Word was concerned.

> *[17]As for these four youths, **God gave them** knowledge and intelligence in every branch of literature and wisdom; Daniel even understood all kinds of visions and dreams.*
>
> *[18]Then at the end of the days which the king had specified for presenting them, the commander of the officials presented them before Nebuchadnezzar. [19]The king talked with them, and out of them all not one was found like Daniel, Hananiah, Mishael and Azariah; so they entered the king's personal service. [20]As for every matter of wisdom and understanding about which the king consulted them, he found them ten times better than all the magicians and conjurers who were in all his realm.*
>
> — Daniel 1:17-20

The qualities the world so greatly valued did not come about through its system of education or the inherent abilities of these particular individuals. They were set apart and attained superior wisdom in the course of their personal faithfulness to God's Word and ways. God's definition of wisdom comes as the result of a practicing faith, which goes a long way toward explaining why the citizens of the world cannot and never will possess it.

Not Just Theology, But Eschatology

Just as the opening chapters of Daniel begin with tests to illustrate the connection between the true wisdom of God and faithfulness to His Word, so it is visited again to close out the book.

> 3*"Those who have **insight** will shine brightly like the brightness of the expanse of heaven, and those who lead the many to **righteousness**, like the stars forever and ever.*
>
> — Daniel 12:3

As is found in many places in Scripture, wisdom and understanding by God's standard is inseparable from righteousness, a quality which only exists in the presence of a lifestyle of obedience to God's Word. To ensure our understanding of this, Daniel in the same chapter documents the opposite condition.

> 10*"Many will be purged, purified and refined, but the wicked will act wickedly; and **none of the wicked will understand**, but **those who have insight will understand**.*
>
> — Daniel 12:10

One cannot "*lead the many to righteousness*" except by the personal example resulting from a life of obedience to God's Word and ways. But to ensure there is no misunderstanding where this spiritual priority is concerned, the absence of adherence to His Word results in a lack of understanding commensurate with the resulting spiritual condition. Wisdom, where God's Word is concerned, cannot be isolated from the issue of personal faithfulness.

> 18***Here is wisdom**. Let him who has understanding calculate the number of the beast, for the number is that of a man; and his number is six hundred and sixty-six.*
>
> — Revelation 13:18

Who knows the total number of books, articles, sermons and even entire websites which have been devoted to the proclamation of those who claim to have in some way "figured it out". (At the time of this writing, last year "they" were all predicting the end with what they called the "Blood Moons"; this year it was an obsession with a particular celestial alignment on September 23rd. Any bets on what it will be next year?) However, the solution is not actually a worldly pursuit by its standards of knowledge and wisdom, but a personal spiritual quest where the personal application of Scripture is concerned. No, in the context of the whole counsel of God's Word on the subject, it is only those with the wisdom derived from a personal, obedient relationship with Christ who are going to bridge the knowledge gap, much in the same way it likewise occurred for Daniel and his companions in their time, and according to God's timing.

The Other Side of the Coin

When it comes to the specific issue of eschatology and in particular as it concerns the topic of the Antichrist, however, we may have over-focused on this important detail concerning the mark to the detriment of something equally critical where this figure is concerned.

> 9*"**Here is the mind which has wisdom**. The seven heads are seven mountains on which the woman sits, 10and they are seven kings; five have fallen, one is, the other has not yet come; and when he comes, he must remain a little while.*
>
> — Revelation 17:9-10

Whereas Revelation 13, like many passages in Scripture, primarily describe the Antichrist from the perspective of an individual, Revelation 17-18 provide a parallel description of him as a ***kingdom***. The biblical mandate where this figure is concerned is actually a two-sided coin where it is just as important to recognize him as an individual man as well as the embodiment of a kingdom. As we shall see, both of these aspects are constantly presented in parallel throughout Scripture.

As elaborated in the *Preface* to this book, this actually makes sense, especially since the primary defining behavior of the Antichrist is to counterfeit Christ in every way possible. Biblically speaking, a "kingdom" is defined as the people who comprise it, and its citizenry becomes more and more like its ruler as it mimics his actions, attitudes and way of thinking and carry out his policies and directions. Just as we in the Body of Christ work to make ourselves individually, and the whole Bride of Christ collectively, more and more into the likeness of our Master by the exclusive working of His Word, so the followers of Antichrist mimic him. One brings us into eternal union with the Godhead, the other into eternal separation and damnation in the Lake of Fire. In the end, each is a direct reflection of the other.

For those who accept and practice His Word, this final series of events we collectively label as the Last Days is not as much of a mystery as many would like for us to believe. The truth for the practicing Christian is that everything God has provided in His Word will either be understood in advance or as it takes place and, as our Wisdom, it is only through Him that we comprehend the difference. But apart from Christ, ***nothing*** will be known until it is too late.

In the mean time, we have an assignment to carry out which involves not just a king, but a kingdom.

Part One:
The Old Testament Foundation

1 ❖ Daniel 2: The Ten Toes

[31]"You, O king, were looking and behold, there was a single great statue; that statue, which was large and of extraordinary splendor, was standing in front of you, and its appearance was awesome. [32]The head of that statue was made of fine gold, its breast and its arms of silver, its belly and its thighs of bronze, [33]its legs of iron, its feet partly of iron and partly of clay. [34]You continued looking until a stone was cut out without hands, and it struck the statue on its feet of iron and clay and crushed them. [35]Then the iron, the clay, the bronze, the silver and the gold were crushed all at the same time and became like chaff from the summer threshing floors; and the wind carried them away so that not a trace of them was found. But the stone that struck the statue became a great mountain and filled the whole earth.

— Daniel 2:31-35

In this first vision, given to an earthly king, the perspective provided shows how it looks from an earthly viewpoint; the parallel vision to this as given to Daniel in chapter 7 will show how these same things are viewed from the heavenly perspective. This is valuable in and of itself as a lesson in the difference between the world's viewpoint and God's.

In this case, the world is fixated on the eye candy: "*fine gold*", "*silver*", "*bronze*" and so forth packaged in an impressive looking monument. As we will later see in Daniel 7, God's prophet Daniel is shown the heavenly perspective from which God sees them in their true spiritual state as various beasts. But by purely earthly standards, they project an image that is "*awesome*" and "*of extraordinary splendor*" until something comes along to not just topple it, but "*crushed... like chaff...and the wind carried them away so that not a trace of them was found*". As with every empire, kingdom and nation-state in the history of history, such have their time and place before being replaced, and as is so often the case, ultimately disappearing from history completely. In this divine revelation, God unveils the entire remaining time line of human history and how it will ultimately conclude.

It must be noted that although there has been a tremendous amount of God's prophetic Word given by many prophets prior to Daniel, that we have to factor in the context both of what was stated through them before the Babylonian Captivity of Daniel's time, and now because of what is finally being revealed. We always have to consider what is relevant for each particular prophet's time and that which has a future fulfillment, paying special attention to the fact that there are often ***multiple*** fulfillments. In other words, that which God spoke through them originally may not only apply to events in that prophet's time or in their very immediate future, but that first historical fulfillment may additionally be recapitulated one or more times in the future. We did not know at the time such were given how they were addressing what would later be revealed in Daniel, being partially concealed in this respect. As with most things prophetic, later revelations often open our eyes to what we did not realize was there all along.

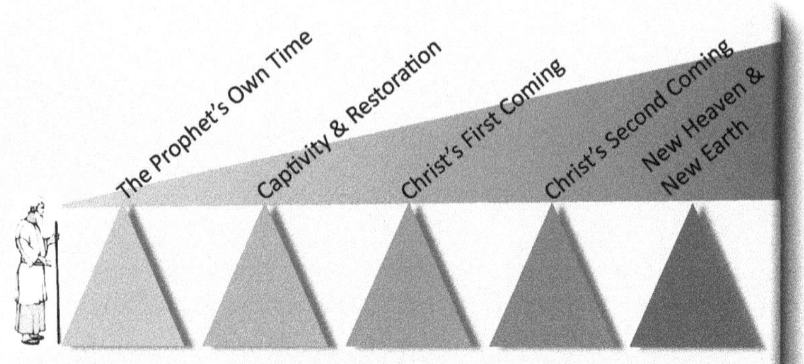

From one point of view, all the peaks appear to be lined up and look like a single mountain rather than different peaks separated by valleys of time. Determine for which time the prophecy is primarily speaking, & then whether there may be multiple recapitulations.

For instance, the Abomination of Desolation spoken of by Daniel occurred twice in the Inter-Testamental Period by Antiochus Epiphanes IV (163 BC) and the Roman General Pompey (63 BC). Yet both Christ and the Apostle Paul speak of it happening again. Not only have there been several fulfillments such as in the course of the destruction of Jerusalem in 70 AD and the Roman erection of a temple to Jupiter on the site of the Temple thereafter, but a number of similar subsequent historical recapitulations of this event. Each is a "shadow" or forerunner teaching us something about the final one yet to come by the ultimate figure of the Antichrist. God's prophetic Word may address multiple fulfillments beyond what is experienced at the time they are given through that particular prophet, resulting in more than just the literal, historical originally taking place.

The greater point for us where Daniel 2 is concerned is to be cognizant that the context of most prophecy prior to Daniel was primarily understood to either be current events in Israel during the life of that prophet, Israel's immediate future up to and including the Babylonian Captivity, or the Messiah, whether in what we now recognize as either His First or Second Coming. The vision in Daniel 2 is the first explicit timeline given by God to illuminate the total sequence of history remaining from the Babylonian Captivity until the Second Coming of Christ for the whole world. That we can return to those previously given Scriptures and find that they absolutely agree with what is given in Daniel testifies to their authorship by the Holy Spirit. But we are only able to understand the overall plan and assign Scripture to its proper place in this sequence because of this foundational revelation. This vision provides God's overall plan for the rest of history commencing ~587 BC until Christ's Millennial Reign still before us. Everything given before and after will adhere to and illuminate further this first, basic timeline, but this is the crucial starting point providing the basics.

The Context in Daniel

> [27]*Daniel answered before the king and said, "As for the mystery about which the king has inquired, neither wise men, conjurers, magicians nor diviners are able to declare it to the king.* [28]*However, there is a God in heaven who reveals mysteries, and He has made known to King Nebuchadnezzar **what will take place in the latter days**. This was your dream and the visions in your mind while on your bed.*
> — Daniel 2:27-28

It is important to note that the way this first vision became known provides a real-world example of an important divine statement in the closing chapter of Daniel which applies to the whole of God's prophetic Word:

> *"...and none of the wicked will understand, but those who have insight will understand.*
> — Daniel 12:10b

Something established in Daniel and affirmed by the rest of God's Word is that those who possess insight, wisdom and/or understanding are all defined as someone who is in a right relationship with the Lord, what today we would identify as a Holy Spirit-filled, Bible practicing Christian. This is who will "*have insight and understand*", as opposed to all those in a lifestyle of sin as describing the "*wicked*". It is a distinct contradiction to all those in the modern Church asserting that when it comes to eschatology, "No one really knows" and therefore no one can be dogmatic in their interpretation or position. Such proponents are separating something God's Word says cannot be disassociated, which is that those who are biblically faithful ***can*** and ***will*** understand the prophetic portions of God's Word.

The unambiguous and plain text leaves no doubt that it pertains to the end of history—"*the latter days*". Daniel, being a student of Scripture, (Dan. 9:2) would most certainly have been aware of that which had already been stated through Isaiah and Micah...

> [2]*Now it will come about that*
> ***In the last days***
> ***The mountain** of the house of the LORD*
> *Will be established **as the chief of the mountains**,*
> *And will be raised above the hills;*
> *And all the nations will stream to it.*
> — Isaiah 2:2

> [1]*And it will come about **in the last days***
> *That **the mountain** of the house of the LORD*
> *Will be established **as the chief of the mountains***
> *It will be raised above the hills,*
> *And the peoples will stream to it.*
> — Micah 4:1

An axiomatic principle of Bible interpretation is that while *everything* God has spoken in His Word is important, that which He repeats is *especially* so. He does this for our benefit and the importance of its connection to this first vision certainly would not have been lost on Daniel. (Keep this in a special place because the use of "mountains" is going to be further visited in future passages concerning the anti-king and his anti-kingdom, and it will be important to know that the meaning was revealed from the very beginning.)

But as New Testament believers, we would naturally be drawn to the words of Christ Himself...

> [42]*Jesus said to them, "Did you never read in the Scriptures,*
>
> *'THE STONE WHICH THE BUILDERS REJECTED,*
> *THIS BECAME THE CHIEF CORNER stone;*
> *THIS CAME ABOUT FROM THE LORD,*
> *AND IT IS MARVELOUS IN OUR EYES'?*
>
> [43]*"Therefore I say to you, the kingdom of God will be taken away from you and given to a people, producing the fruit of it.* [44]*and he who falls on this stone will be broken to pieces; but on whomever it falls, it will scatter him like dust."*
> — Matthew 21:42-44

The connection back to this vision is unavoidable not just in the parallel symbolism, but the accompanying explanation of the ultimate effect in both instances of being crushed and scattered. The bottom line contextually is that this vision is categorically assigned as a revelation of God's plan "*in the latter days*" and not limited to just something in Daniel's time.

The Plain Meaning

As with so many revelations in Scripture, the overall explanation itself is ***also*** provided in Scripture and often corroborated by one or more parallel references. In this case, the plain meaning is not only provided here, but will be affirmed in the explanation of the corollary vision in Daniel 7 to come.

> [36]*"This was the dream; now we will tell its interpretation before the king.* [37]*You, O king, are the king of kings, to whom the God of heaven has given the kingdom, the power, the strength and the glory;* [38]*and wherever the sons of men dwell, or the beasts of the field, or the birds of the sky, He has given them into your hand and has caused you to rule over them all.* ***You are the head of gold****.*
> — Daniel 2:36-38

And so it begins with the Babylonian Empire, at its height during Daniel's time. Represented not only as the head of the whole body but cast in gold, from a fleshly point of view, it will never get better than this where earthly empires are concerned. One of the ways we know that this is referring to the whole world and not exclusively to Israel is by the use of "*the sons of men*" in verse 38. This is a very semitic way of describing all of mankind and never used for Israel exclusively.

But don't rush past the last statement, "***You*** *are the head of gold*". This is proof that in God's Word, a king is ***both*** an individual and the embodiment, or personification, of his kingdom; they are inseparable. We will see that this is not just replayed in future scriptural discussions of the anti-king and his anti-kingdom, but this crucial connection established with the first vision will be equally present in the final one of Revelation. This is affirmed again in the next verse when it is stated that the next kingdom will arise "*after* ***you***" and be "*inferior to* ***you***", textually verifying that God's Word views a king as the embodiment of his kingdom. They are inseparable and interchangeable.

> *[39]"After you there will arise another kingdom inferior to you, then another third kingdom of bronze, which will rule over all the earth.*
> — Daniel 2:39

It is important to note that the first two parts of the vision were fulfilled in Daniel's lifetime when Babylon was overthrown by Medo-Persia in ~538 BC. (Dan. 5:30-31) The third kingdom—Greece, led by Alexander the Great, would rise to overtake them around 330 BC. (We can categorically assert the third kingdom of bronze is Alexander's Greece because we've peeked ahead and know this to be plainly stated to Daniel in a subsequent revelation.)

The second kingdom represented by the chest and two arms comports to the structure of the Medo-Persian Empire which alternated between its two major branches. There will be a much more detailed treatment to come in Daniel of what is presented here as the third and fourth kingdoms.

The phrase "*all the earth*", which is found frequently in Scripture, should be understood as, "the whole world as it is known at that time". This aids in understanding the progressive nature of this vision which shows each phase to be a partial fulfillment of the scope and size of the final anti-kingdom, which will be the first to achieve total domination of the entire globe.

> *[40]"Then there will be a fourth kingdom as strong as iron; inasmuch as iron crushes and shatters all things, so, like iron that breaks in pieces, it will crush and break all these in pieces. [41]In that you saw the feet and toes, partly of potter's clay and partly of iron, it will be a divided kingdom; but it will have in it the toughness of iron, inasmuch as you saw the iron mixed with common clay. [42]As the toes of the feet were partly of iron and partly of pottery, so some of the kingdom will be strong and part of it will be brittle. [43]And in that you saw the iron mixed with common clay, they will combine with one another in the seed of men; but they will not adhere to one another, even as iron does not combine with pottery.*
> — Daniel 2:40-43

More information is given for the fourth kingdom than the previous three, with an accompanying list of specific characteristics:

- "*...as strong as iron...it will crush and break all these in pieces*". (v.40)
- "*...partly of potter's clay and partly of iron, it will be a divided kingdom...*" (v.41)
- "*...it will have the toughness of iron...*" (v.41)
- "*...some of the kingdom will be strong and part of it will be brittle*". (v.42)
- "*...they will combine with one another in the seed of men; but they will not adhere to one another...*" (v.43)

Perhaps the most telling feature of this kingdom is the list of actions which are found in this passage: "*crushes*", "*shatters*", "*breaks*" and additionally "*crush*" and "*break*". The size and scope of the original Roman Empire and its method of working is going to be essential for understanding how the final anti-kingdom likewise rises to full strength...

> [12]*"The ten horns which you saw are ten kings who have not yet received a kingdom, but they receive authority as kings with the beast for one hour.* [13]*These have one purpose, and they give their power and authority to the beast.*
> — Revelation 17:12-13

Although the literal Roman Empire had "*the toughness of iron*", at the same time it exhibited that it was, indeed, "*a divided kingdom*" made of parts which were "*strong*" and others which were "*brittle*". Rome actually subjugated more peoples and nations through negotiation than military conquest, and this created a patchwork empire of sorts. Different nations, and even individual city-states, possessed various rights and wielded varying degrees of influence in the overall scheme of things. This speaks to the nature of the anti-king's "body" being a failed counterfeit of the Body of Christ and that it cannot attain to true unity and its inherent divisiveness will be a major factor in its downfall. The Antichrist and his forerunners can bring groups into a single empire, but they will never become a unified, contiguous people and instead maintain their own identity and culture, an uncontested feature of the ancient Roman Empire. This was likewise carried into the split into two major branches derived from the original as represented by the two legs of the image.

As a sidebar to the reader, one of the issues of confusion which many commentaries bring to this chapter is an attempted rigidness to isolate this vision from the rest of Scripture. In this author's opinion, it is not just unavoidable that we already know of further prophetic revelations, but that to ignore them completely is a mishandling of God's Word. Most academic cases attempting to assign alternate meanings to this chapter by quarantining it from the rest of Scripture will assert things like, "The text doesn't say how many toes the statue has" so they can disconnect this vision from further revelations in Scripture where a parallel ten occurs. Or they discuss what they thought Daniel was thinking or knew at the time, rather than working from the fact that this is actually God speaking. Like many things in the Bible, and especially when it comes to God's prophetic Word, we must be amenable to the process of a "progressive revelation" where there is a continual building upon the previous, not a replacement of it, and not avoid the fact that we already know it. This variation of what I call "The Ostrich Syndrome" only serves to undermine from the outset what we know to be further revealed. We must not allow such a corruption from the outset in order to protect against the greater errors to which it will inevitably lead.The best interpreter of God's Word is always God's Word.

At any rate, these characteristics personified by iron and clay are shared by the first, literal Roman Empire which arose from the four-way break-up of Alexander's Grecian Empire, was even more acute in the subsequent two-way division of the Western and Eastern branches represented by the legs, and ultimately will be realized to its fullest yet to come in a final confederation of ten kingdoms, whose sole purpose is to "*give their power and authority to the beast*". (Rev. 17:13) It is ultimately a futile effort attempted in the power and will of man as stipulated by "*the seed of men*" not being able to "*adhere to one another*". Apart from Christ, there is no unity and never will be. The metals can't mix with each other and remain separate.

It is important to note the decreasing weight and strength of materials from top to bottom to show it to be top-heavy and easy to topple. Humans think civilization is enduring, advancing and getting better with each new age, but it actually rests on brittle feet mixed with clay. Empires may last for centuries, but when each one falls, it falls very quickly, often in a day or so. The value of these elements dramatically decrease from the top down in a representation that mankind is not improving, but cheaper, weaker and although advancing technologically, declining where it counts the most—spiritually and morally. It is also a picture of diminishing beauty and glory. This is also reflected in the decreasing value of the materials from the head to the feet.

Each kingdom has its own strengths, but each one is weaker overall than the previous. The historical iterations of each possessed a different form of government:

- Babylon was ruled by an absolute monarch.
- Medo-Persia had a king who worked through his princes and established laws for which even he was held accountable.
- Greece operated through a king and an army.
- Rome was at times a republic ruled by a Senate, but often giving way to an emperor in combination with laws, both conquering nations outright and negotiating them into the fold.

The representation of Rome is particularly interesting since its origins are found in Greece as a result of the four-way split of that empire upon Alexander the Great's death. Every subsequent Western culture maintains strong roots and influences from these empires even to this very hour, but especially to Greece most often described as Hellenization of a culture.

Rome would first grow as a consolidated empire, but eventually split into distinct Western and Eastern branches as represented by the legs. Although those offshoots clearly possessed a heritage in the original Roman Empire, they were nonetheless ultimately distinct entities, neither one actually centered in the city of Rome nor comprising anywhere near the total geographic area or efficacy of the original, both growing weaker and increasingly divided. Likewise, its last variation still to come in the character of ten toes of mixed material speaks of still retaining the original character, but ultimately being something completely different from all previous variations. There are many throughout history and even at present who insist that the ten toes will be a literal revival of the original Roman Empire. If such is true, it would be a major departure from the established pattern.

- Babylon had a different governmental structure, capital, and boundaries in terms of the nations it occupied.
- Medo-Persia consumed Babylon with its own type of government, a different capital, and expanded area of occupation.
- Greece ultimately encompassed them both with yet another type of government, capital, and occupied area.
- Rome would again share certain characteristics, but its borders, government and capital were, yet again, unique to it alone and swallowed all the others entirely.

With each conquest would come the domination of their respective language, economy and culture, albeit inheriting strong influences from each of their predecessors.

In other words, Medo-Persia was not a clone of Babylon, nor Greece of Medo-Persia, nor Rome of Greece, and neither will the final ten toed iteration. It will be the first empire ever and will absorb the entire planet, not just what it understands to be the known world. The greater takeaway is that since no subsequent kingdom was a clone or exact duplicate of the previous, and merely continued to act in that character while putting forth their own cultural, geographic and political particulars, so it will be for the final "*Babylon the Great*" belonging to the Antichrist, here represented by the ten toes. Like father to son to grandson, each shares similarities and characteristics being descended from the previous, but each is ultimately and uniquely their own person carrying out things in their particular ways. Neither individuals nor whole nations experience a literal "reincarnation", but belong to an overall group by how they act "in the character of" each other.

The Final Kingdom

> 44"*In the days of those kings the God of heaven will set up a kingdom which will never be destroyed, and that kingdom will not be left for another people; it will crush and put an end to all these kingdoms, but it will itself endure forever.* 45*Inasmuch as you saw that a stone was cut out of the mountain without hands and that it crushed the iron, the bronze, the clay, the silver and the gold, the great God has made known to the king what will take place in the future; so the dream is true and its interpretation is trustworthy."*
>
> — Daniel 2:44-45

As to the overall timing, it is important to note exactly what is meant by, "*In the days of **those** kings*". It is not referencing all the kings mentioned in the whole of this vision to this point, but directed solely at the very last manifestation of the ten toes.

One of the great false teachings widely accepted within the Western Church today is a variation of "Kingdom Now Theology", such as Dominionism, Triumphalism, and many similar variants. They will present an interpretation of this passage claiming that this is not referring to the Second Coming of Christ, but His First Coming. In various ways each off-shoot of this fundamental error claims this is speaking about the Messiah coming and spiritually conquering the world by setting up the Church. Their beliefs are commonly rooted in Replacementism—the belief that God is through with Israel, and therefore every instance in Scripture where Israel is mentioned "The Church" should now be substituted to replace it. They assert in some fashion that Christ will not literally return until the Church has led every human on the planet to Christ. They see the rock not as the Messiah, but the Church. Their eisegetical presentation revolves around the notion that the Church, as the kingdom of Christ, spiritually conquers the world in order to trigger His literal return. They think He established His kingdom already as the Church and that it is already growing on its way to consuming the whole earth.

However, the exegetical fact of the matter, verified by the rest of Scripture which we cannot ignore, is that this final form of the Roman Empire represented by the feet and its ten toes has never transpired historically and is the repeated model of the final anti-kingdom of the anti-king.

We are provided a list of the characteristics of this final kingdom crushing all those previous:

- "*...will never be destroyed...will itself endure forever*" (v.44)
- "*...will not be left for another people...*" (v.44)
- "*...will crush and put an end to all these kingdoms...*" (v.44)

Yes, we could say that from a purely spiritual point of view that the Body of Christ as His Kingdom "*will never be destroyed*", "*will itself endure forever*", and "*will not be left for another people*". However, when did it "*crush and put an end to all these kingdoms*"? As my grandfather would say, "'Close' is only good enough for horseshoes and hand grenades—not God's Word". We cannot accept interpretations such as those offered by Replacementists which do not comport to 100% of God's Word. In this case, 75% may be a success story by the world's standards, but it utterly fails to meet God's minimum requirement of 100%. The rock simply cannot be representing the Church.

Equally important in this passage is the designation in verse 44, "*the God of heaven will set up a kingdom*". It is eternal—"*it will endure forever*", and if the first four kingdoms are literal, we cannot all of the sudden spiritualize away this final, eternal one. This will literally "*take place in the future*", according to the text. There is no plausible scenario that at Christ's First Coming He destroyed either a ten nation confederation or any kingdom at any time, up to and including the present.

But finally, consider the stated characteristic that this final kingdom "*filled the whole earth*". (Dan. 2:35) Again, we cannot embrace the literal for the previous four kingdoms and then switch to explaining the last kingdom as something merely symbolic. All of these things combine to clearly point to that which is yet to come, confirmed by more of God's Word to follow, which unlike Daniel at the time, we are acutely aware of and must take into consideration. In New Testament terms, we know how the final spiritual conquest of mankind will reveal itself when this literally takes place...

> *[9]For this reason also, God highly exalted Him, and bestowed on Him the name which is above every name, [10]so that at the name of Jesus* EVERY KNEE WILL BOW, *of those who are in heaven and on earth and under the earth, [11]and that every tongue will confess that Jesus Christ is Lord, to the glory of God the Father.*
> — Philippians 2:9-11

The Ultimate Counterfeit

Although the term "*Antichrist*" ("*antichristos*", Strong's #500) will not be used in Scripture until introduced by the Apostle John, (1 Jn. 2:1, 2; 4:3; 2 Jn. 1:7) it must always be kept in mind that the prefix "anti" does not mean "against", but rather "in place of". The most important attribute of this final figure emphasized when this particular description is used of him is someone who counterfeits the authentic as much as possible with the aim of substituting himself in Christ's place. Therefore something very telling about this statue overall is revealed when it comes to the Antichrist and his primary compulsion to fraudulently parallel all things Christ.

> *[11]And He gave some as apostles, and some as prophets, and some as evangelists, and some as pastors and teachers, [12]for the equipping of the saints* ***for the work of service, to the building up of the body of Christ****; [13]****until we all attain to the unity of the faith****, and of the knowledge of the Son of God, to a mature man, to the measure of the stature which belongs to the fullness of Christ. [14]As a result, we are no longer to be children, tossed here and there by waves and carried about by every wind of doctrine, by the trickery of men, by craftiness in deceitful scheming; [15]but speaking the truth in love,* ***we are to grow up in all aspects into Him who is the head, even Christ,*** *[16]****from whom the whole body****, being fitted and held together by what every joint supplies, according to the proper working of each individual part, causes the growth of the body for the* ***building up of itself in love****.*
> — Ephesians 4:11-16

Christ is the Head of the Body of Christ, Who provided various gifts and offices for the purpose not only of attaining "*the unity of the faith*", but "*to grow up in all aspects into Him*". In other words, the rest of the Body will grow into the image and character of Christ its head, eventually becoming one with Him. Pay particular attention to how this is contrasted by this inaugural image revealed by God which simultaneously shows the Antichrist both as a king and a kingdom. His followers are incapable of attaining to any semblance of spiritual unity, with each iteration bearing some resemblance to the previous ones but ultimately remaining different. The satanic counterfeit of the Head and Body of Christ becomes weaker and weaker, is stratified differently at each level, and ultimately crumbles and blows away. In a stark contrast to one of the chief characteristics of the true Body, this pathetic lookalike ***is*** "*tossed here and there by waves and* ***carried about by every wind*** *of doctrine, by the trickery of men, by craftiness in deceitful scheming*". (Eph. 4:14) That which happens spiritually parallels what takes place in the vision, when "*they were crushed all at the same time and became like chaff from the summer threshing floors; and* ***the wind carried them away*** *so that not a trace of them was found*". (Dan. 2:35) There is always a parallel spiritual cause or condition behind every literal or physical consequence.

Neither silver, bronze, iron nor clay can become gold; they will ***always*** remain ultimately separate; they cannot mix together. Rather than the whole body growing into the head, the satanic counterfeit is not just diverse, but divided. Rather than "*building up of itself in love*", it will attain to everything not just completely contrary to that goal, but actively working against it. Rather than standing firm and ultimately delivered safely into eternity, the imitation will crumble and blow away as it departs into the eternal Lake of Fire. This greatly aids in understanding a detail revealed later that the Antichrist will actually turn against one of the most important members of his constituency which brought him to power. (Rev. 17:16-17) He will, in effect, divorce his woman in the ultimate contrary act to Christ taking His Bride.

While there are previous portions of God's prophetic Word which we now understand further illuminate and expand upon the vision of Daniel 2, in this first overt picture of the final ruler of the world we are provided a parallel image not just of an individual man as represented by the overall monument, but the fact that he is also a kingdom as represented by his various parts so assigned by the explanation of the vision. From this point on in Scripture God will continue to expand on ***both*** of these aspects. He is not just to be understood as a king, but a kingdom. This is the ultimate goal which God's Word is trying to teach where the Antichrist is concerned; he is not just an individual counterfeit of Christ, but of the Body of Christ. And, ultimately, the anti-kingdom will literally form into a confederation of ten earthly kings/kingdoms with a heritage and character derived from this overall monument to earthly empires, but especially beholden to the nature of the Roman Empire, although as individually unique as each previous empire.

In other words, it will not ***be*** Rome, but certainly ***in the character of*** Rome.

2 ❖ Daniel 7: The Fourth Kingdom

[1]In the first year of Belshazzar king of Babylon Daniel saw a dream and visions in his mind as he lay on his bed; then he wrote the dream down and related the following summary of it.
— Daniel 7:1

As stated previously, whereas the vision in Daniel 2 is given to an earthly king from an earthly point of view, a parallel vision is given Daniel by the heavenly King from His heavenly perspective. Instead of a statue composed of four separate metals corresponding to descending body parts as members of the same overall figure, this divine revelation shows each of the four in their true spiritual state in the same sequence, but as the beasts they truly are.

An important linguistic detail we will revisit at times is the fact that a scriptural distinction is made between animals which are, according to the standards of God's Word, clean versus unclean. The translators of the Greek Septuagint—the version of the Old Testament which is most often quoted by the New Testament, renders clean beasts as "*zoon*" (Strong's #2226), and unclean as "*therion*" (Strong's #2342), which is exactly how they also appear in the New Testament. For instance, the four living beings operating in heaven in Revelation 4-5 are "*zoon*", but the beasts we know to be the Antichrist and False Prophet of Revelation 13 are "*therion*". Antichrist figures described as "*beasts*" are the ultimate counterfeit of the Messiah, one of whose primary designations is that of a "*zoa*" (singular of *zoon*), that being the Lamb of God. From the outset, the Septuagint renders all of these beasts in Daniel 7 as *therion*.

The disclosure of the approximate date when this vision occurred should be noted because it would indicate that if the book of Daniel were to be organized sequentially, this event actually takes place before those of chapter 5. This is an important detail because there are a number of books in Scripture which are purposely detached from being strictly sequential. (The Gospel of Matthew is of particular note in this regard.) The Holy Spirit is communicating something to us in each case, and here it may be in the choosing of chapter 7 to begin the second half of the book of Daniel. Whereas the first half is centered around historical events and deals mainly with Gentile figures and nations, the second half is much more focused on the prophetic and future history of Israel. The first six chapters involve what some have described as "court tales"—events directly connected with various Gentile kings, while the last six chapters are organized around a set of four visions concerned with the final aspects of the divine plan of the heavenly King.

Much is also made of the fact (and rightly so) that chapters 1 and 8-12 are written in Hebrew—the native language of Israel, and chapters 2-7 in Aramaic, the lingua franca at that time of the Gentiles. Of even greater interest to Jeopardy enthusiasts, because of the transliteration of the names of musical instruments from their Greek names into Aramaic, this is the only book of the Bible in which all three of its original languages—Greek, Hebrew and Aramaic, are found. There seems to be another pattern to the overall structure as well in a progression from Babylon to Medo-Persia in chapters 1-6 which is repeated again in chapters 7-12. The fact is that the literary structure of this book and its overall organization are important factors pertaining to the greater message conveyed.

But this structure also parallels the fact that in the first six chapters, Daniel interprets and deals with other people's visions, but in the final six chapters reports visions which he personally experienced. And there is a special emphasis corresponding to the 1st and 2nd kingdoms of Nebuchadnezzar's vision concerning Babylon and Medo-Persia, first in the fact that chapters 7 and 8 take place while Daniel served kings of Babylon, but chapters 9 through 12 when he subsequently served kings of Medo-Persia after their conquest of Babylon. This speaks to what may be one of the most overlooked features of the book of Daniel, that its historicity—that is, its documentation of the literal, historical fulfillment of the earliest aspects of the prophecies given, is a testimony in and of itself that God will most certainly fulfill *everything* here revealed. Daniel both experienced and witnessed a partial and beginning fulfillment of the prophetic Word documented in his book. We can be confident that this is not theoretical and entirely committed to some distant future fulfillment, but is already in progress and currently in the process of coming true because Daniel, and recorded history, have witnessed it.

The First Vision

2Daniel said, "I was looking in my vision by night, and behold, the four winds of heaven were stirring up the great sea.
— Daniel 7:2

17'These great beasts, which are four in number, are four kings who will arise from the earth.
— Daniel 7:17

The explanation of the vision is given in the plain text, so there is no need to venture a guess as to what is being represented or depicted. Throughout Scripture, the Gentile nations of the world are repeatedly represented by great bodies of water such as in this case, "*the sea*". The parallel explanation in verse 17 explicitly states, "*from the earth*".

12Alas, the uproar of ***many peoples***
Who roar ***like the roaring of the seas,***
And ***the rumbling of nations***
Who rush on ***like the rumbling of mighty waters****!*
13The nations rumble on ***like the rumbling of many waters,***
But He will rebuke them and they will flee far away,
And be chased like chaff in the mountains before the wind,
Or like whirling dust before a gale.
— Isaiah 17:12-13

*15And he said to me, "****The waters*** *which you saw where the harlot sits,* ***are peoples and multitudes and nations and tongues****.*
— Revelation 17:15

Like the composition of the monument in Daniel 2, each beast is a product of the Gentile world. This will be an important detail revisited when we discuss the primary chapter in Scripture on the Antichrist and False Prophet, Revelation 13, where one comes from the sea and the other from the land. It is puzzling that there is so much debate over the meaning of that particul detail when Scripture itself provides the answer from the outset.

The i "*stirring up the great sea*" is "*the four winds of heaven*", which in parallel biblic present God's judgment or a variety of divine forces which bring about gl oil. Jesus referenced this phenomenon as a feature of the End Times in

> *sun and moon and stars, and on the earth* ***dismay among*** ***roaring of the sea and the waves***, *[26]men fainting from* *things which are coming upon the world; for the* *po en.*

> *[3]And four great b the sea, different from*
> — Daniel 7:3

> *[17]'These great beasts, which are four in number, are four kings who will arise from the earth.*
> — Daniel 7:17

Once again God's Word uses "kings" and "kingdoms" interchangeably. In scriptural parlance, a ruler is the personification of his empire, and the empire is a direct reflection of its primary ruling personality. It is always concerned with ***both*** the king and the kingdom.

An added detail is the specific reference that they are "*different from one another*". Just as in Daniel 2 each is comprised of a different metal and body part, the attention brought to this fact is something we are going to need to carry over until we exhaust all that Scripture provides on this topic. In other words, they may share common characteristics and heritage, they may each be one-in-a-series belonging to a whole, but each is unique in its own right and never an exact duplicate of anything which comes previous or after. This is textual proof that the very last kingdom cannot be a clone of the Roman Empire or any of the beasts in the sequence. Historically speaking, the Babylonian, Medo-Persian, Greek and Roman Empires possessed different political structures, cultural influences, occupied distinct geographical territory, and in many other ways were varied in their size, power and working. But they all still share a common origin and character, particularly as things are understood spiritually.

> *[18]'But the saints of the Highest One will receive the kingdom and possess the kingdom forever, for all ages to come.'*
> — Daniel 7:18

For the first time in either vision, specific mention is made of the fate of "*the saints*" in these matters and will be more fully developed in visions here and yet to come to Daniel. This seems to affirm one of the purposes of prophecy, which is to comfort God's people by assuring them not just of God's ultimate control in spite of earthly appearances to the contrary, but His personal concern for their outcome.

The First Three Beasts

In this recapitulation of the first vision from a heavenly point of view, Daniel does not seek an explanation or further information on the first three beasts, but will rather focus on what concerns him most, the fourth beast. The text moves quickly through the first three before expounding in much more detail both the final earthly and eternal kingdoms yet to come.

[4]"The first was like a lion and had the wings of an eagle. I kept looking until its wings were plucked, and it was lifted up from the ground and made to stand on two feet like a man; a human mind also was given to it.

— Daniel 7:4

[36]"This was the dream; now we will tell its interpretation before the king. [37]"You, O king, are the king of kings, to whom the God of heaven has given the kingdom, the power, the strength and the glory; [38]and wherever the sons of men dwell, or the beasts of the field, or the birds of the sky, He has given them into your hand and has caused you to rule over them all. You are the head of gold.

— Daniel 2:36-38

In supporting Scriptures the king of Babylon as well as the kingdom of Babylon are described both as a lion (Jer. 4:7; 49:14, 22; 50:17, 44; Joel 1:6) and an eagle. (Jer. 49:22; Lam. 4:19; Eze. 17:3; Hab. 1:8) Archaeology has provided historical affirmation by discovering statues and reliefs of winged lions representing the Babylonian Empire. (As well as among the ruins of the former Assyrian Empire, which was entirely engulfed by Babylon.) The references to the plucking of its wings and being given a human mind are most likely referring to the personal experience of Nebuchadnezzar recorded in Daniel 4 when God's judgment caused him to behave like an insane, wild animal for seven years before restoring him upon finally acknowledging the authority and sovereignty of the One True God.

Nebuchadnezzar demonstrated that he did not learn the right personal lesson from his vision, obviously becoming so enamored with his portrayal as a gold head that, as recorded in Daniel 3, he made an image of himself alone entirely of gold and deified himself by demanding all worship him through the image. While we will revisit that again later, it dramatically illustrates the difference between an earthly viewpoint and agenda, and the true spiritual issues actually taking place.

[5]"And behold, another beast, a second one, resembling a bear. And it was raised up on one side, and three ribs were in its mouth between its teeth; and thus they said to it, 'Arise, devour much meat!'

— Daniel 7:5

[39]"After you there will arise another kingdom inferior to you...

— Daniel 2:39a

One of the features of the Medo-Persian Empire is that its two parts were not completely equal, one being greater than the other as represented by the bear "*raised up on one side*". Historically, Persia dominated the alliance with Media. This will also be supported when this kingdom is again revisited in Daniel 8 where the two horns of the ram are explicitly stated to represent "*the kings of Media and Persia*" (Dan. 8:20), and one of the horns "*was longer than the other*". (Dan. 8:3) Many commentators believe the three ribs secondarily refer to the larger part of Persia, which contributed three-fourths of the total size of the confederation.

However, the primary meaning of the "*three ribs...in its mouth between its teeth*" is directly associated with the command, "*Arise, devour much meat!*", symbolizing its consumption of other beasts. In this case, we know from the historical record that Medo-Persia's three most notable conquests were Babylon (539 BC), Lydia (546 BC) and Egypt (525 BC). No other empire prior to this controlled more territory than Medo-Persia.

[6]"After this I kept looking, and behold, another one, like a leopard, which had on its back four wings of a bird; the beast also had four heads, and dominion was given to it.
— Daniel 7:6

...then another third kingdom of bronze, which will rule over all the earth.
— Daniel 2:39b

Considering how a leopard is already renowned for its pure speed, the addition of wings seems to dramatically raise this aspect to another level. When combined with this beast of prey's appetite for blood, we can see the parallels to Alexander the Great's Greek Empire which not only carried out its conquests with lightning speed compared to previous forerunners, but exhibited an insatiable lust for territory. It only took Alexander about ten years to conquer the Medo-Persian Empire and extend his domain to the border of India, an incredibly quick accomplishment by the standards of the ancient world.

In order to understand the meaning of the "*four heads*", a head is often used in Scripture to represent a ruler or government, (Dan. 2:38; Is. 7:8-9) just as in English we use the term "heads of state". This feature, in parallel with its "*four wings*", seems to speak of the key outcome resulting from Alexander's empire. Upon his death in 323 BC, and after a bit of internal struggle and political intrigue, the kingdom was largely carved into four parts among Alexander's generals:

- Greece and Macedonia was initially ruled by Antipater and later by Cassander.
- Thrace and a large part of Asia Minor was subject to Lysimachus.
- Syria, Babylon and much of the Middle East was governed by Seleucus I Nicator.
- Egypt and Palestine were given to the control of Ptolemy I Soter.

This structure is the detailed focus in the following chapters of Daniel, but this is the foundation given from which it will be greatly expanded. In Daniel 8:21-22 this is clearly stated as "*four horns that...represent four kingdoms which will arise from his nation*". But it is the fourth kingdom which will receive greater and greater attention as we move forward in both Daniel and the rest of Scripture.

At this juncture, it is important to remind ourselves that if we study each of these visions exclusively by themselves without visiting their parallels and textual supporting passages in the rest of Scripture, we are most likely to not just miss the greater message to which they are pointing, but even come to a completely wrong understanding of the vision itself. While we will visit this later in much more detail, it is important to note that these three beasts, who we know from the first vision to be members of a single figure represented by the image of various metals, is replayed again in the final Revelation of Jesus Christ in His seminal description of the final Antichrist and False Prophet.

> *[1]And the dragon stood on the sand of the seashore. Then I saw a beast coming up out of the sea, having ten horns and seven heads, and on his horns were ten diadems, and on his heads were blasphemous names. [2]And **the beast** which I saw **was like a leopard**, and his feet were like those of **a bear**, and his mouth like the mouth of **a lion**. And the dragon gave him his power and his throne and great authority.*
> — Revelation 13:1-2

The first three beasts of Daniel 7, which we know to be members of the one image in Daniel 2, are all members of the final beast—that is, the Antichrist, in Revelation 13.

Of note is the fact that from Daniel's point of view, who is looking at the future from his position in the past, sees them in their sequential order going forward as the lion, the bear and the leopard—Babylon, Medo-Persia, then Greece. From the Apostle John's perspective of being in the future and looking back at history fulfilled, he sees them in the reverse order of the leopard, the bear and the lion. But like Nebuchadnezzar's vision of each part being a member of a single figure, so are the beasts of Daniel 7 incorporated into a single figure in John's vision so as to scripturally connect these things together.

But the greater takeaway is that we are gathering more and more information along the way which will ultimately combine into something greater than the sum of its parts should we embrace the whole counsel of God's Word and not isolate each instance to itself alone.

The Fourth Beast

7"After this I kept looking in the night visions, and behold, a fourth beast, dreadful and terrifying and extremely strong; and it had large iron teeth. It devoured and crushed and trampled down the remainder with its feet; and it was different from all the beasts that were before it, and it had ten horns. 8While I was contemplating the horns, behold, another horn, a little one, came up among them, and three of the first horns were pulled out by the roots before it; and behold, this horn possessed eyes like the eyes of a man and a mouth uttering great boasts.

— Daniel 7:7-8

19"Then I desired to know the exact meaning of the fourth beast, which was different from all the others, exceedingly dreadful, with its teeth of iron and its claws of bronze, and which devoured, crushed and trampled down the remainder with its feet, 20and the meaning of the ten horns that were on its head and the other horn which came up, and before which three of them fell, namely, that horn which had eyes and a mouth uttering great boasts and which was larger in appearance than its associates. 21I kept looking, and that horn was waging war with the saints and overpowering them 22until the Ancient of Days came and judgment was passed in favor of the saints of the Highest One, and the time arrived when the saints took possession of the kingdom.

— Daniel 7:19-22

We do not want to risk over-emphasizing a single point of Scripture to the point that it begins to overshadow and reshape the rest of our understanding, but it is important to note that this fourth beast is unique in the sequence. Or as Daniel here observes, "*different from all the others*". Compared to those previous to it, Daniel identifies it as "*exceedingly dreadful*" because "[it] *devoured, crushed and trampled down the remainder*". As devastating and violent were each of the previous empires, this one's propensity for violence and domination leaves them all behind. This is a characteristic visited repeatedly in Daniel. (Dan. 2:34-35, 40, 44; 7:23)

There is something deeper which is being expressed in this particular beast from all the rest in that it defies being categorized or even likened to any earthly creature. While it possess teeth, claws, feet and a head, the multiple horns make it difficult at best to assign it to something common in nature such as the previous associations with a lion, bear and leopard, which Scripture never attempts. This is most certainly one of the earliest hints at not just its satanic nature, but how completely unique the ultimate, final anti-kingdom will be from all its predecessors. Likewise the final beast just visited in Revelation 13, while retaining a few qualities and attributes recognizable in the animal kingdom, is a hybrid attaining to something completely unique and abstract from nature. In that case we can attribute it to the fact that the beast is animated by the dragon—that is, Satan, a unique creation apart from the animal kingdom as well. In fact, there really is no "dragon" in nature, is there?

But as to the point of the fourth kingdom, as the legs of iron represent the Roman Empire, the historical record unquestionably documents its surpassing cruelty and lust for violence. Rome's power and longevity would definitely qualify it as being different from all the empires which came before it and would exceed all others in its ultimate influence not just politically and culturally, but in geographic size. That which we should keep in mind going forward, especially when we visit the last iteration represented by the feet and ten toes, is just as each beast is different from the others but combining into a single, overall picture of the final anti-king/anti-kingdom, the ferocity and other characteristics of the historical Roman Empire will be but a pale shadow compared to the magnitude of that quality found in the ultimate, final fulfillment.

The agenda disclosed by the actions of "*waging war with the saints and overwhelming them*" is the first of other scriptural affirmations of this final figure, especially Revelation 13:7. Every prefigurement of the anti-king and their respective anti-kingdom shares this propensity for violence against God's people, both Jew and Christian, during every historical age.

One of the features of the final kingdom will involve three of the ten being conquered by their new ruler. The use of the term "*uprooted*" denotes a violent overthrow as opposed to a benevolent or negotiated succession. Beside other similarities, a major reason to view Herod the Great as a forerunner of this final figure is the fact that he had ten sons, three of which he executed. But the lack of a clear historical parallel contributes to our understanding that as something to be taken literally, this is an unfulfilled event yet to come.

7 "After this I kept looking in the night visions, and behold, a fourth beast, dreadful and terrifying and extremely strong; and it had large iron teeth. It devoured and crushed and trampled down the remainder with its feet; and it was different from all the beasts that were before it...

— Daniel 7:7a

23 "Thus he said: 'The fourth beast will be a fourth kingdom on the earth, which will be different from all the other kingdoms and will devour the whole earth and tread it down and crush it.

— Daniel 7:23

Thus we see that the references to the violent actions of the beast is not metaphorical or symbolic, but a dramatic way of highlighting its literal nature and behavior. It will not merely exert influence, but complete and violent domination. It is interesting to note that one of the chief names of the Antichrist is "*son of perdition*" (2 Th. 2:3) which can also be translated, "*son of destruction*". It carries with it the dual meaning of not just his ultimate fate, wherein he himself will suffer destruction, but the manner in which he carries out his personal agenda to bring destruction to everything and everyone.

Horns & THE Horn

...and it had ten horns.
— Daniel 7:7b

24'As for the ten horns, out of this kingdom ten kings will arise...
— Daniel 7:24a

The feature of the "*ten horns*" makes its first appearance here, but it is going to be repeatedly associated in Scripture with the anti-king (Rev. 12:3, 18; 13:1; 17:3) and the anti-kingdom. (Dan. 7:20, 24; Rev. 12:7; 17:12, 16) What quickly becomes apparent when studying these references in the overall context of Daniel 7 and Revelation 12, 13 and 17 is that they are constantly crossing back and forth so as to be referring to the ultimate anti-figure as both an individual king and a collective kingdom. This is but the beginning of God's Word providing a picture of not just ten horns representing the ultimate anti-kingdom, but the individual horn assigned to the ultimate anti-king. In fact, the two most used references to the Antichrist are "*beast*" and "*horn*".

8While I was contemplating the horns, behold, another horn, a little one, came up among them, and three of the first horns were pulled out by the roots before it; and behold, this horn possessed eyes like the eyes of a man and a mouth uttering great boasts.
— Daniel 7:8

...and another will arise after them, and he will be different from the previous ones and will subdue three kings. 25He will speak out against the Most High and wear down the saints of the Highest One, and he will intend to make alterations in times and in law; and they will be given into his hand for a time, times, and half a time.
— Daniel 7:24b-25

The fact that the anti-king "*will arise after them*"—that is, ***after*** the final confederation represented by the ten horns, clearly shows that this final anti-kingdom is yet to come. While it is certainly possible that the ten arise as some sort of reconfiguration with a connection to the historical Roman Empire, no clear formation conforming to these scriptural standards has yet taken place, and as previously stated according to Revelation 17:9, it is only going to be discerned by "*the mind which has wisdom*"—that is, through Christ who is the wisdom of those born again. But just as there are signs which we are supposed to recognize preceding the return of Christ for His Church in the *Harpazo*, so it also belongs to those things we are supposed to recognize as an imminent warning of the final appearance of Antichrist.

The little horn is not only presented in verse 8 as possessing the human characteristics of "*the eyes of a man and a mouth*", but in the accompanying explanation in verses 24-26 is persistently called by the pronouns "*he*" and "*his*": "***he** will speak out*", "***he** will intend*", "*given into **his** hand*". Again, Scripture obliterates the difference we might ordinarily assign to a king from a kingdom by the fact of how fluidly it shifts back and forth between them without distinction.

Although it is initially seen as "*a little one*" in comparison to the rest, it is ultimately witnessed in verse 20 as "*larger in appearance than its associates*" and in the course of coming to power over the rest,"*will subdue three kings*". The rise to power above all others of both the anti-king as an individual and the ultimate anti-kingdom is something which we are to take note of in the overall sequence of understanding the final one to come.

The reference to "*eyes like the eyes of a man*" seems to be the first of several references to come which highlight the attributes of wisdom, intelligence and insight, yet his true spiritual condition is betrayed by his speech, which is consistently described in Scripture as blaspheming God in the process of lifting up himself. To the believer this is a revelation of his animation by Satan, but to the vast numbers of unbelievers this will actually be well received, even assigned as being an appealing part of a very charismatic personality by worldly standards. These are parallel features given even more detail in other significant passages of Scripture speaking about this final figure. (Dan. 11:36-37; 2 Th. 2:2-3; Rev. 13:5-6)

The use of a "*ten*" and a subset of "*seven*" is something we will revisit, but even at this early stage in our exploration of Scripture we should keep our eye on a key parallel provided in God's prophetic Word:

> [11]*"The beast which was and is not, is himself also an eighth and is one of the seven, and he goes to destruction.* [12]***The ten horns which you saw are ten kings who have not yet received a kingdom, but they receive authority as kings with the beast for one hour****...* [17]*For God has put it in their hearts to execute His purpose by* ***having a common purpose, and by giving their kingdom to the beast****, until the words of God will be fulfilled.*
>
> — Revelation 17:11-12, 17

This is textual proof showing that we are not just wishing or imagining that the final kingdom of ten toes/ten horns is something future which has not yet taken place, because it occurs near the very end "*for one hour*", a biblical way of describing a very short period near the end. And it further shows the futility of so many who make dogmatic claims about the identity of these ten kingdoms which, like the Antichrist himself, have not yet come into existence, much less been divinely revealed to the saints.

Verse 25 is the first overt revelation that this final figure is not just an enemy of God ("*He will speak out against the Most High...*"), but of God's people ("*...and wear down the saints of the Highest One...*). Likewise is his intention "*to make alterations in times and in law*" one of the first indications of his addiction to acting in the character of God, and as we shall see this developed further, desiring to be equal to the Most High. This is but the first of what will be many disclosures concerning his agenda to counterfeit Christ in every way possible.

During the reign of Antiochus Epiphanes IV in the Inter-Testamental Period circa 163 BC, a person who literally fulfilled to a point many of the things attributed to the Antichrist so as to teach us about the final one to come, much of what he did could be characterized as an attempt "*to make alterations in times and in law*". In his quest to remake Jewish society into a clone of Greek culture, he legislated the imposition of culture, outlawed proper Temple worship and even the reading of the Torah, and attempted to reposition holidays and feasts in line with perceived Greek counterparts. As with various antichrist figures in history who have attempted to implement this similar agenda, they may help to explain what the final figure is going to attempt in this regard. Herod the Great was another who repeatedly attempted to do these kinds of things.

The First Math Lesson

While there is no disputing that through Daniel we will become acutely aware of the mathematics of God's overall time line for the rest of history as expressed in "*weeks*" of years, and that there ***is*** unquestionably a final week of years which is devoted to those coming last in human history counting down to the return of Christ documented in Revelation 19:11-21, the fact is that neither Daniel nor the rest of Scripture focuses much attention on what I prefer to call the 70th Week of Daniel, but overwhelmingly and almost exclusively emphasizes what is first presented here: "*time, times, and half a time*"—that is, 3-1/2 lunar years and some pertinent variations.

This is a main subject presented in great detail in this author's previous book, *And THEN the End Will Come*, so I don't want to exhaustively address the topic here, particularly for those who are already familiar with it. But to whet the appetite a bit for the rest, the fact is that outside of Daniel 9:27 from which we can verify the absolute truth of a final week of years, Scripture does not keep referring back to a final seven year period it calls "***The*** Tribulation" as it has so commonly been accepted in the modern Church. (It has only been a staple of the Church's vocabulary since the early 1800's, which is relatively recent in comparison to its 2,000 year history.)

Whether it is an error by the well-intentioned or fostered as an outright deception by the spiritually false, the fact is that there is no such thing in Scripture by that name. What has happened is that something Jesus designated in the Olivet Discourse to be experienced exclusively by the Church and the Church alone in the course of that final week of years as a period of "*tribulation*"—in the Greek rendered as "*thlipsis*" (Strong's #2347), has been erroneously lifted out of context and reapplied to the entire final week of years.

Look at all that Jesus identifies as features of this period of "*tribulation*" in Matthew 24:9-14; not a single thing applies to the ***world*** but is the exclusive experience of the Church alone. If we examine all the many instances of "*thlipsis*" employed in the New Testament, it will become apparent that they refer to an experience exclusive to believers. It is only when it is accompanied by the qualifier "*megale*", as in "***great*** *tribulation*", that something experienced by the whole world is expressed, and that is also a phase limited in scope within the 70th Week and not describing a whole 3-1/2 year half. (Commentators are quite fond of stating matter-of-factly, "The first half of the seven years is '***The*** Tribulation', and the second half '***The Great*** Tribulation'," or calling the whole final week of years "The World's Tribulation". ***All*** are textually absent from Scripture.)

Your concordance or Bible search program will also confirm that nowhere in the New Testament is a seven year period ever mentioned, other than in reference to the number of years Anna was married before becoming a widow. (Lk. 2:36) In both Daniel and Revelation, where the time spans are specifically quantified, the repeated references are to forms equivalent to 3-1/2 lunar years such as "*time, times and half a time*", "*forty-two months*", "*1,260 days*"and so forth.

But this sidebar has been necessary at this juncture because here, from the very outset, even ***before*** the concept of "*weeks of years*" is revealed to Daniel, the inaugural time span assigned to the Antichrist is 3-1/2 lunar years—"*time, times and half a time*". (That is, one year plus two years plus a half a year.) There are multiple deceptions at work on a wide variety of fronts in the obsession of a "7" so as to blind us from the "3-1/2". We must not reassign the importance, much less engage in renaming and redefining, that which the plain text of Scripture so clearly defines and emphasizes.

Even more importantly should be the fact that, as Bible students who give the priority to Scripture being the best interpreter of Scripture, we should dogmatically adhere to what is plainly specified in God's Word and carefully evaluate whether or not someone is adding, subtracting or outright nullifying what is presented. And in this case, it is particularly noteworthy that from the earliest disclosure of the anti-king we are presented with a 3-1/2, and as it will turn out, it is the ***last half*** of Daniel's 70th Week which receives the most attention.

This would be important in its own right because of all of the other scriptural references to some form of 3-1/2, but it is particularly telling when it comes to his primary tactic of counterfeiting the Messiah. Jesus' public ministry from His baptism to His Ascension spanned 3-1/2 years. Like Jesus who was certainly known by some for 30 years prior to His public ministry, the Antichrist will likewise be around prior to his own formal span of 3-1/2 years, but it is this final half of the 70th Week to which Scripture prolifically assigns the greatest share of the attention.

The Divine Kingdom

> 44*"In the days of those kings the God of heaven will set up a kingdom which will never be destroyed, and that kingdom will not be left for another people; it will crush and put an end to all these kingdoms, but it will itself endure forever.* 45*Inasmuch as you saw that a stone was cut out of the mountain without hands and that it crushed the iron, the bronze, the clay, the silver and the gold, the great God has made known to the king what will take place in the future; so the dream is true and its interpretation is trustworthy."*
> — Daniel 2:44-45

While a chief characteristic of the final kingdom is its appetite for crushing and devouring and trampling, this is taken to the limit when experienced by the kingdom of the One True King. Unlike past empires which, when conquered, are passed along to its conquerers, "*that kingdom will not be left for another people*", an early indication of all that Scripture foretells of the fate of the anti-king's followers and the future for the those of the Messiah. Each of these earthly kingdoms inherited the traits and culture of the previous and passed them along to the next; Christ's will utterly reject and refuse to absorb any of them.

> 9*"I kept looking*
> *Until thrones were set up,*
> *And the Ancient of Days took His seat;*
> *His vesture was like white snow*
> *And the hair of His head like pure wool.*
> *His throne was ablaze with flames,*
> *Its wheels were a burning fire.*
> 10*A river of fire was flowing*
> *And coming out from before Him;*
> *Thousands upon thousands were*
> *attending Him,*
> *And myriads upon myriads were*
> *standing before Him;*
> *The court sat,*
> *And the books were opened.*
> 11*"Then I kept looking because of the sound of the boastful words which the horn was speaking; I kept looking until the beast was slain, and its body was destroyed and given to the burning fire.*
> — Daniel 7:9-11

> 26*'But the court will sit for judgment, and his dominion will be taken away, annihilated and destroyed forever.*
> — Daniel 7:26

We are keenly aware of the many similarities put forth here which are revisited in parallel passages of God's Word, particularly in Revelation where we find these physical descriptions of Christ and the ultimate end of the Antichrist, False Prophet and their followers in the Lake of Fire. (Rev. 19:20-21) Likewise the references to a court and judgment are literally addressed at the "*great white throne*" in Revelation 20:11-15 as the Millennial Kingdom comes to an end and everything transitions to eternity.

> 12 *"As for the rest of the beasts, their dominion was taken away, but an extension of life was granted to them for an appointed period of time.*
> — Daniel 7:12

To the best of my understanding, this is identifying something which will only happen to the very last anti-kingdom which shows it to ultimately be unique from its predecessors. When Babylon ceased to exist, it did not instantly disappear. While its political and military dominance may have ceased, its people were absorbed into the Medo-Persian Empire where it continued to have an influence culturally, morally, and socially. Likewise together with the Medo-Persians, all would be assimilated into the Greek Empire upon its conquest of Medo-Persia, and the Greek and all it had subsumed into the Roman Empire. Each would leave a lingering imprint on the next. Who would argue that even at present Western societies are still heavily influenced by Greece and Rome? But the final anti-kingdom will come to a complete and final end with no residual effect from transferring its population to the next conquerer. There will be no "*extension of life*" for it. This is the final effect of the feet of iron and clay being struck and utterly destroyed by Christ the Stone as originally declared. Christ's kingdom will not absorb anything or anyone as a result of its conquest of the anti-kingdom so as to produce the first kingdom which is "leaven free" from all that these empires passed along to each other.

> 13 *"I kept looking in the night visions,*
> *And behold, with the clouds of heaven*
> *One like a Son of Man was coming,*
> *And He came up to the Ancient of Days*
> *And was presented before Him.*
> 14 *And to Him was given dominion,*
> *Glory and a kingdom,*
> *That all the peoples, nations and men of every language*
> *Might serve Him.*
> *His dominion is an everlasting dominion*
> *Which will not pass away;*
> *And His kingdom is one*
> *Which will not be destroyed.*
> — Daniel 7:13-14

> 27 *'Then the sovereignty, the dominion and the greatness of all the kingdoms under the whole heaven will be given to the people of the saints of the Highest One; His kingdom will be an everlasting kingdom, and all the dominions will serve and obey Him.'*
> — Daniel 7:27

There is quite a contrast of the Kingdom of God to the previous kingdoms of men.

The Messiah coming "*with the clouds of heaven*" is a repeated eschatological feature in Scripture. (Mt. 24:30; 26:6; Mk. 13:2; 14:6; 1 Th. 4:17; Rev. 14:14-15) This very verse in Daniel is quoted by Christ in the Olivet Discourse and at His trial. But there are those who would like to spiritualize away this text to deny this as describing a literal event. Simply put, all the previous kingdoms are real, so there can be no exception for the final one. If we examine this carefully, we will understand that this initiates a new phase of His work where the heavenly and earthly are no longer separate in the way they once were. While there is a temporary earthly institution we commonly call the Millennial Kingdom, His reign does not come to an end with that thousand year period, but transitions into eternity future.

Many Parallels Already

We have already been presented with a lot of information in the earliest visions of the anti-king and his anti-kingdom, and considering this is but a fraction of what is to come, it is worthwhile to pause and document that which has already been given in parallel here at the beginning with that which we are already aware has been provided in the last book of Scripture:

1. The term "*beast*" is interchangeably used to reference the anti-king or his anti-kingdom. (6 times in Dan. 7; 79 times in Rev. 12; 13; 16; 17; 19 & 20)
2. Both beasts are ascribed ten horns. (Dan. 7:7, 20, 24; Rev. 13:1; 17:3, 12, 16)
3. Both are opposed to God, in each case the beast himself engaged in blaspheming God. (Dan. 7:25; Rev. 13:1, 5-6)
4. Both persecute the saints. (Dan. 7:25; Rev. 13:7)
5. Both formally reign for 3-1/2 years. (Dan. 7:25; Rev. 13:5)
6. Both are destroyed upon Christ's Return and establishment of His own kingdom. (Dan. 7:26-27; Rev. 19:19-20)

We have an incredible amount of scriptural material still before us on this subject, and yet from the outset that which is revealed in the final Revelation of Jesus Christ is divulged as a parallel confirmation from the very earliest. These characteristics will repeatedly show up not just in parallel supporting Scripture, but in both historical and biblical types who foreshadow the final one to come. We will find these characteristics not only in the likes of Herod the Great, Absalom, the kings of Babylon, Assyria and Tyre, as well as other forerunners of the Antichrist in Scripture, but in the historical parallels of the likes of Antiochus Epiphanes IV, the Roman emperors, Napoleon, Hitler, Stalin and many, many others. Scripture will continue to expand on these traits and contribute even more, but a fundamental portrait is already being formed.

As mentioned earlier, we do not want to repeat the mistake so many have made of studying these instances in isolation from each other, nor should we pretend that we are not acutely aware of Scripture which comes after Daniel. We will ultimately discover that the Old Testament provides a rich foundation on the anti-king/anti-kingdom which is neither replaced nor rendered obsolete by the New Testament, but on which the final 27 books of the Bible intrinsically depend in order to understand what they are trying to convey for the very same subject.

The Portrait Begins to Take Shape

At this point, we are already provided key characteristics which not only define this final figure not just as an anti-king, but an anti-kingdom, many of which will be revisited in parallel Scripture to come, but all of which steadily paint a portrait of the final one to come:

- "*...different from all the others...*" (Dan. 7:19)
- "*...exceedingly dreadful...*" (Dan. 7:19)
- "*...teeth of iron...*" (Dan. 7:19)

- "*...claws of bronze...*" (Dan. 7:19)
- "*...devoured, crushed and trampled down the remainder...*" (Dan. 7:19)
- "*...three of them fell...*"—that is, he will conquer three of the final ten kingdoms. (Dan. 7:20)
- "*...had eyes...*" (Dan. 7:20)
- "*...a mouth uttering great boasts...*" (Dan. 7:20)
- "*...larger in appearance...*" (Dan. 7:20)
- "*...waging war against the saints and overpowering them...*" (Dan. 7:21)
- "*He will speak out against the Most High...*" (Dan. 7:25)
- "*...wear down the saints...*" (Dan. 7:25)
- "*...intend to make alterations in times and in law...*" (Dan. 7:25)
- "*...they will be given into his hand for a time, times, and half a time.*" (Dan. 7:25)

The first good news is provided to the saints in how it will all ultimately turn out:

- "*...the court will sit for judgment...*" (Dan. 7:26)
- "*...his dominion will be taken away, annihilated and destroyed forever.*" (Dan. 7:26)
- "*...the sovereignty, dominion and the greatness of all the kingdoms under the whole heaven will be given to the people of the saints of the Highest One...*" (Dan. 7:27)
- "*...His kingdom will be an everlasting kingdom, and all the dominions will serve and obey Him.*" (Dan. 7:27)

Even at this earliest stage of all that we know is yet to be provided in addition to this, we have quite a list for this final figure as an individual, as a kingdom, and actions and activities he will undertake in both roles. And so that we will maintain the right spiritual perspective on it all, we are provided the assurance of the greater working of God which we will experience at the end of it all. But not to be overlooked is the caveat established from the very beginning that the most important time span is a 3-1/2 year period, especially considering the weight assigned to seven years so prevalent in the modern Church.

This is really only the beginning.

3 ❖ Daniel 8: The Small Horn

> *[1]In the third year of the reign of Belshazzar the king a vision appeared to me, Daniel, subsequent to the one which appeared to me previously. [2]I looked in the vision, and while I was looking I was in the citadel of Susa, which is in the province of Elam; and I looked in the vision and I myself was beside the Ulai Canal.*
> — Daniel 8:1-2

Although a continuation of the previous visions, Daniel's second vision narrows the focus to the second and third empires of those revelations and broadens our understanding of the final anti-king. Much more detail is provided on the Medo-Persian and Greek Empires because, as it turns out, they are going to have multiple effects on Israel's future, both immediate and intermediate. Additionally, there have already been historical fulfillments of much of what is shown Daniel which will be replayed in the End Times. This is one of the primary examples of how God's prophetic Word is more often a pattern repeating itself until the final, ultimate fulfillment, rather than a one-and-done one-time prediction. It is also an example of God's "progressive revelation" in that He is continuing to provide more detail with each new vision, and narrowing the focus with each pass. Nothing previously given becomes obsolete or superseded, but rather given more detail or greater context.

From the information in the opening verses, we know that, like chapter 7, this took place before the events of chapter 5 and two years after Daniel's first vision. But more significantly, it indicates that the vision places Daniel in the vision to the vicinity of the place and time when, from the historical record, we know Cyrus is establishing the Medo-Persian Empire. Such will overthrow the current Babylonian regime in a relatively short 12 or so years in the future from when Daniel received this vision of those and subsequent events. And it is no small irony that the vision takes Daniel to the place which will become a capital of the Medo-Persian Empire represented as the ram which is about to come to power.

Also of note, as previously visited, is the fact that the portion of Daniel written in Aramaic—the lingua franca of the Gentiles at that time, comes to an end with last verse of chapter 7 (it spans Daniel 2:4-7:28), and from Daniel 8:1 to the end of the book reverts to Hebrew, the language specific to Israel. This linguistic change coincides with the shift in emphasis attesting to its relevance to God's people in particular. There is very little in the first seven chapters of Daniel that exclusively corresponds to Israel, as opposed to the prominent connections present in the rest.

A Word on Secular History

Before completely diving into Daniel 8, the reader will have already realized just from the opening chapters how important the historical record is for a complete understanding of Daniel, and by extension, much of God's given prophetic Word. ***Many*** fulfillments of prophecy are documented in Scripture while a great many others, however, are confirmed from history apart from the biblical text. There are those who are uncomfortable with something or someone secular confirming the fulfillment of a divine revelation, a prime example being the resistance to the Jewish historian Josephus corroborating and even supplementing many things which occurred during Christ's First Coming and shortly thereafter. Or because of the negative connotations of the Apocrypha, do not easily accept the historicity of some of its writings such as the books of Maccabees, for instance. There are some who take the extreme position that if Scripture itself does not document the fulfillment, no other source can be used, or at the least never trusted.

The fact is that Scripture itself at times refers to events only known and documented in the secular historical record. At the top of the list is Christ Himself, who celebrated the "*Feast of Dedication*". (Jn. 10:22) Nowhere in the Scriptures will this Jewish observance be found, which has since come to be commonly known as "Hanukkah". It has no biblical basis or accompanying mandates for being celebrated as its origin is purely the product of history and tradition rather than the Mosaic Law. This is the celebration of the victory over a tyrant we have already referred to by the name of Antiochus Epiphanes IV which occurs in the Inter-Testamental Period—that is, in the biblically undocumented space of approximately 400 years between the books of Malachi (the last book of the Old Testament) and Matthew (the first book of the New). He was overthrown in what is historically known as the Maccabean Revolt (167-160 BC) which is still celebrated within Judaism to this day. The point is that Christ would have known exactly what He was participating in, and it is only known to us from the historical record, without which we would forever wonder, "What was that Feast of Dedication thingy?"

Likewise, there are obvious milestones which are universally accepted and yet only known from the historical record such as the destruction of Jerusalem and the Temple in 70 AD, the Bar Kochba Revolt which led to the Jewish Diaspora (132-136 AD) and so forth. There are other instances where Scripture corroborates an historical event such as when all Jews were expelled from Rome during Emperor Claudius' reign, although neither Scripture nor any of the secular historical accounts provide an exact date. (Acts 18:2) Students of Scripture must also be students of history, always bearing in mind the old saying, "'History' is actually ***His*** Story".

This is especially critical when it comes to the study of Daniel because even non-believing scholars and historians see such unimpeachable parallels to the historical record that they openly argue that the only logical explanation is that Scriptures like the book of Daniel must have actually been surreptitiously written much later ***after*** these things took place and disguised to make it look like they were predicted in advance. To our shame, many Christian scholars are slower and more stubborn in their acceptance of God's literal fulfillment of His Word than many of their secular counterparts.

While we cannot base our doctrine or theology on the historical record, it is invaluable not only in showing the literalness of God's Word, but in teaching something about the nature of future fulfillments. In other words, all the historical kingdoms teach something about the final anti-kingdom to come, but all must conform to the parameters established in Scripture; all of the historical anti-kings teach something about the final Antichrist to come, but each must conform to what has been established in God's Word. History and typology never serve as the basis for something we believe and can only conform to and confirm what is plainly stipulated in Scripture to begin with.

The Vision Explained

> [15]*When I, Daniel, had seen the vision, I sought to understand it; and behold, standing before me was one who looked like a man.* [16]*And I heard the voice of a man between the banks of Ulai, and he called out and said, "Gabriel, give this man an understanding of the vision."*
>
> [17]*So he came near to where I was standing, and when he came I was frightened and fell on my face; but he said to me, "Son of man, understand that the vision pertains to the time of the end."*
>
> [18]*Now while he was talking with me, I sank into a deep sleep with my face to the ground; but he touched me and made me stand upright.* [19]*He said, "Behold, I am going to let you know what will occur at the final period of the indignation, for it pertains to the appointed time of the end.*
>
> — Daniel 8:15-19

In a testament to the fact that when authentic dreams, visions or any form of revelation originates with God, we once again find that it is equally critical for the meaning to also come from God. Just as Nebuchadnezzar needed a divine explanation of his dream, Daniel needs the same for his vision. Remember, Daniel was only the conduit through whom God chose to explain to Nebuchadnezzar God's meaning; Daniel does not possess the power on his own to explain such things and must always rely on God for the answer. There is a greater lesson here testifying to the fact that it is only God-given wisdom which explains the meaning of His prophetic Word, an affirmation for modern believers of the New Testament teaching that ***Christ*** is ***our*** wisdom. There is much confusion in the area of eschatology because of the large number of engaged scholars who are not believers to begin with, and even a sizable number of the believing who are trying to work it all out on their own. Daniel needed an explanation of his vision as much as Nebuchadnezzar. One of the major differences between them is Daniel immediately knew to Whom to go.

Gabriel provides two important details which serve to encapsulate the proper context for Daniel's vision:

- "*...I am going to let you know what will occur* ***at the final period of the indignation****...*"
- "*...for it pertains to* ***the appointed time of the end****.*"

Gabriel actually twice repeats that this concerns "*the time of the end*" in both verses 17 and 19.

"The Indignation"

Special attention should be paid to the phrase, "*the final period of the indignation*". While the term "*indignation*" in its standalone meaning most often refers to the expression of divine anger, (e.g., Lam. 2:6; Is. 10:25; Mic. 7:9; etc.) this period or phase of time labeled "***the*** *indignation*" is later affirmed in the text of Daniel itself as specifying the final phase of the eschaton.

> [36]*"Then the king will do as he pleases, and he will exalt and magnify himself above every god and will speak monstrous things against the God of gods; and he will prosper **until the indignation is finished**, for that which is decreed will be done.*
> — Daniel 11:36

In the Greek Septuagint, it may be most revealing that they chose to render the Hebrew "*za'am*" (Strong's #2195), which the NASB translators here translate "*indignation*", in Greek as "*orge*" (Strong's #3709), which is consistently translated into English in the New Testament as "*wrath*". The final 3-1/2 years of history is characterized by the wrath of Satan who will be unrestrained through the Antichrist, False Prophet and their anti-kingdom when Satan himself is cast out of heaven and down to earth. That particular time as documented in Revelation is also assigned the designation of "*orge*"—that is, "*wrath*".

> [9]*And the great dragon was thrown down, the serpent of old who is called the devil and Satan, who deceives the whole world; he was thrown down to the earth, and his angels were thrown down with him...*[12]*"For this reason, rejoice, O heavens and you who dwell in them. Woe to the earth and the sea, because the devil has come down to you, **having great wrath**, knowing that he has only a short time."*
> — Revelation 12:9, 12

But likewise this time is superseded by "*the day of the Lord*", a phase of the very end spoken of more than any other in Scripture which, more than any other documented characteristic, is repeatedly equated with being the final outpouring of ***God's*** wrath.

> [14]*Near is the great day of the LORD,*
> *Near and coming very quickly;*
> *Listen, the day of the LORD!*
> *In it the warrior cries out bitterly.*
> [15]***A day of wrath is that day**,*
> *A day of trouble and distress,*
> *A day of destruction and desolation,*
> *A day of darkness and gloom,*
> *A day of clouds and thick darkness,*
> — Zephaniah 1:14-15

There is a dual aspect to the character of wrath which personifies "*the indignation*" in that what is expressed satanically is in turn heaped upon them all and to a much greater devastating effect by God. It is a time of wrath upon wrath, so to speak.

As explained in detail in *And THEN The End Will Come*, "*the day of the Lord* " is not to be confused with or assigned as being just another name for the entire final week of years, nor for "*the great tribulation*", which is the final most intense phase within Daniel's 70th Week to be experienced by the entire world, both believers and non-believers alike. It is the defining phase marking the end of that final week of years when the removal of the Church takes place and "*the day of the Lord*" commences. This will be repeatedly reinforced further in Daniel by its emphases on that last half of the final week of years as directly connected to the final anti-king. The entirety of that final 3-1/2 years is characterized by wrath, however, first as initially expressed by the Antichrist from its outset as he publicly takes his place with the inaugural event of the Abomination of Desolation and everything is at its spiritually darkest. But then, with the removal of the Church shortly thereafter, it is God's wrath added in the onset of "*the day of the Lord*" which multiplies this characteristic of wrath to proportions unprecedented in human history to that point. Believers may have to endure the anti-king's wrath, but will be removed and exempted from that of the True King.

The Ram

[3]Then I lifted my eyes and looked, and behold, a ram which had two horns was standing in front of the canal. Now the two horns were long, but one was longer than the other, with the longer one coming up last. [4]I saw the ram butting westward, northward, and southward, and no other beasts could stand before him nor was there anyone to rescue from his power, but he did as he pleased and magnified himself.
— Daniel 8:3-4

[20]"The ram which you saw with the two horns represents the kings of Media and Persia.
— Daniel 8:20

We keep revisiting the historical fact that the Medo-Persian Empire, as expressed in its very name, was composed of two main branches based on an alliance between Media and Persia. That the "*two horns*" represent them is plainly stated in the divine explanation of Daniel's vision. That "*the two horns were long, but one was longer than the other*" reflects what we know from history, that Persia was the more dominant of the two. This is also why many believe that the reference to the second beast in Daniel's previous vision "*resembling a bear...raised up on one side*" (Dan. 7:5) is parallel to this feature of a partnership which is unequal in size, and to Nebuchadnezzar's depiction of the silver torso with two arms to also represent each branch. (Dan. 2:32, 39)

Just as archaeology has uncovered the prolific use of the lion as a symbol which Babylon used of itself, so it has been shown that the ram is the self-assigned emblem of Persia. Likewise the goat was literally used by and therefore associated with Greece. (I guess this is where schools get the notion of a mascot, something which has been handed down to modernity by ancient cultures identifying with something in place of the One True God. Admittedly it is strange to acknowledge this as a present-day descendant of idolatry because we just don't think of them that way.) By using the same earthly symbols these empires offered of themselves, God's visions would not only allow their meanings to be clearly understood by the people of the day to whom these prophecies were first published, but reveals something about the sovereignty of God who is far and away above and beyond these human notions of themselves. He turns back their own things upon them.

*[2]"For in the way you judge, you will be judged; and **by your standard of measure, it will be measured to you**.*
— Matthew 7:2

The reference to the "*ram butting westward, northward, and southward*" in combination with "*no other beasts could stand before him*" mirrors the historical facts of their military conquests. Already possessing lands to the east where the known map of the ancient world is concerned, the Medo-Persian Empire would successfully overthrow Babylon, Syria and Lydia in Asia Minor to the west, Scythia and the region in and around Armenia to the north, and to the south, Egypt and Ethiopia. The land of Israel and its immediate neighbors would have been folded into this empire because of the Southern Kingdom of Judah's acquisition by Babylon directly, or the earlier appropriation into the Assyrian Empire which first carried away the population of the area belonging to the ten tribes which formed what we refer to as the Northern Kingdom of Israel. But as we shall see in Daniel 11, Israel is caught in a perpetual tug-of-war between the Seleucid and Ptolemaic Empires and repeatedly passed between them in a cycle which will historically repeat itself until the very end.

The final characteristic listed, "*he did as he pleased and magnified himself*", is a trait of both the anti-king and anti-kingdom which is revisited in parallel Scriptures. But it should not be overlooked that while Scripture is clearly depicting a kingdom, notice the pronouns: "***he*** *did as* ***he*** *pleased and magnified* ***himself***". Likewise, the accompanying explanation provides the simultaneous reference to both a king and a kingdom by stipulating "*the two horns represents the* ***kings***". We can be assured that this individual is singularly defined as someone who will do as he pleases and magnifies himself. Every antichrist figure shares this propensity for self-deification which is ultimately realized to its fullest by the final one in the Abomination of Desolation.

The Goat

> *5While I was observing, behold, a male goat was coming from the west over the surface of the whole earth without touching the ground; and the goat had a conspicuous horn between his eyes. 6He came up to the ram that had the two horns, which I had seen standing in front of the canal, and rushed at him in his mighty wrath. 7I saw him come beside the ram, and he was enraged at him; and he struck the ram and shattered his two horns, and the ram had no strength to withstand him. So he hurled him to the ground and trampled on him, and there was none to rescue the ram from his power. 8Then the male goat magnified himself exceedingly. But as soon as he was mighty, the large horn was broken; and in its place there came up four conspicuous horns toward the four winds of heaven.*
>
> — Daniel 8:5-8

> *21"The shaggy goat represents the kingdom of Greece, and the large horn that is between his eyes is the first king. 22The broken horn and the four horns that arose in its place represent four kingdoms which will arise from his nation, although not with his power.*
>
> — Daniel 8:21-22

Again, while Scripture provides the plain meaning which cannot be disputed or spiritualized away into something else, it is important to note that this refers to both a king ***and*** a kingdom as "*the shaggy goat represents the* ***kingdom*** *of Greece*" and "*the large horn...is the first* ***king***". Scripture persistently presents an interchangeable teaching of both a king and a kingdom and visions which simultaneously speaks of them symbiotically.

The actions assigned to the goat, as with the previous, parallel the historical record. His "*coming from the west over the surface of the whole earth without touching the ground*" corresponds to the speed, by ancient standards, with which Alexander the Great established his empire's boundaries, engulfing Medo-Persia, the ram. This was a chief characteristic as well of the previous vision embodied by the representation of the leopard with wings. (Dan. 7:6) Whereas the two horns of the ram represent the two kings of the cooperating branches of the Medo-Persian Empire, the single "*conspicuous horn*" of the goat is the person of Alexander. While each image is an overall representation of the ultimate anti-kingdom, their respective ruling personalities are identified within to simultaneously reveal the ultimate anti-king.

While the horns of the ram representing the Medo-Persian Empire were "*shattered*" by the one, greater horn of the goat representing Alexander, and "*there was no one to rescue the ram from its power*" foretelling of one earthly power overcoming another, take note of the absence of any citation of an earthly factor being responsible when "*the large horn was broken*". True to the text, his empire having reached its pinnacle of success, he did not die by human agency. The conflicting accounts of his death have in common the factors of an excess of alcohol compounded by disease, but he was not overcome by the working of another person. He died in the city of Babylon which he planned to make his capital, an interesting parallel to the final anti-king who is so closely associated with "Babylon the Great".

Either of Alexander's two sons would have been the likely heirs of the empire, but were murdered. After a period of internal strife, the Greek Empire was partitioned and distributed among four of Alexander's Greek military leaders, or what is described in the vision as, "*in its place there came up four conspicuous horns toward the four winds of heaven*". Cassander to the west would rule Macedonia, Greece and Thrace, Lysimachus to the east controlled Lydia, Ionia, Phrygia and other parts of present-day Turkey, Seleucus to the north ruled present-day Iran, Iraq, Syria and parts of Central Asia, with Ptolemy to the south occupying Egypt and neighboring regions, initially including Israel. There were smaller enclaves, but these were the four main ones which together overlay most of the original empire.

This four-way division and their formal occupation in this manner had the multiplied effect of bringing the Greek culture and language to the whole of the then-known world which is still felt in the Western world to this day. This facilitated a universal acceptance of the Greek language so that by the time of Christ's First Coming, His message could be disseminated to all those nations and people groups, not to mention serve as a seminal influence for us personally by what would eventually develop into the English language.

Israel will find itself caught in the middle between the Seleucid and Ptolemaic Empires, which is why we find further revelation in Daniel which narrows the focus to these two kings/kingdoms and almost no further reference to the others. Over time the map will change again, of course, but this four-fold division and influence will exist as a political and cultural undertow even to this day, and it is worth paying attention to the parallels at present in the way that confederations roughly corresponding to the originals appear to be playing out yet again. In particular, from a biblical point of view, is the northern alliance to come identified in Ezekiel 38-39 anchored by modern-day Russia, Turkey and Iran which revisits many parallels to the historic Seleucid Empire. As of the time of this writing, we see them active in this area again in Syria, seeming to draw everyone else there as well.

As to the four kingdoms, however, as stated in Daniel 8:22, although they would rise in Alexander's place, it was with far less efficacy—"*not with his power*".

The Small Horn

9Out of one of them came forth a rather small horn which grew exceedingly great toward the south, toward the east, and toward the Beautiful Land. 10It grew up to the host of heaven and caused some of the host and some of the stars to fall to the earth, and it trampled them down. 11It even magnified itself to be

21"The shaggy goat represents the kingdom of Greece, and the large horn that is between his eyes is the first king. 22The broken horn and the four horns that arose in its place represent four kingdoms which will arise from his nation, although not with his power.

23"In the latter period of their rule,

equal with the Commander of the host; and it removed the regular sacrifice from Him, and the place of His sanctuary was thrown down. [12]And on account of transgression the host will be given over to the horn along with the regular sacrifice; and it will fling truth to the ground and perform its will and prosper.

[13]Then I heard a holy one speaking, and another holy one said to that particular one who was speaking, "How long will the vision about the regular sacrifice apply, while the transgression causes horror, so as to allow both the holy place and the host to be trampled?"

[14]He said to me, "For 2,300 evenings and mornings; then the holy place will be properly restored."

— Daniel 8:9-14

When the transgressors have run their course,
A king will arise,
Insolent and skilled in intrigue.
[24]His power will be mighty, but not by his own power,
And he will destroy to an extraordinary degree
And prosper and perform his will;
He will destroy mighty men and the holy people.
[25]And through his shrewdness
He will cause deceit to succeed by his influence;
And he will magnify himself in his heart,
And he will destroy many while they are at ease.
He will even oppose the Prince of princes,
But he will be broken without human agency.
[26]The vision of the evenings and mornings
Which has been told is true; But keep the vision secret,
For it pertains to many days in the future."

— Daniel 8:21-26

Again, if we were to treat this in isolation from the rest of Scripture, we might come to a conclusion which stands apart from that which the whole counsel of God's Word is teaching. The fact is that, unlike Daniel at the time, we ***do*** have the rest of Scripture by which the Holy Spirit provides additional insight so as to greatly illuminate the meaning of what is stated here. And, of course, we know from history the things which has taken place which may have fulfilled God's Word, as opposed to that which has yet to be fulfilled, and with the aid of Scripture, those which are recapitulated yet again until an ultimate and final fulfillment is achieved.

Prefiguring the Final Figure

In this case, such combine to introduce what is initially presented as "*a rather small horn*" which comes out of what we know to be the four-way division of the Greek Empire. Particularly because of what will be further revealed in Daniel 11 in combination with the historical record, we know that Antiochus Epiphanes IV, a ruler arising from the Seleucid Dynasty, fulfilled many of these events. We will also come to understand that, as a major type of the Antichrist, this was a forerunner of a final fulfillment yet to come. The manner in which Epiphanes acted has much to teach about the final figure to come who will replay these events, but to an even greater, multiplied degree.

While we will discuss this in more detail when visiting Daniel 11, we can be sure that prophecy often works as a repeating pattern until its final fulfillment because of the Abomination of Desolation itself. (Dan. 11:31) Epiphanes will fuel the Maccabean Revolt (167-160 BC) when, among other things, he desecrates the Temple by erecting within it a statue of Zeus using his own face in an act of self-deification, and sacrifices a pig (an unclean animal) on its altar. However, about a hundred years later, the Roman General Pompey will desecrate the temple as well by unlawfully entering into the Holy of Holies.

Even though the Jews understood the Abomination of Desolation to have already taken place twice in these events, in the Olivet Discourse Jesus says it will happen yet again (Mt. 24:15; Mk. 13:14), and in his letter to the Thessalonians, so does the Apostle Paul. (2 Th. 2:3-4) General Titus would lead the Roman destruction of the Temple in 70 AD, and Emperor Hadrian would even build and dedicate a temple to Jupiter on that very spot which would not just include a statue of Jupiter, but one of himself, again replaying an antichrist figure effecting self-deification.

There have been a number of desecrations subsequent to this including Constantine's nephew's failed attempt, and what may be considered a perpetual desecration to this day with the establishment of the Al-Aqsa Mosque. The many abominations prefigure the final one to come in an example of how prophecy often works as a pattern, or what Christ called "*birth pangs*" which repeat yet gain in intensity until the final "birth", so to speak. As painful as each increasing birth pang might be, they are nothing compared to the actual birth.

So from the one horn of the goat, which we know to be Alexander the Great, arose the four empires described previously, and the horn among the four which represents the Seleucid Empire produces Antiochus Epiphanes IV, here initially described as "*a rather small horn which grew exceedingly great*" who will prefigure the final one to come. He was not actually the rightful heir to the throne, but through bribery and flattery (what might be characterized as "*intrigue*") succeeded in taking the place of his nephew. His rise to power corresponded historically with campaigns which grew his empire "*toward the south, toward the east, and toward the Beautiful Land*"—that is, Israel itself.

The True Source of Their Character

Daniel 8:10 is a revealing insertion into the text to let us know that there is more than just a human historical figure being described:

> [10]*It grew up* ***to the host of heaven*** *and caused some of the host and some of the stars to fall* ***to the earth****, and it trampled them down.*
> — Daniel 8:10

This relates to one of the famous scriptural provisions of the character and actions directly attributed to Satan:

> [4]*And his tail swept away a third of the stars of heaven and* ***threw them to the earth****.*
> — Revelation 12:4a

In other words, a textual reference to Satan is provided to remind us that the ultimate fulfillment of the figure being described is going to be the Antichrist, someone who is unique in being ***satanically*** possessed; not merely demon-possessed, but indwelt by Satan personally when he is permanently cast out of heaven and having to carry out his schemes in the earthly arena "*knowing that he has only a short time*". (Rev. 12:7-12)

One of Satan's defining traits is his earnest desire to be like God, which Scripture documents with the accompanying description of Satan himself having both fallen from heaven and as that of a star:

> [12] *"**How you have fallen from heaven,***
> ***O star of the morning**, son of the dawn!*
> *You have been cut down to the earth,*
> *You who have weakened the nations!*
> [13] *But you said in your heart,*
> *'I will ascend to heaven;*
> ***I will raise my throne above the stars of God,***
> *And I will sit on the mount of assembly In the recesses of the north.*
> [14] *I will ascend above the heights of the clouds;*
> *I will make myself like the Most High.'*
> — Isaiah 14:12-14

But in this particular case, there seem to be two different groups being addressed by the distinction that he caused "*some of the **host***" as opposed to "*some of the **stars***" to not just fall in both instances, but trampled. Sometimes Scripture uses the metaphor of "*stars*" to represent believers:

- "*...and I will greatly multiply your seed **as the stars** of the heavens...*" (Gen. 22:17; 26:4; Ex. 32:1)
- "*...and **eleven stars** were bowing down to me.*" (Gen. 37:9)
- "*...you are this day **like the stars of heaven** in number.*" (Dt. 1:10)

In other words, the reference to "*the host*" may be describing the fall which Satan caused among the angels, while "*the stars*" is the fall, what we commonly call "apostasy", among God's people. Great apostasy is a repeated staple of the End Times and frequently associated with the activities of the Antichrist and antichrist figures. However, a reasonable case can be made for assigning "*host*" to those on earth and "*stars*" to those in heaven, but regardless, to Satan is attributed a spiritual falling away from the ranks of ***both*** the earthly and the heavenly.

This is further referenced in Daniel 8 by describing the milieu out of which he arises as, "*When the transgressors have run their course*" (Dan. 8:23), "*transgressors*" having the biblical definition of someone actively rebelling against God's Word and ways. The text then shows how he capitalizes on this to even greater effect when, "*He will cause deceit to succeed by his influence*". (Dan. 8:25) A major part of Satan's nature to deceive is often taught in Scripture when associating him with a serpent. But where deception fails to get the job done, he takes up the character of his other major scriptural personification as a dragon whose chief tactic is persecution.

- "*He will destroy mighty men and the holy people*". (Dan. 8:24)
- "*And he will destroy many while they are at ease*". (Dan. 8:25)

These primary features are present in every figure from history or Scripture who prefigures the final Antichrist to come. They are masters of deception who eventually betray their true agenda by transitioning to open persecution and warfare.

Historical Parallels

Epiphanes invoked a failed campaign against Egypt, seeming to take out his vengeance on Israel when turned back, plundering the Temple and, according to the historical accounts of the apocryphal books of Maccabees, slaughtered tens of thousands. He outlawed biblical worship, the reading of the Torah, observing the Sabbath and dietary practices, and enacted many laws in an attempt to completely replace not only Judaism as a religion, but dissolve the entire Jewish culture to instead become completely Hellenized. He actively persecuted those who would not comply.

The reference this comes about "*on account of transgression*" is a feature of the historical record during the time of Epiphanes that many in Israel were not faithful to begin with and readily adopted both Greek religion and culture. There would even be those who, for a time, sided with those fighting against Epiphanes who would then betray the faithful and willingly go back under him. When God exercises divine judgment, it is often executed through earthly agency as in the examples of Assyria and Babylon so it would not be unprecedented to see Epiphanes as a tool of that judgment. And so Epiphanes controlled the land and culture for a number of years and halted the Temple rites, here specified as "*removed the regular sacrifice from Him*". During this period he exerted absolute power to "*perform his will and prosper*".

By suppressing and even attempting to destroy biblical Judaic teaching and practices, he mirrored the scriptural prediction that this figure "*will fling truth to the ground*". The historical record discloses that as many copies of the Torah as were found were gathered, shredded and burned with fire. In fact, an automatic death sentence was assessed on anyone found in possession of God's Word. This consequence was even extended to those simply found to be practicing anything documented in Scripture. As has happened many times since, a satanically animated tyrant comes to power who not only attempts to not just legislate God's Word and ways out of existence, but eliminate any who attempt to abide by it. First the public places of worship are closed, then the worshipers are pursued even into their very homes.

It is important to note that "*evenings and mornings*" is the biblical way of describing a single day. This comes from the Creation Narrative in Genesis, where for each of the creation events listed, it is followed up with, "*there was evening and there was morning, one day*" (Gen. 1:5), "*there was evening and there was morning, a second day*" (Gen. 1:8) and so on through the entire account. Even to this day Judaism defines a day as occurring from nightfall to nightfall. Much confusion concerning the biblical handling of time comes from trying to impose our modern, Western calendar and clock whereas Scripture is consistently attached to the lunar cycle and its biblical parameters. In those terms, this is speaking of a period of approximately 6 years and 5 months according to a lunar accounting.

Nonetheless, scholars have already provided the tedious work (which I will spare the reader and not revisit) of confirming that 2,300 lunar days was, indeed, the length of time corresponding to the activities of Epiphanes, at the end of which on our calendar is calculated to have been December 14, 164 BC, when Judas Maccabeus led the cleansing and re-dedication of the Temple. This is celebrated within Judaism to this day as "Hanukkah", but observed by Jesus in His time as "*the Feast of Dedication*". (Jn. 10:22) As Daniel 8:14 predicted, after the specified length of time, "*then the holy place will be properly restored*", and the historical record stipulates that is exactly what happened.

The reference that this figure "*will be broken without human agency*" (Dan. 8:25) could be said of Epiphanes if some historical accounts are accurate that he committed suicide by drowning himself, but even more so if the account of Second Maccabees is correct:

> 5 But the all-seeing Lord, the God of Israel, struck him with an incurable and invisible blow. As soon as he stopped speaking he was seized with a pain in his bowels, for which there was no relief, and with sharp internal tortures— 6 and that very justly, for he had tortured the bowels of others with many and strange inflictions. 7 Yet he did not in any way stop his insolence, but was even more filled with arrogance,

> breathing fire in his rage against the Jews, and giving orders to drive even faster. And so it came about that he fell out of his chariot as it was rushing along, and the fall was so hard as to torture every limb of his body. [8]Thus he who only a little while before had thought in his superhuman arrogance that he could command the waves of the sea, and had imagined that he could weigh the high mountains in a balance, was brought down to earth and carried in a litter, making the power of God manifest to all. [9]And so the ungodly man's body swarmed with worms, and while he was still living in anguish and pain, his flesh rotted away, and because of the stench the whole army felt revulsion at his decay. [10]Because of his intolerable stench no one was able to carry the man who a little while before had thought that he could touch the stars of heaven.
>
> — 2 Maccabees 9:5-10

The very last detail scripture divulges about this final figure is that his fate concludes with the return of Christ who ends the satanically animated reign by casting both the Antichrist and False Prophet alive into the Lake of Fire:

> [20]*And the beast was seized, and with him the false prophet who performed the signs in his presence, by which he deceived those who had received the mark of the beast and those who worshiped his image;* ***these two were thrown alive into the lake of fire*** *which burns with brimstone.*
>
> — Revelation 19:20

Unlike all of their biblical and historical precursors, they are the ultimate meaning of what it means to be "*broken without human agency*".

But for sanity's sake, we must revisit an important detail which was specified in this vision so that we know with confidence that what took place in the Inter-testamental Period as an historical fulfillment in the antics of Antiochus Epiphanes IV is, to be sure, going to be replayed again, and that is the very first and last thing Gabriel revealed to Daniel:

> [17]*So he came near to where I was standing, and when he came I was frightened and fell on my face; but he said to me, "Son of man,* ***understand that the vision pertains to the time of the end****."*
>
> — Daniel 8:17

Gabriel repeats this important caveat again as he concludes his explanation of the vision:

> [26]*"The vision of the evenings and mornings*
> *Which has been told is true;*
> *But keep the vision secret,*
> *For* ***it pertains to many days in the future****."*
>
> — Daniel 8:26

Yes, I mentioned this at the outset of this study, but like Gabriel, I am reinforcing its importance again at the end. Everything in God's Word is important, but that which is repeated is especially so.

Obviously, although much of what is stated both here and in Daniel 11 to come unquestionably experienced such a literal fulfillment that even secular scholars do not deny these historical parallels, such did not herald "*the time of the end*". Subsequent parallel passages of Scripture pertaining to the Antichrist and False Prophet, especially through other foreshadowing types both biblical and historical, will restate and even provide additional illumination on these particulars. But of all the historical forerunners of the Antichrist, none are more vital than Epiphanes in teaching about the ultimate anti-king to come and the true operation of the final anti-kingdom.

Are We Really Sure?

Now there are those who will put forth the reasonable objection, "How can the Antichrist replay the life of Epiphanes when Epiphanes came from the Seleucid Empire, and it appears the Antichrist rises from a revived Roman Empire? How can one be a mirror of the other if they are not absolutely identical?" The answer is provided by understanding that this question is not entirely based on the correct assumption of how typology works. A "type" or foreshadowing figure is ***not*** a pure, 100% clone; they are ***not a mirror*** of each other. Rather, each iteration leading up to the final one in the series shares common characteristics, or as stated earlier, acts "***in the character of***".

As in Nebuchadnezzar's statue, each is a part of one body, sharing the same characteristics, but individually they are different metals and different body parts. They belong to the same overall image, but are still individually unique within it. Likewise in Daniel's corresponding vision, they share common traits and behaviors passed down to the final figure, but are individually distinct in and of themselves.

Babylon passed its characteristics to Medo-Persia, which had its own enunciated geography, government, culture and so forth. And although Medo-Persia and then Greece after it would likewise be distinct in these things, still carried within them the same character of their forerunners. The final kingdom has roots in Rome, but the original itself first split into two halves as represented by the two legs (which are often referred to as the "Western Roman Empire" and the "Eastern Roman" or "Byzantine Empire"), and ultimately into something different in its final form as the ten toes. (The final one ***has*** to be different since it will consume the entire planet!) Each engulfed or completely swallowed the previous empire and adopted its character and influence into their own, but none are clones or copies of anything which came before it. They share a common spiritual heritage, passing those characteristics down just like genetic and behavioral traits are transmitted from father to son to grandson. But in this case, the "father", so to speak, is always Satan.

Whereas a genetic lineage may weaken over time as more generations inherit the previous predispositions and deficiencies, what is taking place in this case is that more and more of the satanic is coming through with each passing round until in the end, when he is literally cast to the earth, he and the final figure of the Antichrist become one. There are no more allusions to Satan as in all the past types and figures; the final one is fully merged and operating with no distinction between them. So one would be right to say that the final Antichrist will not be an identical twin of Antiochus Epiphanes IV (or any other prefiguring type), only that they share traits, which although were horrific as performed by the Seleucid king, will be many times multiplied and magnified in the last figure to come. Forerunners such as Epiphanes are influenced and even animated by Satan; the final Antichrist will be ***possessed*** by him.

This is an aspect of the book of Revelation which can be easily overlooked, that one of its major features is to show how the distinctions and barriers between the heavenly and the earthly are dissolving. Satan is thrown to earth, both angels and demons at times are no longer hidden from view but visibly observed and working in our earthly venue, and of course Christ literally comes and brings the kingdom of Antichrist to a close as He inaugurates the Millennial Kingdom on earth. We see this same progressive revelation in the many anti-kings and anti-kingdoms which prefigure the final ones both biblically and historically; the satanic is progressively revealed until literally coming to an earthly residence in the final anti-king, and becomes fully visible on earth.

More for Our Checklist

Daniel 8 provides yet additional distinctives identifying what is ultimately to come. To our previous list from Daniel 7 of what defines the ultimate anti-king/anti-kingdom we may add:

- He causes "*some of the host and some of the stars to fall to the earth, and it trampled them down.*" (v.10)
- Will magnify himself "*to be equal to the Commander of the host...*" (v.11)
- Removes "*the regular sacrifice...*" (v.11)
- "*...will fling truth to the ground...*" (v.11)
- "*...will...perform its will and prosper.*" (v.11)
- His public appearance corresponds to "*when the transgressors have run their course*"—that is, a time of great spiritual rebellion or apostasy. (v.23)
- "*Insolent and skilled in intrigue.*" (v.24)
- "*His power will be mighty, but not by his own power*". (v.24)
- "*...He will prosper and destroy to an extraordinary degree...*" (v.24)
- "*...He will...prosper and perform his will*". (v.24)
- "*He will destroy mighty men and the holy people.*" (v.24)
- "*...through shrewdness he will cause deceit to succeed by his influence...*" (v.25)
- "*...he will magnify himself in his heart...*" (v.25)
- "*He will even oppose the Prince of Princes...*" (v.25)
- "*He will be broken without human agency.*" (v.25)
- "*...both the holy place and the host* [will be] *trampled...*[for] *2,300 evenings and mornings...*" (v.13-14)

When we consider this list of 16 characteristics together with the 18 listed at the end of our discussion of the vision in Daniel 7, we can see that more than just a casual portrait of the final figure as both a king and kingdom is provided in Scripture, even at this early stage. Already we are seeing the emerging pattern of common traits which are revisited in Scripture, such as prolific deception, self-deification, persecution of the faithful and reward for the unfaithful, making maximum use of all things military and political, a deliberate attempt to halt any adherence to God's Word and ways, a textbook narcissistic personality which is simultaneously charismatic in its influence and a master manipulator of others, and an obsession for taking the very place dedicated to God, the Temple. He uses it as his own platform for elevating himself while at the same time attempting to erase all things pointing to the One True God.

In some respects he is the ultimate counterfeit of Christ in the course of his rise to prominence, but at its peak, plainly and without apology makes every effort to completely replace the Messiah for real. First he pretends to be the authentic Messiah (uses deception), then he attempts to take His actual place (uses force and persecution).

It has surely not gone unnoticed by the reader that the events replayed within the borders of Israel during the reign of Epiphanes are at least incipiently present worldwide at this very time, a testament to the previous assertion that such historical examples are but a shadow of what is many more times multiplied in the last and final fulfillment.

4 ❖ Daniel 9: The Weeks of Years

*[20]Now **while I was speaking and praying, and confessing my sin and the sin of my people Israel, and presenting my supplication** before the LORD my God in behalf of the holy mountain of my God, [21]**while I was still speaking in prayer**, then the man Gabriel, whom I had seen in the vision previously, came to me in my extreme weariness about the time of the evening offering. [22]He gave me instruction and talked with me and said, "O Daniel, **I have now come forth to give you insight with understanding**.*

— Daniel 9:20-22

One of the chief lessons to be learned from the Prophet Daniel is that he is a both a man of prayer and God's Word. In spite of his example and even the many teachings of Christ that these are exactly the qualities He most values in the End Times believer, so few seem to see this critical connection in Scripture at large, but especially as it is repeatedly revealed within eschatological passages. Christ concludes the Olivet Discourse with parables which have in common whether believers will be found to be faithful servants as defined by their practice of prayer and commitment to His Word both for their selves individually, and as they minister to others. In the book of Daniel, this is one of the most common, recurring themes:

- In chapter 1 we are provided the example of Daniel and his companions who went to great lengths and even personal risk to obey God's Word rather than man's, and received both earthly and heavenly rewards for their faithfulness.
- In chapter 2, the "impossible" answer to Nebuchadnezzar's dream was obtained by Daniel and his companions praying (Dan. 2:17-18), followed by Daniel's documented praise to God for receiving the answer in that manner. (Dan. 2:19-23).
- In chapter 3, Daniel's companions passed their test of faith and public witness to all that, "*we are not going to serve your gods or worship the golden image you have set up*" (Dan. 3:18) in a dramatic display of obedience to God's Word and ways even unto death.
- In chapter 6 we find Daniel not just engaged in regular prayer three times a day, but "*making petition and supplication before his God*". (Dan. 6:10-11) An attempt is made to use this against him with the earthly king, but as we all know, Daniel was delivered from this test and in the process won over Darius to the Heavenly King.

- In chapter 7, when Daniel does not understand the meaning of the divine vision imparted to him, he prays, as he will again do for the vision to come two years later in chapter 8.
- In chapters 10-12 (all of which are a single, uninterrupted passage), the answer to his vision again comes at his request—in other words, prayer. (Dan.10:12)
- In chapter 12, Daniel is assured that biblical understanding of God's prophetic Word comes to those "*who lead the many to righteousness*" (Dan.12:3) which can only be achieved by someone who is a practitioner of prayer and obedient to God's Word, and equally assured that "*none of the wicked will understand*" (Dan. 12:10), the antithesis of the condition of righteousness.

But chapter 9 in its own right is one of the greatest lessons recorded in Scripture, something which demonstrates the believer's need to incorporate the Word of God into their prayer, what Scripture most often refers to as meditating—that is, the application of God's Word in our personal approach to God as Daniel in this chapter demonstrates.

Prayer & Eschatology

> *1In the first year of Darius the son of Ahasuerus, of Median descent, who was made king over the kingdom of the Chaldeans— 2in the first year of his reign, I, Daniel, **observed in the books** the number of the years which was revealed as **the word of the LORD to Jeremiah** the prophet for the completion of the desolations of Jerusalem, namely, seventy years. 3**So I gave my attention to the Lord God to seek Him by prayer and supplications, with fasting, sackcloth and ashes**.*
>
> — Daniel 9:1-3

What is Daniel doing? He is ***prayerfully*** studying prophecy, and upon realizing its significance for his day, what does he do? Develop a chart? Host a blog or website? Initiate a series of conferences or embark on a speaking tour? Walk the streets wearing a sandwich board proclaiming, "The End Is Near"? No, he realizes that with the literal and impending fulfillment of God's prophetic Word that it cannot be properly processed without an accompanying compliance with the whole of His Word in the believer's life! His immediate concern is not whether or not prophecy is going to come true, but whether or not God's people are ***spiritually prepared*** for its inevitable fulfillment. Daniel is more concerned whether God's people are ready than anything else. In a fascinating parallel, this is actually Christ's greatest concern as he closed the Olivet Discourse.

- In the *Parable of the Faithful vs. Evil Slave* (Mt. 24:45-51), in either case a "*slave*" by definition being someone belonging to and appointed by God to do His work, the issue upon His return is whether they are found to be feeding and caring for the rest of the household, a metaphor for ministering the Word to the Church. The faithful is blessed and promoted, the evil immediately assigned to hell. It expresses Christ's primary concern that the Word is being both properly taught and consumed by His followers.
- In the *Parable of the Ten Virgins* (Mt. 25:1-13), even though all are "*virgins*", which by definition means only those who belong to the Church, the "*wise*" are Holy Spirit-filled practitioners of the Word as represented by having oil in their lamps, but the "*foolish*" as lacking the same. Those properly prepared through the Word

were ready and entered in with the bridegroom, the others shut out. It expresses Christ's concern that His followers be individually prepared and ready in the Word when He returns.

- In the *Parable of the Talents* (Mt. 13:14-30), all are identified as "*slaves*" so that everyone addressed again belongs to and is appointed by God to do His work. The faithful carry out the Master's business and are rewarded upon His return, the "*wicked, lazy slave*" is not merely found unprepared and wanting, but identified as "*worthless*" and immediately cast into hell. It expresses Christ's concerns that practitioners of His Word are doing so not just within the Church as in the previous examples, but in the course of their ministry to the world at large.

None of these warnings involves non-believers, who by definition have no clue what is really coming, but each example is hyper-directed at ***believers*** alone who are responsible to be ***spiritually*** ready for His return by being practitioners of His Word individually, within the Church, and in the course of their outreach and ministry to the world. In fact, each of the fourteen recorded warnings issued by Jesus in the parallel accounts of the Olivet Discourse in Matthew, Mark and Luke are exclusively directed at believers alone because they are the only ones who can possibly be aware of what is actually taking place in the Last Days. Likewise, Daniel's initial reaction is to pray for the spiritual state of God's people, whom Daniel recognized were not prepared for the impending fulfillment of God's Word in their time.

It Begins With Sincere Repentance

3So I gave my attention to the Lord God to seek Him by prayer and supplications, with fasting, sackcloth and ashes.
— Daniel 9:3

Not just "*prayer*", but "*supplication*", a term which describes appealing for a heartfelt response from someone who has something to give to one who has a need. The greater context of "*supplication*" involves an inferior subordinate who has no real claim or justification for gracious treatment seeking it from someone superior who can provide it if they so choose. It carries with it the overtones of compassion, mercy and sympathy. In its most rudimentary expression, it might be thought of as imploring God, "Even though I don't deserve it, please take pity on me." In Scripture it is used overwhelmingly as an appeal to Yahweh to request grace for something completely undeserved. A prime example is the penitent thief on the cross next to Jesus.

But the additional "*with fasting, sackcloth and ashes*" is the Old Testament expression of sincere repentance accompanied by mourning. This is not merely saying one is sorry or asking for forgiveness, but painfully aware of what they have done, and because of their earnest desire to never repeat this mistake, makes a sincere public commitment in this manner to no longer re-visit that behavior, action or breech of faith. All of these things combine to visibly convey a truly changed heart, mind and soul.

Notice that Daniel does not seek another vision or some kind of additional information about the prophecy he now understands God is about to fulfill, but that the desire is "*to seek Him*"—that is, something on a very personal, faith-based level. When a Christian comes to believe the Rapture will take place soon, their first impulse should be "*to seek Him*", not the event itself.

It is Followed Up With God's Word

> *[4]I prayed to the LORD my God and confessed and said, "Alas, O Lord, the great and awesome God, who keeps His covenant and lovingkindness for those who love Him and keep His commandments, [5]we have sinned, committed iniquity, acted wickedly and rebelled, even turning aside from Your commandments and ordinances. [6]Moreover, we have not listened to Your servants the prophets, who spoke in Your name to our kings, our princes, our fathers and all the people of the land.*
> — Daniel 9:4-6

There is an immediate contrast drawn between God who "***keeps** His covenant*" with those who prove their love because they in turn "***keep** His commandments*", and the confession of the root cause of sin, iniquity, wickedness and rebellion as "***turning aside from** your commandments and ordinances*". The character of God is that He always "*keeps*" His Word; the sinner, wicked and rebellious all have in common "*turning aside from*" His Word. If someone is going to achieve the biblical definition of repentance wherein the problem of sin is permanently abandoned and no longer repeated, such will not be possible without a corresponding change in behavior which does not merely listen to the Word, but puts it into practice and becomes consistently obedient to it.

An exclamation point for this problem is provided in the additional stipulation, "*Moreover, we have not listened to Your servants the prophets*". In other words, they had not only rejected God's written Word, but His spoken Word through the many additional messengers "*who spoke in Your name to our kings, our princes, our fathers and all the people of the land*". A true return to His Word and ways involves not just embracing written Scripture, but those preaching and presenting it for the present context of our life. Such is the primary lesson of what a believer needs to do in the face of the imminent fulfillment of God's prophetic Word.

Not Just the Individual

> *[7]"Righteousness belongs to You, O Lord, but to us open shame, as it is this day—to the men of Judah, the inhabitants of Jerusalem and all Israel, those who are nearby and those who are far away in all the countries to which You have driven them, because of their unfaithful deeds which they have committed against You. [8]Open shame belongs to us, O Lord, to our kings, our princes and our fathers, because we have sinned against You.*
> — Daniel 9:7-8

The contrast of God's "*righteousness*" and the people's state of "*shame*" is presented in the context of taking responsibility for the current consequences having come about by "*unfaithful deeds which they have committed against You*", fully acknowledging that their current status cannot be attributed to God "*because we have sinned against You*". Personal accountability in such matters is first confessed and presented before offering the same for the whole group involved. Although Daniel is never recorded as committing any sin, much less personally contributing to this problem by participating in this root cause, he does not point the finger at others but as a member of the group assumes responsibility for the group so as to intercede on their behalf. Such is the primary lesson for what the Church needs to do in the face of imminent fulfillment of God's prophetic Word.

The Dual Working of the Word

[9]"To the Lord our God belong compassion and forgiveness, for we have rebelled against Him; [10]nor have we obeyed the voice of the LORD our God, to walk in His teachings which He set before us through His servants the prophets. [11]Indeed all Israel has transgressed Your law and turned aside, not obeying Your voice; so the curse has been poured out on us, along with the oath which is written in the law of Moses the servant of God, for we have sinned against Him. [12]Thus He has confirmed His words which He had spoken against us and against our rulers who ruled us, to bring on us great calamity; for under the whole heaven there has not been done anything like what was done to Jerusalem.

— Daniel 9:9-12

One of the first things Joshua led Israel to do upon entering the Promised Land was to direct half of them to stand on Mt. Ebal to recite the curses provided in God's Word for failure to observe His Word, and the other half on Mt. Gerizim to recite the corresponding blessings for keeping it. (Dt. 27-28) The consequences were not only quite specific, but included what came to transpire historically in the ultimate removal of Israel from the land into the very captivity they were suffering in Daniel's lifetime. They were additionally experiencing the consequences of what the prophets specifically and repeatedly warned them against, and were therefore doubly responsible for their own present circumstances.

*[13]Yet the LORD warned Israel and Judah through all His prophets and every seer, saying, "Turn from your evil ways and keep My commandments, My statutes according to all the law which I commanded your fathers, and which I sent to you through My servants the prophets." [14]However, **they did not listen**, but stiffened their neck like their fathers, who did not believe in the LORD their God. [15]**They rejected His statutes and His covenant which He made with their fathers and His warnings with which He warned them.** And they followed vanity and became vain, and went after the nations which surrounded them, concerning which the LORD had commanded them not to do like them.*

— 2 Kings 17:13-15

*[11]Then the king of Assyria carried Israel away into exile to Assyria, and put them in Halah and on the Habor, the river of Gozan, and in the cities of the Medes, [12]**because they did not obey the voice of the LORD their God**, but transgressed His covenant, even all that Moses the servant of the LORD commanded; **they would neither listen nor do it**.*

— 2 Kings 18:11-12

Daniel, one of the foremost students and practitioners of God's Word recorded in the whole of Scripture, begins by acknowledging the contrast between a righteous God who is defined by keeping His Word as opposed to the rebellious and wicked who turn aside from it, then assumes personal responsibility before assigning corporate liability in this regard to the whole of Israel, and ultimately takes ownership that the consequences currently experienced came about not only as a result of a lapse of obedience to His written Word, but to His further warnings and admonitions presented through His prophets.

(As a side note, perhaps a major part of the answer to the oft posed question of why the Church, at least in its present condition in the West, has been largely unresponsive to the many and obvious fulfilled prophecies of the past half century is that when those who should know better fail to keep His Word where their personal walk is concerned, spiritual blindness always results for the greater things. And just as it was in those times, but to an even greater degree today because of modern media and particularly the Internet, we have turned a deaf ear to more voices applying God's Word to our times than probably all previous generations combined. Daniel's example addresses a current problem which information alone cannot remedy, that repentance and a return to God's Word is the critical need of the moment in order to be properly prepared for the complete fulfillment which is about to come.)

> [13]*"As it is written in the law of Moses, all this calamity has come on us; yet we have not sought the favor of the LORD our God by turning from our iniquity and giving attention to Your truth.* [14]*Therefore the LORD has kept the calamity in store and brought it on us; for the LORD our God is righteous with respect to all His deeds which He has done, but we have not obeyed His voice.*
>
> — Daniel 9:13-14

This is the ultimate conundrum in the presence of God's judgment. Near the opening of Daniel's prayer he identified the consequences resulting from the human side of the equation "*because of* ***their unfaithful deeds*** *which they have committed against You*" (v.7) to God being "***righteous with respect to all His deeds*** *which He has done*", and the net result has been, "*but we have not obeyed His voice*". Even so, God is characterized as holding back the consequences and not immediately acting in His merciful character in stating He "*has kept the calamity in store*". It is only the persistent pursuit of sin and resistance to turning back which eventually "*brought it on us*". Nonetheless, there is no attempt here to avoid responsibility or shift it somewhere else.

> [15]*"And now, O Lord our God, who have brought Your people out of the land of Egypt with a mighty hand and have made a name for Yourself, as it is this day—we have sinned, we have been wicked.* [16]*O Lord, in accordance with all Your righteous acts, let now Your anger and Your wrath turn away from Your city Jerusalem, Your holy mountain; for because of our sins and the iniquities of our fathers, Jerusalem and Your people have become a reproach to all those around us.* [17]*So now, our God, listen to the prayer of Your servant and to his supplications, and for Your sake, O Lord, let Your face shine on Your desolate sanctuary.*
>
> — Daniel 9:15-17

It is important to note that Daniel does not lead with this, but after properly visiting the issue of personal and corporate sin, repentance, and the handling of God's Word, he appeals to God's past working in what were considered the greatest benefits to both Israel at large and its individual constituents. Without God they would still be slaves in Egypt; without God they would have never obtained the Promised Land, much less Jerusalem and the Temple therein. And Daniel correctly understands that Israel and all these things were effected to bring glory and honor to the One True God, stipulating that in the course of the Exodus God's working "*made a name for Yourself*" and that the consequences of "*Your wrath*" which came on "*Your city Jerusalem*" and its "*desolate sanctuary*" were solely "*because of our sins and the iniquities of our fathers*". In the shadow of the fulfillment of God's promise to bring an end to these things is an accompanying commitment from God's people to not just accept personal responsibility for past unfaithfulness, but to commit going forward to the only solution by pursuing consistent faithfulness to His Word and ways so as to be truly and authentically ready for what is to come. One of the critical steps in the process is the sincere realization it is not about ***our*** name, honor and glory, but our sincere and earnest desire for ***His***.

Hear and Forgive

18"O my God, incline Your ear and hear! Open Your eyes and see our desolations and the city which is called by Your name; for we are not presenting our supplications before You on account of any merits of our own, but on account of Your great compassion. 19O Lord, hear! O Lord, forgive! O Lord, listen and take action! For Your own sake, O my God, do not delay, because Your city and Your people are called by Your name."

— Daniel 9:18-19

A friend once succinctly summed up life by intoning, "He's God, and I'm not". Such is expressed here on the macro level. One of the things all the great spiritual examples in Scripture share is the earnest, sincere desire bordering on obsession for God's glory and honor and a complete indifference when it comes to their own. These are qualities best suited for those properly prepared for His return—that is, for the complete fulfillment of His Word. Daniel highlights "***Your*** *ear*", "***Your*** *eyes*", "***Your*** *name*" (twice), "***Your*** *great compassion*", "***Your*** *own sake*", and ultimately "***Your*** *city and* ***Your*** *people*" because they "*are called by* ***Your*** *name*". It is entirely a grace-based appeal which categorically rejects a justification involving "*any merits of our own*". Daniel makes an appeal to what God was working in His own name and glory, praying according to God's ***already given Word*** rather than seeking something new.

A Personal Agenda

I am sure that of those who went to the trouble to invest their own time and expense to read this book, most have probably not only been a Christian for some time, but are more than casually acquainted with the prevailing issues of eschatology. When you came to the title of this chapter, "The Weeks of Years", and began reading a lengthy exegesis of Daniel's prayer, did you become a little anxious and wonder, even in passing, "Is he ever going to get to that?"

I readily admit that for most of my life my habit was to go directly to such portions of God's Word as Daniel 9:24-27 and not bother with what appeared to not have much, if anything, related to it in the whole account of chapter 9. It took me much longer than it should have to treat the portions of God's prophetic Word the same way I handle the rest where I resist lifting a verse or passage out of the greater context in which it is presented. This is one of the primary reasons there is so much more confusion when it comes to eschatology than the other areas of doctrine and theology because even Bible teachers and scholars make the mistake of changing their hermeneutics—their rules for Bible interpretation, when it comes to something touching the prophetic, and even ignoring the verses around something they believe is more important eschatologically.

Ordinarily we would never take a few verses out of their surrounding context as the majority of us have done to Daniel's "*weeks of years*" in the three closing verses of this chapter and build an entire doctrine around it. If this was Scripture devoted to something related to salvation, justification or sanctification, for instance, we would never abandon the rest of chapter 9 to only and always fixate on just these last three verses, and at the least we would always give due consideration to the immediate context in the verses surrounding it. Outside of God's prophetic Word speaking of the Messiah, there is probably no more important or visited verses of prophecy than Daniel 9:24-27 and, sadly, an accompanying, monumental ignorance of the true context in which they were given. For various reasons, the overriding rule that context matters where the rest of God's Word is concerned is in this case given an unwarranted exception and jettisoned more often than not.

What Was Daniel Seeking?

> *[20]Now while I was speaking and praying, and confessing my sin and the sin of my people Israel, and presenting my supplication before the LORD my God in behalf of the holy mountain of my God, [21]while I was still speaking in prayer, then the man Gabriel, whom I had seen in the vision previously, came to me in my extreme weariness about the time of the evening offering. [22]He gave me instruction and talked with me and said, "O Daniel, I have now come forth to give you insight with understanding. [23]At the beginning of your supplications the command was issued, and I have come to tell you, for you are highly esteemed; so give heed to the message and gain understanding of the vision.*
>
> — Daniel 9:20-23

While indulging me with my visiting of each sentence of Daniel's prayer in the opening 19 verses, did you notice that Daniel ***never*** asked God for a vision? Daniel made no inquiries about God's intentions for the future other than to intercede for His people's right response to His Word by their repentance and return to His already given Word. One of the most important and influential revelations in the whole of God's Word was given to someone who was not even actively pursuing knowledge of something new or future in the realm of the prophetic, but attempting to resolve past human failure to properly respond to what was already known prophetically and having an impact in the present.

Daniel plainly documents that this seminal revelation came "*while I was still speaking in prayer*", the very details of which are provided in the opening 19 verses, none of which even slightly hint at requesting the revelation to come. No, there is a far greater lesson here that adhering to all that God has ***already*** given in His Word, being in compliance with the past and present working of His Word, and a priority on personal faithfulness where His Word is concerned is the most important prerequisite for what is yet to come. Just as you would not allow your carpenter apprentice to build a house when they can't hammer a nail yet or saw a two-by-four, neither will the deeper things of God be revealed to those who never left the proverbial shallow end of the pool.

As noted previously, an association is made in the pages of Daniel between understanding and righteousness (Dan. 12:3) and a direct link between the lack of understanding and wickedness. (Dan. 12:10) In our rush to chart the End Times or focus our attention on what we think is a core issue, we continue to miss the fact that consistently accompanying God's prophetic Word are instructions and examples of what to do to be spiritually qualified to not just understand it, but put it into effect. As in everything truly belonging to biblical Christianity, it is much more a test of faith than a test of knowledge.

I have personally attended far more of my share of so-called "prophecy conferences", admittedly mostly due to supporting someone who was one of the featured speakers, where I tired of the majority taking the podium who were at best "lecturers" but never pastor/teachers of God's Word. A true shepherd is not an information giver, and the sheep are not information gatherers. So few were actually engaged in any kind of real ministry when not on their lecture circuits, much less fulfilling the biblical mandate of not just discipling others, but growing in the Word themselves. I know how harsh this sounds, but the fact is that I often pursued God's Word in the same manner, as something studied in preparation for a presentation instead of obeyed and put into personal practice. Real shepherds live with the sheep and experience what they experience rather than visit them once a year to tell them what life in the pasture is supposed to be like, or worse, their opinion of what it should be.

Where Is The Concern?

In Daniel, and in particular in the greater context of what is inarguably one of the most important passages of God's prophetic Word, the very lesson of what to do with God's Word is at the heart of the context in which it was given. If we were truly pursuing God's future Word, we would be first and foremost dedicated to upholding His past and present Word. If we truly recognize at this time that much of God's prophetic Word has already come true and confirms we are in the shadow of the ultimate fulfillment of all that we know is shortly ahead of us, shouldn't we, like Daniel, be more concerned for the current lack of compliance by His people of the Word He has already given and fulfilled than personal quests for further or new revelations? Perhaps one of the aspects of Christ's warning that in the Last Days, "*Because lawlessness is increased, most people's love will grow cold*" (Mt. 24:12) has as one of its casualties the wrong pursuit of eschatology. After all, "*lawlessness*" is a direct reference to a failure of obedience where His Word is concerned.

Neither did Daniel ask God if the prophecies given through Jeremiah were indeed about to be fulfilled, but by faith took God's written Word for it and addressed them in prayer to God as "future fact"—something Daniel believed would come true by a faith which saw it as if it was already fulfilled. Most notably, this model of prayer, faith and God's Word produced an immediate reaction because of the stark realization, "We aren't ready for this!" Knowing that the people of his time were not properly spiritually prepared when it came to God's already given Word, Daniel was acutely aware of how ill-prepared they were for what His Word portended was about to arrive. Daniel did not celebrate and become enthusiastic that he was about to witness something divinely predicted come true, but understanding its true spiritual impact, immediately empathized the consequences for the spiritually ill-prepared.

This has been the world's longest Christian public service announcement to ask what would happen if we were to emulate Daniel in this regard for our own generation, whom we are convinced are about to imminently experience the fulfillment of God's prophetic Word on an even greater scale than all previous generations combined? What if each time we visited this seminal teaching on the "*weeks of years*", we also revisited the context in which it was given? What if we became more concerned about the lack of preparedness among God's people and what it means than for the satisfaction of unlocking the meaning of three verses?

There is a greater issue of faith at work in Daniel 9 for each of us personally than one purely pertaining to knowledge, isn't there?

The Timing of the King & Anti-King

> *22He gave me instruction and talked with me and said, "O Daniel, I have now come forth to give you insight with understanding. 23At the beginning of your supplications the command was issued, and I have come to tell you, for you are highly esteemed; so give heed to the message and gain understanding of the vision.*
> — Daniel 9:22-23

There is something very interesting taking place in looking at the content of what is here called "*your supplications*". For Daniel this began as a realization that the plain text of Jeremiah was about to be fulfilled, "*I...observed in the books the number of years which was revealed...to Jeremiah the prophet for the completion of the desolations of Jerusalem, namely, **seventy years***". (Dan. 9:2)

> [10] *"For thus says the LORD, 'When seventy years have been completed for Babylon, I will visit you and fulfill My good word to you, to bring you back to this place.*
> — Jeremiah 29:10

Daniel was not asking the Lord what this meant or seeking an alternative or deeper meaning of the seventy literal years which were about to come to pass. Unlike the countless failed attempts throughout the whole of history since, where a number found in Scripture is lifted completely out of context and fancifully manipulated into some vain attempt to claim something prophetic is about to take place, Daniel accepted the seventy years for ***exactly*** what they were: seventy literal years which were about to conclude. It is ***God*** who initiates a response which provides a revelation not involving the seventy literal years of the Babylonian Captivity as it relates to Israel, but seventy ***weeks*** of years as it relates to God's plan for the whole world. For those tempted to continue the tradition of making more out of numbers than what the plain text of Scripture provides, in both cases they are ***literal*** years which cannot be spiritualized away or reassigned some kind of symbolic or metaphorical meaning. The vision of this "seventy" is given in the shadow of accepting the literalness of the first "seventy".

But again, Daniel's initial prayer was addressing the impending end of Israel's seventy year Captivity and their return to the land, yet God reveals the world's final seventy ***weeks*** of years which will again centrally involve what takes place in the land of Israel, but this time not just for Israel alone. Daniel's prayers concerning Israel, Jerusalem and the Temple experienced a divine response which went far beyond what would simply happen to those things in Daniel's immediate future, but their ultimate fate on the world stage for all mankind.

> [24] *"**Seventy weeks** have been decreed for your people and your holy city, to finish the transgression, to make an end of sin, to make atonement for iniquity, to bring in everlasting righteousness, to seal up vision and prophecy and to anoint the most holy place.* [25] *So you are to know and discern that from the issuing of a decree to restore and rebuild Jerusalem until Messiah the Prince there will be **seven weeks** and **sixty-two weeks**; it will be built again, with plaza and moat, even in times of distress.*
> [26] *"Then after the **sixty-two weeks** the Messiah will be cut off and have nothing, and the people of the prince who is to come will destroy the city and the sanctuary. And its end will come with a flood; even to the end there will be war; desolations are determined.* [27] *And he will make a firm covenant with the many for **one week**, but **in the middle of the week** he will put a stop to sacrifice and grain offering; and on the wing of abominations will come one who makes desolate, even until a complete destruction, one that is decreed, is poured out on the one who makes desolate."*
> — Daniel 9:24-27

There seems to be a different emphasis placed on the "*seventy weeks*" overall from a subdivision of "*seven weeks and sixty-two weeks*", which obviously totals sixty-nine (but is never called that), and that final week completing it all. So before we jump to that final week of years, it is important to first understand the "*seventy weeks*" overall and then why it is not only divided into a "*sixty-two*" and "*seven*" to cover the first sixty-nine weeks, but ultimately calling out that last and final week of years on its own. There are two aspects presented in the "*seventy*", the sixty-nine subdivided into "*seven*" and "*sixty-two*", and the very last week of years.

As it turns out, the two major figures associated with this sequence are the "*Messiah the Prince*" (v.25)—that is, Jesus Christ in both His First and Second Comings, and the "*one who makes desolate*"—that is, the figure we most commonly refer to as the Antichrist. (v.27)

> [8]*Then that lawless one will be revealed whom the Lord will slay with the breath of His mouth and bring to an end by the appearance of His coming;* [9]*that is, the one whose coming is in accord with the activity of Satan, with all power and signs and false wonders,* [10]*and with all the deception of wickedness for those who perish, because they did not receive the love of the truth so as to be saved.*
> — 2 Thessalonians 2:8-10

The Context of the Seventy Weeks

The first caveat concerning the "*seventy weeks*" is that it is has "*been decreed for your people and your holy city*". To the very end, this involves the people of Israel and Jerusalem.

We live at a time when far too much of the Church, at least in the West, has embraced some form of Replacementism—that is, the false notion Israel had their chance and blew it, God is through with Israel and has transferred all His attention and blessings upon the Church, so every time you come across a reference to "Israel" in Scripture just cross it out and replace it with "the Church". There are many variations, but whether it calls itself "Kingdom Now Theology", "Dominionism", "Triumphalism", "Manifest Sons of Destiny", or whatever, they all basically form their position from this false premise. Many take it to an extreme to even make the claim that it is only when the Church finally wins every person to Christ that He will return, meaning that the Church conquering the earth initiates His return, and by some accounts, this is when the Millennial Kingdom will take place.

If there has even been the remotest tug on the reader's mind at one time or another which even allowed for the possibility of such a teaching to be true, read these verses again and, like Daniel, accept God's Word for its plainly stated truth. There is no mention of such a replacement much less a scenario where human agency is responsible for completing God's work. In fact, the Apostle Paul devoted Romans 9-11 specifically for the purpose of addressing exactly what God's plans are for Israel in relationship to the Church, and it outright rejects every variation of Replacementism ever offered.

> [24]*"Seventy weeks have been decreed for your people and your holy city,* ***to finish*** *the transgression,* ***to make an end of*** *sin,* ***to make atonement for*** *iniquity,* ***to bring in*** *everlasting righteousness,* ***to seal up*** *vision and prophecy and* ***to anoint*** *the most holy place.*
> — Daniel 9:24

A detailed list is provided as to the purpose of the "*seventy weeks*":

- "*...to finish the transgression...*"
- "*...to make an end of sin...*"
- "*...to make atonement for iniquity...*"
- "*...to bring in everlasting righteousness...*"
- "*...to seal up vision and prophecy...*"
- "*...to anoint the most holy place.*"

From the outset it must be stated that ***this*** is how we know the difference between a partial fulfillment or forerunner and the ultimate, final event. We know that an antichrist figure in Antiochus Epiphanes IV committed an abomination of desolation which desecrated the Temple, and that after overcoming him and taking back the Temple, the Jews of that time replaced the desecrated alter on which he sacrificed a pig and went through the tedious process of cleansing and consecrating the Temple according to the Mosaic Law. Yet we know that as close as this event mirrored so many things revealed through Daniel, because it neither brought an end to "*transgression*","*sin*" and "*iniquity*" nor ushered in "*everlasting righteousness*", it was a precursor teaching us something about the final one yet to come.

A staple provided by many of Walk with the Word's teachings visits the fact that although they share many similarities and may even be thought of as "cousins", the fact is that "*transgression*", "*sin*" and "*iniquity*" are not the exact, same thing. They actually describe three specific yet related conditions:

- "*Sin*"—in Hebrew "*chatta-ah*" (Strong's #2403), is failing to meet the standard of God's Word. Anyone and everyone can "miss the mark" where God's standards are concerned.
- "*Transgression*"—in Hebrew "*pesha*" (Strong's #6588), is the act of rebelling against the standard of God's Word. It is consciously knowing the difference and making a conscious contrary choice.
- "*Iniquity*"—in Hebrew "*avon*" (Strong's #5771), carries with it the meaning of "to bend", "to twist" or "to deviate from the way". It is the twisting of God's Word so as to justify one's self or actions in spite of the true standard of God's Word.

That which is presented here is intended to cover the entire spectrum of sinful behavior. So it is not referring to a time when just another kingdom comes to power on earth in the usual manner, but addressing the end to the real root cause of all mankind's ills initiated by the Fall in the Garden. That which came through Adam and Eve's encounter with the serpent—whom we know to be Satan, is finally brought to a permanent end along with that provocateur himself. But in this specific context, we cannot overlook the fact that "*transgression*" has been highlighted and elevated above all "*sin*" and all "*iniquity*" by designating that God is going to bring an end to "***the*** *transgression*".

It has already been revealed to Daniel that "***the*** *transgression*" is that time when the Antichrist operates out of the Temple for himself alone, a period initiated by the Abomination of Desolation, his public act of self-deification.

> [13]*Then I heard a holy one speaking, and another holy one said to that particular one who was speaking, "How long will the vision about the regular sacrifice apply, while* ***the transgression causes horror****, so as to allow both the holy place and the host to be trampled?"* [14]*He said to me, "For 2,300 evenings and mornings; then the holy place will be properly restored."*
>
> — Daniel 8:13-14

The culmination of the "*seventy weeks*" coincides not only with an end to the general sin-based spiritual conditions, but those belonging to the ultimate "*man of sin*" (2 Th. 2:3)—that is, the Antichrist. This initiates not only the onset of the complete opposite of sin, iniquity and transgression—that is, "*everlasting righteousness*", but a restoration of the "*qodesh qadashim*"—"*the most holy place*".

The global view provided for the entirety of the "*seventy weeks*" is to permanently address the greater spiritual issues which have been the undercurrent for all of history in the elimination of the antagonist who first and continually fomented sin, and that very behavior in general. That vacuum is immediately replaced with "*everlasting righteousness*" and the restoration of the central biblical symbol of right worship, "*the most holy place*". The battle originally initiated between the Godhead and Satan which carried over into the ranks of mankind comes to end both for the literal figures involved and the greater spiritual conditions in play.

The Context of "Seven" & "Sixty-Two"

> *25"So you are to know and discern that from the issuing of a decree to restore and rebuild Jerusalem until Messiah the Prince there will be seven weeks and sixty-two weeks; it will be built again, with plaza and moat, even in times of distress.*
> — Daniel 9:25

The main objective for understanding the first sixty-nine of the seventy weeks is what we call the First Coming. Daniel was specifically told that "*a decree to restore and rebuild Jerusalem*" would initiate a countdown when the Messiah would come and then "*be cut off*", followed by the final antics of the anti-Messiah which concluded with his "*complete destruction*".

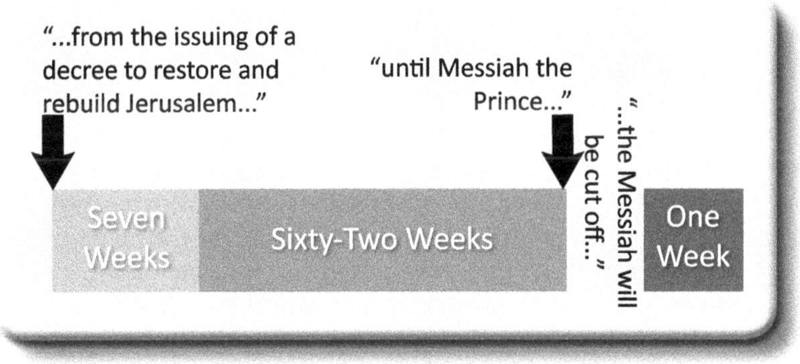

One of the initial difficulties we have to navigate is that the biblical record holds that there was more than a single decree issued relating to the Temple or Jerusalem. The first was issued by Cyrus for the Jews to return to Jerusalem and rebuild the Temple:

> *1Now in the first year of Cyrus king of Persia, in order to fulfill the word of the LORD by the mouth of Jeremiah, the LORD stirred up the spirit of **Cyrus king of Persia**, so that he **sent a proclamation** throughout all his kingdom, and also put it in writing, saying: 2"Thus says Cyrus king of Persia, 'The LORD, the God of heaven, has given me all the kingdoms of the earth and He has appointed me **to build Him a house in Jerusalem, which is in Judah**.*
> — Ezra 1:1-2

It is important to note that the intention was not to restore Jerusalem itself, and that the specific designation of "*Judah*" indicates the recognized area around Jerusalem, but not the whole of the original land of Israel.

> *1Then **King Darius issued a decree**, and search was made in the archives, where the treasures were stored in Babylon. 2In Ecbatana in the fortress, which is in the province of Media, a scroll was found and there was written in it as follows: "Memorandum—3In the first year of King Cyrus, Cyrus the king issued a decree: 'Concerning the house of God at Jerusalem, let the temple, the place where sacrifices are offered, be rebuilt and let its foundations be retained...*
> — Ezra 6:1-3a

Work on the Temple began but was interrupted because of local interference. The appeal to resume the work took place during the new reign of King Darius who found King Cyrus' original decree in the government archives and re-issued the original king's order to rebuild the Temple. In order to preclude any further local interruptions, King Darius issued his own order which would allow the work to be completed:

> [7]*"Leave this work on the house of God alone; let the governor of the Jews and the elders of the Jews rebuild this house of God on its site.*
> — Ezra 6:7

However, this second decree was also limited to the Temple and not a license for the greater restoration of Jerusalem as a whole.

The third recorded decree issued by King Artaxerxes empowered Ezra and the priests and Levites who were to operate the Temple to return to Jerusalem and initiate the continual operation of the Temple with a special offering from the king himself:

> [14]*"Forasmuch as you are sent by the king and his seven counselors to inquire concerning Judah and Jerusalem according to the law of your God which is in your hand,* [15]*and to bring the silver and gold, which the king and his counselors have freely offered to the God of Israel, whose dwelling is in Jerusalem,* [16]*with all the silver and gold which you find in the whole province of Babylon, along with the freewill offering of the people and of the priests, who offered willingly* ***for the house of their God which is in Jerusalem****;* [17]*with this money, therefore, you shall diligently buy bulls, rams and lambs, with their grain offerings and their drink offerings and offer them on the altar of* ***the house of your God which is in Jerusalem****.* [18]*Whatever seems good to you and to your brothers to do with the rest of the silver and gold, you may do according to the will of your God.*
> — Ezra 7:14-18

Conspicuous by its absence from this decree as well is permission to rebuild Jerusalem and still restricts activities to the Temple proper. It is with Nehemiah, after the restoration of the Temple as both a facility and its required operations, when the focus shifts to Jerusalem:

> [1]*The words of Nehemiah the son of Hacaliah. Now it happened in the month Chislev, in the twentieth year, while I was in Susa the capitol,* [2]*that Hanani, one of my brothers, and some men from Judah came; and* ***I asked them concerning the Jews who had escaped and had survived the captivity, and about Jerusalem****.* [3]*They said to me, "The remnant there in the province who survived the captivity are in great distress and reproach, and the wall of Jerusalem is broken down and its gates are burned with fire."* [4]*When I heard these words, I sat down and wept and mourned for days; and I was fasting and praying before the God of heaven.*
> — Nehemiah 1:1-4

Nehemiah then beseeches God in prayer "*to make Your servant successful today and grant him compassion before this man*" (Neh. 1:11) before making his request of King Artaxerxes for the restoration of Jerusalem. Whereas Ezra oversaw the rebuilding of the Temple, it is under Nehemiah's direction that the rebuilding of the city of Jerusalem takes place.

> [7]*And I said to the king, "If it please the king, let letters be given me for the governors of the provinces beyond the River, that they may allow me to pass through until I come to Judah,* [8]*and a letter to Asaph the keeper of the king's forest, that he may give*

> *me timber to make beams for **the gates of the fortress** which is by the temple, for **the wall of the city** and for the house to which I will go." And **the king granted them** to me because the good hand of my God was on me.*
> — Nehemiah 2:7-8

What we learn from the books of Ezra, Haggai and Zechariah is that it took forty-nine years—that is, the first "*seven weeks*" of years of the sixty-nine, to complete the construction of the Temple, at which time the rebuilding of Jerusalem under the direction of Nehemiah took place.

While this can be extremely confusing in an effort to first navigate the various decrees and then perform the tedious task of calculating the dates between each edict and where they fall in relation to Christ's First Coming (especially since Scripture is using a lunar calendar of years comprised of 29.5 day months and we no longer are), it is sufficient to note that there have been many studies calculating the various possibilities which suitably align themselves to confirm the accuracy of what Scripture predicted. To understand and evaluate them all, however, would take an additional monumental discussion as to how one interprets, "*Then... the Messiah will be cut off and have nothing*". (Dan. 9:26) It ranges from the Crucifixion to the destruction of the Second Temple some 36 years after.

Because Daniel's prophecy does not mention restoration of the Temple but just Jerusalem alone, and that is the sole focus of the fourth decree given Nehemiah, this is the preference which many much more math-enabled academicians have used to calculate these sixty-nine weeks as ending with the day Jesus rode into Jerusalem in what we contrarily call "The Triumphal Entry". I say "contrarily", because it was not actually a triumph for Israel but its very worst day when in seeing through their temporary false acceptance of Him Jesus said...

> 39 *"For I say to you, from now on you will not see Me until you say, 'BLESSED IS HE WHO COMES IN THE NAME OF THE LORD!' "*
> — Matthew 23:39

While it may be argued as to which milestone is the actual target of Daniel's prophecy for when "*the Messiah will be cut off*", there is still a problem here because the initial "*seven weeks*" of years has already passed with building of the Temple, and the prophecy says, "*from the issuing of a decree to restore and rebuild Jerusalem...there will be seven weeks **and** sixty-two weeks*". A fulfillment is already underway when this particular decree is issued.

Again, there have been successful calculations for each decree which coincide with the sixty-nine weeks concluding in a close relationship with something parallel to the Messiah's First Coming, but to this author's mind, there has yet to be a fully satisfying explanation of why Scripture specifies a decree which it then provides recorded instances of decrees instead of only reporting on the one that matters. Something else must be going on here.

A Modern Application

Allow me to suggest why this somewhat involved exercise of navigating through the various decrees might actually have a greater use and benefit to us in the here and now.

We are all familiar with the scriptural basis for understanding that there are ***many*** false christs, who among many other supporting reasons, have as a primary agenda serving to disguise and make it difficult to discern the final actual one. There are also ***many*** false prophets who serve the same function, disguising and making it difficult to unmask the ultimate False Prophet. And as discussed already, there have been ***many*** Abomination of Desolations prefiguring the final one yet to come. Satan sends a flood of what we might call "pre-counterfeits" because his agenda is to make it as difficult as possible to determine what is ultimately authentic, but God turns each around to the Holy Spirit-filled faithful to teach them something about the final one to come. Satan has his purposes for the "many", but God has His.

Nonetheless, there are many antichrists, many false prophets, many abominations of desolations, and even many Babylons from the very first on the plains of Shinar in Genesis to the last "*Babylon the Great*" in Revelation and those in between. This author suggests that this maze of decrees we have had to navigate concerning the Temple and Jerusalem is a counterfeited feature of the Last Days. There are ***many*** treaties.

Ultimately we hold as axiomatic from the plain text of Scripture that the Antichrist will make a covenant with Israel, which for the first time in Scripture is overtly stated in this very passage in Daniel 9:27. It is obvious from this and supporting texts that this is going to involve not just Jerusalem, but a third temple, what many of us call the "Tribulational Temple" which The Temple Institute in Israel, supported by a reconstituted Sanhedrin, has already prepared in advance and is waiting to build as we sit here today.

Although we have yet to witness ***this*** covenant, the fact is that there have already been ***many*** treaties and negotiations that have already taken place in the form of the Olso Accords, the Camp David Accords, or many other lesser attempts. Nary a week goes by when it is not reported that someone is negotiating something to do with Israel or Jerusalem. Many do not realize that the Clinton administration put forth a proposal that specifically included the Temple as one of its chief points.

In other words, there has ***already*** been ***many*** treaties obfuscating the final one to come just as we have already had many antichrists, many false prophets, and many abominations. The many decrees accompanying the historical restoration of Jerusalem and the Temple seem to be a counterfeit feature of the Antichrist's intentions for Jerusalem and the Temple in that final week of years.

This also should encourage us to make the effort at some point to delve into Ezra, Nehemiah, Haggai and Zechariah because they address the issues which were involved with re-establishing both the Temple and Jerusalem, two major issues consuming the entire world at present. Although the modern nation-state of Israel was instituted in 1948, it was not until 1967 that a partial return of Jerusalem was effected. It has never come under complete, autonomous control of Israel much less gained more than casual access to the Temple Mount itself. This conflict which was first played out in Old Testament times on a local level between Jews and Gentiles has now taken a multiplied leading role on the world stage. It is difficult to find anyone without an iron in the fire, so to speak, when it comes to not just the land of Israel, but Jerusalem itself. As with almost everything prophetic, what happened then is the best teacher for what will happen next.

Just as historically Jerusalem was "*built again, with plaza and moat, even in times of distress*" (Dan. 9:25) as recorded by Ezra, Nehemiah, Haggai and Zechariah, so it has been to an even greater degree for what has already taken place in the modern era, with an obviously larger obstacle of distress yet to come for it to be completed.

We must also consider that in the difficulty of navigating these decrees in the Old Testament that it is a precursor to the principle that no one will know the day or the hour. There is not a clear path to precisely calculating this divine decree, and likewise the satanic counterfeit is difficult to pinpoint because the rest of Scripture, the New Testament included, is silent where the treaty is concerned. Again, this may be telling us that this is one of those details which will only be understood in hindsight.

The Context of What (Or Who) Comes After

> [26]*"Then after the sixty-two weeks the Messiah will be cut off and have nothing, and the people of the prince who is to come will destroy the city and the sanctuary. And its end will come with a flood; even to the end there will be war; desolations are determined.* [27]*And he will make a firm covenant with the many for one week, but in the middle of the week he will put a stop to sacrifice and grain offering; and on the wing of abominations will come one who makes desolate, even until a complete destruction, one that is decreed, is poured out on the one who makes desolate."*
> — Daniel 9:26-27

To correctly understand the text it is important to see that there are two figures mentioned here. The first is obviously "*the Messiah*", and the second is identified by the entire description, "*the prince who is to come*", who we would call the Antichrist. Especially because of supporting Scripture, the things which are attributed to this "*prince*" without a capital "p" here are affirmed as some of his chief activities:

- "*...destroy the city and the sanctuary.*"
- "*...there will be war...*"
- "*...desolations are determined.*"
- "*...make a firm covenant with the many for one week...*"
- "*...in the middle of the week he will put a stop to sacrifice and grain offering...*"
- "*...on the wing of abominations...makes desolate...*"

It is here where we derive the concept of a final "week of years" because not only is a final seven year period designated from the outset, but having explained what takes place with the initial sixty-nine we do not have to guess that this is addressing the final anti-king and anti-kingdom specified as at work during this final timespan. For even the casual Bible student, these are the main things which usually come to mind when picturing the Antichrist. We have already been provided many features supporting this basic list and many, many more are coming to enhance a very in-depth portrait which revisits these activities at the core of them all.

But without jumping full-steam ahead, it is worth noting at this juncture the parallels at present with what Jesus presented in the Olivet Discourse:

Daniel	Jesus
"...destroy the city and the sanctuary."	*"But when you see Jerusalem surrounded armies, then recognize that her desolation is near." (Lk. 21:20)*
"...there will be war..."	*"You will be hearing of wars and rumors of wars." (Mt. 24:6)*
"...desolations are determined."	*"...fainting from fear and the expectation of the things which are coming upon the world..." (Lk. 21:26)*

<table>
<tr><td>"...make a firm covenant with the many for one week..."</td><td rowspan="3">"Therefore when you see the ABOMINATION OF DESOLATION which was spoken of through Daniel the prophet, standing in the holy place (let the reader understand), then those who are in Judea must flee to the mountains. (Mt. 24:15-16)</td></tr>
<tr><td>"...in the middle of the week he will put a stop to sacrifice and grain offering..."</td></tr>
<tr><td>"...on the wing of abominations...makes desolate..."</td></tr>
</table>

> *...even until a complete destruction, one that is decreed, is poured out on the one who makes desolate."*
> — Daniel 9:27b

But it does not end with "*the one who make desolate*"—one of the prime traits of the Antichrist, but his complete and permanent end.

> [1]*Then I saw another sign in heaven, great and marvelous, seven angels who had seven plagues, which are the last, because* ***in them the wrath of God is finished****.*
> — Revelation 15:1

The basic timeline and accompanying sequence established in Daniel is leveraged and greatly enhanced in supporting Scriptures to come, but in its simplest expression it provides that the Messiah comes the first time to address the issue of sin and will come again to permanently remove Satan and his surrogates. The Old Testament Scriptures actually develop this into two major themes depicting the Messiah in the First Coming as coming in the character of the patriarch Joseph in what many call "The Suffering Servant" and Jews call "*HaMaschiach ben Jozef*"—the Messiah the Son Joseph, where His primary work is in regard to the cross and sin, and in the Second Coming as "The Conquering King", or by the Jews as "*Hamaschiach ben David*"—the Messiah the Son of David, in the character of King David when He overthrows Satan and establishes the Millennial Kingdom on earth. (Although strictly speaking, unbelieving Judaism still maintains the real Messiah is yet to come and somehow fulfills both of these roles in a single coming.)

In effect, in the course of Christ's First Coming He addresses the "*end of sin*" and "*atonement for iniquity*" to the degree that it is offered to those who accept Him as their Savior. This can be thought of as a partial fulfillment which comes to full realization with the final disposition of His Second Coming and we see additionally witness "*everlasting righteousness*", anointing of "*the most holy place*", and the end of the need for "*vision and prophecy*" which are sealed up since we have Christ, the Word of God, Himself.

The issue which most often arises is why there is a break between the sixty-nine weeks we know to have been already completed, and the one final week which has not. And the best example I have come across to illustrate this situation is akin to a clock stoppage at a sporting event. As long as they are attending an injury on the field, the clock is stopped, and there is always, so to speak, one minute left in the game. It can take five minutes, ten minutes, it may be so serious they have to call and wait for an ambulance, but until the officials resume the game, we are suspended until it commences again. In effect, we are always one minute away from God resuming the "*weeks of years*" clock.

A Final Caveat

There is a very important omission which must be highlighted at this point.

One would have to either have just become a Christian last week or been living in unusual seclusion to not know that the entire field of study academia calls "Eschatology" revolves around this final week of years. One of the few things which seems to be universally accepted for a subject whose debate has spilled over into countless thousands upon thousands of sermons, articles, websites, books and even entire conferences is a final seven year period. But having read these four verses for yourself, have you wondered why everyone calls it "***The***Tribulation"? And, yes, it is most often capitalized in near-universal acceptance that whenever the term is encountered the reader automatically knows it is referring to Daniel's final week of years.

So we have ***Pre***-Tribulationism, ***Mid***-Tribulationism, ***Post***-Tribulationism, and at times we have even encountered ***Pan***-Tribulationism. In each of these cases, the appended "-Tribulationism" refers to the final seven years, and the prefix affixes the proposed timing of the Rapture in relationship to it. "Pre" believe the Rapture occurs before the seven years entirely, "Mid" to its occurrence in the exact middle of the seven years, "Post" to the end, and "Pan" to a small group of the tired-of-arguing-about-it who will accept it happening at any time. ("Pre-Wrath" is relatively new to the field, but it still expresses their timing of the Rapture in relationship to the final seven years just after its midway point.) The average teaching presented in any written, oral or video format by any holder of these different views all begin with the assumption that there ***is*** a final seven year period called "***The***Tribulation" and that the timing of the removal of the Church is intrinsically tied to it. (Yes, there are minority or one-off exceptions, but this is the general occurrence.)

So if that is not stated here in Daniel where the unassailable concept of a final "week of years" originates, then it surely must appear somewhere else in supporting Scripture, right? Just as so many things pertaining to the prophetic are repeated, substantiated and provided deeper and more thorough explanations in parallel passages of God's Word, surely there must be verses referring to "***The***Tribulation" as another designation for the final week of years, stipulating that it is bounded by this seven year structure. This is a major point presented in this author's previous book, *And THEN The End Will Come* for those more than casually interested, but we still have to deal here with the fact that there is ***no such thing*** to be found in God's Word.

How Did This Happen?

There is an old-time seminary saying originally attributed by D. A. Carson to his father, a variation of which I favor from Jacob Prasch which asserts, "A text out of context from its co-text is a pretext". Something has been lifted out of its original scriptural context and then used so often it has become assumed to be axiomatically true in the mainstream.

If you pull out your trusty concordance or use your Bible software's search features, there is only one reference to "*seven years*" in the whole Bible which has an eschatological connection, and it has nothing to do with Daniel's 70th Week.

> 9 *"Then those who inhabit the cities of Israel will go out and make fires with the weapons and burn them, both shields and bucklers, bows and arrows, war clubs and spears, and* ***for seven years they will make fires of them****.*
> — Ezekiel 39:9

In what is most often referred to as the End Times Gog and Magog scenario of Ezekiel 38-39, the weapons left over from the conflict are burned over a subsequent seven year period, and there is absolutely nothing remotely provided in the text to suggest even the most tenuous connection to Daniel's final week of years, much less referring to it as "***The*** Tribulation".

There are certainly some other references to "*seven years*" in the Old Testament, but none of these are eschatological much less pointing to the 70th Week of Daniel. And in the New Testament, there is a single, lone reference to "*seven years*" which has nothing to do with it either:

> [36]*And there was a prophetess, Anna the daughter of Phanuel, of the tribe of Asher. She was advanced in years and had* ***lived with her husband seven years after her marriage****,*
>
> — Luke 2:36

Due solely to the fact that Daniel 9:27 categorically states, "*in the middle of the week he will put a stop to sacrifice*", we understand that both Christ and Paul indirectly refer to the final week of years when they speak of that milestone slated to take place at its exact midway point. (Mt. 24:15; Mk. 13:14; 2 Th. 2:3-4) That this is the halfway milestone is further stipulated to Daniel in the closing chapter, specifying it kicks off the last half of the final week of years:

> [11]*"From the time that the regular sacrifice is abolished and the abomination of desolation is set up, there will be 1,290 days.*
>
> — Daniel 12:11

What we will find in Scripture is that although there is unquestionably a final seven year structure, God's Word will over-emphasize its last half. Before ever encountering Daniel 9, in his vision many years previous which was recorded in Daniel 7, this is what was first disclosed as a timing issue concerning the Antichrist:

> [25]*'He will speak out against the Most High and wear down the saints of the Highest One, and he will intend to make alterations in times and in law;* ***and they will be given into his hand for a time, times, and half a time****.*
>
> — Daniel 7:25

God's Word is not playing some kind of game with us where it briefly flashes the seven years but then takes it away, but it is attempting to convey something more important by emphasizing in particular its second half. In other words, it is not Scripture which provided us the term "***The*** Tribulation", but man.

Again, where did this come from?

The Tribulation

> [9]*"Then* ***they*** *will deliver* ***you*** *to* ***tribulation****, and will kill you, and you will be hated by all nations because of My name.* [10]*At that time many will fall away and will betray one another and hate one another.* [11]*Many false prophets will arise and will mislead many.* [12]*Because lawlessness is increased, most people's love will grow cold.* [13]*But the one who endures to the end, he will be saved.* [14]*This gospel of the kingdom shall be preached in the whole world as a testimony to all the nations, and then the end will come.*
>
> — Matthew 24:9-14

In the Olivet Discourse, Jesus opens with warnings about many false christs, wars and rumors of wars, famines, earthquakes and the like all characterized as a progressive series of "*birth pangs*". (Mt. 24:3-8) These things fade in over the beginning of what we would call the Last Days or the eschaton. And then he identifies a new follow-on phase, "***Then** they will deliver **you** to tribulation*". Jesus uses the term "*tribulation*" to describe a time when "***they***"—the whole world, "*will deliver **you***"—believers, into a time of unprecedented persecution. No one in the world experiences this except believers. It is not the world's tribulation, not Israel's tribulation, it is singularly limited to no one but the ***Church***. Look at each thing Jesus specifies to happen when this takes place:

- "*...they...will kill you...*"
- "*...you will be hated by all nations because of My name.*"
- "*...many will fall away...*"
- "*...many...will betray one another and hate one another.*"
- "*Many false prophets will arise and will mislead many.*"
- "*...most people's love will grow cold.*"

This is persecution, apostasy and deception hyper-focused on no one but the Church. And notice that there is a greater purpose, which is always the by-product of persecution which can only be assigned to the Church, "*This gospel of the kingdom shall be preached in the whole world*". Christ's instruction in Acts 1:8 will finally be realized by the Church where the Gospel is concerned. There is no accompanying guarantee that it will be well and properly received, only that it will accomplish the global goal of being preached to everyone.

This period of persecution is marked by a milestone:

> [15]*"Therefore when you see the ABOMINATION OF DESOLATION which was spoken of through Daniel the prophet, standing in the holy place (let the reader understand), [16]then those who are in Judea must flee to the mountains.*
> — Matthew 24:15-16

Now we arrive at the scripturally mandated midway point of Daniel's 70th Week even though there is no mention of "*seven years*". With the public disclosure of the Antichrist, now the whole world experiences a tribulation right alongside the Church which He calls "*great tribulation*":

> [21]*"For **then** there will be a **great tribulation**, such as has not occurred since the beginning of the world until now, nor ever will. [22]Unless those days had been cut short, no life would have been saved; but for the sake of the elect those days will be cut short.*
> — Matthew 24:21-22

This is not a 3-1/2 year phase either, but a time which is "*cut short*" by the removal of the Church described in Matthew 24:29-31. This signals the onset of what Scripture prolifically describes as "*the day of the Lord*" when all that is left is the wrath of God to be poured out on the anti-king and the members of his anti-kingdom.

"***The*** Tribulation" is a manmade device which has incorrectly lifted the text in isolation from its co-text to create a pretext which has, unfortunately, entered into mainstream acceptance. And as we will see further, this is no trivial thing, but produces a chain of unacceptable consequences. Remember, Jesus Himself established that false teaching acts like leaven, and though only introduced in a very small amount, eventually permeates everything. (Mt. 16:11-12)

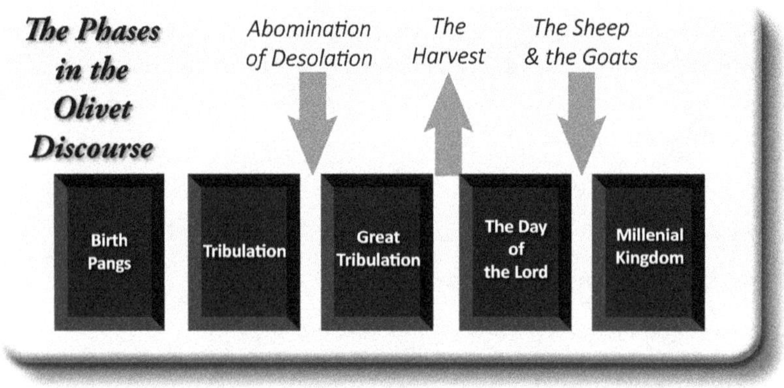

In Conclusion

The Prophet Daniel serves as a model for what a believer should do in the Last Days:

- He was deep into God's Word.
- He accepted the plain meaning of God's prophetic Word.
- He was regularly engaged in prayer.
- He had a burden for God's people and interceded for them.

This is a very valuable example in and of itself, which as pointed out earlier, mirrors the very same behaviors with which Christ ended the Olivet Discourse as to what He expects to find in believers upon His return.

Daniel's prayer for Israel and the impending fulfillment of God's prophetic Word about to literally take place was supplemented by a divine revelation involving the whole world:

- Daniel prayed about Israel's seventy years; God disclosed the entire world's situation for ***its*** remaining "*seventy weeks of years*".
- Daniel prayed about the disposition of the spiritual condition and return of Israel in the foreseeable future; God disclosed both Israel's at the Messiah's First Coming and the whole world's conclusion with His Second Coming.
- Daniel prayed concerning the end of the desolations of the times to Jerusalem and its Temple; God disclosed the end of the ultimate and final desolations to come.
- Daniel prayed for Jerusalem and the Temple and their restoration; God disclosed what would take place with them in the much longer term and their ultimate disposition.
- Daniel prayed for the people sins, iniquities and transgressions; God disclosed when He would bring an end to these very same things for the whole world.

One might say that while pursing the immediate—the micro, God responded for all time with the macro. God additionally disclosed more concerning the working and character of the anti-king and his anti-kingdom, but with specific time parameters to serve as a fundamental foundation into which everything subsequent, both in Daniel and the whole of God's Word, will dovetail not just eschatologically, but theologically.

We are not in need of a new or additional revelation from God, if only we would approach what He has already given in His written Word in the same manner Daniel did for our own times, knowing that the seventy ***weeks*** are about to be concluded.

5 ❖ Daniel 10-12: The Latter Days Milieu

[14]"Now I have come to give you an understanding of what will happen to your people in the latter days, for the vision pertains to the days yet future."
— Daniel 10:14

A very good way to evaluate a commentary to determine whether its author truly believes in the divine authorship of Scripture is to examine what they say about these final chapters in Daniel. Whenever someone discounts even a small portion of God's Word as being something not originally God-given and purposely inserted by man, we can be sure that they will challenge the authenticity of Scripture in other ways in their writings. This is one of those sections of Scripture which is not just a test ***of*** faith, but a test ***for*** faith.

When the substance of Daniel's last vision as detailed in chapter 11 is compared to the historical record, such an unquestionable accuracy is encountered that it challenges the reader's faith so as to betray whether or not they actually believe God can predict future events. Even though they cannot deny its accuracy for what took place historically, it is no surprise that a non-believer of any kind rejects the premise this was all revealed before it occurred, but the number of professing believers who reject it for the same reason is quite astonishing. There are many self-professed "Christian" scholars who, like their secular counterparts, believe it was impossible for Daniel to so accurately predict future events. So their common prevailing theory is that long after Daniel died, and especially ***after*** these events took place in history, someone else added these last chapters to the original book to only make it look like it was all predicted beforehand. Of course, we know that Daniel did not "predict" ***anything***, immediately revealing when someone has taken God out of the equation and assumes the Bible is actually just the writings of man.

Some have the academic honesty to attribute this to a theoretical figure they call "Deutero-Daniel", a pseudonym for a second unnamed writer who appended additional pages to the original book long after the original, historical Daniel had died. (This has never even come close to being historically authenticated, but they believe it and teach it nonetheless.) This same approach is applied to other Scriptures and figures as well, as seen by such parallels in the suggestion of a "Deutero-Isaiah" for the same reasons. When a commentator uses these designations outright, he is honestly conveying to the reader from the outset this position that the text was purposely inserted after the fact by someone who came along later and not provided by the original historical figure. The problem is not all are so forthcoming, but a bit of patient reading of their comments never successfully hides this belief for very long.

Unfortunately, no one has to be a Holy Spirit-filled, born again Christian to get a degree in religion or theology, or to write books or even be employed as a professor by those institutions. By definition, non-believers do not believe in God to begin with, but concede that if He does exist, He does not speak to man, and if He did, He certainly would not tell them the future, much less anything else. To them it is either a myth, a delusion or a con. However, the influence of unsaved academicians throughout the history of the Church to the present has been so pervasive that their assertions, which actually undermine the authority and divine inspiration of Scripture, have worked their way into the beliefs of many of their saved counterparts. It is a strange variation of the *Parable of the Tares* (Mt. 13:24-30, 36-43) at work in the fields of Christian academia, except in this case, the wheat seems to endorse and accept the tares as equals. They fail to realize the consequences for those who come to their field, looking to be fed, only to find far more of the counterfeit fruit than the authentic.

If we have accepted the plain text of what has been presented in the first nine chapters, we cannot abandon that approach and create a new set of rules for that which is offered in the last three; or worse, just ignore or dismiss them as an invention of man. While every verse of God's Word is important, what we are about to study is particularly so, not just because it provides more detail in depth of things previously disclosed, but serves to teach us about the true working of God's prophetic Word as a repeating pattern with an ultimate fulfillment rather than a one-and-done cul-de-sac.

This is especially important when it comes to understanding the scriptural attributes of the final anti-king/anti-kingdom, as we will be introduced to a level of detail previously unvisited which has already been partially fulfilled historically with an unrealized future completion. And this will establish our field of understanding as to what, exactly, 1st century listeners and readers would have understood when not just Jesus Himself, but the Apostles Paul and John, would be referring to when speaking of things like the Abomination of Desolation, the "*son of perdition*", "*false christs*", and the "*Antichrist*".

Although in the modern era we understand Revelation 13 to be the definitive chapter when it comes to the Antichrist, comparatively little new data is provided there when juxtaposed against the wealth of information already in the hands of the Old Testament reader. When Jesus and the Apostles spoke about these things, the majority of what is scripturally divulged was in their possession along with historical events already transpired which they knew to be directly reflecting them. Therefore the few new items which the New Testament brought to their understanding stood out in a dramatic way unfamiliar to present-day Christians who have not only grown up with the whole Bible, but are overly discipled in the New Testament so as to overshadow that which was originally presented beforehand. Such is why this author chose to expose the topic closer to the order given in Scripture because the fact is that much more is known about this from the Old Testament than the New.

Another important reason is to address the serious side-effect all too commonly encountered where the very last God-given information in the book of Revelation is assigned the first priority and as the starting point over all the previous, often discounting or ignoring it altogether in favor of just Revelation which came last. This is often done at the expense of the rest of Scripture, particularly the Old Testament, making all that came before John's final vision subordinate to, or sometimes nullified by, this last book of the canon. In truth, the very first Christian readers of Revelation accepted it as an authentic member of God's Word because they understood how perfectly it conformed to and was confirmed by all the Scriptures which came before it, not the other way around as it is often found in the modern Church.

Such is the powerful nature of these final chapters of the book of Daniel, that it causes this kind of re-evaluation of not just our principles of Bible interpretation and the way we handle Scripture, but challenges the depth of our trust in God's Word as the best interpreter of God's Word.

Not the Same as Previous Experiences

> [1]*In the third year of Cyrus king of Persia a message was revealed to Daniel, who was named Belteshazzar; and the message was true and one of great conflict, but* ***he understood*** *the message* ***and had an understanding*** *of the vision.*
> — Daniel 10:1

As it has been the pattern in Daniel, he provides a date for when this event takes place by specifying at what point a particular king is in power at the time of the vision. In this case, what might be most interesting is this indicates that the return from the Babylonian Captivity as led by Ezra is already underway. Daniel lived to witness the fulfillment of much of the prophecy provided through him, but in particular Israel's imminent return which he took to be true by accepting God's Word on its face as seen in chapter 9. Unlike so many of the prophets recorded in Scripture, Daniel did not have to take it by faith that the Word of God given through him would eventually come true future to his own lifetime. (Heb. 11:39) There is also the interesting pattern that Daniel's visions occurred in the first and third years of Belshazzar and the first and third years of Cyrus.

We cannot help but read the Bible knowing full well not just the whole canon of its sixty-six books, but the parallel history for these past millennia since Daniel's time, so it may be difficult for us to reconstruct his point of view at that very instant because of what we now know. With so much of God's Word fulfilled during his lifetime, and even as the return from the Captivity was taking place, how would those things revealed which were not yet fulfilled going to come about? Surely a wise and biblically-grounded man such as this was acutely aware of Israel's past cyclical behavior of falling away, returning to God, falling away, returning to God—what was next? Were they just going to return to the same old thing?

It is always interesting when mortal man, who is a slave to the celestial motion of time and measures all things in relationship to the finite number of days of his life, has an encounter with the immortal God of the universe Who in eternity stands apart from time and divulges what is to come, because His viewpoint is never limited to just the earthly lifespan of the inquirer. But it is most telling that each subsequent vision recorded in Daniel is really an extension of the very first originally interpreted for Nebuchadnezzar, just with much more detail for particular aspects of it, and that seeing God beginning to fulfill it during Daniel's lifetime provided an assurance of faith for the future fulfillments yet to come for the rest.

In this final vision which so many find difficult, the stark contrast to other visions stand out, "*he understood the message and had an understanding of the vision*". His reaction to something which he understood from the outset sets this experience apart from those previous. And this vision is especially unique in that it did not involve symbols such as animals or beasts or the great sea and the like, or deciphering a cryptic divine message, but was directly given and understood from the outset. And yet being in full possession of its meaning, Daniel's reaction was not quite what we think we would have if we were given absolute clarity of God's plans. True encounters with the God in Scripture are repeatedly characterized as completely humbling and overwhelming, an indictment of the false presentations so commonly the fodder on display with fake recreations on YouTube.

After a lengthy preparation for the vision in the text of Daniel 10:1-11:1, the content will be fully provided in Daniel 11:2-12:3 before a closing set of instructions in Daniel 12:4-13. (This is one of those places where the 16th century insertion of verse and chapter markings is slightly askew.) What is provided in chapter 10 can be thought of as a very thorough introduction which also divulges the work and interest of angels and demons in the affairs of man, something further developed in the book of Revelation yet to come. In those final years of history, the heavenly begins to visibly merge with the earthly and this is initially revealed in the book of Daniel.

An Unexpected Reaction

> *2In those days, I, Daniel, had been mourning for three entire weeks. 3I did not eat any tasty food, nor did meat or wine enter my mouth, nor did I use any ointment at all until the entire three weeks were completed.*
> — Daniel 10:2-3

Daniel "*understood the message*" and yet his reaction is the ultimate expression of mourning. All we know at this point is "*the message was true and one of great conflict*", but as Daniel understood what these chapters will reveal to us, we will see that although a rescue is eventually featured, the body of this vision is a series of conflicts with unavoidable consequences for Israel in the middle of it all.

It may aid in knowing that this deep reaction is depicted in Scripture as a continual, ongoing state of mourning as seen expressed over such things as mourning for the dead (Gen.37:34), over sin (Ezra 10:6) or over calamity coming about by the wrath of God. (Eze. 7:12) Such would even be exemplified by Nehemiah's reaction to the apostatizing of Israel so quickly after the return from Captivity. (Neh. 1:4) That which Daniel is experiencing is far deeper than mere concern or temporary sorrow. This is actually the kind of response which Scripture associates with a true knowledge of that time of the end called "*the day of the Lord*", when God's wrath is ultimately poured out on the world:

> *18Alas, you who are longing for the day of the LORD,*
> *For what purpose will the day of the LORD be to you?*
> *It will be darkness and not light;*
> *19As when a man flees from a lion*
> *And a bear meets him,*
> *Or goes home, leans his hand against the wall*
> *And a snake bites him.*
> ***20Will not the day of the Lord be darkness instead of light,***
> ***Even gloom with no brightness in it?***
> — Amos 5:18-20

It is not worth starting a cult over, but if we were to translate this literally from the Hebrew, Daniel's time of mourning lasted "three sevens of days"—in other words, three "weeks" of days in a parallel usage to the previous chapter's "*weeks of years*" metric. This just shows that our English translations can be right in what they represent, but may obscure some of the original details of the presentation of the text itself which lends to teaching something deeper or in parallel. It at least contributes to our understanding of the way time was handled in ordinary things in a similar fashion to God's prophetic Word.

The Divine Revelation

[4]On the twenty-fourth day of the first month, while I was by the bank of the great river, that is, the Tigris, [5]I lifted my eyes and looked, and behold, there was a certain man dressed in linen, whose waist was girded with a belt of pure gold of Uphaz. [6]His body also was like beryl, his face had the appearance of lightning, his eyes were like flaming torches, his arms and feet like the gleam of polished bronze, and the sound of his words like the sound of a tumult.

[7]Now I, Daniel, alone saw the vision, while the men who were with me did not see the vision; nevertheless, a great dread fell on them, and they ran away to hide themselves. [8]So I was left alone and saw this great vision; yet no strength was left in me, for my natural color turned to a deathly pallor, and I retained no strength. [9]But I heard the sound of his words; and as soon as I heard the sound of his words, I fell into a deep sleep on my face, with my face to the ground.

— Daniel 10:4-9

The text does not specify this connection openly, but we cannot help but notice that Daniel's period of prayer and fasting comes around the same time as Passover and the Feast of Unleavened Bread. As this vision is also taking place simultaneous to the first of three major returns of Israel out of the Babylonian Captivity to the Promised Land, it may be no coincidence that a man of prayer and Scripture like Daniel sees parallels to the original Exodus taking place with Israel's emigration from its captor Babylon, and he is concerned for both their literal and spiritual deliverance. If so, this may aid in understanding his reaction to the vision. He sees both the historical and prophetic pattern in both.

The description of the appearance of this "*certain man*" certainly fits with parallel features in other passages of Scripture depicting a holy being, but from the fact that Daniel had already encountered Gabriel and fails to call him by that name and the reactions of Daniel and all around him, this favors this being someone new. It is most likely that this is a Christophany—that is, an Old Testament appearance of Christ, not just because of similar descriptions in parallel Scriptures (Eze. 1:27; Rev. 1), but also because of something this figure will do at the close of Daniel:

*[7]I heard the man dressed in linen, who was above the waters of the river, as **he raised his right hand and his left toward heaven, and swore by Him who lives forever** that it would be for a time, times, and half a time; and as soon as they finish shattering the power of the holy people, all these events will be completed.*

— Daniel 12:7

This appears to be the declaration of a divine oath promising the unconditional fulfillment of all that was revealed to Daniel. Angelic messengers are known to confirm the truth and authenticity of the message they have delivered, but they are not normally guarantors of a divine outcome, hence the strong suspicion that, just like the case of the Apostle John, Jesus is making a direct revelation to Daniel.

To be fair, however, because of the statement in verse 11, "*I have now been sent to you*", which would mitigate against this being a Christophany, this may be referring to two individuals who are involved, Christ giving the vision as depicted here, and then an angel who is actually giving Daniel the interpretation as there seems to be another conversation taking place between them at times. This is also parallel to what transpired in Revelation with the Apostle John when he experiences a personal encounter with Christ (Rev. 1:12-20), but the bulk of the message is subsequently provided by Christ through His angelic messengers. (Rev. 7:13-14; 17:1; 21:9;

22:16) We see this back-and-forth interaction where some things are spoken directly by Christ and others by Him through an angel.

> [6]*And he* [the angel] *said to me, "These words are faithful and true"; and the Lord, the God of the spirits of the prophets, sent His angel to show to His bond-servants the things which must soon take place.* [7]*"And behold, I* [Christ] *am coming quickly. Blessed is he who heeds the words of the prophecy of this book."*
> — Revelation 22:6-7

In a similarity to Paul's experience when encountering Christ, (Acts 9:1-7), Daniel alone witnessed these events although those in the vicinity felt a supernatural presence, which is another supporting feature lending credence to this being an encounter with the divine rather than just an angelic messenger. Daniel's reaction, "*I fell into a deep sleep on my face*" is a parallel to a similar reaction Abraham experienced in his own encounter with God. (Gen. 15:12)

This accompanying context in which the meat of the message is recorded in chapter 11 is an important feature because it is establishing the very things which secular and skeptical Christian scholars forsake or willfully ignore, that Daniel did not "predict" ***anything***. When any part of God's Word is reassigned as authored by man instead of the divine, this is ultimately their admission of having no faith in Him whatsoever. This is especially reinforced by the fact of Christ Himself conveying this message, since we know that it is Christ Himself who ***IS*** the very Word of God. (Jn. 1:1) But of all the large number of parallels between the respective visions of the Prophet Daniel and the Apostle John, this detail is perhaps the most important because it establishes the true, divine authorship of Christ over man.

The Angelic Explanation

> [10]*Then behold, a hand touched me and set me trembling on my hands and knees.* [11]*He said to me, "O Daniel, man of high esteem, understand the words that I am about to tell you and stand upright, for I have now been sent to you." And when he had spoken this word to me, I stood up trembling.*
>
> [12]*Then he said to me, "Do not be afraid, Daniel, for from the first day that you set your heart on understanding this and on humbling yourself before your God, your words were heard, and I have come in response to your words.* [13]*But the prince of the kingdom of Persia was withstanding me for twenty-one days; then behold, Michael, one of the chief princes, came to help me, for I had been left there with the kings of Persia.* [14]*Now I have come to give you an understanding of what will happen to your people in the latter days, for the vision pertains to the days yet future."*
> — Daniel 10:10-14

In other words, Daniel experiences the vision which is the reason he "*had been mourning for three entire weeks*". (Dan. 10:2) The angel was sent to "*give you an understanding*", and immediately dispatched at the beginning of Daniel's prayer and fasting, but is delayed in the interim so that he arrives at the end of those three weeks.

Something important is revealed here in that we are made aware that there is, indeed, heavenly warfare taking place in parallel with earthly events. It may be difficult for us to fully understand the nature of this delay and the necessity for Michael to intervene for this angel against "*the prince of the kingdom of Persia*", but as previously stated, this is an eschatological feature which is particularly emphasized in Revelation where every time major events take place on earth, they are preceded by a look into what is taking place in heaven. This is also something revealed in the very first book of Scripture whose known content was around even before the Torah—Job. (Job 1:6-9; 2:1-3) From the outset it was revealed how those in the heavenly realm are involved in what takes place down here.

As things progress to their ultimate conclusion, the distinction between the earthly and heavenly realms dissolve as a prelude to Christ coming to establish His Millennial Kingdom on earth. In Revelation there are angelic messengers visible in the sky, heavenly beings such as a message-proclaiming eagle are witnessed, Satan himself is thrown down to the earth, and even demon hordes are released from the abyss. Things which were previously out of sight in the heavenly begin to visibly merge into earthly view.

> [12]*For our struggle is not against flesh and blood, but against the rulers, against the powers, against the world forces of this darkness, against the spiritual forces of wickedness in the heavenly places.*
>
> — Ephesians 6:12

But there is also a detail stated here which must not be overlooked because of the greater context of this book. Notice that it was not just "***the prince*** *of the kingdom of Persia*", but "***the kings*** *of Persia*". In other words, once again Scripture addresses not just a king, but a kingdom, and these again being satanically animated.

The most important textual context for all that is about to be given is prefaced that this is "*what will happen to your people in the latter days, for the vision pertains to the days yet future*". Daniel would understand from this that he should not expect to witness any portion of this vision to be fulfilled in his remaining lifetime, unlike elements of previous revelations he was party to. For us with our present perspective, the vision will narrow our focus to the final antics of the anti-king/anti-kingdom, at first replaying the events effected by Antiochus Epiphanes IV, and then extending into the last part of the vision which has never realized any historical fulfillment whatsoever and is the sole property of "*the days yet future*".

Parallel Assignments

> [15]*When he had spoken to me according to these words, I turned my face toward the ground and became speechless.* [16]*And behold, one who resembled a human being was touching my lips; then I opened my mouth and spoke and said to him who was standing before me, "O my lord, as a result of the vision anguish has come upon me, and I have retained no strength.* [17]*For how can such a servant of my lord talk with such as my lord? As for me, there remains just now no strength in me, nor has any breath been left in me."*
>
> [18]*Then this one with human appearance touched me again and strengthened me.* [19]*He said, "O man of high esteem, do not be afraid. Peace be with you; take courage and be courageous!"*
>
> *Now as soon as he spoke to me, I received strength and said, "May my lord speak, for you have strengthened me."*
>
> [20]*Then he said, "Do you understand why I came to you? But I shall now return to fight against the prince of Persia; so I am going forth, and behold, the prince of Greece is about to come.* [21]*However, I will tell you what is inscribed in the writing of truth. Yet there is no one who stands firmly with me against these forces except Michael your prince.*
>
> — Daniel 10:15-21

If nothing else, we are clearly presented with the revelation that just as mankind is involved in an epic struggle on earth which is really an extension of spiritual warfare, so the same is taking place in parallel in the heavenly realm.

Notice that Daniel does not address this figure as God, which the NASB would normally show by using small capital letters as in "Lord", but the Hebrew "*adown*" (Strong's #113) which is closer to the English "sir", another indication that the explainer of the vision is an angel. Daniel nonetheless holds this messenger in higher regard than himself.

This parenthetical statement by the angel of having to "*return to fight against the prince of Persia...and...the prince of Greece*" is going to be an important supporting detail for the heart of the prophetic message about to be articulated. The angel's involvement with Persia and Greece is going to parallel what is going to take place with Israel at their hands, covering specific events which will take place over the next two hundred or so years before jumping to the very final years of history. That which directly affects Israel through these earthly kings and kingdoms is experiencing a heavenly parallel in which this angel participates. This is also why the detail of Michael's involvement is noted as he is directly connected to the health and welfare of Israel. But this additionally reveals that the agendas of earthly kings are actually those of the spiritual forces behind them, as in this brief passage we have been exposed to not only Michael as "*your prince*"—that is, for Israel, but both a demonic prince of Persia and one of Greece. This reveals the satanic influence which animates each forerunner of the final one to come.

Something to take note of is that the source of the explanation for this vision will come from "*what is inscribed in the writing of truth*". It should not be surprising to learn of heavenly documentation of God's plans, as we are told that the Book of Life was something likewise written "*from the foundation of the world*". (Rev. 13:8; 17:8) But this again reinforces the fact that when commentators of any proclaimed spiritual condition assign to Daniel as a person the contents of this vision, they are completely dismissing God Himself and publicly divulging not just a lack of faith in His Word, but an absence of belief in Him personally.

The Sequence of the End

> 1 *"In the first year of Darius the Mede, I arose to be an encouragement and a protection for him.*
>
> — Daniel 11:1

The explanation of the vision begins with a sort of parenthetical remark by the angel as to his involvement in these matters, which also serves as an earthly, historical milestone from which extends the rest of the sequence so that we know it begins with Darius. Daniel 11:2-34 has parallel historical fulfillments, but beginning in verse 21 with the introduction of Antiochus Epiphanes IV, we are presented with events which will be replayed again in the End Times. We understand this from the fact that we will see him literally fulfill specific things which previous visions in Daniel assigned to that final figure, but textual provisions will be made which show him to fall short of a final fulfillment yet to come. This particular anti-king and his anti-kingdom foreshadow the ultimate one to come of whom the remainder of the chapter speaks. In the third section beginning with verse 35 to the end of the chapter, none of what is revealed has experienced even a partial fulfillment and is assigned to the final Antichrist alone.

So the first part is history fulfilled, the second part is a partial fulfillment of history to be replayed again, and the final and third part is future history still to come which has not experienced any previous partial fulfillment. This first part is not something completely unrelated to the Antichrist, but provides a look at the milieu out of which this final figure and his kingdom arise, parallel to Christ's teaching of the "*birth pangs*" leading up to the metaphorical "birth" of the final fulfillment of God's prophetic Word.

The following chart provides a graphical depiction of the four major divisions of Alexander's Empire and the lineage of the two main branches which are consistently referred to in Daniel 11 as "*the king of the North*" and "*the king of the South*". What began with the overall picture provided in Nebuchadnezzar's dream has steadily narrowed through the subsequent visions in Daniel to two of the four divisions of Alexander's Empire which not only mirror what will take place in the Last Days, but from which will rise the final anti-king and his anti-kingdom.

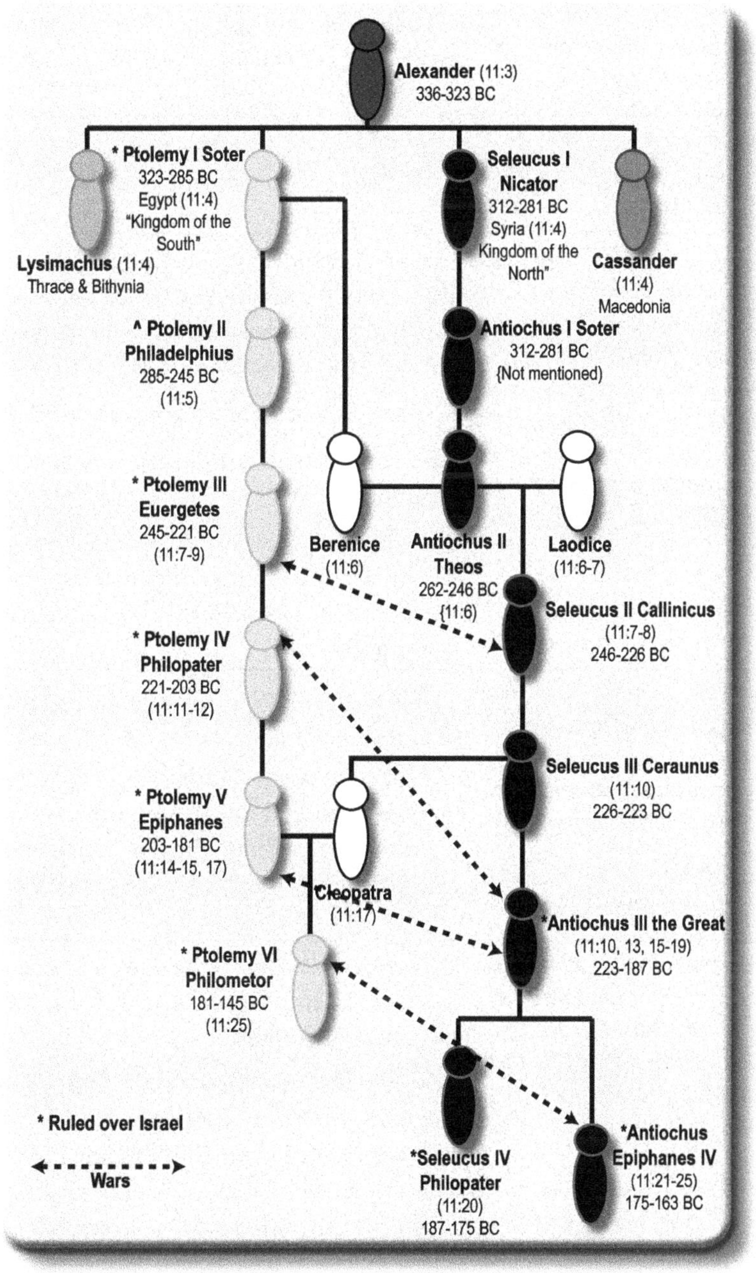

The following format will provide the historical fulfillments for each of verses 2-34, and then we will continue with those specific to the final anti-king in Daniel 11:35-45, which have no past parallels and are assigned to that which only the final, ultimate Antichrist will perform.

The Historical Fulfillment

2	*And now I will tell you the truth. Behold, three more kings are going to arise in Persia. Then a fourth will gain far more riches than all of them; as soon as he becomes strong through his riches, he will arouse the whole empire against the realm of Greece.*	• Three Kings = Cambyses (aka "*Ahasuerus*" in Ezra 4:6), Pseudo-Smerdis (aka "*Artaxerxes*" in Ezra 4:7), Darius Hystaspes (aka, "Darius" in Ezra 4:24) • 4th King = Xerxes, who attempted to invade Greece in 480 BC. • "*Arouse the whole empire*": Xerxes spent 4 years assembling an army of 2,641,000 troops from all corners of his empire.
3	*And a mighty king will arise, and he will rule with great authority and do as he pleases.*	• Alexander, the one-horned goat in chapter 7, invades Persia in 334 BC.
4	*But as soon as he has arisen, his kingdom will be broken up and parceled out toward the four points of the compass, though not to his own descendants, nor according to his authority which he wielded, for his sovereignty will be uprooted and given to others besides them.*	• Upon Alexander's death his generals divided the empire into 4 kingdoms: Lysimachus took Thrace and Bithynia, Cassander took Macedonia, Ptolemy I Soter took Egypt and Seleucus I Nicator took Syria. • None of them were descendants of Alexander. • None of them accrued the power and authority of Alexander. • "*Others besides them*": Refers to all the other smaller parts of Alexander's kingdom that were taken by lesser rulers. The four mentioned above merely possessed the largest portions.
5	*Then the king of the South will grow strong, along with one of his princes who will gain ascendancy over him and obtain dominion; his domain will be a great dominion indeed.*	• King of the South = Ptolemy I Soter of Egypt (323-285 BC) • "*One of his princes*": Seleucus I Nicator, when the empire was united under Alexander, was a subordinate or "satrap" of Ptolemy. But now Seleucus has become a king in his own right over Syria and the surrounding area.
6	*After some years they will form an alliance, and the daughter of the king of the South will come to the king of the North to carry out a peaceful arrangement. But she will not retain her position of power, nor will he remain with his power, but she will be given up, along with those who brought her in and the one who sired her*	• "*Form an alliance*": They agreed to end years of war between Ptolemy I and Seleucus I that has extended into their sons' reigns. • Daughter of the king of the South = Berenice, the daughter of Ptolemy II Philadelphus, who is given in marriage to Antiochus II Theos, king of the North at this time, who in turn divorces his current wife Laodice for the sake of this arrangement.

	as well as he who supported her in those times.	• "*She will not retain her position, nor will he remain in power*": When Ptolemy dies, Antiochus takes back Laodice (his original wife) who poisons Antiochus and has Berenice and her son put to death so that Laodice's son, Seleucus II Callinicus, becomes king.
7	*But one of the descendants of her line will arise in his place, and he will come against their army and enter the fortress of the king of the North, and he will deal with them and display great strength.*	• "*One of her descendants*": Berenice's brother, Ptolemy III Euergetes, takes the Egyptian throne to become the next "*king of the South.*" • Ptolemy III avenged his sister's death by overrunning the Syrian kingdom ("*king of the North*") all the way to the Euphrates and even put Laodice to death for killing his sister.
8	*Also their gods with their metal images and their precious vessels of silver and gold he will take into captivity to Egypt, and he on his part will refrain from attacking the king of the North for some years.*	• Ptolemy III returned to Egypt not just with great treasure but with over 2,400 images—including Egyptian idols—that the kings of Persia had taken when they conquered Egypt and ruled the Middle East previously. The Egyptians were so gratified that they gave him the name "Euergetes", which means "benefactor." • "*Refrain from attacking*": Ptolemy III lived 4 years longer than Seleucus II, not warring with the "king of the North" for a time.
9	*Then the latter will enter the realm of the king of the South, but will return to his own land.*	• Seleucus II does not foray far or long into Egypt against Ptolemy III.
10	*His sons will mobilize and assemble a multitude of great forces; and one of them will keep on coming and overflow and pass through, that he may again wage war up to his very fortress.*	• "*His sons*": Seleucus III Ceraunus and Antiochus III the Great. • "*One of them*": Antiochus III warred with next king of the South Ptolemy IV Philopater until he recovered all the parts of Syria lost to Ptolemy III. • "*Up to his very fortress*": Refers to Antiochus III's incursions all the way to the fortified city of Raphia in Gaza.
11	*The king of the South will be enraged and go forth and fight with the king of the North. Then the latter will raise a great multitude, but that multitude will be given into the hand of the former.*	• Ptolemy IV defeated Antiochus III's army of 70,000 infantry and 4,000 cavalry. 10,000 were slain and 4,000 taken captive.
12	*When the multitude is carried away, his heart will be lifted up, and he will cause tens of*	• Instead of pursuing Antiochus III and completely overtaking the "*king of the North*" Ptolemy IV makes peace, thus delaying "*the problem*" to another day.

	thousands to fall; yet he will not prevail.	• "*Cause tens of thousands to fall*": Ptolemy IV's depraved lifestyle/beliefs in which he now indulges in to lead the people astray are well documented.
13	*For the king of the North will again raise a greater multitude than the former, and after an interval of some years he will press on with a great army and much equipment.*	• Antiochus III conducts successful military campaigns against Persia and India. • 14 years after his defeat at Raphia, Antiochus III engages the new "*king of the South*"—Ptolemy V Epiphanes—who has just taken the throne as a child.
14	*Now in those times many will rise up against the king of the South; the violent ones among your people will also lift themselves up in order to fulfill the vision, but they will fall down.*	• "*Many will rise up*": Antiochus III was joined by Philip the king of Macedon and Egyptian rebels to war against Ptolemy V. • "*The violent ones among your people*": Refers to Jews that aided and provisioned Antiochus III as he moved through Palestine against Ptolemy V. • "*They will fall down*": Antiochus III attacks the Egyptian garrison in Jerusalem but Israel is not freed.
15	*Then the king of the North will come, cast up a siege ramp and capture a well-fortified city; and the forces of the South will not stand their ground, not even their choicest troops, for there will be no strength to make a stand.*	• Antiochus III defeats the Egyptian general Scopas at the city of Paneas near the source of the Jordan river. Scopas flees to Sidon. • In vain Egypt sends its choicest army under the command of Eropus, Menocles and Damoxenus who are unable to rescue Scopas' army.
16	*But he who comes against him will do as he pleases, and no one will be able to withstand him; he will also stay for a time in the Beautiful Land, with destruction in his hand.*	• Israel comes under the control of Antiochus III but rather than gaining political independence or freedom, Israel becomes a base of military operations and the site of much of the conflict between the warring kingdoms.
17	*He will set his face to come with the power of his whole kingdom, bringing with him a proposal of peace which he will put into effect; he will also give him the daughter of women to ruin it. But she will not take a stand for him or be on his side.*	• Antiochus III gives his daughter, Cleopatra, to Ptolemy V in marriage and includes Judea and part of Syria as a dowry. Antiochus' plan is to acquire the Egyptian kingdom through this marriage but Cleopatra favors her husband over her father and thus the scheme is defeated.
18	*Then he will turn his face to the coast lands and capture many. But a commander will put a stop to his scorn against him; moreover, he will repay him for his scorn.*	• Antiochus III, in his warring with Rome, captured many islands of the Aegean. • The Roman general Lucius Scipio Asiaticus turned Antiochus III back at Magnesia in 190 BC. • "*His scorn*": A way of stating that this conflict with Rome was personal more than political.

19	*So he will turn his face toward the fortresses of his own land, but he will stumble and fall and be found no more.*	• Compelled by Rome to relinquish all of the territory west of the Taurus, and to pay tribute to defray the cost of the war between the two, Antiochus III garrisons the cities that are left to him. • Antiochus III is slain in an insurrection of his own soldiers at Elymais when he attempts to plunder its temple of Jupiter in order to raise the money he's required to pay Rome.
20	*Then in his place one will arise who will send an oppressor through the Jewel of his kingdom; yet within a few days he will be shattered, though not in anger nor in battle.*	• Antiochus III's son Seleucus IV Philopater ascends to the throne. • Seleucus IV sends Heliodorus to Jerusalem to plunder the Temple and take back the "dowry" of Judea, etc. promised with the marriage of Cleopatra. • A few years later Heliodorus poisons Seleucus IV in attempt to usurp the throne. But Antiochus IV Epiphanes—Seleucus IV's brother—ascends to the throne, supplanting Seleucus IV's son (Demetrius) who is visiting Rome at the time.

In the centuries leading up to the First Coming of Christ, Israel was repeatedly caught in the middle of world powers and politics tussling back and forth not only over the physical land, but the very culture and religion of God's people themselves. Anyone with even a minimum knowledge of the history of the Levant knows that this epic struggle between kings and kingdoms has been a persistent staple of history. Entire empires have fought and passed control of Israel back and forth between them in the many centuries since the Seleucids and Ptolemies, there were the many Crusades, and even in the modern era when the British Empire was involved in shaping and reshaping that part of the world in the 18th and 19th centuries, along with other involvements. That which led up to the establishment of the modern state of Israel, as well as all that we are painfully aware which has taken place in and around Israel since 1948, echoes the very same back and forth conflicts originally documented in Daniel 11. Nothing garners more annual attention from the United Nations than issues involving Israel.

This is exactly the kind of geopolitical tumult which is not only specified by Scripture, but which we have all been witnessing in our very lifetime. It is just that, like birth pangs, it gets more and more powerful with each wave and begins to occur closer and closer together as the final event approaches. What by modern standards of warfare began as minor skirmishes between Israel and her neighbors with the withdrawal of Great Britain has escalated to not just wars between many pairs of nations in the Middle East, but invoking two major incursions by the United States and coalition forces. At present, things have escalated in Iraq and Syria to the point where there are boots on the ground not just from the U.S., but Russia, Turkey, Iran and a number of European countries.

It would be hard to make a case of any present-day country which is not involved in some way when it comes to the issues of either Israel or Jerusalem, and certainly at no time in history have all the major powers of the world been so drawn there simultaneous to each other as is currently transpiring.

As it happened before it is taking place yet again, but on a multiplied scale as never previously experienced. And out of this will arise a specific figure who is now introduced who is going to show us the early stages of working for the final one to come. Scripture continues by then revealing those things which the final figure alone will accomplish to distinguish him from all previous forerunners, both historical and scriptural.

6 ❖ Daniel 10-12: The Latter Days Forerunner

> [35] *"Some of those who have insight will fall, in order to refine, purge and make them pure until the end time; because **it is still to come at the appointed time**.*
> — Daniel 11:35

This is a key verse which clearly identifies the prophetic nature of what is taking place and providing the assurance that any historical fulfillment does not end things here. As repeatedly visited, prophecy is far more often pattern and fulfillment in order to teach about the last one to come. We are provided many examples, both in Scripture and history, of the final anti-king to come. While he may be a difficult figure to parse from the flood of counterfeits supplied by Satan in an effort to screen his identity for as long as possible, one of the most reassuring provisions in Daniel is that in the end, "*none of the wicked will understand, but those who have insight will understand*". (Dan. 12:10) This is one of the stark indicators of the Western Church's true current spiritual state, that the blindness to what is taking place is in such parallel detail to not just what is provided in Scripture, but as it has prophetically occurred before. The contrast of the minority who are drawn to what is happening as opposed to the majority who are willfully ignoring it is a betrayal of the true, deeper spiritual condition which was foretold in God's Word as characterizing the last state of the Church in the shadow of these things.

On the historical stage of the sequence presented in Daniel 11 we are introduced to Antiochus Epiphanes IV who is the ultimate legacy of what began with Nebuchadnezzar and subsequently spawned the chain of kings and kingdoms producing this final figure. At this point we might call him the most important historical type of the Antichrist, and although his name does not ever appear in Scripture, it is not as if he exists as one of the many purely historical examples who are completely absent from the scriptural record. Because of that which God's Word teaches about the final anti-king/anti-kingdom we can know that the myriad of secular figures such as Hitler or Napoleon are historical prefigurements even though they are not remotely referred to in God's Word. But the literal documenting of Epiphanes' activities in Scripture in this case is, without a doubt, provided in God's Word, so we have to at least technically consider him as straddling both the scriptural and historical.

When either the topic of the Abomination of Desolation or someone coming as a false messiah was presented in New Testament times, it is Epiphanes who would first and foremost come to mind. The revolt which removed him and the ensuing reestablishment of Temple worship is still celebrated within Judaism to this day. Now known as Hanukkah, at His First Coming Jesus participated in this non-Mosaic mandated holiday then called the "*Feast of Dedication*". (Jn. 10:22) Here again the figure of Epiphanes is not entirely absent from Scripture as the annual celebration of the end to his existence is clearly recorded by the Apostle John by referring to this observance. And from this documented New Testament reference it does not take a quantum leap to acknowledge that Epiphanes is at least obliquely referenced in the pages of the Bible. Without Epiphanes, there is no "*Feast of Dedication*" as continued to this very day by the observance of Hanukkah.

It is unfortunate that the misuse of the books in that which we categorize as the Apocrypha have stigmatized them for most believers because of Catholic sanctioning, but especially when it comes to the Hasmonean Period and what took place with Epiphanes in particular, 1 and 2 Maccabees are legitimate historical material contributing much to our understanding of what took place with this figure. While such may not be included in the formal canon of Scripture, as with other parallel historical accounts, they have much to teach us about what took place at that time which most certainly has already begun to be recapitulated again at present. One has to at least give due consideration why those historical works show in detail the fulfillment of what is initially presented here in Daniel 11. It is an interesting contradiction to this author's mind when someone wholeheartedly endorses the historical writings of Josephus for Christ's time and yet rejects these equally authoritative historical writings for the Inter-Testamental Period.

Nonetheless, we will first read through the entire account of Epiphanes' activities before undertaking the manner in which they parallel that final figure and his kingdom to come.

The Overlapping Fulfillment

21 *In his place a despicable person will arise, on whom the honor of kingship has not been conferred, but he will come in a time of tranquility and seize the kingdom by intrigue.*	• "*Epiphanes*" means "illustrious" but he is often called "Epimanes", a play of words meaning "madman". Some of the unkingly behavior he exhibited was carousing with people of low character, bathing with them in the public baths, and throwing stones at passers-by. (First "frat boy" recorded in history.) • "*Seize the kingdom by intrigue*": Antiochus IV never had the kingship formerly conferred on him but obtained it through "*flattering*" Eumenes and Attalus of Pergamos to help him as well as by conducting a campaign among the Syrian people of personally embracing one and all.
22 *The overflowing forces will be flooded away before him and shattered, and also the prince of the covenant.*	• Antiochus IV Epiphanes invades Egypt. • "*The prince of the covenant*" refers to the new king of Egypt, Ptolemy VI Philometor, the son of Cleopatra, the sister of Antiochus IV. (Translation: Ptolemy IV is Antiochus IV's nephew.) • Ptolemy VI's guardians initiated a war with Antiochus IV to win back the dowry of Judea and such but were soundly defeated.

23	*After an alliance is made with him he will practice deception, and he will go up and gain power with a small force of people.*	• Antiochus IV feigned friendship with young Ptolemy VI and offered to help "organize" Ptolemy VI's kingdom. Antiochus IV took possession of Memphis and all Egypt proper, throwing off suspicion by using such a small force.
24	*In a time of tranquility he will enter the richest parts of the realm, and he will accomplish what his fathers never did, nor his ancestors; he will distribute plunder, booty and possessions among them, and he will devise his schemes against strongholds, but only for a time.*	• Antiochus IV takes all the strongholds/major cities of Egypt with the exception of Alexandria.
25	*He will stir up his strength and courage against the king of the South with a large army; so the king of the South will mobilize an extremely large and mighty army for war; but he will not stand, for schemes will be devised against him.*	• Antiochus IV conducts formal, open warfare throughout Egypt with his army. • "*Schemes*": Antiochus IV leaves Ptolemy VI in Memphis as a puppet power, making it look like all of Antiochus IV's actions were being taken on behalf of his nephew.
26	*Those who eat his choice food will destroy him, and his army will overflow, but many will fall down slain.*	• "*Those who eat his choice food*": The young Ptolemy VI's advisors did not warn him as to Antiochus IV's real motives and schemes. • Antiochus IV subdued the Egyptian army at Pelusium.
27	*As for both kings, their hearts will be intent on evil, and they will speak lies to each other at the same table; but it will not succeed, for the end is still to come at the appointed time.*	• Each tries to manipulate the other for their own personal agenda but God's agenda is what will prevail.
28	*Then he will return to his land with much plunder; but his heart will be set against the holy covenant, and he will take action and then return to his own land.*	• On his way back to Syria, Antiochus IV attacks and takes Jerusalem killing 80,000, taking 40,000 prisoner, and selling an additional 40,000 as slaves. • Antiochus IV enters the Temple, takes away the gold and silver vessels, sacrifices swine on the altar and sprinkles the sacrifice throughout the Temple.

29 *At the appointed time he will return and come into the South, but this last time it will not turn out the way it did before.*	• Antiochus IV assembles a great fleet and army for another invasion of Egypt, also demanding the ceding to him of Cyprus, Pelusium and everything around the mouth of the Nile. Ptolemy hires Greek mercenaries to meet him in battle. • The Roman ambassador Popilius Loenas meets Antiochus IV in Eleusis—4 miles from Alexandria—to deliver Rome's demand that he turn back. Antiochus IV submits.
30 *For ships of Kittim will come against him; therefore he will be disheartened and will return and become enraged at the holy covenant and take action; so he will come back and show regard for those who forsake the holy covenant.*	• The Roman delegation actually arrived in Grecian ships from Kittim, another name for Cyprus, one of the lands Antiochus IV was demanding. • On his way home, Antiochus IV sends Apollonius in 167 BC to destroy Jerusalem, 2 years after he first subjugated it. From a fortress outside the Temple worshipers were ambushed and killed as they came to the Temple, thus ending Temple worship. Sources indicate that Antiochus IV's forces were aided by rebel Jews and the high priest, Menelaus, himself. • Antiochus IV issued a decree that everyone had to conform to the Greek religion and the temple is dedicated to Jupiter Olympius.
31 *Forces from him will arise, desecrate the sanctuary fortress, and do away with the regular sacrifice. And they will set up the abomination of desolation.*	• An idol-altar and image of Jupiter are erected upon the temple's alter of burnt offerings.
32 *By smooth words he will turn to godlessness those who act wickedly toward the covenant, but the people who know their God will display strength and take action.*	• Apostasy abounds for those Jews who assisted Antiochus IV's forces and embraced the new religion, but the Maccabees and their followers revolt.
33 *Those who have insight among the people will give understanding to the many; yet they will fall by sword and by flame, by captivity and by plunder for many days.*	• Largely a guerrilla campaign conducted by the Maccabees and their followers for about 3 years, there are many casualties inflicted on the Jews, to include Antiochus IV ordering that some be roasted alive. Many are slain on the Sabbath when they refuse to fight and profane the Lord's day.
34 *Now when they fall they will be granted a little help, and many will join with them in hypocrisy.*	• Freedom is short-lived as the Romans and Herodians soon take control of Judea, but a great many of the apostates that had gone over to Antiochus IV's side switch to the Maccabeans upon their victory.

> 35"*Some of those who have insight will fall, in order to refine, purge and make them pure until the end time; because* ***it is still to come at the appointed time****.*
> — Daniel 11:35

As stated at the opening of this chapter, verse 35 serves as a sort of hinge on the door swinging between the historical figure of Epiphanes which prefigures the early stages of the final Antichrist, and the remainder of Daniel 11 which has yet to be visited by any figure and appears to be exclusively applied to the final anti-king alone. A case for a partial localized fulfillment of this verse in the course of this historical fulfillment can certainly be made but falls short of meeting the full requirements, "*to come at the appointed time*".

This is a biblical phrase which is often associated in Scripture with the specific and final fulfillment of something divinely authored and controlled:

- The miraculous birth of a son to Abraham and Sarah in their old age comes "***at the appointed time*** *of which God has spoken to them*". (Gen. 21:2)
- The Torah specifies that the mandated feasts are to be observed "***at the appointed time***". (Ex. 23:15; 34:18)
- When God sent a plague on Israel for sin, it continued until "***the appointed time***" before coming to an end. (2 Sam. 24:15)
- This is used four times in Daniel alone to specify something working in concert with God's specific timing. (Dan. 8:19; 11:27, 29, 35)

Perhaps "*the appointed time*" is best explained to Habakkuk:

> 3"*For the vision is yet for* ***the appointed time****;*
> *It hastens toward the goal and it will not fail.*
> *Though it tarries, wait for it;*
> *For it will certainly come, it will not delay.*
> — Habakkuk 2:3

So this is not speaking about earthly circumstances or timing as in something like, "It will happen under the right circumstances", but is speaking specifically to a divinely set zero hour.

Lessons from Epiphanes

The author is assuming that the reader possesses at least the minimal working knowledge of New Testament Scripture when it comes to the Antichrist and End Times, so the details to follow will not exhaustively treat that material as if the reader has never read the Bible before. The three definitive New Testament references would be the Olivet Discourse (Mt. 24-25; Mk. 13; Lk. 17 & 21), Paul's teaching on the Antichrist and "*the day of the Lord*" in 2 Thessalonians 2:1-12, and not just the overall sequence of Revelation, but in particular chapters 12-13 as the definitive reference on the anti-king and Revelation 17-18 corresponding to the anti-kingdom. There are the already given attributes in the previous chapters of Daniel as well. As we will visit each of these in much more depth to come, apologies are offered if the assumed connections to those things are not yet as apparent to the reader as they are to the author.

The Initial Stages

> *[21]"In his place a despicable person will arise, on whom the honor of kingship has not been conferred, but he will come in a time of tranquility and seize the kingdom by intrigue.*
>
> — Daniel 11:21

The Antichrist is repeatedly characterized as a very intelligent and devious character who seems to be a master of manipulation and deception. He mimics the two core traits of Satan represented in Scripture as the serpent and the dragon—that is, the biblical representations of deception and persecution. Like his master Satan, he begins with deception and then escalates to persecution when the facade of deception has taken him as far as it can get. As seen here, he does not rise to power legitimately, and in a counterfeit of Christ—and we will see he is constantly trying to counterfeit the true Messiah in every way possible, "*he will come in a time of tranquility*", a false peace in imitation of the Prince of Peace.

This is starkly presented in the 1st Seal of Revelation 6:1-2 when the Antichrist pre-counterfeits Jesus by trying to imitate His coming on a white horse (Rev. 19:11-16) and making an effort from the outset to resemble Him.

A False Peace & Prosperity

> *[22]"The overflowing forces will be flooded away before him and shattered, and also the prince of the covenant. [23]After an alliance is made with him he will practice deception, and he will go up and gain power with a small force of people. [24]In a time of tranquility he will enter the richest parts of the realm, and he will accomplish what his fathers never did, nor his ancestors; he will distribute plunder, booty and possessions among them, and he will devise his schemes against strongholds, but only for a time.*
>
> — Daniel 11:22-24

A well-known feature of the Antichrist is the covenant he will make with Israel (Dan. 9:27), but this is actually just the pinnacle agreement among the many he makes along the way leading up to it. As pointed out from previous prophecies in Daniel, because he acts in the character of Rome, we can expect that, like them, he will negotiate many into voluntarily coming into submission, and like Rome, will resort to force only when deception as practiced through negotiation fails. This may also contribute to the previous discussion of "many" treaties serving to disguise this final one with Israel.

Nonetheless, he will not need a large supporting military presence to bring him to power. The historical effectiveness of "*a small force of people*" has been witnessed in the modern era with the likes of both Hitler and Stalin (and many other historical dictators) whose primary reputation for persecution and violence was earned after an inaugural time primarily characterized by their deceptive negotiations and alliances. But such nearly always begin with a small supporting cast which exerts influence beyond their numbers on behalf of the antichrist figure.

Historical examples such as Hitler in the initial stages of their rise to prominence not only are capable of inducing for at least a short time a false peace in contrast to the tumult of their times, but often a false return to prosperity by various forms of wealth redistribution. But they all have in common that they can never make it last long and their artificial efforts typically last "*only for a time*", and in nearly every case their initial period of deception gives way to a much longer and more intense time of persecution. Their need to fund a false peace often necessitates the transition to warfare.

His Initial Campaign

[25]"He will stir up his strength and courage against the king of the South with a large army; so the king of the South will mobilize an extremely large and mighty army for war; but he will not stand, for schemes will be devised against him. [26]Those who eat his choice food will destroy him, and his army will overflow, but many will fall down slain. [27]As for both kings, their hearts will be intent on evil, and they will speak lies to each other at the same table; but it will not succeed, for the end is still to come at the appointed time. [28]Then he will return to his land with much plunder; but his heart will be set against the holy covenant, and he will take action and then return to his own land.

— Daniel 11:25-28

Without getting too distracted from our main topic here, there is first of all a very similar, as yet unfulfilled event provided in Ezekiel 38-39 which is most commonly called the Gog and Magog scenario, "Gog" actually being recognized as a name for Satan as its leader. A larger coalition than maintained by Epiphanes and his forbearers collectively known as "*the king of the North*" is satanically assembled and led involving what at this time we would call Russia, Iran and Turkey. The actions of Epiphanes and his predecessors of coming into conflict over the Middle East is but a part of Gog and Magog's greater End Times forays extending to the entire Arabian Peninsula and significant parts of Africa as well. But there are documented issues and setbacks, particularly as applied to Israel, which are experienced in similar fashion to those of Epiphanes' time. There are parallels which cannot automatically be ignored for a possible ultimate fulfillment of that which took place with Epiphanes on a much larger scale in the End Times in concert with Ezekiel's as yet unfulfilled revelation.

As with many things borrowed from the Old Testament, it is significant that Islam has co-opted the Gog and Magog scenario for themselves so that not only the apostate portions of Christianity, but Judaism and Islam as well all at present have built-in predispositions to this combined military and spiritual coalition which they associate with the Messiah, but will be led by the ultimate false one.

One of the features of this campaign identified in Daniel is the prominent distinction that "*much plunder*" is a prime motivating factor, as well as some kind of dissatisfaction which arises out of all of this toward Israel specifically. Nonetheless, Scripture sets the expectation that it is not what is popularly called the last Battle of Armageddon which will involve the land of Israel in the Last Days, but a series of conflicts involving not just the Holy Land itself, but the entire region from Libya to Ethiopia to the Saudi Peninsula and the spheres of influence of this final Russia-Iran-Turkey coalition. That which was played out in Epiphanes' time is recapitulated in a much larger, final fulfillment. And just as the Seleucid Empire came into repeated conflict with the Ptolemaic Empire in Egypt, it has been repeatedly seen in our lifetime that Egypt has often been uncooperative with its Arab counterparts, not just initiating its own treaties with Israel, but controlled far more by its military elements than that portion of its own Islamic population. That they will eventually come into conflict with other Arab states is often put forward even by secular observers because of these inherent modern differences which actually replay the historical.

The Abomination of Desolation

[30]"For ships of Kittim will come against him; therefore he will be disheartened and will return and become enraged at the holy covenant and take action; so he will come back and show regard for those who forsake the holy covenant. [31]Forces from him will arise, desecrate the sanctuary fortress, and do away with the regular sacrifice. And they will set up the abomination of desolation.

— Daniel 11:30-31

Firstly, "*ships of Kittim*" as it took place historically describes the Roman incursion into the affairs between "*the king of the North*" and "*the king of the South*". Perhaps this will evolve into something more substantive along these lines, but we have already seen heavy European involvement in the Middle East, and even more so by the European Union (EU). A scenario where their intervention temporarily turns the final figure back is not completely inconceivable and even plausible just based on recent history. Neither the historical Seleucid Kingdom nor any Middle Eastern powers at present have had a formidable naval presence like Imperial Rome or its modern-day European descendants.

Secondly, Jesus specifically warns that a precursor to the Abomination of Desolation is a formal military campaign brought against Jerusalem and even sets this as the trigger for the time to flee without hesitation:

[20]"But ***when you see Jerusalem surrounded by armies, then recognize that her desolation is near****. [21]Then those who are in Judea must flee to the mountains, and those who are in the midst of the city must leave, and those who are in the country must not enter the city; [22]because these are days of vengeance, so that all things which are written will be fulfilled.*

— Luke 21:20-22

[15]"Therefore ***when you see the ABOMINATION OF DESOLATION which was spoken of through Daniel the prophet****, standing in the holy place (let the reader understand), [16]then those who are in Judea must flee to the mountains. [17]Whoever is on the housetop must not go down to get the things out that are in his house. [18]Whoever is in the field must not turn back to get his cloak.*

— Matthew 24:15-18

This should be considered the seminal End Times milestone above all the others which are to be experienced prior to the Church's removal because it is the one not just documented in both Testaments, but by Christ Himself. While the whole of Daniel's 70th Week is not referenced in the New Testament, we undeniably know of its presence by the specific mention of this defining midway point.

[27]"And he will make a firm covenant with the many for one week, ***but in the middle of the week*** *he will put a stop to sacrifice and grain offering; and on the wing of abominations will come one who makes desolate, even until a complete destruction, one that is decreed, is poured out on the one who makes desolate."*

— Daniel 9:27

The parallel actions of these forces under the direction of Satan through the Antichrist are something Christ calls "*the times of the Gentiles*":

> [24]*and they will fall by the edge of the sword, and will be led captive into all the nations; and Jerusalem will be* ***trampled under foot by the Gentiles*** *until* ***the times of the Gentiles*** *are fulfilled.*
> — Luke 21:24

This is further illuminated in Revelation:

> [1]*Then there was given me a measuring rod like a staff; and someone said, "Get up and measure the temple of God and the altar, and those who worship in it.* [2]*Leave out the court which is outside the temple and do not measure it, for it has been* ***given to the nations; and they will tread under foot*** *the holy city* ***for forty-two months****.*
> — Revelation 11:1-2

The broader geopolitical interests of the Antichrist in the greater boundaries of mid-Africa to the whole of the Middle East into Iran, Turkey and Russia become focused exclusively on Israel itself not merely in the political realms, but to affix worldwide attention to what takes place there spiritually. As with all antichrist prefigurements, because of this defining attribute of the final one, they all at some point become self-appointed replacement gods who demand to be worshiped, and they love to do it in Jerusalem.

The Apostasy & Persecution

> [32]*"By smooth words he will turn to godlessness those who act wickedly toward the covenant, but the people who know their God will display strength and take action.* [33]*Those who have insight among the people will give understanding to the many; yet they will fall by sword and by flame, by captivity and by plunder for many days.* [34]*Now when they fall they will be granted a little help, and many will join with them in hypocrisy.* [35]*Some of those who have insight will fall, in order to refine, purge and make them pure until the end time; because it is still to come at the appointed time.*
> — Daniel 11:32-35

One of the main effects witnessed during every historic round of persecution of God's people is to spiritually "*refine, purge and make them pure*". Likewise such is also accompanied by those who initially leave the faith and "*turn to godlessness*" and those who apostatize and even "*join them in hypocrisy*". The physical events are always motivated by more powerful underlying spiritual influences.

Jesus characterizes the time leading up to the Abomination of Desolation as a time of focused persecution of the Church:

> [9]*"Then* ***they*** *will deliver* ***you*** *to tribulation, and will kill you, and you will be hated by all nations because of My name.* [10]*At that time* ***many will fall away*** *and will betray one another and hate one another.*
> — Matthew 24:9-10

The advent of the Abomination of Desolation then kicks off an even more intense period of spiritual darkness and accompanying violence and persecution, but this time not exclusively poured out on the Church alone, but the whole world for believer and non-believer alike:

*[21]"For **then there will be a great tribulation**, such as has not occurred since the beginning of the world until now, nor ever will. [22]Unless those days had been cut short, no life would have been saved; but for the sake of the elect those days will be cut short.*

— Matthew 24:21-22

In Revelation 17-18 we will learn that a time comes when the Antichrist will turn on those who actually brought him to power because he will not be satisfied with followers who worship him through these surrogates, but in his bid to become equal to God Himself will remove the "middle man", so to speak, so that he can be publicly and directly worshiped without the aid of any intermediaries. First he does everything possible to eliminate those such as Christians and Jews who never succumb to worshiping him, then he will turn on those surrogates who channel and direct that worship toward him in order to become the direct, ultimate replacement for Christ.

These will be the most difficult and traumatic times for Christians, surpassing all previous periods of persecution and apostasy combined. But to those who endure, Christ promised:

[18]"Yet not a hair of your head will perish. [19]By your endurance you will gain your lives.

— Luke 21:18-19

In Revelation this is repeatedly expressed with the accompanying qualifier, "*he who overcomes*". (Rev. 2:7, 11, 17, 26; 3:5, 12, 21; 21:7)

In the days of the Maccabees in their fight against Epiphanes, they were mostly organized in small bands, had a huge problem with traitors in their ranks, and had to deal with the fact that a large number of the population embraced the enticements to Hellenize their culture and religion. One of their most potent enemies became Menelaus, the High Priest himself in a foretaste of one of the top problems during the First Coming which is magnified in the Second, the compromised and corrupt ranks of the religious elite. As it was then, we are already experiencing herculean deception and even at times persecution coming from seminary graduates even within so-called Evangelicism as the leaders and purveyors of wave after wave of false movements are becoming outspoken enemies of anything still clinging to biblical orthodoxy. As it was historically, a time will come when a civil war of sorts will finally break out as the remaining faithful remnant recognizes them for the enemy of the cross that they have truly become, but that betrayal by leadership has already incipiently begun.

Such will be experienced by the Church until "*the appointed time*", a particularly intense escalation before the faithful are removed:

[22]"Unless those days had been cut short, no life would have been saved; but for the sake of the elect those days will be cut short.

— Matthew 24:22

The Fulfillment Yet To Come

*[36]"Then the king will do as he pleases, and he will exalt and magnify himself above every god and will speak monstrous things against the God of gods; and **he will prosper until the indignation is finished**, for that which is decreed will be done.*

— Daniel 11:36

The transition begun in verse 35 takes a firm hold in verse 36. As previously visited, "*the indignation*" is initiated by the Abomination of Desolation and characterizes the entire time of rule alloted the Antichrist, which is provided in Scripture both as "*a time, times and half a time*" (Dan. 7:25; 12:7) and "*forty-two months*" (Rev. 13:5), various expressions of 3-1/2 lunar years. The remainder of Daniel 11 from verse 35 on is the focus of the following chapter.

The Example of Epiphanes

As a forerunner of the ultimate anti-king, our list of attributes and behaviors is greatly expanded:

- "*...a despicable person...*" (Dan. 11:21)
- "*...will arise, on whom the honor of kingship has not been conferred...*" (Dan. 11:21)
- "*...will come in a time of tranquility...*" (Dan.11:21)
- "*...will...seize the kingdom by intrigue*". (Dan. 11:21)
- Will make "*an alliance*". (Dan. 11:23)
- "*...will practice deception...*" (Dan. 11:23)
- "*...will go up and gain power with a small force of people*". (Dan. 11:23)
- "*...he will accomplish what his fathers never did, nor his ancestors...*" (Dan. 11:24)
- "*...he will distribute plunder, booty and possessions...*" (Dan. 11:24)
- "*...he will devise his schemes against strongholds, but only for a time*". (Dan. 11:24)
- "...[heart] *intent on evil...*" (Dan. 11:27)
- "*...will speak lies* [while negotiating]..." (Dan. 11:27)
- "*...his heart will be set against the holy covenant...*" IDan.11:28)
- "*...he will be disheartened and will return and become enraged at the holy covenant and take action...*" (Dan. 11:30)
- "*...he will come back and show regard for those who forsake the holy covenant*". (Dan. 11:30)
- "*By smooth words he will turn to godlessness those who act wickedly toward the covenant...*" (Dan. 11:32)

Likewise to the characteristics and actions of the ultimate anti-kingdom gleaned to this point we can add:

- "*...overflowing forces will be flooded away before him and shattered...*" (Dan.11:22)
- "*In a time of tranquility he will enter the richest parts of the realm...*" (Dan. 11:24)
- "*He will stir up his strength and courage against the king of the South with a large army...*" (Dan. 11:25)
- "*...so that the king of the South will mobilize an extremely large and mighty army for war...*" (Dan. 11:25)
- "*...but he* [the king of the South] *will not stand, for schemes will be devised against him*". (Dan. 11:25)
- "*...the end is still to come at the appointed time*". (Dan.11:27)
- "*...he will return to his land with much plunder...*" (Dan. 11:28)

- "...*he will take action and then return to his own land*". (Dan. 11:28)
- "*At the appointed time he will return and come into the South, but this last time it will not turn out the way it did before*". (Dan. 11:29)
- "...*ships from Kittim will come against him*..." (Dan. 11:30)
- "*Forces from him will arise, desecrate the sanctuary fortress, and do away with the regular sacrifice*..." (Dan. 11:31)
- "...*they will set up the abomination of desolation*". (Dan.11:31)
- "*Those who have insight...will fall by sword and by flame, by captivity and by plunder for many days*". (Dan. 11:33)
- "...*many will join with them* [those who have insight] *in hypocrisy*". (Dan. 11:34)

This list is sizable in itself, but when combined with what is provided in the previous visions in Daniel, we can see that the 1st century listener during Christ's First Coming would have possessed in exhaustive detail not just the characteristics of someone carrying out the Abomination of Desolation or acting as a counterfeit messiah, but how they were enacted in the historical example of Epiphanes. Since they still celebrated their victory over him, Epiphanes would not have left their memories even after nearly 200 hundred years had passed when John documents in Jesus' time "The Feast of Dedication".

After we take stock of the final list of traits to be divulged in the remaining verses of Daniel 11 in the next chapter, we will assemble an inventory of these features which combine into a formidable portrait of this final figure and provide the foundation for its New Testament completion. But as stated previously, well over 90% of what is biblically divulged about this figure and his kingdom is first revealed in the Old Testament, which would make any additional details sharply stand out to 1st century believers in a manner unfamiliar to us. Again, this is mainly due to the fact that as Christians who have never lived without the whole canon of both Testaments, and especially having been first grounded in the New Testament before visiting the Old in the depth necessary, cannot possibly view Scripture in the precise, same way as our earlier counterparts in this regard.

In this case this has the reverse effect of causing them to be much smarter than us on this topic because when we first came across the New Testament references to the Antichrist and the Abomination of Desolation, for instance, at that point we attempted to understand them without this depth of prior defining information the Old Testament or the supporting historical record. The new details which are to come in the New Testament are extremely important, but can be misinterpreted and even overblown without the basic yet thorough foundation previously provided.

7 ❖ Daniel 10-12: The Latter Days Final Figure

[36]"Then the king will do as he pleases, and he will exalt and magnify himself above every god and will speak monstrous things against the God of gods; and he will prosper until the indignation is finished, for that which is decreed will be done...[45]yet he will come to his end, and no one will help him.
— Daniel 11:36, 45b

In the broadest sense, the Antichrist is the ultimate example of an unrepentant sinner whose short and selfish temporal time in this life gives way to the worst eternal consequences. He is the quintessential poster child exemplifying the model of every individual and collective sinful behavior. One of his assigned names is even the *"man of lawlessness"* (2 Th. 2:3) to emphasize his complete and personal opposition to God's Word and ways. Biblical love has no greater example than Christ selflessly giving His life on the cross so that all might live, so it should be no surprise that the Antichrist is the polar opposite who cares for no one but himself. Christ ministered for 3-1/2 years to bring eternal life through the grace of God; Antichrist for his 3/1-2 years brings eternal death and the wrath of God.

As discussed earlier, the chief defining characteristic of this final figure, and all his forerunners for that matter, is to counterfeit:

- Christ is the King, so he comes as a counterfeit king;
- Christ has a Body of believers who are growing into His very image and likeness, but the parallel in the Antichrist image is of separate metallic parts of different parts of the body which are ultimately crushed and blown away;
- Through Christ comes the worship of the One True God, through Antichrist the worship of Satan.

Such a list could go on with many more parallels, but it comes down to the difference between Heaven and the Lake of Fire and the respective paths to each, but in much parallel counterfeit detail in a satanic imitation of the authentic. Yes, for a time *"he will prosper...yet he will come to his end..."*

A Time Limit

*[35]"Some of those who have insight will fall, in order to refine, purge and make them pure until the end time; because **it is still to come at the appointed time**.*
— Daniel 11:35

As previously visited, "*the appointed time*" is repeatedly found in Scripture referring to something taking place according to God's timing. We can also confirm this by consulting the Greek Septuagint to find that this instance of "*time*" was translated by those Jewish scholars from the Hebrew into the Greek word "*kairos*" (Strong's #2540). When found in an eschatological context, *kairos* carries with it the meaning of a timed event or something bounded by a specific timespan. This is as opposed to sometimes finding the underlying Greek word "*chronos*" (Strong's #5550), which eschatologically refers to a sequence that is not necessarily confined to a stopwatch. "*Chronos*" is the basis for the English word "chronology".

Some things in God's scheme of things are a *chronos*—a sequence which moves forward depending on when each successive step is completed. "A" must be fulfilled before moving on to "B", which must be finished before advancing to "C" and so forth. Other parts of God's plan are a *kairos* which either have a specific start time, end time, or both. One of the problems we encounter when attempting to determine a time for something eschatological is not determining from the outset if it is definitely a timed event rather than a sequence. The tension between these two mechanisms only conflicts with our modern notions of time and timing, sometimes failing to understand that God uses and is in control of both.

> 6*So when they had come together, they were asking Him, saying, "Lord, is it at* ***this time*** [chronos] *You are restoring the kingdom to Israel?"*
> 7*He said to them, "It is not for you to know* ***times*** [chronos] *or* ***epochs*** [kairos] ***which the Father has fixed by His own authority;***
> — Acts 1:6-7

Here is a plain scriptural example showing that God uses and is in control of both *kairos* and *chronos*. They were asking if this is the *chronos*—"*this time*", or the place in the sequence of Christ's overall working when He would now restore "*the kingdom to Israel*", having fulfilled what we now know to be the sequence of His First Coming defined by His work on the cross. Jesus did not say that such a restoration would not take place, but responded to affirm that His followers have a more important mission in the overall sequence which must come before what is commonly referred to as the Millennial Reign. He is saying, "First ***this*** must come before ***that***." This was an extension of the parables He gave closing out the Olivet Discourse which all featured Him as the Master or Bridegroom returning to find out in each case whether His own were carrying out their assignments in the interim. We are supposed to trust in God's timing for both set dates and times and the overall sequence.

When it comes to the End Times, our perspective is not provided a clearly defined starting point when we can undeniably hear the metaphorical starter's pistol formally initiating the final week of years. Jesus rather describes a progression in the character of "*birth pangs*" coming in concentric waves which become more frequent and powerful the nearer we approach and enter into that final week of years. In other words, it begins as a *chronos*, a sequence whose initial schedule is not quantified as we experience it, but provided in the order in which to expect it. This is what makes the Abomination of Desolation our most important fixed milestone (short of the *Harpazo*), because it signals a transition from the *chronos*—the longer opening sequence, to the final *kairos* of specified length. Scripture speaks of this final time as various expressions of 3-1/2 lunar years with many accompanying references to something which is not simply timed, but expires altogether. The eschaton is ***both*** a *chronos* and a *kairos*, and yet God is equally in control of it all.

Although Jesus' formal public ministry was but 3-1/2 years in length, the First Coming actually began approximately 31-1/2 years prior with the first appearance of Gabriel to Zacharias. (Lk. 1:5-20) In fact, an accounting of the Old Testament prophecies which Christ would fulfill from Gabriel's appearance to His Ascension show that approximately 14% of them were fulfilled in those 31 or so years prior to the initiation of that ministry commencing with His baptism by John. While many provisions in God's prophetic Word pertaining to the eschaton are surely confined to the boundaries of Daniel's 70th Week, as it was in the First Coming, a significant body of them characterize a much longer period leading up to it. Not everything is a *kairos.*

Although we cannot be sure how long it takes him to rise from obscurity to power and worldwide prominence, there are several assignments of *kairos* to the anti-king/anti-kingdom, and they all seem to focus on the last half of Daniel's 70th Week. In other words, at the beginning of the eschaton we experience a longer *chronos* which at the very end gives way to a divinely specified *kairos.*

The Time of Persecution

> 25 *'He will speak out against the Most High and* ***wear down the saints*** *of the Highest One, and he will intend to make alterations in times and in law;* ***and they will be given into his hand for a time, times, and half a time****.*
>
> — Daniel 7:25

It may seem nit-picky, but while the general activities of blasphemy and imitating God are mentioned, the key endeavor which is twice emphasized is, "*He will...wear down the saints*" and "*they will be given into his hand*".

If we were reading the Bible for the very first time, we might notice that this first reference of timing assigned to the Antichrist comes in Daniel 7 ***before*** the concept of "*weeks of years*" is first introduced in Daniel 9. At the least, it would seem that from the very outset a special emphasis is established not on "the seven", but the 3-1/2, and of all his behaviors and undertakings, his persecution of God's people is nearly always mentioned when this subject comes up throughout God's Word.

The Time of Transgression

> 13 *Then I heard a holy one speaking, and another holy one said to that particular one who was speaking, "How long will the vision about the regular sacrifice apply, while the transgression causes horror, so as to allow both the holy place and the host to be trampled?"*
>
> 14 *He said to me, "For 2,300 evenings and mornings; then the holy place will be properly restored."*
>
> — Daniel 8:13-14

There is much debate as to whether this particular instance has multiple fulfillments, or is limited exclusively to Epiphanes and no one else. This is, however, probably the most abused number in the Bible second only to "666".

Many have done this, but most notably it was the infamous Millerites in the 19th century who rallied around the error of treating this as 2,300 ***years*** and calculating that the Rapture would take place in 1843. When it did not happen, many realized they had forgotten to account for year "0" so as to miscalculate it a year early, and thus repeated it all over again in 1844.

Their legacy continues to this day in subsequently spawning both the Jehovah's Witnesses and the Seventh-day Adventists, both of whom vie for the record of most failed date predictions.

Jews have always used the Genesis account to define a day, which is why even today they see it as extending from nightfall to nightfall. In the Creation Narrative, at the end of each of God's divine acts, Scripture records, "*And there was evening and there was morning, one day*", (Gen. 1:5), "*And there was evening and there was morning, a second day*" (Gen. 1:8) and so on through the entire account. When Scripture speaks of "*evenings and mornings*" as it does in Daniel, it is referring to the biblical definition of a literal day. It does not use a twenty-four hour clock measuring things from midnight to midnight like we do, and it certainly cannot be allegorized into anything ***but*** a literal day.

This period, roughly the equivalent of 6.4 lunar years, also turns out to be the precise length of time the historical record attributes to the antics of Epiphanes who "*trampled*" both the "*holy place and the host*" and committed the first recorded Abomination of Desolation.

One of the reasons we cannot simply cast aside the notion that this may be an instance of a one-time prophetic fulfillment with no future recapitulation is that at the end of Epiphanes' reign, it is clearly documented that the restoration of the Temple was effected. This is not specified in Scripture as something which will happen to the third Tribulational Temple in which the Antichrist deifies himself and co-opts as his center of worship. Rather, because of the worldwide devastation of the final earthquake in Revelation 16:18 ("*...such as there had not been since man came to be upon the earth...*"), and so much textual real estate devoted in the closing chapters of Ezekiel to the building of what might be called the fourth "Millennial Temple", no restoration of that third Temple takes place as revealed by Scripture.

Additionally, since there are no scriptural parallels to "*2,300*" in the same manner that variations of 3-1/2 lunar years support and play off each other, this author is hesitant to make the same case for something which theologians categorize as "*hapax legomenon*"—that is, a term only used one, single time in the whole of God's Word. It is unwise to form an entire opinion, and especially doctrine, that is based on a single, remote reference in Scripture.

However, this is something to keep in prayerful consideration so as to not become dogmatically attached in some way without allowing for the possibility that, like many prophetic items, it has yet to be revealed for a subsequent, ultimate fulfillment. The parallels to other passages makes it impossible to outright dismiss with absolute certainty that there is no prophetic connection whatsoever, but the fact that it does not correspond to any of the other quantities of seven or 3-1/2 in God's Word provides a reasonable basis to consider it does not belong to that category. It may have been included for the very purpose of bringing to our attention the historical figure of Antiochus Epiphanes IV.

The Time of the Covenant

> 27 *"And he will make a firm covenant with the many for one week, but in the middle of the week he will put a stop to sacrifice and grain offering; and on the wing of abominations will come one who makes desolate, even until a complete destruction, one that is decreed, is poured out on the one who makes desolate."*
>
> — Daniel 9:27

This author had an eye-opening experience when going to Google, selecting to perform an image search, and typing in "tribulational chart", which produced what appears to be thousands of graphical representations of the End Times timeline. Like snowflakes, no two seem to be exactly alike. But the overwhelming common feature found in most of them is to assign as the very first event in the final seven years the 1st Seal of Revelation 6:1-2. While this may or may not be correct, this is simply never stated as such anywhere in Scripture. The one thing which ***is*** categorically stated is missing from these charts most of the time: "*And he will make a firm covenant with the many for one week*". In this verse we are provided not just the definitive beginning and end, but the precise midway point.

- The beginning is the making of this agreement;
- 3-1/2 years later is the midway milestone of the Abomination of Desolation when the covenant is broken;
- The end is seven years from the treaty going into effect and 3/1-2 years from the Abomination.

The end of the final week of years is the end of the Antichrist when "*a complete destruction, one that is decreed, is poured out on the one who makes desolate*".

However, this initiating feature of instituting a covenant is never again addressed in Scripture (not even the New Testament), and instead it is the Abomination of Desolation—that is, the halfway point, which keeps reappearing to be established as the focal point initiating that ***last half*** of Daniel's 70th Week. We see this in the Olivet Discourse where, again, Jesus refers to everything leading up to it as coming in the character of "*birth pangs*", and heaping most of the attention on this halfway milestone.

> 15 *"Therefore when you see the* ABOMINATION OF DESOLATION *which was spoken of through Daniel the prophet, standing in the holy place (let the reader understand),*
> 16 *then those who are in Judea must flee to the mountains.*
> — Matthew 24:15-16

The beginning seems to be purposely obscured, fading in as a *chronos*—a sequence, before unmistakably becoming the final *kairos*—a timed, final countdown kicked off by the Abomination of Desolation. Like many prophetic fulfillments documented for the First Coming in the Gospels, this may be something which will only be clearly understood in hindsight in its totality, but this middle milestone is unmistakable.

For those who think a treaty cannot be concealed from public view, during the past year prior to the time of this writing it was disclosed for the first time that the Vatican had entered into a treaty with the Palestinians two years earlier of which no one was previously aware. (This was not ***the*** treaty, just an example of concealment.) Scripture renders unmistakable our recognition of the middle and ending of the final week of years, but not necessarily that this precise beginning will be equally unavoidably recognized.

As visited previously when discussing the difficulty of figuring out which of the four biblically-recorded decrees we should use to measure the distance to Christ's First Coming, and the Antichrist's repeated tactic of making agreements as he rises to power, this seems to be replayed in the timing of this seminal negotiated agreement. A case can be made for the repeated scriptural pattern of a *kairos* whose beginning can only be discerned in hindsight, but whose subsequent milestones are clearly witnessed.

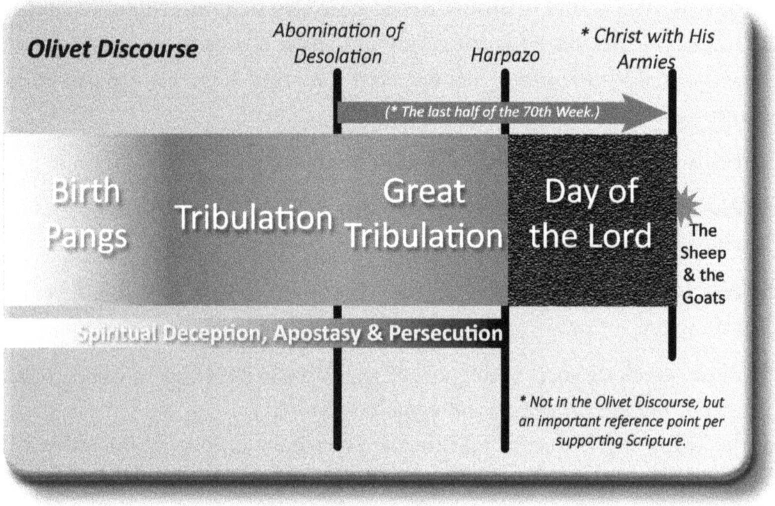

The Time Until the End

> *[6]And one said to the man dressed in linen, who was above the waters of the river, **"How long will it be until the end of these wonders?"** [7]I heard the man dressed in linen, who was above the waters of the river, as he raised his right hand and his left toward heaven, and swore by Him who lives forever that it would be for a time, times, and half a time; and as soon as they finish shattering the power of the holy people, all these events will be completed.*
> — Daniel 12:6-7

Persecution is again a featured point, but the emphasis is placed on assigning the expiration date for the final 3-1/2 lunar years.

This is followed with an interesting puzzle, when all of the sudden "*times*"—that is, lunar years, are exchanged for literal "*days*".

> *[11]"From the time that the regular sacrifice is abolished and the abomination of desolation is set up, there will be **1,290 days**. [12]How blessed is he who keeps waiting and attains to the **1,335 days**!*
> — Daniel 12:11-12

Christ's prophetic disclosure to the Apostle John will introduce two units of measure which on the surface appear to be equal to 3-1/2 lunar years: "*1,260 days*" (Rev. 11:3; 12:6) and "*forty-two months*". (Rev. 11:2; 13:4-7) A perfect lunar year consists of 12 months (new moons) and 360 days, so a perfect 3-1/2 year lunar period would total both 42 months and 1,260 days. However, there is no reference in Daniel to "*1,260*" and likewise absent from Revelation is "*1,290*" and "*1,335*".

In truth, there is no such thing as a perfect lunar year totaling 360 days without some manmade help to synchronize its shortfalls with the solar cycle of 364-1/4 days. A lunar year is based on twelve lunar months, defined as one full moon to the next. This is actually a very steady and celestially regulated 29.5 days. In other words, a lunar month alternates from being either 29 or 30 days in length so there can never be twelve in a row of the same size.

Because the requirements for Temple operations required a new moon sacrifice, the Talmud has very detailed instructions for calculating lunar months and years, and a small nation like

Israel where bad weather could prevent everyone from knowing when a new month began required a somewhat involved process for determining when it occurs. (There are modern-day websites devoted to keeping track of this for practitioners of Judaism.) Adjustments had to be made, otherwise the calendar would become disassociated from the seasons, so it was calculated that a year had to have at least four, and no more than ten, thirty day months, each of the remaining being twenty-nine. In other words, in actual practice, a biblical lunar year fluctuates between 352 and 358 days—it ***always*** falls short of the theoretical 360. To make up for the growing distance with the solar calendar, instead of adding exactly what was needed to make up the difference as we now do, they would insert an entire "leap month" by adding an additional month of Adar at the beginning of a year. (They literally have two beginning months of Adar when this happens.) In other words, there would be years which actually had ***thirteen*** months and ***more*** than 360 days to help bring it back into balance with nature's seasonal cycles.

This is a long-winded explanation that "*1,290 days*" is simply a 3-1/2 year period which includes a leap month. In such a case, "*time, times, and half a time*" and"*1,290 days*" are the exact, same thing. A 3-1/2 year lunar period containing a leap month was still considered just a 3-1/2 year period overall.

Although rare, there have been documented times when an excess of 29 day months were experienced so close together that a particular three year period experienced the insertion of two leap months to compensate for this shortfall, which makes for 1,320 days, just 15 days shy of the "*1,335 days*". It has been pointed out by Jacob Prasch of Moriel Ministries that there may be eschatological implications provided in the book of Esther where Purim is curiously celebrated on the 15th of Adar in walled cities such as Jerusalem (Est. 9:20-21), meaning that there may be an explanation for this longest designation, something to keep in prayerful consideration going forward.

The greater point is that there is a logical explanation for the "*1,290 days*", and perhaps a scriptural basis for the "*1,335 days*", which warrants further investigation, reducing the mysteriousness of these assigned parallels to the final 3-1/2 lunar years of history. But the main textual meaning of this particular *kairos* of the Antichrist is to define the end and doubly reinforce the last half of Daniel's 70th Week of years.

The Time of His Formal Reign

> *5There was given to him a mouth speaking arrogant words and blasphemies, and authority to act* ***<u>for forty-two months</u>*** *was given to him. 6And he opened his mouth in blasphemies against God, to blaspheme His name and His tabernacle, that is, those who dwell in heaven. 7It was also given to him to make war with the saints and to overcome them, and authority over every tribe and people and tongue and nation was given to him.*
>
> — Revelation 13:5-7

In the Apostle John's vision the features of blaspheming God, a formal time of authority for the Antichrist's reign, transgressing the Temple and persecution of God's people are revisited, but assigned an alternate *kairos* of "*forty-two months*" to set it apart for some reason from the previous iterations.

In Revelation, "*1,260 days*" is used when addressing the activities of the "good guys"—that is, the Two Witnesses (Rev. 11:3) and Israel (Rev. 12:6), personified as the woman fleeing into the wilderness; "*forty-two months*" is assigned to "bad guys"—the Gentiles trampling Jerusalem

(Rev. 11:2) and the reign of the Beast (Rev. 13:4-7) So even if we want to avoid the tediousness of the lunar calendar, we can see that the Holy Spirit is trying to bring a distinction to our attention by emphasizing their spiritual natures through the use of different time designations. Those belonging to the light are not confused with those in darkness by their respective numerical assignments.

When it comes to the number "42" specifically in Scripture, it seems to be the numerical expression of apostasy, derived from multiplying the number of man,"6", by the number of perfection", "7", so as to illustrate man's spiritual corruption of the perfect. In Scripture we find instances when it is associated with this kind of behavior:

- It was 42 apostate youths who taunted Elisha about the rapture of Elijah who were devoured by the bears. (2 Ki. 2:23-25)
- It was 42 apostate sons of the king of Northern Israel killed by God's assassin, Jehu. (2 Ki. 10:12-14)
- It is recorded that the unfaithful generation wandering in the wilderness camped at 42 places in the Wilderness. (Num. 33)
- It was 42,000 who were killed in the time of Jephthah. (Jg. 12:1-7)

At the least the biblical references to "42" seem to be associated with someone or something contrary in obedience to God's Word and ways.

Scripture provides a *chronos*—a sequence of events which gradually intensify leading into a final *kairos* expressed in various forms of 3-1/2 lunar years which appear with various designations so as to differentiate a variety of functions and even greater underlying spiritual conditions. A separate, dedicated study would need to be pursued in order to determine whether every recorded instance of some variation of 3-1/2 all synchronize with each other or instead overlap in some fashion, but when it comes to how they are applied to the Antichrist, they are commonly assigned to the second half of Daniel's 70th Week. With each instance, the Holy Spirit is not just reinforcing the overriding importance of the last 3-1/2 years of history, but trying to bring to our attention specific activities and spiritual conditions.

The Final Anti-King to Come

> 35 *"Some of those who have insight will fall, in order to refine, purge and make them pure until the end time; because it is still to come at the appointed time.*
>
> 36 *"Then the king will do as he pleases, and he will exalt and magnify himself above every god and will speak monstrous things against the God of gods; and he will prosper until the indignation is finished, for that which is decreed will be done.* 37 *He will show no regard for the gods of his fathers or for the desire of women, nor will he show regard for any other god; for he will magnify himself above them all.* 38 *But instead he will honor a god of fortresses, a god whom his fathers did not know; he will honor him with gold, silver, costly stones and treasures.* 39 *He will take action against the strongest of fortresses with the help of a foreign god; he will give great honor to those who acknowledge him and will cause them to rule over the many, and will parcel out land for a price.*
>
> — Daniel 11:35-39

We may wonder why some traits are repeated in so many of the passages referring to the final Antichrist or his many prefiguring counterparts, but it is this textual repetition which greatly aids in making that very connection. In Daniel's final list we will understand the relationship to previous passages by the inclusion of shared characteristics or activities, and therefore be able to identify the new additions in each which are being assigned exclusively to that final figure.

Verse 35 serves as a transition or sort of "hinge", if you will, allowing the door to swing either back to Epiphanes as a historical prefigurement or forward to the yet to be encountered final figure, by the reference to the greater spiritual purpose of persecution where God's people are concerned. But the included reference of something"*still to come*" provides a caveat that while this may have experienced a partial fulfillment historically, there is slated a more complete future fulfillment.

To our list of the characteristics of the anti-king we can add:

- "*...will do as he pleases..*" (v.36)
- "*...he will exalt and magnify himself above every god...*" (v.36)
- "*...will speak monstrous things against the God of gods...*" (v.36)
- "*...he will prosper until the indignation is finished...*" (v.36)
- "*He will show no regard for the gods of his fathers...*" (v.37)
- "*He will show no regard...for the desire of women...*" (v.37)
- "*...nor will he show regard for any other god, for he will magnify himself above them all*". (v.37)
- "*...he will honor a god of fortresses, a god whom his fathers did not know...*" (v.38)
- "*...he will honor him* [a god of fortresses] *with gold, silver, costly stones and treasures*". (v.38)
- "*He will take action against the strongest of fortresses with the help of a foreign god...*" (v.39)
- "*...he will give great honor to those who acknowledge him and will cause them to rule over the many...*" (v.39)
- "*...will parcel out land for a price*". (v.39)

Here we are provided a deeper treatment of the specifics of his self-deification, false worship practices, and inducements for following him. It is an interesting highlighted detail that the satanic nature of his spiritual condition is reflected in his personal relationships where women are concerned. Scripture repeatedly illustrates faithfulness as a committed marriage and unfaithfulness as adultery which, when pursued, deteriorates to the worst condition described as a parallel to prostitution. This final figure is the very definition and ultimate personal example of apostasy and the textbook portrait of spiritual unfaithfulness. His literal issue with women is a symptom of a deeper spiritual disease.

The Final Anti-Kingdom to Come

> *40"At the end time the king of the South will collide with him, and the king of the North will storm against him with chariots, with horsemen and with many ships; and he will enter countries, overflow them and pass through. 41He will also enter the Beautiful Land, and many countries will fall; but these will be rescued out of his hand: Edom, Moab and the foremost of the sons of Ammon. 42Then he will stretch out his hand against other countries, and the land of Egypt will not escape. 43But he will gain control over the hidden treasures of gold and silver and over all the precious things*

of Egypt; and Libyans and Ethiopians will follow at his heels. [44]But rumors from the East and from the North will disturb him, and he will go forth with great wrath to destroy and annihilate many. [45]He will pitch the tents of his royal pavilion between the seas and the beautiful Holy Mountain; yet he will come to his end, and no one will help him.

— Daniel 11:40-45

Although there are obviously activities in every list which an individual king cannot effect by himself, this second section is more oriented in the dual expression of his anti-kingdom. As repeatedly stipulated, just as Christ is both the King and a Kingdom comprised of believers, the Antichrist is essentially a pursuit to counterfeit both.

European or Middle Eastern?

There is a particular point which needs to first be discussed that the anti-king is here identified as "*the king of the North*", which is the moniker assigned all the Seleucid kings in the previous verses, and of Epiphanes in particular. This provides justification for stipulating that many, if not all of their actions will be replayed by this last figure and bridges this final anti-king to Epiphanes specifically. But anyone who has sampled the fare from the smörgåsbord of the various eschatological schools of thought are more than familiar with the popular assertions that the Antichrist arises as the head of a European confederation in the character of a revived Roman Empire. There is no shortage of commentators expressing as factual he is Roman, operates out of Rome, and heads a reconstituted Roman Empire.

This will be visited in more detail to come, especially when we consider Revelation's references to "*Babylon the Great*" as the final anti-kingdom, but it is worth noting that rarely has this author found a dogmatic proponent of the Antichrist leading a European coalition provide a parallel explanation for why he is categorically assigned in Daniel as "*the king of the North*", whom none of those advocates would dispute was a Middle Eastern/Asia Minor empire based out of what is designated on modern maps as Syria and Iraq. This gets even more interesting still with the tension of various theories resolving the timing, role and nature of the Gog and Magog coalition specified in Ezekiel 38-39, which share much of the same agenda and similar actions as specified in these final verses of Daniel 11.

An important lesson to be gleaned from the previous visions in Daniel is that ***none*** of the kings or kingdoms are identical twins, or clones, of the previous. Instead, as previously stipulated, they act "in the character of" each other, sharing the same common spiritual heritage and satanically animated tendencies. Each kingdom was unique from each other in their geography, government, capital, language and culture. Each unquestionably provided a lasting influence on those to follow, but each iteration is ultimately unique from the rest. Even in the final composition of Nebuchadnezzar's image representing Rome, it fragmented into Western and Eastern branches as represented by the two legs, each continuing to have strong connections to the original unified Roman Empire, but ultimately becoming something distinctly different. Likewise, the final "Roman Empire" to come as depicted by the ten toes is "in the character of" those previous iterations but evolves a uniqueness not seen in any previous variation.

*[12]"The ten horns which you saw are ten kings who have not yet received a kingdom, but **they receive authority as kings with the beast for one hour**. [13]These have one purpose, and they give their power and authority to the beast.*

— Revelation 17:12-13

The salient takeaway is that there are those scriptural attributes which will be ultimate fulfillments "in the character of" the forerunners of the anti-king and anti-kingdom, which should not be confused with scriptural designations which make a specific assignment as to their identity. The Antichrist and his empire clearly operate in the character of the past examples of Babylon, Medo-Persia, Greece and Rome, but is singled out as replaying the Seleucid Empire as seen in the wealth of detail provided in Daniel 11.

The notion of an ultimate European Empire has had many proponents throughout history, but its status was greatly accelerated by the popular adoption of Hal Lindsey's seminal work, *The Late, Great Planet Earth*. But there have always been at least a very vocal minority who insist that in order to also deceive the Jews, the Antichrist must of necessity be ethnically Jewish. It is also noteworthy that over the past twenty years in particular a growing number of advocates have come forward favoring not just an ethnically Gentile Antichrist, but an Arab one specifically. While we will deal with this in depth when considering Revelation 13, it is in that portion of God's prophetic Word we learn that the Antichrist is actually ***two*** figures working in tandem, the other whom we call the False Prophet. In other words, there is some latitude for both camps where one figure is ethnically Gentile and the other of Jewish descent. However, every single antichrist figure in Daniel is an ethnically Gentile political ruler with a penchant for self-deification.

But when it comes to the actual empire and the empire which is formed exclusively for his purposes alone, the textual evidence provided in Daniel 11 is that he recapitulates the Seleucid Empire, but on an obviously much grander global scale. The initial vision of the image in Daniel 2 is subsequently narrowed in subsequent visions so that in this final one, the final figure is most closely associated with the Seleucid Empire. The final one will ultimately still be unique from all the previous even though he shares the same characteristics.

Attributes of the Anti-Kingdom

- "*...the king of the South will collide with him...*" (v.40)
- "...[he] *will storm against him* [the king of the South] *with chariots, with horsemen and with many ships...*"
- "*...he will enter countries, overflow them and pass through*". (v.40)
- "*He will also enter the Beautiful Land...*" (v.41)
- "*...many countries will fall...*" (v.41)
- "*...but these will be rescued out of his hand: Edom, Moab and the foremost of the sons of Ammon*". (v.41)
- "*...he will stretch out his hand against other countries...*" (v.42)
- "*...Egypt will not escape*". (v.42)
- "*...he will gain control over the hidden treasures of gold and silver and over all the precious things of Egypt...*" (v.43)
- "*...Libyans and Ethiopians will follow at his heels*". (v.43)
- "*...rumors from the East and from the North will disturb him...*" (v.44)
- "*...he will go forth with great wrath to destroy and annihilate many*". (v.43)

- "*He will pitch the tents of his royal pavilion between the seas and the beautiful Holy Mountain...*"(v.45)
- "*...he will come to his end, and no one will help him*". (v.45)

There is a certain ebb and flow represented here which mimics the same back and forth actions which historically took place between the Seleucid and Ptolemaic Empires, identified in Daniel 11 as "*the king of the North*" and "*the king of the South*". These also provide many parallels to the yet to be realized Gog and Magog scenario of Ezekiel 38-39 which seem to correspond to those of the Seleucid Empire but on a much larger scale. It would seem that the revisited turmoils and conflicts centering on the Levant have been an almost perpetual reminder to every generation of what is to be ultimately concluded there. They are all a precursor to the ultimate culmination in what is to come at Armageddon when the forces of Satan finally come face to face with those accompanying Christ.

What took place in the repeated back-and-forth forays of the Seleucid and Ptolemaic Empires were preceded by similar moves and counter-moves employed by the Egyptian, Assyrian, Babylonian, Medo-Persian and Grecian Empires before them. This not only continued after them under Rome, but through various players for the next two millennia up to this very hour with various incursions, crusades and nearly every world's empire providing some kind of political intrigue there. At the time of this writing, nearly every nation, coalition, and then some are involved militarily in the Middle East, and the major religious influences of Christianity, Judaism, Islam and Catholicism are in constant conflict over Jerusalem. Since its institution, no political issue has been more legislated in the United Nations than Israel and Jerusalem.

> [2]*"Behold, I am going to make Jerusalem a cup that causes reeling to all the peoples around; and when the siege is against Jerusalem, it will also be against Judah.* [3]*It will come about in that day that I will make Jerusalem a heavy stone for all the peoples; all who lift it will be severely injured. And all the nations of the earth will be gathered against it.*
>
> — Zechariah 12:2-3

8 ❖ Daniel 10-12: The Latter Days Focus

Daniel's final vision, which actually began in chapter 10, now continues uninterrupted into chapter 12. We are provided a summary which is primarily focused on the future, ultimate fulfillment of Daniel's 70th Week, but begins by once again showing the correspondence between the earthly and the heavenly.

> [1]*"Now at that time Michael, the great prince who stands guard over the sons of your people, will arise. And there will be a time of distress such as never occurred since there was a nation until that time; and at that time your people, everyone who is found written in the book, will be rescued.*
>
> — Daniel 12:1

There are several other biblical references to Michael which reveal his activities, but this instance is focused on the fact that he not only "*stands guard over the sons of your people*"—that is, Israel, but parallel to this final time of the anti-king, Michael "*will arise*". It would appear that mention of this is purposely inserted at this point in the text to narrow down the view to Israel. This is further confirmed in this passage when it states that "*there will be a time of distress such as never occurred* ***<u>since there was a nation</u>***". This is a way of stating, "in all of ***<u>Israel's</u>*** history" there has never been something this bad.

We know from Revelation 12 that Michael oversees throwing Satan and his demons out of heaven, casting them down to earth, (Rev. 12:7-9) and that there is strong evidence this is something which coincides with the Antichrist's public revealing at the Abomination of Desolation. In other words, although he is active prior to the final 3-1/2 years, in a replay of the inauguration of Christ's ministry at His baptism by John when God the Father and God the Holy Spirit were heard and seen confirming the deity of the Son to inaugurate His 3-1/2 year public ministry, a satanic counterfeit is effected by his going into the Temple, being possessed by Satan now cast to earth, and together with the endorsement of the False Prophet visibly and publicly declaring himself to be God to inaugurate his own 3-1/2 (and final) years. Christ's baptism took place humbly in the wilderness on the other side of the Jordan; the counterfeit enacts an ostentatious public display in the Temple in Jerusalem to make it look credible from an earthly perspective.

It is also at this time in the Olivet Discourse when Jesus warns those who are in Judea who witness this to flee, another feature of Revelation 12 which helps tie the timing of Satan's begrudging arrival on earth and this Antichrist declaration in the Temple. Both events are closely associated with a flight from Israel into the wilderness.

Another interesting parallel can be drawn to what the King James calls "*the time of Jacob's **trouble***" and the NASB "*Jacob's **distress***":

> [7]*'Alas! For that day is great,*
> *There is none like it;*
> *And it is the time of Jacob's distress,*
> *But he will be saved from it.*
> — Jeremiah 30:7

Both not only reference "*distress*" but a rescue as well.

There is a point in the Olivet Discourse when Christ provides a parallel description which is disclosed as coming on the heels of the Abomination of Desolation and the accompanying flight out of Israel:

> [21]*"For then there will be a great tribulation, such as has not occurred since the beginning of the world until now, nor ever will.*
> — Matthew 24:21

Contrary to popular notions to the contrary, this is an intense phase of the final week of years (not the whole thing or just one of its halves) which occurs just before the removal of the Church:

> [29]*"But **immediately after the tribulation of those days** THE SUN WILL BE DARKENED, AND THE MOON WILL NOT GIVE ITS LIGHT, AND THE STARS WILL FALL from the sky, and the powers of the heavens will be shaken.* [30]*And then **the sign of the Son of Man will appear in the sky**, and then all the tribes of the earth will mourn, and **they will see the SON OF MAN COMING ON THE CLOUDS OF THE SKY** with power and great glory.* [31]*And He will send forth His angels with A GREAT TRUMPET and **THEY WILL GATHER TOGETHER His elect** from the four winds, from one end of the sky to the other.*
> — Matthew 24:29-31

A case can be made that this reference in Jeremiah is describing that time upon the Church's removal when God's focus returns to Israel and all the remaining as yet unfulfilled promises of God's Word for them are realized in the course of the most prolific acceptance in the whole of Israel's history of Yeshua as their Messiah. In other words, the literal flight ***out*** of Israel is simultaneously a spiritual flight ***to*** Christ. It is a much larger recapitulation of what occurred in the First Coming when many went into the wilderness across the Jordan to be baptized by either John the Baptist or Jesus' disciples. (Lk. 3:2-3; Jn. 4:1-2) Although not expressly provided in Scripture, this may be a plausible explanation for the exemption from the Antichrist's control of Edom, Moab and Ammon, the immediate geographic locations to which those exiting Israel are most likely to immediately emigrate in an emergency evacuation scenario. (Dan. 11:41)

According to as yet unfulfilled prophecy in Zechariah, only a third of Israel will survive, an indication of how severe things will become in "*the time of Jacob's distress*". But it also specifies that the remaining third do not simply experience a physical rescue, but a spiritual one as well:

> [8]*"It will come about in all the land,"*
> *Declares the LORD,*
> *"That two parts in it will be cut off and perish;*
> *But the third will be left in it.*
> [9]*And I will bring the third part through the fire,*
> *Refine them as silver is refined,*

And test them as gold is tested.
They will call on My name,
And I will answer them;
I will say, 'They are My people,'
And they will say, 'The LORD is my God.' "
— Zechariah 13:8-9

However the particulars play out, it would appear from the text that the focus has been narrowed further to not just Israel at the center of the struggle between world powers, and still further to the Antichrist's interest in Israel alone, but to their very outcome in the overall scheme of things. But that this is exclusively applied to Israel, note in Jeremiah 30:7 that it states,"***he*** *will be saved from it*" as a firm, textual indication that this is something spoken of literal Israel alone.

The Resurrection

2Many of those who sleep in the dust of the ground will awake, these to everlasting life, but the others to disgrace and everlasting contempt.
— Daniel 12:2

The very end defined by what happens to "*those who sleep*" as opposed to "*the others*" echoes Jesus' own assurance of the very same outcome:

28"Do not marvel at this; for an hour is coming, in which all who are in the tombs will hear His voice, 29and will come forth; those who did the good deeds to a resurrection of life, those who committed the evil deeds to a resurrection of judgment.
— John 5:28-29

Daniel 12:2 is particularly notable for being the very first time the phrase "*everlasting life*" is used in the Old Testament, for which the New Testament prolifically employs "*eternal life*". Likewise it is interesting that the Hebrew word "*dara'own*" (Strong's #1860) here translated as "*contempt*" is only used one other time in the Old Testament, and that in the very last verse of Isaiah in an eschatological context of the very end:

22"For just as the new heavens and the new earth
Which I make will endure before Me," declares the LORD,
"So your offspring and your name will endure.
23And it shall be from new moon to new moon
And from sabbath to sabbath,
All mankind will come to bow down before Me," says the LORD.
24Then they will go forth and look
On the corpses of the men
Who have transgressed against Me.
For their worm will not die
And their fire will not be quenched;
And they will be an ***abhorrence*** *to all mankind."*
— Isaiah 66:22-24

It seems to describe an object of ultimate aversion which suffers eternal consequences.

Although there are certainly other references, Daniel 12:2 is widely recognized as the most explicit reference of an individual's resurrection in the Old Testament. (Job 19:26; Ps. 17:15; Is. 26:19) However, the reader is cautioned that we should never base our understanding of doctrine on a single verse, and in this case if we visit the whole counsel of God's Word (e.g., Rev. 20:4-6), we will understand this better in the context not just of the underlying theology, but the overall timing.

This briefest of verses manages to capture the doctrinal soul of the biblical concept of resurrection:

- It is a literal, ***bodily*** resurrection.
- The body is raised from the grave and given new life.
- The new body is immortal.
- Both believer and non-believer alike spend eternity in a bodily form.
- The saved will "*awake to everlasting life*", but the unsaved to "*everlasting contempt*".

The Proof of Biblical Wisdom

> *[3]Those who have insight will shine brightly like the brightness of the expanse of heaven, and those who lead the many to righteousness, like the stars forever and ever.*
> — Daniel 12:3

This is a valuable standalone lesson in itself which teaches that biblical wisdom is proven not just by personal obedience to God's Word and ways, but leading others in the same in order to achieve "*righteousness*".

> *[30]But by His doing you are in **Christ Jesus, who became to us wisdom from God**, and righteousness and sanctification, and redemption,*
> — 1 Corinthians 1:30

> *[16]**Let the word of Christ richly dwell within you, with all wisdom teaching and admonishing one another** with psalms and hymns and spiritual songs, singing with thankfulness in your hearts to God.*
> — Colossians 3:16

For believers, Jesus is our wisdom which is not something intended to solely enrich us individually, but intended for "*teaching and admonishing one another*". An important aspect of this, especially in the context of Daniel 12:3, is that ***none*** of God's Word, not even the prophetic portions, are purely informational. As with the whole of Scripture there is the responsibility on the part of ***both*** the discipler and the discipled to put it into practice. That which we might label eschatological is always accompanied by instructions as to what to do with it. When we stop at publishing a chart of our timeline or limit the content of a prophecy conference to what really amounts to no more than a lecture, we are failing to achieve this minimum standard.

Conceal and Seal

> *[4]But as for you, Daniel, conceal these words and seal up the book until the end of time; many will go back and forth, and knowledge will increase."*
> — Daniel 12:4

In what begins the final instructions given to Daniel, it should be noted that "*seal up the book*" as referred to here means that Daniel was writing this all down. He is not being told to keep it a secret, but the command to "*conceal...and seal up*" is best understood within the overall context as yet another textual proof that what was given through Daniel was not for his time alone or its immediate future, but in an ultimate realization for that very last phase of human history. And in the context of the time when a "*book*" was really a scroll, this could not possibly apply to just the last vision in Daniel 10-12, but the ***whole*** book of Daniel inscribed on one, continuous page.

One of the ways that we know that ever since Christ's Ascension we have been living in the Last Days is because near the end of the Apostle John's vision, he was instructed to do the opposite:

> [10]*And he said to me, "**Do not seal up** the words of the prophecy of this book, for the time is near.*
> — Revelation 22:10

The New Testament frequently speaks in terms of our ***already*** being in the Last Days:

> [1]*God, after He spoke long ago to the fathers in the prophets in many portions and in many ways, [2]**in these last days** has spoken to us in His Son, whom He appointed heir of all things, through whom also He made the world.*
> — Hebrews 1:1-2

> [20]*For He was foreknown before the foundation of the world, but has appeared **in these last times** for the sake of you [21]through Him are believers in God..."*
> — 1 Peter 1:20-21a

The Greek word "*apokalupsis*" (Strong's #602) which we translate as the English "*revelation*" carries with it the meaning of an unveiling. The closer to the door or window we get, the clearer we see until the veil is fully lifted and we are able to walk through. But one of the ways we know that it was not just to John's vision alone to which this unsealing applies is the fact that the tremendous number of parallels between the two books has served to explain so much of their meaning. What began in the visions of Daniel has many supporting scriptural counterparts, but none deeper and more important than Revelation.

This does not mean, however, the veil is gone, only that we are closer than ever before, and for those who are putting His Word into practice, the remaining understanding necessary will be provided by Christ at the proper place and time.

The Final Stretch

The Two Witnesses

> [5]*Then I, Daniel, looked and behold, two others were standing, one on this bank of the river and the other on that bank of the river. [6]And one said to the man dressed in linen, who was above the waters of the river, "How long will it be until the end of these wonders?"*
> [7]*I heard the man dressed in linen, who was above the waters of the river, as he raised his right hand and his left toward heaven, and swore by Him who lives forever that it would be for a time, times, and half a time; and as soon as they finish shattering the power of the holy people, all these events will be completed.*
> — Daniel 12:5-7

This is not just bringing the final vision to a close, but concluding the whole book of Daniel. One of the things which lets us know for sure that Daniel's experiences are particularly important in God's economy is this divine affirmation in sending two witnesses. A pair of witnesses is an important accompanying feature of many events recorded in Scripture such as the two angels at Sodom and Gomorrah, the two angels at Jesus' tomb and Ascension and so forth. While many of the pairs found in Scripture certainly contribute to our understanding of the ultimate Two Witnesses provided in Revelation 11, there is an overall principle of God's Word that "*on the evidence of two or three witnesses a matter shall be confirmed*". (Dt. 19:15) The many pairs in Scripture first and foremost are meeting this godly requirement, and if necessary God will accomplish this by angelic agency. In the case of Christ Himself, John the Baptist is not only called "*a witness*" (Jn. 1:7), but at Jesus' baptism was the testimony of both God the Father and God the Holy Spirit (Mt. 4:16-17) in the most authoritative example of this. In fact, Christ affirmed His divinity by specifying His own self-witness was enough, but that it was still dually substantiated by the Father as well:

> [31]*"If I alone testify about Myself, My testimony is not true.* [32]*There is another who testifies of Me, and I know that the testimony which He gives about Me is true.*
> — John 5:31-32

In the previous discussion concerning the identity of those bringing this final vision to Daniel, notice that there are the two men on opposite banks of the river and in addition "*the man dressed in linen*" above the river between them which we identified as a Christophany—that is, an Old Testament appearance of Christ. Again, this is due to the fact that He confirms these things with an oath in God's name in combination with the other factors previously discussed. But this is also a kind of exclamation point attached by the presence of these two witnesses who are cast in the dual role of not just confirming Daniel's experience, but the divine authority who was the greater Author of the book of Daniel.

Unsealing the Sealed

> [8]*As for me, I heard but could not understand; so I said, "My lord, what will be the outcome of these events?"*
> [9]*He said, "Go your way, Daniel, for these words are concealed and sealed up until the end time.*
> — Daniel 12:8-9

We cannot help but notice some similarities with the way Jesus is directly involved with the closing out of the book of Daniel and the closing out of the book of Revelation.

> [6]*And he said to me, "These words are faithful and true"; and the Lord, the God of the spirits of the prophets, sent His angel to show to His bond-servants the things which must soon take place.* [7]*And behold, I am coming quickly. Blessed is he who heeds the words of the prophecy of this book."*
> — Revelation 22:6-7

> [10]*And he said to me, "Do not seal up the words of the prophecy of this book, for the time is near.*
> — Revelation 22:10

There is a divine confirmation attesting not just to the authority, but the authenticity of each book, but particularly for Revelation and Daniel. These two works act as "bookends", so to speak, with the book of Daniel originally "***concealed and sealed up*** *until the end time*", but with the initiation of the End Times (Heb. 1:1-2; 1 Pe. 1:20), Revelation marks the point of release with, "'***Do not seal up*** *the words of the prophecy of this book, for the time is near*'". There is no doubt that with this coming at the very end of not just Revelation but the final book closing out the canon of Scripture that this applies to the whole of God's Word as well as the releasing of Daniel in the process. (Dt. 4:2; Prov. 30:6; 1 Co. 4:6)

The offer in Revelation, "*Blessed is he who heeds the words of the prophecy of this book*" expand upon those in Daniel referring to those with true biblical understanding "*who lead the many to righteousness*" and "*will understand*" these things, both testifying to the need to not just read God's Word, but to put it into practice.

As previously touched on, the fact is that no one short of a Holy Spirit-filled, Bible-practicing follower of Christ is going to understand such things, and no intense curiosity or academic credential will make up for it. To challenge the authorship of Daniel, believing much of it was written by someone else after the fact to only make it ***look*** like predictions were made in advance is not actually a challenge to the person of Daniel, but Christ Himself who personally attests to the true Source of the book.

End Times Behavior

> *10Many will be purged, purified and refined, but the wicked will act wickedly; and none of the wicked will understand, but those who have insight will understand.*
> — Daniel 12:10

The closing remark that "*the wicked will act wickedly*" echoes in the closing of Revelation:

> *11Let the one who does wrong, still do wrong; and the one who is filthy, still be filthy; and let the one who is righteous, still practice righteousness; and the one who is holy, still keep himself holy."*
> — Revelation 22:11

This is testifying to the fact that the way everyone will act and react upon witnessing for themselves the fulfillment of these End Times events will conform to their lifestyle. In other words, if one is living a lifestyle of obedience to God's Word and ways now, that is how they will be found when this takes place; if instead it is one of sin or wickedness, such will continue adhering to that behavior unchanged by these events. When these things transpire it will be too late for anyone to change, whether biblically "*filthy*" or "*righteous*", and will therefore not do so because of a sign, wonder or irrefutable fulfillment of a prophecy, but continue "business as usual". We will be ***then*** as we are ***now***.

This has been repeatedly demonstrated in Scripture, with such examples as Pharaoh and the Egyptians in the Exodus who were never truly changed by Moses' and Aaron's testimony and signs or even the ten plagues themselves. Or at Sodom and Gomorrah where even after being struck blind, "*they wearied themselves trying to find the doorway*". (Gen. 19:11) Like a drug addict who will do anything to get the next fix, they scratched and clawed at the door in pursuit of their wicked behavior even after being struck by God, leading to His ultimate striking of the whole area. Repeatedly we are shown that signs work to the opposite effect in the hearts of those following God from those rejecting Him, to the one an affirmation of their faith, but the other serving to judge and condemn them for their disbelief. Several times Revelation pauses to point out that the wicked continue to act wickedly, unchanged by all that is taking place. (Rev. 9:20-21; 16:9-11, 21)

The True Nature of the End

> *11From the time that the regular sacrifice is abolished and the abomination of desolation is set up, there will be 1,290 days. 12How blessed is he who keeps waiting*

and attains to the 1,335 days! 13But as for you, go your way to the end; then you will enter into rest and rise again for your allotted portion at the end of the age."
— Daniel 12:11-13

The original question initiating this closing sequence was, "*How long will it be until **the end of these wonders**?*" (Dan. 12:6) Pay attention to the wording because this is not asking how long it will be until these things finally ***begin*** to take place, but rather how long will they ***continue*** once they begin to transpire. This is why the answer is not provided as the whole of Daniel's 70th Week. The first milestone initiating this closing period is once again given as the Abomination of Desolation. And, again, this alludes to the nature of the awareness of those experiencing these things, that although there is unquestionably a final seven year period, the beginning is not the discernible "beginning of the end", but rather the midway milestone.

Just as this final vision begins with a prolonged milieu out of which the Antichrist rises, and only narrows the timing down by assigning the Abomination of Desolation as the trigger for the final 3-1/2 years of history, this is exactly what Christ does in the Olivet Discourse. The *chronos* (sequence or chronology) of the gradually increasing "*birth pangs*" gives way to the *kairos* (a fixed schedule) Christ likewise identifies as the Abomination of Desolation.

Not just because this is the topic of this book, but it is beyond important to note that Christ through Daniel, the Apostles John and Paul, and even singularly through His giving of the Olivet Discourse repeatedly affirms a final period of history which is dominated and characterized by the actions of the Antichrist upon the whole world, God's people included. And yet, one of the most popular notions put forth and held by so many in the Western Church today is that there is no need to worry about, much less study in detail, the Antichrist because the Church will be removed before he even begins to work, quite a number dogmatically insisting ***long*** before he even appears. There are many on both sides of the aisle who tell us that we cannot argue about the timing of the Rapture because it is not an essential doctrine of the faith, and yet the error of Pre-Tribulationism is leaving millions unprepared for that which Jesus Himself repeatedly warns over and over and over again in His Word. Yes, it actually does matter. The wrong assertion of the timing is leading to an even more consequential error from something the Church will experience beforehand.

There is also the disproportionate influence of the false notions that it is the Church who will conquer the whole world for Christ which triggers His return, and yet Scripture is steadfast in its assertion that the End Times is not characterized by anything ***but*** an increase in wickedness, evil and a steadfast rejection of Him "*just as it happened in the days of Noah*" (Mt. 24:37; Lk. 17:26; 1 Pe. 3:20) and "*the same as happened in the days of Lot*". (Lk. 17:28) There are even variations of teachings about second chances in spite of living through and being unchanged by these events. By rendering us unfaithful and disobedient now, Satan knows we will be unfaithful and disobedient then.

But in Daniel's twice being told "*go your way*" (v.9 & 13) we are provided instructions as to how, exactly, to deal with not having all the answers when, like Daniel, we ask, "*what will be the outcome of these events?*" This is not a rebuke, but an admonition to go about one's life being personally faithful and obedient to God's Word knowing that whether we meet the Lord through the one-time event of the Rapture or through the more common end of mankind through death and resurrection, we will be saved because we followed through our belief in Christ by our lifestyle in Christ. This is exactly what Christ teaches in each of the concluding parables of the Olivet Discourse with each scenario featuring Christ as the Master or Bridegroom returning and immediately making a determination as to the faithfulness, or not, of those who call themselves His own.

> [8]*"I tell you that He will bring about justice for them quickly. However, when the Son of Man comes, will He find faith on the earth?"*
> — Luke 18:8

We have already dealt with the issue of the various descriptions of the final 3-1/2 years, but it is unfortunate that so many come to these final verses and exclusively fixate on the two numerical values given, ignoring the greater and more valuable accompanying message of this book's benediction. That which appears to present itself as a mathematical mystery is wrapped in the assurance that in the absence of a full and complete understanding of such individual details, the full and complete personal practice of God's Word resolves everything in God's much larger view of what is most important in eternity.

A Personal Commentary

> [11]*For the grace of God has appeared, bringing salvation to all men,* [12]*instructing us to deny ungodliness and worldly desires and to live sensibly, righteously and godly in the present age,* [13]***looking for the blessed hope and the appearing of the glory of our great God and Savior, Christ Jesus,*** [14]*who gave Himself for us to redeem us from every lawless deed, and to purify for Himself a people for His own possession, zealous for good deeds.*
> — Titus 2:11-14

In the years since Jacob Prasch published his ground-breaking work on the Antichrist, *Shadows of the Beast*, we were not so naive as to think it would be universally welcomed with unicorns and glitter and cotton candy parades. Having been a pastor, missionary and conference speaker for more than 30 years, Jacob was painfully aware of the academic landscape, and there were many reactions as expected. But there was an unanticipated one whose impact, if thoroughly considered, can be quite devastating in its eventual consequences for the believer.

The phrase which seems to be used more than almost any other by those holding to Pre-Tribulationism is "*the blessed hope*", as they have co-opted this phrase as their synonym for the Rapture. This meaning is perfectly reasonable as the underlying Greek word in this Scripture for the *"appearing"* is "*epiphaneia*" (Strong's #2015), which in parallel usages by Paul means "to manifest oneself", not to merely visit or make an appearance as the English may alternatively infer.

> [14]*that you keep the commandment without stain or reproach until* ***the appearing*** *of our Lord Jesus Christ,*
> — 1 Timothy 6:14

> [10]*but now has been revealed by* ***the appearing*** *of our Savior Christ Jesus, who abolished death and brought life and immortality to light through the gospel,*
> — 2 Timothy 1:10

> [1]*I solemnly charge you in the presence of God and of Christ Jesus, who is to judge the living and the dead, and by* ***His appearing*** *and His kingdom:*
> — 2 Timothy 4:1

> [8]*in the future there is laid up for me the crown of righteousness, which the Lord, the righteous Judge, will award to me on that day; and not only to me, but also to all who have loved* **His appearing**.
>
> — 2 Timothy 4:8

Exegetically, it is obviously not exclusively constrained to just the Rapture, because for believers who die prior, they are resurrected first at Christ's "*appearing*" and will actually meet their raptured counterparts. (1 Th. 4:15-17) It equally applies to the resurrected as well as the raptured, so it is not wrong to speak of the Rapture as ***also*** being "*the blessed hope*", but it is not ***limited*** to that one, single meaning.

Numerous and loud voices from this camp, consistently shouting this phrase from Scripture (and often accompanied with intense derision) invoked this as a rebuttal for some kind of incontrovertible scriptural argument that the Church will neither encounter nor have to experience the Antichrist, and further put forth the accompanying accusation, "You're not looking for the appearance of Christ! You're looking for the appearance of Antichrist!" It's the age-old tactic of attacking the messenger instead of dealing with the message.

This particular "ism" bases their entire position on the assumption that because "*the day of the Lord*" is a time of God's wrath from which Christians are exempt, and "***The*** Tribulation" (all seven years) is wholly and completely "*the day of the Lord*", the Rapture "has" to take place entirely before those final seven years. Therefore, they further stipulate, the Church will never encounter the Antichrist. To them, teaching the Church anything about the Antichrist is not just a waste of time, but is taking up a heretical position against the Rapture, against Christ Himself, and completely going over to the dark side to instead promote Satan himself. (One notable personality went so far as to lecture his large, university audience that if the Bride of Christ is allowed to enter the Tribulation, then Christ is a wife abuser, while other notable personalities have called all non-Pre-Trib positions "satanic".)

But what does Scripture actually state?

> [1]*Now we request you, brethren,* ***with regard to the coming of our Lord Jesus Christ and our gathering together to Him***, [2]*that you not be quickly shaken from your composure or be disturbed either by a spirit or a message or a letter as if from us, to the effect that the day of the Lord has come.* [3]***Let no one in any way deceive you***, *for* ***it will not come unless the apostasy comes first, and the man of lawlessness is revealed***, *the son of destruction,* [4]*who opposes and exalts himself above every so-called god or object of worship,* ***so that he takes his seat in the temple of God, displaying himself as being God***.
>
> — 2 Thessalonians 2:1-4

First comes the apostasy—a massive spiritual falling away from the faith, followed next by the "*apokalupsis*"—the "*revelation*" of the Antichrist, and afterward "*the day of the Lord*". Scripture unquestionably teaches that the Church most certainly does not experience "*the day of the Lord*", but "*the day of the Lord*" does not come until ***after*** the Antichrist is publicly revealed. And what will he do so that we know who and what he is?

> *...he takes his seat in the temple of God, displaying himself as being God.*
>
> — 2 Thessalonians 2:4b

He commits the Abomination of Desolation! Yes, in spite of Scripture's clear and unambiguous teaching that the Abomination of Desolation takes place precisely at the midpoint of the final week of years, the holders of this position insist we will not even see it. The timing is confirmed through Paul that we will witness both the apostasy and the Abomination of Desolation before *"the day of the Lord"* takes place, which precisely matches that which Jesus taught in the Olivet Discourse.

But the textual icing on the cake where the error of this position is concerned is found in the use of "*appearance*"—that is, "*epiphaneia*" as we continue in the same passage:

> *8Then that lawless one will be revealed whom the Lord will slay with the breath of His mouth and bring to an end **by the appearance of His coming**; 9that is, the one whose coming is in accord with the activity of Satan, with all power and signs and false wonders, 10and with all the deception of wickedness for those who perish, because they did not receive the love of the truth so as to be saved.*
> — 2 Thessalonians 2:8-10

The use of "*epiphaneia*" in this passage cannot possibly be referring to the Rapture as something coming before the entire, final seven years because the Antichrist is clearly documented to experience this outcome at ***the very end of*** the final seven years when Christ's "*epiphaneia*"—"*the appearing of His coming*" takes place. This contradicts those who dogmatically assert that "*epiphaneia*" only and exclusively applies to the Rapture. In this context it is describing His appearing at the very ***end*** of the final seven years when He returns with His armies and brings Daniel's 70th Week, and the Antichrist, to an end. (Rev.19:11-21) In an example of what happens when something is lifted out of context and in isolation from the rest of God's Word, we are provided with a real-life example of a pretext.

In what I can only describe as a turn of events that is beyond sad and, of course, reason, if it has not happened yet, the reader is sure to encounter a growing popular notion that is being put forth by that camp which is a complete violation of God's repeated command not to alter His Word. More and more are endorsing the reaching down into the Greek text of 2 Thessalonians 2:3 and claiming that instead of "*apostasia*" (Strong's #646) which means a spiritual falling away or spiritual departing, the word should be replaced with "*aphistemi*" (Strong's #868) which can be used to mean a physical "departing" as in someone leaving. You will hear them make the very strange and unbiblical case that the verse therefore now actually means, "First the ***Rapture***—that is, a ***physical*** departing, then the Antichrist" to align it with their timing. Such have dogmatically clung to an error for so long and so deeply that they will violate other Scripture in a vain attempt to maintain their view. This isn't about a difference of opinion where the timing of the Rapture is concerned, but Christ's servants failing to give the proper food at the proper time. (Mt. 24:45) But it is also a modern-day recapitulation of Peter's warning about those who distort the teachings of Paul. (2 Pe. 3:14-18) [For a complete explantion, see *Appendix A: When Change Is Expressly Forbidden.*]

The Bottom Line

Daniel's revelation of the final seven year period is ***defined*** by the appearance and activities of the Antichrist and his kingdom's ultimate dissolution. It is initiated by the Antichrist's covenant with Israel, its precise middle annotated by the seminal public display of the Antichrist committing the Abomination of Desolation, and its end measured from that midway milestone when it is not just Christ's appearance which takes place, but the ultimate demise of this final figure and everything/everyone associated with him. It is a time completely dominated by the documented activities of the Antichrist, who is given the same amount of time on earth as Christ was provided in His First Coming.

But even more so do we encounter this with the sizable number of references to variations of 3-1/2 lunar years. Every one of them is connected to the Antichrist, even the references to the "good guys". In the use of "*1,260 days*" for the flight of Israel into the wilderness, the is a flight ***from*** the Antichrist, and one of the main feature of the activities defining the Two Witnesses of Revelation 11 assigned this timespan is a running confrontation ***with*** the Antichrist. Amongst a list of many additional items, the final expressions of 3-1/2 are defined in relation to either a time of persecution by the Antichrist, the length of his official authority, or as a measurement of how long the desecration of God's temple will go on until the end. Even in the closing references to "*1,290 days*" and "*1,335 days*" it is, "*From the time...the abomination of desolation is set up...*" (Dan. 12:12)

Yes, we are to be "*looking for the blessed hope*" by doing exactly what Paul says in the greater context of the verses in which this phrase is presented: "*deny ungodliness and worldly desires and to live sensibly, righteously and godly in the present age*". (Titus 2:12) But is the purpose of "*the blessed hope*" tied exclusively to the Rapture alone? Again, in the context given, its greater purpose is followed by, "*to redeem us from every lawless deed, and to purify for Himself a people for His own possession,* ***zealous for good deeds***". (Titus 2:14) Those with "*the blessed hope*" are characterized as such obedient practitioners of His Word and ways that they are producing the spiritual fruit so as to be found dressed and ready whether He comes for them tonight through death and Resurrection, or tomorrow by the one-time event we call the Rapture. One has "*the blessed hope*" by being a faithful practitioner of His Word, work and ways in this life knowing that one way or the other, Christ is coming for us and we need to be spiritually prepared and qualified whenever that occurs.

We are not "***looking*** for the Antichrist". Like Daniel when he saw that the seventy years were almost up, we are looking for the fulfillment of God's prophetic Word, accepting by faith that it will take place ***exactly*** as He has stated. The difficult times ahead are going to be multiplied for those who are not prepared to take God at His Word, and His Word says to recognize what is coming. What kind of hope will come for those who fail to do that?

In Daniel's time, he interceded for God's people, concerned that they were not spiritually prepared for what was about to be fulfilled in God's prophetic Word. Perhaps we should likewise be more concerned for the current state of the Church, seeing as so many of its members are presently ill-prepared as well.

> *However, when the Son of Man comes, will He find faith on the earth?"*
> — Luke 18:8b

9 ❖ The Early Portrait

The depth of what was known about the anti-king and anti-kingdom by the Old Testament believer is not just impressive, it is actually nearly complete. One of the chief benefits resulting from Christ's First Coming is His opening the hearts and minds of His followers to the meaning of God's Word as never before. (Lk. 24:32, 45; 1 Jn. 5:20) It would not just contribute certain additional features, but illuminate what was previously recorded and already embedded in the text. That which was known at this point is not just comprehensive, but will be foundational for the additional details the New Testament supplies to complete this portrait. As the New Testament does in every case, it will reveal much which was always residing in plain sight in the Old Testament which now comes forward, but of course nothing is replaced or rendered obsolete, but further affirmed and reinforced.

1st Century Understanding

For the 1st century Jewish audience to whom Christ publicly ministered, it would have been impossible for them to not understand what had transpired in history in parallel to God's given Word to that point, and especially so when it came to the book of Daniel. Daniel's contribution could have been used exclusively as a standalone history book simply to teach what took place beginning with the Babylonian Captivity leading up to that very time:

- The Babylonian Empire
- The Medo-Persian Empire
- The Greek Empire
- The Roman Empire

We can see why there were such high expectations in the extra-biblical Jewish literature of the Second Temple Period leading up to and into the time of the First Coming in their expectations for the Messiah, because God's plan had come true exactly as given. Here they were, living in that very last empire before the Messiah would come and replace it all with ***His*** kingdom exactly as foretold. We might now better understand why there was this repeated assumption recorded in the Gospels that it was time for the Messiah to remove all the earthly kingdoms and establish His own, something which even the Apostles brought up in their final face-to-face meeting with Him. (Acts. 1:6-8) Not fully understanding the gap between Daniel's 69th and 70th weeks, they were fixated on the very next thing they understood to come which would replace the Roman Empire:

[34]"You continued looking until a stone was cut out without hands, and it struck the statue on its feet of iron and clay and crushed them. [35]Then the iron, the clay, the bronze, the silver and the gold were crushed all at the same time and became like chaff from the summer threshing floors; and the wind carried them away so that not a trace of them was found. But the stone that struck the statue became a great mountain and filled the whole earth.
— Daniel 2:34-35

[44]"In the days of those kings the God of heaven will set up a kingdom which will never be destroyed, and that kingdom will not be left for another people; it will crush and put an end to all these kingdoms, but it will itself endure forever. [45]Inasmuch as you saw that a stone was cut out of the mountain without hands and that it crushed the iron, the bronze, the clay, the silver and the gold, the great God has made known to the king what will take place in the future; so the dream is true and its interpretation is trustworthy."
— Daniel 2:44-45

But because that generation did not quite have a handle on how the whole counsel of God's Word, as given to that point, spoke of what we now clearly understand to be "one Messiah, two comings", the expectation was for the imminent crushing of Rome "*like chaff*" and "*carried... away so that not a trace of them was found*". So many would find the chief preparatory message of the Messiah's forerunner difficult, or at best as a mixed message of sorts for the kind of crushing and removal required first:

[17]"His winnowing fork is in His hand to thoroughly clear His threshing floor, and to gather the wheat into His barn; but ***He will burn up the chaff*** *with unquenchable fire."*
— Luke 3:17

Or that of the Messiah Himself:

[42]Jesus said to them, "Did you never read in the Scriptures,

'THE STONE WHICH THE BUILDERS REJECTED,
THIS BECAME THE CHIEF CORNER stone;
THIS CAME ABOUT FROM THE LORD,
AND IT IS MARVELOUS IN OUR EYES'?

[43]"Therefore I say to you, the kingdom of God will be taken away from you and given to a people, producing the fruit of it. [44]And ***he who falls on this stone will be broken to pieces; but on whomever it falls, it will scatter him like dust****."*
— Matthew 21:42-44

Before the fall of the earthly empires there would have to come the personal capitulation of the throne of each heart. Ironically, for those who will successfully navigate the eschaton, this is exactly what must still take place for the Second Coming.

Nonetheless, they knew how each of the major empires leading up to the one in control at the time were not just foretold in Scripture and represented something satanically animated in opposition to the One True God, but were keenly aware of the parallel fulfillment not just by the Seleucid and Ptolemaic Empires in general, but how they narrowed down to Antiochus Epiphanes IV himself and on to their own hour under Roman rule. They were the last in a series of generations who had been living out the precise sequential fulfillment of Daniel's visions, conscious that they had arrived at the end of the given sequence. Or so it may have seemed.

So maybe we can better empathize with the overall context of the First Coming, that not everyone was a Zealot or Herodian who sought a Messiah whose chief purpose would be to take down the Romans politically and elevate Israel in its place, but there would be many who subscribed to this because of their beliefs in the biblical timing of the Messiah and their misunderstanding of the gap which would separate His two comings. Many of them were so attached to their interpretation, that even while witnessing an alternate fulfillment, they steadfastly processed it incorrectly. They saw contradictions to their preconceived conceptions as confirmations that these actual fulfillments were instead proof of a deception, or worse, yet another in a long line of false messiahs already encountered.

That particular generation was more like us than we probably would care to admit. They were painfully aware that they were living in the last days, so to speak, on the cusp of witnessing the fulfillment of God's prophetic Word as they understood it to that point, and in full expectation of the Messiah's arrival. And as noted, one of our primary hermeneutics is that much of what took place in the First Coming foreshadows that which is replayed to a greater degree in the Second Coming. They were aware of prophecy, we are aware of prophecy; they expected the Messiah, we expect the Messiah; prophetic fulfillments had already taken place to fuel their expectations of its imminent conclusion in their lifetime; we have already witnessed the earthly "*birth pangs*" to assure us of the final climax to come in our own. But will we replay the general failure to properly recognize and act upon it correctly? Which of our own closely held misconceptions will we cling to? The majority's rejection of what literally took place in the First Coming is replaying even now in the ever-increasing apostasy setting the stage for what should be the first anticipated appearance of the Antichrist before the final one of Christ, and yet so many are poised to embrace a lethal reversal of the authentic.

But particularly when Jesus spoke of the Abomination of Desolation, they clearly understood the parallel history of what was provided through Daniel and how it literally played out in not just Epiphanes' reign and the Maccabean Revolt nearly 200 years earlier, but the incursion into the Holy of Holies by the Roman General Pompey nearly 100 years after that. To those at that time a clear connection would have been made not just with visions of Daniel mirroring the sequence of ascendant empires and kings, but accepting as absolute fact the historical fulfillment of each step from Nebuchadnezzar to Epiphanes' desecration to the current rise of the Roman Empire.

> 15 *"Therefore when you see the* ABOMINATION OF DESOLATION *which was spoken of through Daniel the prophet, standing in the holy place (**let the reader understand**),*
> — Matthew 24:15

Just as Daniel himself was found to be immersed in and searching God's Word, so Christ issues the same challenge to revisit God's Word given through Daniel. Jesus did not issue the command to just ***listen*** to what He was saying at the time, but to examine it in light of what Scripture had already provided. (This is a great lesson in how all things are tested against the standard of God's Word.) Jesus ***as*** the very Word of God is directing attention ***to*** the very Word of God.

Even for the Early Church, who not only received the indwelling and guidance of the Holy Spirit but Christ's explanation of the Scriptures to them, such would exist for approximately 15 years after Christ's Ascension before James would author the first book of what would later be included in the New Testament canon. The first 22 New Testament books—all but the 5 authored by the Apostle John, are not even written until a period of 15-30 or so years after Pentecost, and it will still take some time for them to be duplicated and distributed as individual letters, and as much as 100 or so years before being collected into the formal structure of the New Testament. The fact is that for the very first generation in particular, but for quite a time after, where God's written Word was concerned, it was still about the Old Testament. Just as the Bereans tested and verified Paul's New Testament teachings against the measure of the Old Testament writings (Acts 17:10-12), so it would continue to be used to supplement and confirm what was heard firsthand from the Messiah and subsequently conveyed by His Apostles, and even the following generations of their disciples.

It is going to take even longer before the Church possesses the entire New Testament canon since John's contributions will come so late in the 1st century. Considering the time it took not just to hand-copy scrolls, in addition to the months if not years it took to send something from city to city in the ancient world, much less country to country; it is going to be some time before Christians are fully able to leverage all that the New Testament provides. It is even more impressive, then, to consider all that a 1st century believer would have known on the cusp of inheriting all that was to additionally come in the New Testament.

The Historical Record

The Old Testament most certainly contains more about the anti-king/anti-kingdom than our study which, to this point, has centered on the book of Daniel. We have made this our exhaustive starting point because this ***is***, unquestionably, the foundation for all that is to follow. While we could probably find those at the time of or leading up to the First Coming who were at least piecing together the other references in parallel to Daniel to be found in the Tanakh, the fact is that it is really only with the full knowledge and disclosure of the substance of the New Testament by which we are able to fully revisit many things previously concealed which are now revealed. What is given in Daniel, however, is the public text into which everything else will fit. We will visit many of them in the course of proceeding into the next section dealing with the New Testament. But long before Revelation was actually written, and even before the rest of the additional canon of Scripture, believers would have had an impressive wealth of knowledge of the historical figures and institutions foreshadowing the final ones to come.

- They would know the details of each preceding empire and how they absorbed and influenced one another "in the character of" a common, yet deteriorating, moral and spiritual disposition.
- They would understand Nebuchadnezzar personally and all the historical kings of these empires on down to Antiochus Epiphanes IV as "*the king of the North*" as the various personifications of the final king to come.
- They would immediately associate the Abomination of Desolation with what took place literally with both Epiphanes and Pompey, envisioning this upon hearing both Christ and the Apostle Paul assert that it would take place yet again.

And it is an interesting additional detail provided in the New Testament that Judaism had already experienced a number of false messiahs which could be understood as prefiguring the final one to come:

> *[36]"For some time ago Theudas rose up, claiming to be somebody, and a group of about four hundred men joined up with him. But he was killed, and all who followed him were dispersed and came to nothing. [37]After this man, Judas of Galilee rose up in the days of the census and drew away some people after him; he too perished, and all those who followed him were scattered.*
> — Acts 5:36-37

The First Coming shares a common experience with many of the same things to come in the shadow of the Second Coming, albeit on a much larger, world scale:

> *[5]"For many will come in My name, saying, 'I am the Christ,' and will mislead many...[11]"Many false prophets will arise and will mislead many.*
> — Matthew 24:5, 11

The problem of false messiahs and false prophets in the First Coming in their concentration on Israel is multiplied in the Last Days on the world stage. Satan was, in effect, attempting to discredit or at least diminish the impact of the authentic Christ in the First Coming, but with the imminent arrival of his own complete substitute, Satan multiplies counterfeits of the counterfeit in a magnified strategy presaging the final return of the authentic. At present, we not only have an incredible number of impostors around the globe claiming to be Jesus who are obviously animated by the spirit of antichrist, but there are those claiming to actually be ***THE*** Antichrist. The Apostle John will document that this trend continued to proliferate even to the end of the 1st century:

> *[18]Children, it is the last hour; and just as you heard that antichrist is coming, **even now many antichrists have appeared**; from this we know that it is the last hour.*
> — 1 John 2:18

As it was then, even more so is it coming to pass now.

The Scriptural Portrait of the Anti-King

Here is a compilation of the traits and behaviors which can be gleaned from Daniel which can be expected to found not just in the final figure, but many of which are shared by both biblical and historical forerunners. We understand the prefigurements in the way they will feature so many of these characteristics, but it is the final one to come who will own them all.

He is a Beast

- ❑ *"...a fourth beast, dreadful and extremely strong..."* (7:7)
- ❑ *"...it had large iron teeth."* (7:7)

He is a Horn

- ❑ *"...another horn...possessed eyes like the eyes of a man and a mouth uttering great boasts".* (7:8)
- ❑ *"...larger in appearance than its associates."* (7:20)
- ❑ *"...will arise after them* [the ten horns]*...will be different from the previous ones..."* (7:24)
- ❑ *"...a rather small horn which grew exceedingly great toward the south, toward the east, and toward the Beautiful Land."* (8:9)

He is a King

- ❑ *"...a king will arise..."* (8:23)
- ❑ *"It devoured and crushed and trampled down the remainder with its feet..."* (7:7)
- ❑ *"...The fourth beast will be a fourth kingdom on the earth..."* (7:23)
- ❑ *"...different from all the other kingdoms and will devour the whole earth and tread it down and crush it."* (7:23)

He is a Conqueror

- ❑ *"...another* [horn] *will arise after them, and he will be different from the previous ones and will subdue three kings."* (7:24)
- ❑ *"His power will be mighty, but not by his own power..."* (8:24)
- ❑ *"...he will destroy to an extraordinary degree..."* (8:24)
- ❑ *"...he will...prosper and perform his will..."* (8:24)
- ❑ *"He will destroy mighty men and the holy people."* (8:24)
- ❑ The conflicts with the King of the South will replayed again. (11:40)
- ❑ *"He will enter the Beautiful Land, and many countries will fall, but these will be rescued out of his hand: Edom, Moab and the foremost of the sons of Ammon."* (11:41)
- ❑ *"...he will stretch out his hand against other countries, and the land of Egypt will not escape."* (11:42)
- ❑ *"...he will gain control over all the precious things of Egypt..."* (11:43)
- ❑ *"...Libyans and Ethiopians will follow at his heels."* (11:43)
- ❑ *"...rumors from the East and from the North will disturb him, and he will go forth with great wrath to destroy and annihilate many."* (11:44)

He is s Despicable Person, Yet Successful

- ❑ *"...a despicable person will arise..."* (11:21)
- ❑ *"...he will prosper until the indignation is finished..."* (11:36)

He is Self-Promoting & Self-Deifying

- ❑ *"...the sound of the boastful words which the horn was speaking..."* (7:11)
- ❑ *"He will speak out against the Most High..."* (7:25)
- ❑ *"...he will intend to make alterations in times and in law..."* (7:25)
- ❑ *"It even magnified itself to be equal with the Commander of the host..." (8:11)*
- ❑ *"...he will magnify himself in his heart..."* (8:25)
- ❑ *"...the king will do as he pleases..."* (11:36)
- ❑ *"...he will exalt and magnify himself above every god..."* (11:36)
- ❑ *"...*[he] *will speak monstrous things against the God of gods..."* (11:36)
- ❑ *"He will show no regard for the gods of his fathers..."* (11:37)

- "*…nor will he show regard for any other god…*" (11:37)
- "*…he will magnify himself above them all [any other god],*" (11:37)

He is Personally & Spiritually Disturbed

- "[He will show no regard] *for the desire of women…*" (11:37)
- "*…he will honor a god of fortresses, a god whom his fathers did not know; he will honor him with gold, silver, costly stones and treasures.*" (11:38)
- "*He will take action against the strongest of fortresses with the help of a foreign god…*" (11:39)

He is a Master of Deception

- "*…it will fling truth to the ground and perform its will and prosper.*" (8:12)
- "*…Insolent and skilled in intrigue.*" (8:23)
- "*…through his shrewdness he will cause deceit to succeed by his influence…*" (8:25)
- "*After an alliance is made with him he will practice deception…*" (11:23)
- "*..he will accomplish what his fathers never did, nor his ancestors…*" (11:24)
- "*…he will devise his schemes against strongholds…*" (11:24)

He is an Agent of Apostasy

- "*…he will come back and show regard for those who forsake the holy covenant.*" (11:30)
- "*By smooth words he will turn to godlessness those who act wickedly toward the covenant…*" (11:32)
- "*...they* [the people who know their God] *will be granted a little help, and many will join with them in hypocrisy.*" (11:34)

He Persecutes God's People by Open Warfare

- "*…that horn was waging war with the saints and overpowering them…*" (7:21)
- "*…He will…wear down the saints of the Highest One…*" (7:25)
- "*…they will be given into his hand for a time, times, and half a time.*" (7:25)
- "*…it would be for a time, times, and half a time; and as soon as they finish shattering the power of the holy people, all these events will be completed.*" (12:7)
- "*The overflowing forces will be flooded away before him and shattered, and also the prince of the covenant.*" (11:22)
- "*…he will go up and gain power with a small force of people.*" (11:23)

He Takes Down Heavenly Beings as Well as People

- "*It* [horn] *grew up to the host of heaven and caused some of the host and some of the stars to fall to the earth, and it trampled them down.*" (8:10)

He Makes & Breaks a Treaty

- ❑ *"…he will make a firm covenant with the many for one week, but in the middle of the week he will put a stop to sacrifice and grain offering…"* (9:27)
- ❑ *"After an alliance is made with him he will practice deception…"* (11:23)

He Commits the Abomination of Desolation

- ❑ *"…it removed the regular sacrifice from Him…"* (8:11)
- ❑ *"…the place of His sanctuary was thrown down."* (8:11)
- ❑ *"…on account of transgression the host will be given over to the horn along with the regular sacrifice…"* (8:12)
- ❑ *"…'How long will the vision about the regular sacrifice apply, while the transgression causes horror, so as to allow both the holy place and the host to be trampled?'…'For 2,300 evenings and mornings, then the holy place will be properly restored."* (8:13-14)
- ❑ *"…on the wing of abominations will come one who makes desolate, even until a complete destruction, one that is decreed, is poured out on the one who makes desolate."* (9:27)
- ❑ *"From the time that the regular sacrifice is abolished and the abomination of desolation is set up, there will be 1,290 days. How blessed is he who keeps waiting and attains to the 1,335 days!"* (12:11-12)
- ❑ *"Forces from him will arise, desecrate the sanctuary fortress, and do away with the regular sacrifice."* (11:31)
- ❑ *"…they will set up the abomination of desolation."* (11:31)

He Acts Against the Godhead

- ❑ *"He will even oppose the Prince of princes…"* (8:25)
- ❑ *"…his heart will be set against the holy covenant, and he will take action and then return to his own land."* (11:28)
- ❑ *"…he will be disheartened and will return and become enraged at the holy covenant and take action…"* (11:30)

He Takes Up Residence in Israel

- ❑ *"He will pitch the tents of his royal pavilion between the seas and the beautiful Holy Mountain…"* (11:45)

His End Will Come

- ❑ *"…the beast was slain…"* (7:11)
- ❑ *"…its body was destroyed and given to the burning fire."* (7:11)
- ❑ *"…until the Ancient of Days came and judgment was passed in favor of the saints of the High One…"* (7:22)
- ❑ *"…and the time arrived when the saints took possession of the kingdom."* (7:22)
- ❑ *"But the court will sit for judgment, and his dominion will be taken away, annihilated and destroyed forever."* (7:26)

- ❑ *"Then the sovereignty, the dominion and the greatness of all the kingdoms under the whole heaven will be given to the people of the saints of the Highest One…"* (7:27)
- ❑ *"…he will be broken without human agency."* (8:25)
- ❑ *"…he will come this end, and no one will help him."* (11:45)

The Scriptural Portrait of the Anti-Kingdom

Granted, many of the above listed attributes have an obvious cross-over application with his kingdom, so these are additional attributes and activities expressing that fundamental character on a larger scale.

It Will be a Powerful, Yet Divided, Kingdom

- ❑ *"…a fourth kingdom as strong as iron…"* (2:40)
- ❑ *"…feet and toes, partly of potter's clay and partly of iron…"* (2:41)
- ❑ *"…it will be a divided kingdom…"* (2:41)
- ❑ *"...it will have the toughness of iron..."* (2:41)
- ❑ *"…some of the kingdom will be strong and part of it will be brittle.."* (2:42)
- ❑ *"…it had ten horns."* (7:7)
- ❑ *"...different from all the other kingdoms..."* (7:23)
- ❑ *"...will devour the whole earth and tread it down and crush it."* (7:23)
- ❑ *"...three of the first horns wee pulled out by the roots before it..."* (7:28)
- ❑ *"…ten horns…ten kings…"* (7:24)

It is an Improper Mixture

- ❑ *"…the iron mixed with clay, they will combine with one another in the seed of men, but they will not adhere to one another…"* (2:43)

It Brings a Temporary False Peace & Prosperity

- ❑ *"…he will destroy many while they are at ease."* (8:25)
- ❑ *"…he will come in a time of tranquility and seize the kingdom by intrigue."* (11:21)
- ❑ *"In a time of tranquility he will enter the richest parts of the realm…"* (11:24)
- ❑ *"…he will distribute plunder, booty and possessions among them…"* (11:24)
- ❑ *"…he will give great honor to those who acknowledge him and will cause them to rule over the many, and will parcel out the land for a price."* (11:39)

To Sum Up

How complete ***is*** our New Testament understanding of the Antichrist and his kingdom without this Old Testament foundation?

Ultimately he is discerned by those whose wisdom is derived from Christ. And as Christ ***is*** the very Word of God, it should not come as a surprise that it ***is*** the very Word of God which thoroughly foretells his identity by the extensive list supplied of his character, behavior, and actions. The wisdom of Christ has already revealed much to us, yet it will be impossible to work out his identity ***then*** if we have not completely exhausted all that God's Word has already revealed ***now***.

Part Two:
The New Testament Continuation

10 ❖ The Early Church's Understanding

That which the Early Church knew about the Antichrist continued to be sourced primarily from the book of Daniel and actually had nothing to do whatsoever with the book of Revelation. We seem to so easily set aside the fact that John will not receive that vision until nearly 60 years ***after*** Pentecost, and that every book of the New Testament, even the Epistles and Gospel authored by John himself, would all be written ***without*** knowing what would be revealed on Patmos. That those 26 books would all conform to and confirm the contents of that final 27th is an impressive proof of its divine authorship, but the "Early Church" who witnessed the ministry of Christ and were raised by the founding Apostles were all but gone by the time John, achieving an unusual geriatric age even by modern standards, could pass on the last book of the canon of Scripture. In point of fact, no one in the seven churches to whom Revelation is addressed belonged to that original, founding generation which was 100% Jewish (or converts to Judaism), limited to geographic Israel, and firsthand witnesses of Christ and the Apostles. Such were no longer the demographic core of the Church when Revelation was written.

Between Pentecost and Patmos would pass nearly 60 years. Survivors from Jesus' time would be an especially rare find some six decades later in the conditions of the ancient world with perennial war, disease, famine, and such rudimentary medical remedies, even without that which is specific to Christians, persecution. Lifespans were much shorter on the average. Statistically speaking, by the time Revelation is given, the Church is actually well into its ***third*** generation—twice removed from Christ's earthly ministry and that of all the original Apostles save the last standing John. In other words, the strictest definition of who was a member of the very first generation would be those who either witnessed Christ's ministry or came to faith under one of the original Apostles, all of whom except John would be gone by the time the Temple was destroyed in 70 AD. The second generation would be those who came to faith by way of a first generation believer, perhaps having only the briefest of encounters with one of the Apostles before they died. And this second group already removed from the very first would be those through whom the third generation entered the Church.

So by the time of John's exile on Patmos, the majority of those who belonged to the Church had never met either Christ or the Apostles (with the lone possibility of John), nor had much if any contact with those directly discipled and taught by the founding figures, and would have largely come to faith through witnesses who could only at best provide second- or third-hand testimony of Christ and the Apostles. They were the first to at least be aware of all the writings being copied and circulated which would eventually become accepted as 26 of the 27 books of the New Testament, and in the 60 year history of the Church to that point, the very first ones to know about Revelation.

Another unavoidable distinction between the third generation now firmly embedded as the majority demographic of the Church in 95 AD when John received Revelation is that the Church was now mostly ethnically Gentile and far larger in its sheer numbers outside of Israel proper. It was quite a gap of years just between Pentecost and Peter's vision at Cornelius' house (Acts 10) to get the Apostles to openly minister to Gentiles, and still it would take further persecution of the first generation to move them out of geographic Israel and Samaria (Acts 11:19) to finally begin the process of taking the Gospel "*even to the remotest part of the earth*" (Acts 1:8) as mandated by Christ in His final instruction to the Apostles.

The term "Early Church" is often synonymously applied to "the 1st century Church" as if everyone living in the 1st century personally saw and met Christ and the Apostles. But for the first 15 or so years the Church was composed of believing Jews who had yet to venture out of geographic Israel, and over the following 20 or so years thereafter would experience the booms not just characterized by the Pauline missionary journeys, but the authorship of the first 22 books of the New Testament. By the time of the destruction of Jerusalem and the Temple in 70 AD, all but the Apostle John were gone and the Church was now spreading and growing far larger outside of Israel. It would be another 25 years before the advent of the book of Revelation, not long before which would come John's Epistles and Gospel, all written to a completely different audience.

It is a bittersweet irony that the present-day Christian is so frequently found to be lacking a basic knowledge of the history and timeline of the Old Testament, especially as it relates to Israel, God's people of the Covenant, and yet are even less educated when it comes to the New Testament history, timeline and sequence of Scripture as God's people of the New Covenant. Knowing, for instance, when the message through Joel took place as opposed to Zechariah makes a difference when it is understood that they are on completely different sides of the Babylonian Captivity. Likewise are the benefits of knowing that nearly all of the Epistles were written and in circulation before any of the Gospels. We have grown up carrying the whole, intact Bible around but give little consideration to the historical context and timing for each book, much less the fact that it was not even in the possession of what we so broadly refer to as the "Early Church" in the present way.

In fact, what each generation of the 1st century Church knew depends on when, exactly, they lived and died. It is going to take nearly 15 years before the first book is even written, the Epistle of James, and from thence until just shortly before the Temple's destruction in 70 AD all 22 of the New Testament works not authored by John would come into existence and begin to be copied and shared. None of those 22 works were aware of anything written in any of John's Epistles or his Gospel, although his teachings most certainly may have been known and perhaps influenced some of them. But even those which John would contribute much later in that century were completely unaware of what was to come in the final Revelation in approximately 95 AD. The Church operated for around 60 years ***without*** Revelation, and by the end of approximately 30 years began to function for the next 30 with none of John's writings.

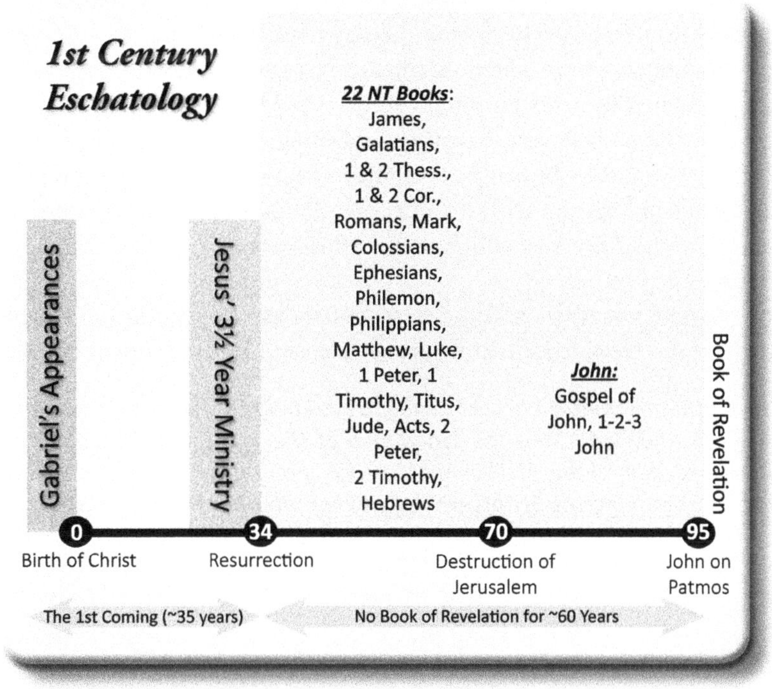

The Earliest Eschatology

This has been a necessary, if prolongated, preliminary discussion because for these 1st century generations of the Early Church, and especially those who witnessed firsthand the ministries of Christ and the Apostles, their "Bible" was still primarily the Old Testament. We need to understand that the first priority which Christ imparted to the Church where God's Word is concerned is understanding the Old Testament so that they would be properly prepared and qualified to author and impart the New Testament. We cannot overlook the detail that upon His Resurrection, for the first time Christ imparted the Holy Spirit to His followers after which "*He opened their minds to understand the Scriptures*"—that is, of course, the only Scriptures existing at the time as what would later be called the Old Testament:

> *20And when He had said this, He showed them both His hands and His side. The disciples then rejoiced when they saw the Lord. 21So Jesus said to them again, "Peace be with you; as the Father has sent Me, I also send you." 22And when He had said this, He breathed on them and said to them, "**Receive the Holy Spirit**. 23If you forgive the sins of any, their sins have been forgiven them; if you retain the sins of any, they have been retained."*
>
> — John 20:20-23

> *44Now He said to them, "These are My words which I spoke to you while I was still with you, that all things which are written about Me in the Law of Moses and the Prophets and the Psalms must be fulfilled." 45**Then He opened their minds to understand the Scriptures**,*
>
> — Luke 24:44-45

Although throughout the course of His ministry Christ often explained the true meaning of God's Word, those listening were limited in their own understanding, even those in His closest inner circle. It was upon His crucifixion when a change in the working of the Holy Spirit began to take place, first by Jesus personally imparting Him to His followers, and then upon the whole Church and all believers thereafter beginning with Pentecost. Their understanding of God's Word, however, did not really come until finally receiving the indwelling of the Holy Spirit personally in combination with the direct revelation by Christ of the proper meaning of the Old Testament, the entirety of which at that time was referred to as "*the Law of Moses and the Prophets and the Psalms*".

The Old Testament was never replaced or rendered obsolete, and in fact was the continuing standard by which the New Testament messengers' authority and authenticity was measured:

> [10]*The brethren immediately sent Paul and Silas away by night to Berea, and when they arrived, they went into the synagogue of the Jews.* [11]*Now these were more noble-minded than those in Thessalonica, for they received the word with great eagerness,* ***examining the Scriptures daily to see whether these things were so****.*
> — Acts 17:10-11

And the New Testament writings themselves are rich with Old Testament references to both explain and justify New Testament teaching.

When Christ, and later Paul, spoke of the Abomination of Desolation, the first thing 1st century Christians thought of was the book of Daniel and the parallel historical fulfillments during the Hasmonean Period with Antiochus Epiphanes IV and the later incursion of General Pompey. Even when the Apostle John much later in the century specifically called this figure "*antichristos*" (Strong's, #550)—literally rendered in English as "*Antichrist*", it was understood in light of Daniel through the prism of the Olivet Discourse. All the teachings by Christ and the Apostles and what would be recorded in their writings for the first 60 years prior until the publication of Revelation let stand unchanged what was known from Daniel. This was necessary in order to affirm that what took place in the Inter-Testamental Period was not ***the*** fulfillment, but only a prefiguring example of an ultimate one yet to come.

For those first generations of believers during the first 60 years of the Church's existence, having no knowledge of the future book of Revelation, their primary guide for understanding all things related to eschatology was Christ's milestone teaching of the Olivet Discourse. This served to bring into focus not only the Old Testament portions of God's prophetic Word provided before Christ's First Coming, but would provide the context for all the apostolic writings, even the latest by John prior to Revelation, for what was to come in the Second Coming. Everything eschatological referenced in the New Testament in its first 26 books is being viewed through the Olivet Discourse, even when making a connection to the Old Testament.

This is examined in detail in the author's previous book, *And THEN The End Will Come*, but it is still essential for a minimal visitation of the basic issues because the truth is that Revelation cannot be fully and properly understood without the foundation of the Olivet Discourse, which not only affirms that which was provided by Daniel as the foundational End Times timeline, but combine together to properly understand Revelation itself.

The Problem of Textual Reversal

One of the main contributing causes of so much confusion seen in the many and varied opinions and interpretations presented in the name of eschatology is a process this author refers to as "textual reversal".

A concept which has near universal acceptance across nearly all theological divides is commonly referred to as "the progressive revelation of God". Some may apply it more rigidly than others, but it basically boils down to accepting that God did not disclose everything all at once from the very beginning, but has been progressively revealing Himself and the Word. There are certain milestones where we see that more of God's plan and Word is revealed than previously experienced. That which was revealed to Noah was a leap forward from what previous generations back to Adam had understood, and going forward we would see such milestones with the likes of Abraham and then Moses. Nothing previous was ever replaced or made obsolete, but rather built upon that foundation to our greater advantage in knowing God's Word and will.

While an exhaustive study of this process would divulge many reasons for God's choosing to work like this, a chief one when it comes to the prophetic portions of God's Word is that it provides a sequence of establishing the elementary and fundamental basics required for attaining to the most advanced levels of understanding. Just as no one begins as a rocket scientist, basic mathematics must first be learned before moving on to algebra in order to then enfold geometry, and on to trigonometry and calculus before finally having the proper skill set to master the higher mathematics involved. Calculus does not nullify or replace basic math or algebra—in fact, it is impossible without them, but there is a sequence building up of the necessary disciplines for such an advanced skill. Attempting to take a shortcut to the top without the prerequisite knowledge and training is exactly what "textual reversal" describes.

In other words, far too often, and even among the scholarly, the approach to eschatology is to ***begin*** with the book of Revelation and ***then*** piece everything else from Scripture into it as if it were given first. In such instances it is not unusual to find that all the rest of God's Word, even though it was given first and long before the very last book of the canon of Scripture, is subordinated to Revelation, and in many cases, declared to be replaced or no longer in effect because of the overriding authority they ascribe to it.

A primary example of textual reversal is the growing number of Christian scholars, authors and commentators who insist that the Olivet Discourse does not apply to the Church, but only to Israel in "***The*** Tribulation" ***after*** the Church's Rapture. This is impossible, of course, just from the fact that for the first 60 years of its existence the Church's expectations for His return were first and foremost the Olivet Discourse, but it is a modern aberration which, among other contributing factors, comes from making Revelation the source and then working backwards.

The Context of the Times

An undisputed historical phenomenon of the 1st century is that this was a time which for awhile gave rise to a new form of literature which we categorize as "apocalyptic". In a satanic strategy which might best be described as "pre-counterfeiting", there was a lot of Jewish literature which employed similar usages of symbolism and dramatic depictions of prophetic themes, often with great similarities to the book of Revelation. But none of them, or any of the prolific Gnostic imitations of the rest of the emerging New Testament canon, were accepted by the Church. How would the 1st century Christians sort and reject the counterfeit from the authentic? In the same way the Bereans did, by measuring all things against the standard of God's Word.

Regardless of authorship, if ***anything*** in Revelation contradicted God's given Word to that point, it would have been summarily rejected as a member of the canon of Scripture. And when it came to eschatology, for more than 60 years the standard by which all things pertaining to the End Times was first measured was the Olivet Discourse. If Revelation in even the smallest way replaced or rendered obsolete even a single detail in the Olivet Discourse, it would have been rejected outright from the outset. And, as we shall see, the Olivet Discourse affirms exactly what was originally established in Daniel, only with additional detail.

In other words, even at its earliest, Revelation never served as a replacement for what previously came in God's Word, nor was it elevated to the starting position where God's prophetic Word is concerned. It was confirmed and understood in the context of coming last in the sequence of all prophetic revelation and understood in light of all that was established previously. It was not a God-given Etch A Sketch™ shaking everything clean to start over anew, but the remainder of the overall portrait progressively provided by all the previous portions of God's Word. (Apologies for the unintended, dramatic alliteration.)

Therefore, before ***we*** jump ahead to Revelation, it is necessary to prepare our eyes to see it in the same context experienced by 1st century believers. We are not giving a priority to their opinions, but rather establishing how the progressive revelation of God's prophetic Word provides the right understanding of that final step in completing the whole picture as revealed to us by God in the combined whole of His Word.

The Olivet Discourse & the Book of Daniel

As previously stated, although we unquestionably know from Daniel 9:27 that there is absolutely, without a doubt, a final "*week of years*", this is never revisited against in Scripture in its entirety as a seven year whole, much less ever textually labeled "***The*** Tribulation". The one, solitary New Testament reference to "*seven years*" is the length of time Anna was married before becoming a widow. (Lk. 2:36) Instead, the overwhelming emphasis in both Daniel where the seven years is established, and in Revelation to come, are variations which associate themselves with a 3-1/2 year lunar period, nearly always referring to the latter half of Daniel's 70th Week.

That beginning, middle and end of that seven years is defined by things directly associated with the Antichrist, but Scripture's subsequent emphasis is heavily weighted from the halfway milestone to the end:

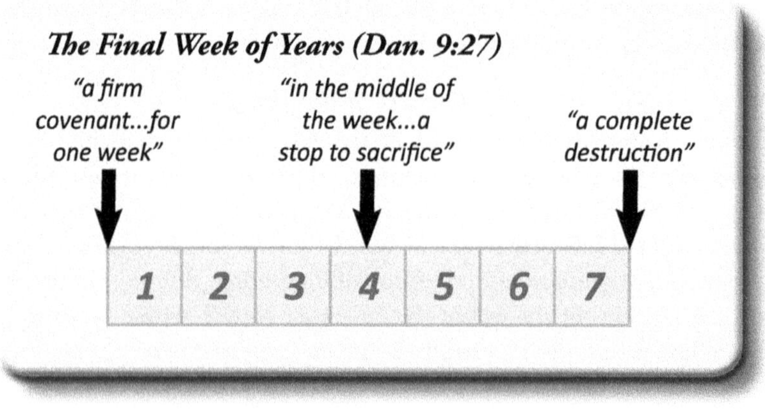

Daniel's 70th Week is triggered by the Antichrist making a treaty with Israel which he will break when, at the exact 3-1/2 year mark, he commits the Abomination of Desolation, and it concludes 3-1/2 years later with his destruction. When Scripture then re-visits the sequence, it keeps referring to the latter half beginning with the Abomination of Desolation. One might say that the emphasis is on the ***beginning*** of the end, so to speak.

Notice how every instance of a "3-1/2" involves some significant aspect of the Antichrist, and is often anchored in some way to the Abomination of Desolation:

> *[25]'He will speak out against the Most High and wear down the saints of the Highest One, and he will intend to make alterations in times and in law; and they will be given **into his hand for a time, times, and half a time**.*
>
> — Daniel 7:25

> *[6]And one said to the man dressed in linen, who was above the waters of the river, "How long will it be until the end of these wonders?" [7]I heard the man dressed in linen, who was above the waters of the river, as he raised his right hand and his left toward heaven, and swore by Him who lives forever that **it would be for a time, times, and half a time; and as soon as they finish shattering the power of the holy people**, all these events will be completed.*
>
> — Daniel 12:6-7

> *[11]"**From the time that the regular sacrifice is abolished** and the abomination of desolation is set up, there will be 1,290 days. [12]How blessed is he who keeps waiting and attains to the 1,335 days!*
>
> — Daniel 12:11-12

> *[3]"And I will grant authority to **my two witnesses, and they will prophesy for twelve hundred and sixty days**, clothed in sackcloth."*
>
> — Revelation 11:3

The Two Witnesses operate until, "*...they have finished their testimony, the beast that comes up out of the abyss will make war with them, and overcome them and kill them.*" (Rev. 11:7) Their ministry seems to be characterized as a running conflict with the Antichrist and his followers with their end specifically assigned to him.

> *[2]"Leave out the court which is outside the temple and do not measure it, for **it has been given to the nations; and they will tread under foot the holy city for forty-two months**.*
>
> — Revelation 11:2

Daniel specifies that it is his Gentile armies who initiate and then enforce not just the occupation of Jerusalem, but the Abomination of Desolation on behalf of the Antichrist. (Dan. 9:26; 11:31)

> *[6]Then **the woman fled into the wilderness** where she had a place prepared by God, so that there she would be nourished **for one thousand two hundred and sixty days**.*
>
> — Revelation 12:6

Israel ("*the woman*") flees from Satan/Antichrist in a parallel to the flight Jesus specifies in confluence with the Abomination of Desolation taking place.

> [13]*And when the dragon saw that he was thrown down to the earth, he persecuted the woman who gave birth to the male child.* [14]*But the two wings of the great eagle were given to the woman, so that she could fly into the wilderness to her place, where **she was nourished for a time and times and half a time, from the presence of the serpent**.*
>
> — Revelation 12:13-14

> [5]*There was given to him* [the beast] *a mouth speaking arrogant words and blasphemies, and **authority to act for forty-two months was given to him**.*
>
> — Revelation 13:5

As Jesus Tells It

Although covered in previous chapters, this summary of all the references to 3-1/2 are necessary to scripturally verify exactly what Jesus is referring to in the Olivet Discourse and how it is using and affirming this very sequence, placing the emphasis on the second half of the 70th Week:

> [15]***"Therefore when you see the ABOMINATION OF DESOLATION*** *which was spoken of through Daniel the prophet, standing in the holy place (let the reader understand),* [16]*then those who are in Judea must flee to the mountains.*
>
> — Matthew 24:15-16

Take note of how this unmistakable milestone of the middle of the 70th Week is anchored with the sequence Christ provides in the Olivet Discourse:

1. "*But all theses are merely the beginning of* ***birth pangs***". (Mt. 24:4-8) A series of general, worldwide events such as "*wars and rumors of wars*", "*famines and earthquakes*", and "*plagues*", and "*terrors and great signs from heaven*" (Lk. 21:11)
2. "*Then* ***they*** *will deliver* ***you*** *to* ***tribulation***". (Mt. 24:9-14) A time of deception, apostasy and persecution solely directed at and experienced by believers alone which will enable the Gospel to "*be preached to the whole world*". (Mt. 24:14)

Notice that there was no hard beginning, no mention of the one thing which Scripture categorically states will trigger the 70th Week, the Antichrist treaty. The beginning is shrouded by events concentrically coming with increasing power and frequency, giving way to the worst period of persecution and apostasy in the history of history, and right at the end of this in Matthew 24:14, Jesus specifies, "*and* ***then*** *the end will come*". What is the next thing He provides in the sequence? The "*abomination of desolation*".

In other words, the first unmistakable milestone for he Church He fixes attention to is the very same "beginning of the end", the last half of the 70th Week of Daniel.

3. "*Therefore when you see the* ***ABOMINATION OF DESOLATION***". (Mt. 24:15-20) Luke captures the detail that this will coincide with "*Jerusalem surrounded by armies*" (Lk. 21:20) and all three synoptic Gospels follow this up with the command to immediately flee from Judea into the wilderness in a parallel to the flights of Israel associated with that final half of the 70th Week.
4. "*For* ***then*** *there will be a* ***great tribulation***". (Mt. 24:21-23) Whereas the previous "*tribulation*" was heaped exclusively on the Church by the world, the entire world now experiences a phase of "*great tribulation*". This is an unprecedented phase which if unchecked would take every life on the planet, "*but for the sake of the*

elect those days will be cut short". (Mt. 24:22) In other words, it does not go on for the entire 3-1/2 remaining years which commenced with the Abomination of Desolation for believers, but their endurance ends with the next step in the sequence.

5. "*But* ***immediately after*** *the tribulation of those days*" (Mt. 24:29) there are three events which take place in very quick succession:

   a. "*...THE SUN WILL BE DARKENED, AND THE MOON WILL NOT GIVE ITS LIGHT, AND THE STARS WILL FALL from the sky, and the powers of the heavens will be shaken*". (Mt. 24:29) These are the same signs repeatedly found in Scripture which are associated with the onset of the final outpouring of God's wrath most commonly called "*the day of the Lord*".

   b. "*And then* ***the sign of the Son of Man will appear in the sky****, and then all the tribes of the earth will mourn, and* ***they will see the SON OF MAN*** *COMING ON THE CLOUDS OF THE SKY with power and great glory*". (Mt. 24:30) Not a "secret" Rapture, but a very visible announcement of what is unmistakably about to take place.

   c. "*And* ***He will send forth His angels*** *with A GREAT TRUMPET and* ***THEY WILL GATHER TOGETHER His elect*** *from the four winds, from end of the sky to the other.*" (Mt. 24:31) For believers, the Rapture cuts short the "*great tribulation*", leaving the remaining behind to undergo the remainder of that last half of the 70th Week which now embodies "*the day of the Lord*". The Church escapes the wrath of God which must be experienced by those left behind.

That which Jesus presents in the Olivet Discourse is not something new, but in reality is a more detailed affirmation of the 70th Week of Daniel with the same emphasis on the latter half as with the rest of Scripture. It is, however, given from the Church's viewpoint. He never describes one entire half as "***The*** Tribulation" or the last as "***The*** Great Tribulation", but uses those terms for specific phases within the sequence of the last week of years.

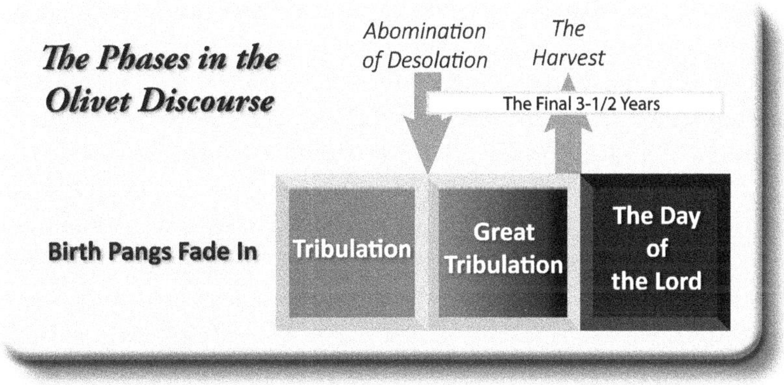

After stipulating that the 70th Week is initiated by the treaty, its omission in the rest of Scripture, and by Christ Himself in the Olivet Discourse, is most likely telling us that, like many things in Scripture, it may only be fully realized in hindsight. Or perhaps like many of the events associated with the Nativity Narrative and Christ's childhood, no one (other than

His parents) noticed or were even party to all the prophetic signs of fulfillment, and few in number were those who saw any of them. Even when the Magi testified, "'*We saw His star in the east*", and Herod the Great specifically inquired "*where the Messiah was to be born*", and even though Herod "*was troubled, and all Jerusalem with him*" (Mt. 2:1-8), no one joined with the Magi.

However, what is repeatedly affirmed by Scripture is the unmistakable milestone of the Abomination of Desolation, the formal initiation of his final 3-1/2 year reign corresponding to and counterfeiting Christ's 3-1/2 year public ministry commencing with His baptism.

The Standard in the First Coming

The baseline assumption by 1st century believers as to the Return of Christ was not based on something entirely new, but was a continuation of the next, more detailed exposure to God's progressive revelation of His plan originally articulated through Daniel. The main difference in the four consecutive and interfacing visions recorded in Daniel and this one given in the Olivet Discourse by Christ is perspective. Jesus revisits and even discloses even more information about the activities of the Antichrist, but in this instance almost exclusively for that which ***the Church*** will personally experience. The same timeline is revisited for those things believers will have to endure, but only up until their removal. Events provided in Daniel, and to be expanded upon in Revelation, which describe what will happen during "*the day of the Lord*" after the Church's removal are absent from the Olivet Discourse. They obviously do not apply to the Church. In Matthew's account, the next event visited after the harvest of believers is the separation of the sheep and goats (Mt. 25:1-13) to inaugurate the Millennial Kingdom. In other words, the sequence skips over "*the day of the Lord*" and picks up again with His thousand year reign where the Church is concerned.

Jesus did not alter anything provided by Daniel, and let everything provided in God's Word remain the standard structure for the eschatology of the 1st century Church. For the next 60 years, each successive generation would understand the eschaton—that general period signaling the close of history which Christ repeatedly called "*the end of the age*" (Mt. 13:39-40, 43; 24:3; 28:20), through the prism of the Olivet Discourse. All of the books of the New Testament, when explaining any aspect of Christ's anticipated Return, having absolutely no possible knowledge of the distant arrival of the book of Revelation, are all commentaries on Christ's teachings, particularly the Olivet Discourse.

At the risk of putting too fine a point on it, for those increasingly loud assertions that the Olivet Discourse has no application to the Church and was given only for Israel after the Church's removal, does it really make any sense at all that God allowed the first 60 formative years of the Church to pass with no direction regarding Christ's return other than what the angels told the Apostles at His Ascension? (Acts 1:9-11) No, the Olivet Discourse was not only their (and our) chief road map, but they took it a step further.

When Revelation was finally available to those very first readers, when they had to make the decision as to whether this was an authentic Word from God or just another in the sea of counterfeit apocalyptic literature, the reason it passed the test and was accepted into the canon of Scripture is precisely ***because*** the book of Revelation conforms to and is confirmed by the Olivet Discourse. Pundits who reverse their order of study by assigning Revelation as the starting point and then working backwards may not see it this way, but as detailed in *And THEN The End Will Come*, those who are properly grounded in God's Word first given arrive at Revelation marveling at the symmetry and intersection it provides with all that came before it.

Have you ever watched one of those television shows where an artist teaches the step-by-step process of making a complete painting? To get to the finished product, one must work backwards. The entire background is roughed in with the most distant objects inserted first. Then comes progressive rounds with each providing more detail working toward the very front, even going back and highlighting and giving even more substance to things previously inserted. It isn't until the very last round that the final highlights and details are effected in the foreground that the clear genius of the picture finally comes into full, glorious view. That is exactly the meaning of "*apokalupsis*"—"*revelation*": a gradual unveiling which allows for more and more detail to be seen the closer we get, until it is completely lifted and everything comes into perfect view.

1st century believers, having the indwelling of the Holy Spirit and Christ's personal explanation of the Scriptures handed down to them through His disciples, had a much clearer view than their Old Testament predecessors. Rather than replace one portrait with another, Jesus simply brought a level of detail to the same portrait never before experienced.

11 ❖ Paul & the Thessalonians

In the 60 or so years between the Olivet Discourse and the book of Revelation, the scriptural contributions concerning the Antichrist are not quantitatively large, but nonetheless essential. The space that they devote to this figure does not deal with the aspects of a kingdom, but as the individual figure to come.

In general, outside of the Gospels and Revelation, it is Peter, Paul, James and John who provide in their writings the majority of the New Testament contributions to eschatology, and it is overwhelmingly focused on how a believer should live and behave in the shadow of His imminent return. Their teachings are not strictly referring to the Rapture, but equally apply whether we "meet" Jesus tonight through death and resurrection or tomorrow in that one time supernatural removal. Either way, Christian living in concert with His Word and ways is the overwhelming emphasis with healthy and constant reminders of the greatest, always present dangers of deception, false teaching and substandard Christian living. Specific mention is repeatedly made of false apostles, false prophets, false teachers and false believers. Apostasy and deception are the things which Jesus warns of more than any other in the Olivet Discourse, and this is the banner most often and prominently displayed by the New Testament writers.

Because the Epistles are essentially apostolic commentaries on Christ's teachings, it is not surprising that when they touch on something eschatological it both conforms to and confirms Christ's primary teaching in the Olivet Discourse. And like all that Jesus taught in relation to "*the end of the age*", it is understandable that they reinforce that which Jesus emphasizes is most important for believers, which is to be "dressed and ready"—that is, found by Christ to be a faithful, biblically practicing Christian both in our ministry to the Church and in our witness to the world. When it comes to the topic of the Antichrist, however, the New Testament contribution is basically limited to Paul and John on whom we will concentrate, dealing with Paul first.

The Thessalonian Problem

The one New Testament "hot spot", if you will, when it comes to the issue of the End Times is in the church at Thessalonica. Acts 17 records that Paul had to cut short his time there and literally flee for his life due to persecution initiated and fomented by local jealous and unbelieving Jews, who would later follow him to Berea and stir things up there as well. In his letters to the Thessalonians, Paul discloses that false teachers came in behind him and rather than introduce an entirely new false teaching, twisted that which Paul had taught into something unintended. The deceivers apparently took the sequence and timing foundational to Paul's teaching and misrepresented it. In other words, they did not introduce some kind of outright substitute, but took the Word of God as conveyed through this Apostle and rearranged it. Ironically, this is ***exactly*** what is taking place today. The Apostle Peter's warning for the Christians at the time becomes even more relevant for Christians today:

> [15]*...just as also* ***our beloved brother Paul****, according to the wisdom given him, wrote to you,* [16]*as also in all his letters, speaking in them of these things, in which are some things hard to understand,* ***which the untaught and unstable distort, as they do also the rest of the Scriptures, to their own destruction****.* [17]*You therefore, beloved, knowing this beforehand,* ***be on your guard so that you are not carried away by the error of unprincipled men and fall from your own steadfastness****,* [18]*but grow in the grace and knowledge of our Lord and Savior Jesus Christ. To Him be the glory, both now and to the day of eternity. Amen.*
>
> — 2 Peter 3:15b-18

At present, when it comes to eschatology, there is no section of Scripture under direct attack and at the center of outright manipulation more than 2 Thessalonians 2:1-12. Ironically, this is Paul's correction given to the Thessalonians for the errors introduced, which is itself being twisted today in the vain effort to alter Paul's teachings yet again. For those interested in a detailed explanation of all that is presently going on with this issue, reader's are encouraged to read *Appendix A: When Change Is Expressly Forbidden*. There is also a very thorough teaching on this in Jacob Prasch's book *Harpazo* in chapter 22, "Imminency and the Harpazo" which is highly recommended.

Each of Paul's letters seem to deal with what was problematic in each particular church, which is why, of all his writings, eschatology is addressed in his letters to the Thessalonians more than all the others combined. This was a big problem for them.

A Dual Working

> [13]*But we do not want you to be uninformed, brethren, about those who are asleep, so that you will not grieve as do the rest who have no hope.* [14]*For if we believe that Jesus died and rose again, even so* ***God will bring with Him those who have fallen asleep in Jesus****.*
>
> — 1 Thessalonians 4:13-14

There was such great anticipation of Christ's return in their lifetime that the question arose as to what will happen to those who have already passed away when He comes for the remaining, still living Christians. It is interesting that Paul does not say, "Don't worry, they're already looking down at you from heaven and you'll be reunited with them some day", as is so often what we might say to comfort someone, or even our self. Paul's explanation is that from our earthly point of view that although they "*have fallen asleep*", they are not actually going to miss out on that event; they are going to participate in the Rapture first.

> [15]*For this we say to you by the word of the Lord, that we who are alive and remain until* ***the coming of the Lord****, will not precede those who have fallen asleep.* [16]*For the Lord Himself will descend from heaven with a shout, with the voice of the archangel and with the trumpet of God, and* ***the dead in Christ will rise first.*** [17]***Then we who***

> ***are alive and remain will be caught up together with them in the clouds to meet the Lord in the air**, and so we shall always be with the Lord.*
> — 1 Thessalonians 4:15-17

In other words, where believers are concerned, the Resurrection and Rapture are two sides of the same coin, two aspects of the dual working of the same thing.

"*The **coming** of the Lord*" is translated from the Greek "*parousia*" (Strong's #3952) and best describes the entire eschaton—that is, the complete sequence of what Jesus calls "*the end of the age*" when all history draws to a close for believer and non-believer alike. All of the things involved with the End Times, including the 70th Week, are all part of the greater *Parousia*. Christ's coming is described in Scripture as something which is a progression of final events and not always speaking about the specific, final return documented in Revelation 19:11-16. The specific mechanics as to how Christ comes for believers in that environment is the English rendering "*caught up*", derived from the underlying Greek word "*harpazo*" (Strong's #726)—to snatch away or to seize violently. (The term "Rapture" is our adaptation of the Latin term "*rapturo*" which the Latin Vulgate used for the Greek "*harpazo*".) Of the terms used to describe this supernatural removal, it is the one which best describes the physical act which will take place. But Paul reveals that this specific event is not simply limited to those who are alive at the time to experience this removal, but are actually the second wave in what is taking place:

1. "*For the Lord Himself will descend from heaven...*
2. "*...with a shout,*"
3. "*...with the voice of the archangel...*"
4. "*...and with the trumpet of God...*"
5. "*...and the dead in Christ will rise first*".
6. "*Then we...will be caught up* [harpazo] *together with them...*
7. "*...in the clouds to meet the Lord in the air...*
8. "*...and so we shall always be with the Lord*".

The modern-day manipulation of Paul's teaching is on display when compared to this sequence where the *Harpazo* is immediately preceded by a visible sighting of Christ accompanied by a "*shout*", "*the voice of the archangel*" and "*the trumpet of God*". This completely refutes the false notion of a "secret" Rapture which is often portrayed as taking place with no prior notice and without any of these accompanying signs.

A typical example is an oft-viewed YouTube video produced by a well-meaning church which shows a few hundred people at a Sunday morning service, when without any warning whatsoever a huge thunderclap sound effect synchronizes with all but a handful of the congregants instantly disappearing, the remaining few falling to their knees in instant repentance and acknowledgment of being left behind. This "secret" Rapture as this video depicts it is not what Scripture provides will take place. That which Paul describes may occur very close together, even perhaps in such quick succession that they occur almost on top of each other, but it nonetheless does not take place in "secret" with absolutely no warning. And it does not happen only for those believers who happen to be alive on earth at the time, but they are actually the follow-on participants joining the Resurrected. An air raid siren may only provide a few minutes warning before enemy planes arrive, but it still signals what is about to take place in advance of it actually happening.

The Day of the Lord

We must remember that in the original text of Paul's letter there were no verse or chapter markings. Paul's teaching continues uninterrupted. Paul now identifies the *Harpazo* with the onset of "*the day of the Lord*", that part of the Last Days which is spoken of more than any other aspect in the whole of Scripture, a time when God's final and ultimate wrath is poured out on earth as the final stage of the end. Because believers are exempt from God's wrath, Paul affirms that believers will be removed as a primary sign signaling the beginning of that particular and final phase of Christ's overall *Parousia*—all that is involved with His coming. But, like Christ, Paul continues by reminding them that "*you do not know the day nor the hour*" (Mt. 25:13) as he continues the teaching.

> [1]*Now as to the times and the epochs, brethren, you have no need of anything to be written to you.* [2]*For you yourselves know full well that the day of the Lord will come just like a thief in the night.*
> — 1 Thessalonians 5:1-2

This an extremely important detail that before "*the day of the Lord*" actually commences, and perhaps even as the very first event which triggers it, the Resurrection and Rapture of believers takes place.

> [3]*While they are saying, "Peace and safety!" then destruction will come upon them suddenly like labor pains upon a woman with child, and they will not escape.* [4]*But* ***you, brethren, are not in darkness, that the day would overtake you like a thief****;* [5]*for you are all sons of light and sons of day. We are not of night nor of darkness;* [6]*so then let us not sleep as others do, but let us be alert and sober.* [7]*For those who sleep do their sleeping at night, and those who get drunk get drunk at night.*
> — 1 Thessalonians 5:3-7

Paul is providing the same explanation Jesus gave in the Olivet Discourse that although non-believers will be taken completely by surprise as in the example Christ gave of the days of Noah, that believers should pay attention to the signs of the times and "*recognize that He is near, right at the door*". (Mt. 24:32-33) Like Christ, Paul affirms the sequence of the End Times as it leads up to the *Harpazo* and transitions to "*the day of the Lord*".

> [8]*But since we are of the day, let us be sober, having put on the breastplate of faith and love, and as a helmet, the hope of salvation.* [9]*For* ***God has not destined us for wrath****, but for obtaining salvation through our Lord Jesus Christ,* [10]*who died for us, so that whether we are awake or asleep, we will live together with Him.*
> — 1 Thessalonians 5:8-10

And so Paul ties the whole discussion together by reaffirming that a biblically faithful Christian will be aware of what is about to take place in the End Times, and they are "*not destined for wrath*"—not going to experience "*the day of the Lord*", but whether through the Resurrection of Rapture—"*whether we are awake or asleep*", all believers are going to "*live together with Him*" in further building upon the initial disclosure of the *Harpazo* which brings them both to Jesus.

A Reversal of the Order

Between Paul's letters, false teachers confuse the Thessalonians. Rather than provide an outright replacement for Paul's teachings, they present their error wrapped in a rearrangement of the sequence of events. They do not make something up which would outright contradict God's Word or could never be verified by it, so instead they basically say, "Yes, Paul was right in what he said, except 'the day of the Lord' has ***already*** come". An entirely false teaching is generated not by making something up from scratch, but by twisting what was known from God's Word to be true. In other words, they redefine "*the day of the Lord*". (Just like today.)

> [1]*Now we request you, brethren, with regard to the coming of our Lord Jesus Christ and our gathering together to Him,* [2]***that you not be quickly shaken from your composure or be disturbed*** *either by a spirit or a message or a letter as if from us,* ***to the effect that the day of the Lord has come****.*
> — 2 Thessalonians 2:1-2

Paul refers to the *Parousia*—"*with regard to the* ***coming*** *of our Lord Jesus Christ*", and makes the direct connection to the dual working of the Resurrection and *Harpazo* as "***our gathering together*** *to Him*", and affirms once again that it takes place prior to "*the day of the Lord*" because they have been "*shaken*" and "*disturbed*" by the false teachers' assertion that "*the day of the Lord has come*". That which Paul previously established in hist first letter is again affirmed as he corrects the false convolution of the sequence Paul originally taught.

> [3]*Let no one in any way deceive you, for* ***it will not come unless the apostasy comes first, and the man of lawlessness is revealed****, the son of destruction,* [4]*who opposes and exalts himself above every so-called god or object of worship, so that he takes his seat in the temple of God, displaying himself as being God.* [5]*Do you not remember that while I was still with you, I was telling you these things?*
> — 2 Thessalonians 2:3-5

So what does "*it*" mean when Paul says, "***It*** *will not come unless...*"? Obviously "*the day of the Lord*" which he has already established comes ***after*** the *Harpazo* when both the Resurrected and Raptured come together before Christ. But now Paul provides two additional details which must happen before the *Harpazo* triggers "*the day of the Lord*" as well: "*the apostasy comes first, and the man of lawlessness is revealed*".

Aside from providing us with two additional names for the Antichrist in "*the man of lawlessness*" and "*the son of destruction*" which summarize many of the character traits already divulged in Scripture concerning this final figure, we are provided a more detailed description of what exactly takes place when he commits the Abomination of Desolation:

- "*...opposes and exalts himself above every so-called god or object of worship...*"
- "*...takes his seat in the temple of God...*"
- "*...displaying himself as being God*".

Self-deification and self-promotion have been characteristics repeatedly disclosed in Scripture concerning this figure, (Dan. 7:11, 25; 8:11, 25; 11:36-37) and it was an unmistakable act performed by Antiochus Epiphanes IV in the first historical illustration of this behavior. It was what Nebuchadnezzar did in Daniel 3 with his own golden image. Through Paul this unmistakable act is provided even more detail.

Jesus provides the very same sequence in the Olivet Discourse in first describing the increasing deception, apostasy and persecution which leads up to the Abomination of Desolation. The sequence provided by both Christ and Paul are identical in stipulating an initial time of growing spiritual darkness characterized by apostasy—a great spiritual falling away, then the public milestone of the halfway point of the 70th Week with the Abomination of Desolation, after which comes what Jesus and Paul both describe as the "*episunagoge*" (Strong's #1997)—that is, the "***gathering*** *together to Him*" of all believers to Christ.

> [31]*"And He will send forth His angels with* A GREAT TRUMPET *and* THEY WILL **GATHER** [episunagoge] TOGETHER *His elect from the four winds, from one end of the sky to the other.*
> — Matthew 24:31

> [1]*Now we request you, brethren, with regard to the coming of our Lord Jesus Christ and our* ***gathering*** [episunagoge] *together to Him,*
> — 2 Thessalonians 2:1

Scripture stipulates that the *Harpazo* will not take place ***before*** the appearance of the Antichrist. Yes, although our hope and faith are set on the coming of Christ, in the Last Days, however, an unmistakable sign of Christ's imminent return which we are to expect is the preceding appearance of the Antichrist.

On the remote chance that the reader is not fully grasping why so much time is being devoted to this aspect of the Antichrist, it is because one of the most popular teachings ***within*** the Church today dogmatically insists that believers will be raptured ***before*** the Antichrist ever makes an appearance. This position is arrived at by doing the very same thing which occurred historically in Thessalonica, by changing the sequence. They insist that the entire final seven years is "*the day of the Lord*", and knowing that believers will be removed before "*the day of the Lord*", they rearrange the sequence to misrepresent both the timing of the *Harpazo* and the appearance of the Antichrist. They change the order of Paul's teaching. Some are even going to the unscriptural lengths of actually changing the text of 2 Thessalonians 2:3, something which even the original false teachers in Thessalonica did not do. [For an in-depth explanation, see *Appendix A: When Change Is Expressly Forbidden.*]

> [6]*And you know what restrains him now, so that in his time he will be revealed.* [7]*For the mystery of lawlessness is already at work; only he who now restrains will do so until he is taken out of the way.*
> — 2 Thessalonians 2:6-7

These two verses are at the center of polarizing interpretations as well, but with different eschatological positions. Again, for a detailed explanation, Jacob Prasch's book *Harpazo* is recommended for the chapters in "Part Three: The Sequence of Prophetic Events Climaxing with the Harpazo". This author subscribes to this being a function of the Holy Spirit who worked on an individual basis under the Old Covenant, but with the advent of the Church Age obviously works much differently. This was expressed by Christ as one of the benefits for believers:

> [7]*"But I tell you the truth, it is to your advantage that I go away; for if I do not go away, the Helper will not come to you; but if I go, I will send Him to you.* [8]*And* ***He, when He comes, will convict the world concerning sin and righteousness and judgment;*** [9]*concerning sin, because they do not believe in Me;* [10]*and concerning righteousness,*

> *because I go to the Father and you no longer see Me; [11]and concerning judgment, because the ruler of this world has been judged.*
> — John 16:7-11

It would seem that as "*the day of the Lord*" approaches in concert with the rise of the Antichrist, that the Holy Spirit reverts to His Old Testament way of working on an individual basis. But regardless of the interpretation of these verses to which one subscribes, Paul is providing yet another condition which must be met before "*the day of the Lord*", preceded by the *Harpazo*, takes place. Once this apostasy and dramatic change in the spiritual environment become palpable to believers, Paul again says the unmistakable appearance of the Antichrist will take place.

A Confirmation of Attributes

> *[8]Then that lawless one will be revealed whom the Lord will slay with the breath of His mouth and bring to an end by the appearance of His coming; [9]that is, the one whose coming is in accord with the activity of Satan, with all power and signs and false wonders, [10]and with all the deception of wickedness for those who perish, because they did not receive the love of the truth so as to be saved.*
> — 2 Thessalonians 2:8-10

We have already observed Scripture which speaks to the destructive nature of the Antichrist (Dan. 7:24; 8:24; 11:40-44), and the destruction which will in turn be visited back upon him (Dan. 7:11, 22, 26-27; 8:25; 11:45) in a parallel affirmation of that which Paul summarizes here, as well as his chief and repeated employment of deception. (Dan. 8:12, 23, 25; 11:23-24, 30-34)

But take special note that Christ's "*coming*" in verse 8—"*parousia*", is preceded by the Antichrist's "*coming*" in verse 9, also using the same term "*parousia*". To those present-day emotional respondents who try to substantiate their rearrangement of the sequence and say, "You're not looking for the coming of Christ, you're looking for the coming of the Antichrist!", the truth is that this is ***exactly*** what is specified by Scripture. Only we are not "looking for" the same thing in the same way; the Antichrist is a crucial sign that what we ***are*** truly looking forward to is about to take place.

> *[11]For this reason God will send upon them a deluding influence so that they will believe what is false, [12]in order that they all may be judged who did not believe the truth, but took pleasure in wickedness.*
> — 2 Thessalonians 2:11-12

And here we are provided an expanded explanation of what Daniel originally disclosed, "*none of the wicked will understand, but those who have insight will understand*". (Dan. 12:10) A lifestyle of wickedness does not merely engender even more sin, but leads to being given over to it so that the end result is a completely false moral and spiritual compass leading to the ultimate worst destination possible. Those who follow the "*man of lawlessness*" end up in a total state of lawlessness.

But a new detail will stick out from verse 9, "*the one who is coming is in accord with the activity of Satan*". This is the first direct textual connection between the Antichrist and the devil.

Yet Another Parallel

Although Paul's exposition is brief, it not only parallels the sequence provided by Christ in the Olivet Discourse, but once again presents the Antichrist and Daniel's 70th Week in the context of what the ***Church*** is to expect and experience.

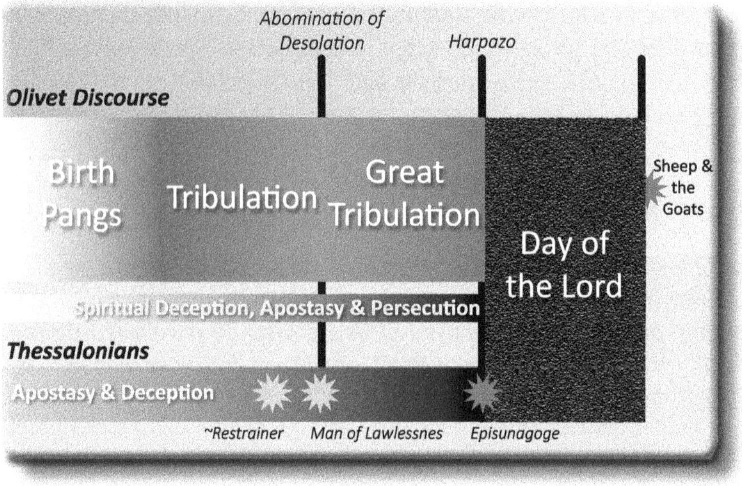

For the New Testament believer who is not going to experience the complete reign of the Antichrist and the whole working of his kingdom, the New Testament writers align themselves with Christ to disclose those elements to which they will be exposed and witness. And the key feature which anchors all the timelines, whether in the Old Testament or the New, whether for ethnic Israel or the Church, is the working of the Antichrist, in particular his unmistakable revelation by the Abomination of Desolation.

Just as Christ's emphasis is on the environment Christians are to expect leading up to the Abomination of Desolation which signals their imminent removal, so does Paul likewise affirm with the additional details that spiritual restraints will be removed just prior to this figure's public appearance who is now unambiguously known to be directly animated by Satan himself. These are likewise not things which non-believers will understand, but are provided solely for believers to recognize and expect.

The Didache

Most Christian references place Paul's writing to the Thessalonians at approximately 49-51 AD and John's Epistles and Gospel being authored between 85-95 AD. So there is something like a 35-45 year gap between them. For more than 50 years since the Church's inauguration at the Day of Pentecost (~34 AD), the first 22 books of the Bible have taken hold as the primary teachings of the Church, and in particular, the synoptic Gospels of Matthew, Mark and Luke. Probably the earliest extant Christian writing from that period is what we call *The Didache*, whose full name is "The Teaching of the Twelve Apostles". It is a compendium of teachings which so closely parallel those found in the first 22 books of the New Testament that it was considered a finalist to be included in the canon of Scripture. One of the reasons we can assign its publication to as early as this 1st century gap in time is the absence of material quoting John's five books.

Its total size is roughly that of the book of Ephesians and is organized by topics. There are many free, online postings of the entire text in English, and even though it may not be considered a part of the sanctified canon of God's Word, it is nonetheless extremely valuable as a parallel Christian resource serving to confirm not just early Christian history, but the biblical text as well. However, if it had been accepted as one of the books of the New Testament, it would not have been found to add anything new or change any existing Scripture, but rather mirror texts already present in the books which have been accepted as such.

As with most important ancient literature, scholars have assigned chapter and verse markings, and its topical arrangement has been organized into 16 short chapters, chapter 16 being the one devoted to eschatology. It is particularly interesting how it parallels the Olivet Discourse:

> WATCH for your life. Let not your lamps be quenched, and let not your loins be ungirded; but be ye ready, for ye know not the hour in which our Lord cometh. 2And be frequently gathered together seeking the things which concern your souls; for the whole time of your faith shall not profit you except ye be made perfect in the last season. 3For in the last days the false prophets and the corrupters shall be multiplied; and the sheep shall be turned into wolves and love shall be turned into hatred; 4for when lawlessness waxeth great, they shall hate and persecute and betray one another; ***and then shall appear the deceiver of the world as the Son of God; and he shall work signs and wonders, and the earth shall be delivered into his hands, and he shall work iniquities such as have never been from everlasting.*** 5Then shall the work of men come into the fire of trial, and many shall be offended, and shall perish; but they that endure in their faith shall be saved by the curse itself. 6And then shall appear the signs of the truth; first the sign of a spreading out in heaven; next the sign of the sound of a trumpet; 7and the third a resurrection of the dead; howbeit not of all, but as it was said, the Lord shall come and all His Saints with him; 8then shall the world see the Lord coming upon the clouds of heaven.
>
> Allen, G. C. (Trans.). (1903). The Didache or The Teaching of the Twelve Apostles Translated with Notes (pp. 9–10). London: The Astolat Press.

Not only does it obviously follow the basic sequence provided in the Olivet Discourse, but the parallels to 2 Thessalonians in the above verse 4 are habitually cited by commentators. In particular is noted the affirmation of the timing of first a time of apostasy, then the appearance of the Antichrist before the *Harpazo* of the Church. At the least it shows that the early Christians who still had not received the book of Revelation were dogmatic about keeping to the literal text provided both by Christ in the Olivet Discourse and the Apostle Paul in his writings.

12 ❖ John & the Early Church

When those early readers first processed Revelation, especially chapter 13 devoted to the Antichrist, they would first and foremost measure it against what was established by Christ, Daniel, Paul, and even John's earlier writings of his Gospel and Epistles which preceded it. If there had been a perceived contradiction with these antecedent writings, Revelation would have ***never*** been accepted as an authentic member of the biblical canon of Scripture.

When Christ provided the Olivet Discourse, He not only let stand what was known to that point from Daniel, but even directed that Daniel be studied even further. (Mt. 24:15) With the exception of a very few details, nothing provided in the 26 books of the New Testament preceding the last in Revelation altered any believer's understanding of the Antichrist as already established in Scripture, not even the Apostle John's Epistles and Gospel which although came later than most of the rest of the writings, still had no awareness of what was to come in Revelation. But there are a couple of points provided by Paul and John which will broaden our understanding and begin to open the door to what already given Scripture has been concealing all along. Together with specific disclosures to come in Revelation, we will once again find many things which are backward compatible, so to speak. John's vision will turn out to not be an unveiling—a revelation fixated solely on future events, but more so an unveiling of many portions of God's ***already*** given written Word which have much to contribute to the overall future fulfillments.

At the risk of belaboring the point for the immediate issue in our own time, my first reaction when I am accused, "You're not looking for the coming of Christ, but the coming of Antichrist!" is actually an overwhelming compulsion to quote the Apostle John. It is most interesting that because of his teachings he is nicknamed "The Apostle of Love", and yet he has more to say not just about the Antichrist, but the spirit of antichrist, than all the other New Testament writers combined. And he is not limiting his teachings about the Antichrist to just a future eschatological context, but having to address the issue that there are already figures rising up and claiming to be Christ even before he has received his vision on the Isle of Patmos. Why does the Apostle John, by his own hand, command Christians to look for ***both*** the antichrist working at all times as well as the ultimate figure to come?

Many Antichrists Already

We know from the conversation of the Sanhedrin in Acts 5 that there were false messiahs, two of which Gamaliel mentions by name in Theudas and Judas of Galilee. And from the historical record, others followed such as one of the most famous yet to come in Simon bar Kochba, who initiated the revolt against the Romans in 132 AD which three years later resulted in more than just Israel's conquest and total destruction; this would bring about the final end of the Jewish state and initiate the dispersement of all the Jews into the Diaspora from which it would take nearly two millennia to even begin to recover. According to what John is writing about, the phenomenon of antichrists is not strictly limited to something happening within the confines of Judaism proper, but has become a problem for the Church in that 60 or so year period between the Day of Pentecost and the writing of the book of Revelation.

John's references to this issue should also be noted as being given in the context of a reminder from him that this issue was apparently so important that it was not only a part of his regular teaching to that point, but deemed so critical that it still warranted mentioning again; it is not presented as brand new material never before heard. And to this body of what appears to be well-known previously transmitted information, John addresses the concept of "*the spirit of antichrist*" which establishes a satanic pattern of working in ***every*** historical period of the Church up until the very Return of Christ.

This issue of the importance of the Antichrist dovetails with the Olivet Discourse in that while there are many signs coming out of the milieu of the "*birth pangs*" over a longer, preliminary period which are not necessarily individually distinguishable to make a positive identification as to the start date of the eschaton, one of the first unambiguous events specified as impossible for believers to ignore is when the Antichrist commits the Abomination of Desolation. The Apostle John not only affirms the Olivet Discourse's contention that there will be a proliferation of false christs and false prophets in general, but by providing how to identify them alludes that this will lead to being able to recognize the ultimate, final one.

"Lawlessness" & "Perdition"

Paul introduced an additional name for the Antichrist which conveys a significant part of his character, "*the man of lawlessness*". (2 Th. 2:3) The biblical definition of "*lawlessness*" (Greek "*anomia*", Strong's #458) is not to be taken as referring to any and every rule of law, but exclusively attached to ***the*** Law—God's Word. Furthermore, it is not referring to the mere absence of God's Law, but violating God's divinely instituted Law. This can be seen in the Apostle John's given definition:

> [4]*Everyone who practices sin also practices lawlessness; and sin is lawlessness.*
> — 1 John 3:4

Notice the twice repeated accompanying "*practices*" so as to identify something which is not a one-time case of backsliding or temporary stumbling, but describing a continual action, or lifestyle, of purposely transgressing God's Word. Paul enhances this meaning by showing how it is not just connected to sin, but is completely contrary to what is practiced by a true believer so as to avoid it:

> [19]*I am speaking in human terms because of the weakness of your flesh. For just as you presented your members as **slaves** to impurity and **to lawlessness, resulting in further lawlessness**, so now present your members as **slaves to righteousness, resulting in sanctification**.*
> — Romans 6:19

Paul's additional assignment to him of "*the son of destruction*", (Greek "*apoleia*", Strong's #684) which can also be literally translated, "*the son of perdition*", describes something which is fully and completely obliterated, not merely damaged. The New Testament most often associates this with the second death or exclusion from Christ's kingdom:

> [13]*"Enter through the narrow gate; for the gate is wide and the way is broad that leads to* ***destruction****, and there are many who enter through it.*
> — Matthew 7:13

> [28]*in no way alarmed by your opponents—which is a sign of* ***destruction*** *for them, but of salvation for you, and that too, from God.*
> — Philippians 1:28

By showing that the opposite of "*destruction*" is "*salvation*", Paul provides a very clear definition of the full biblical meaning of the term.

But Paul provides something never previously brought out into the open before, which John will build upon, that Judas and Antichrist are assigned the exact, same title:

> [12]*"While I was with them, I was keeping them in Your name which You have given Me; and I guarded them and not one of them perished but* ***the son of perdition****, so that the Scripture would be fulfilled.*
> — John 17:12

When we examine God's word chronologically in terms of the order in which Scripture was published so as to know what was known at a particular point in time, this is the first time a reference to the Antichrist is presented which is ***not*** connected with an ethnically Gentile figure, nor to a ruler with a prominent political position. After the canon of Scripture is closed upon the giving of Revelation, and a retroactive examination of all God's Word is undertaken, something is disclosed which is far more likely to take place within the ranks of future generations of believers to come after the 1st Century. Like many aspects of God's Word, details concerning this figure which were previously hidden or too difficult to discern will definitely arise from the rest of God's Word.

One of the reasons for the difference in the emphasis upon "*the son of perdition*" in John 17 and the same Greek words alternatively translated into English as "*the son of destruction*" in 2 Thessalonians 2 is that it is believed the phrase "*the son of perdition*" is a Hebrew idiom designating someone specifically destined for destruction rather than merely acting in the character of someone so bound. It is a ***literal*** outcome, not just a commentary on their nature or temperament. This certainly describes both Judas' and Antichrist's ultimate appointment with the Lake of Fire, and may relate to a detail about Judas revealed when the Apostles were selecting his replacement:

> [24]*And they prayed and said, "You, Lord, who know the hearts of all men, show which one of these two You have chosen* [25]*to occupy this ministry and apostleship from which* ***Judas turned aside to go to his own place****."*
> — Acts 1:24-25

Taken altogether, we can see why the priority where End Times Christians are concerned are repeated warnings against deception and apostasy, staple conditions and behaviors associated with someone not just leading a rebellion against God's Word, but providing a path to embracing the counterfeit who is attempting to be worshiped and take His place.

> [4]*who opposes and exalts himself above every so-called god or object of worship, so that he takes his seat in the temple of God, displaying himself as being God.*
> — 2 Thessalonians 2:4

This is exactly what was designated by Daniel and referenced by Christ, but which also conformed to what had been experienced by the historical fulfillment of Antiochus Epiphanes IV. In the Olivet Discourse, it is at this point that Jesus warns those living in Judea to flee upon witnessing this seminal milestone.

> [6]*And you know what restrains him now, so that in his time he will be revealed.* [7]*For the mystery of lawlessness is already at work; only he who now restrains will do so until he is taken out of the way.*
> — 2 Thessalonians 2:6-7

"*The mystery of lawlessness*", or in many translations, "*the mystery of iniquity*", when we understand the unbreakable connection of "*lawlessness*" to overtly refusing to put God's Word into practice, allows us to see that this is much more about people's resistance to accept and come to Christ. Their refusal, however, does not prevent Christ from executing His plan. But this important aspect of the working of the Antichrist will dovetail with John's disclosure of "*the spirit of antichrist*" to show that the lawlessness leading to destruction both spiritually and literally is a feature at work during every historical age, even when the final figure is not yet present.

It is the Last Hour

> [18]*Children,* ***it is the last hour; and just as you heard that antichrist is coming, even now many antichrists have appeared; from this we know that it is the last hour****.*
> — 1 John 2:18

The Apostle John establishes that a sign of "*the last hour*" is not merely "*that antichrist is coming*", but the final figure is preceded by many counterfeits in a direct parallel to the very first opening line Christ put forth in the formal giving of the Olivet Discourse:

> [4]*And Jesus answered and said to them, "See to it that no one misleads you.* [5]*For many will come in My name, saying, 'I am the Christ,' and will mislead many.*
> — Matthew 24:4-5

We are finally presented with the label "*antichrist*" as opposed to the Olivet Discourse's preferences of "*false Christs*". By this time in Church history, no one has to speculate what this means because John is speaking about something which is actually and literally taking place at that time. In fact, even to this present hour and throughout every age of history, when has there not been the problem of figures originating within both Christianity and Judaism claiming to be the Messiah? But John does make a distinction that there are "*many antichrists*" preceding the final, ultimate Antichrist. Such are betrayed by the fact that they no longer live according to God's Word and ways.

An Important Type

> *[19]They went out from us, but they were not really of us; for if they had been of us, they would have remained with us; but they went out, so that it would be shown that they all are not of us. [20]But you have an anointing from the Holy One, and you all know.*
>
> — 1 John 2:19-20

This may be a powerful parallel to the ultimate figure in Scripture representing the Antichrist in the person of Judas. It was not until Jesus identified him to the Apostles in the course of the Last Supper when it could be fully realized he was not really one of them, even though they had already figured out some of his personal shortcomings. (Jn. 12:4-6; 13:24-30) Jesus knew from the beginning, of course, (Jn 7:70-71) but for a long time Judas appeared to be one of them. It was not until Jesus' revelation concerning Judas at Passover and his immediately leaving to go make arrangements to consummate the betrayal that his identity became clear to all. It is no coincidence that upon being identified and exiting to embark upon his treason that Scripture specifies, "*and it was night*", (Jn. 13:30) the biblical metaphor for spiritual darkness, and the arrest, betrayal and falling away of many which immediately followed gives us some idea of what the "*great tribulation*" will be like. The fact that Judas will return with a force comprised of both Jew and Gentile cannot be overlooked when drawing comparisons to the ultimate Antichrist figure he portrays.

It is very possible that one of the details which will literally play out in the course of the final figure to come is that just as Judas could only be understood for who and what he truly was by the direct revelation of Christ, so will the ultimate revelation of the final figure only come about in the same manner. However, there are things which we need to take into consideration.

The first is that at that time the Apostles had not yet received the Holy Spirit as all believers have now received. John specifically states, "*But **you have** an anointing from the Holy One, **and you all know***". (1 Jn. 2:20) John even goes so far as to state that the very reason he is bringing up this whole issue of the many antichrists preceding the final Antichrist is, "*because you **do know** it* [the truth]". (1 Jn. 2:21)

The second is that it was never clear from the outset that one of the Apostles would betray Christ; it was only understood when Christ announced it in the course of His earthly ministry. (Jn. 6:70) Although it is now obvious this final figure will provide some kind of spiritual resume with a Christian heritage so he will have "*went out from us*" (1 Jn. 2:19), we have huge amounts of unambiguous Scripture and Christ's own personal warnings concerning the coming of the final anti-king. Perhaps there is an ultimate divine revelation to confirm His Word in us, but it is certainly well-known in advance, and raises the question, "Why so much information up front if it is impossible to discern?"

And finally there is Christ's own statement in the Olivet Discourse provided in the midst of the warnings about the many antichrists to not be deceived by directly qualifying it all with, "*Behold, I have told you in advance*". (Mt. 24:25)

The parallel of Judas only being revealed in the very last hours of the First Coming by Christ personally may be illustrating how it will come late in the sequence of the Second Coming, rather than being literally replayed as a complete mystery even to the inner circle of believers. At the very least, with all the repeated scriptural returns to the seminal event of the Abomination of Desolation, there is simply too much Scripture plainly referring to and describing this event for it to escape the notice of any Holy Spirit-filled believer.

But the textual connection between this statement of John and Paul's designation that the Antichrist is also called "*the son of perdition*" promotes Judas to being the primary example of the Antichrist:

- Both are called by the same name.
- Both are not merely demonically possessed, but uniquely ***satanically*** possessed.
- Both are so clever and difficult to discern that they appear for a time to be members of the ranks of believers.
- Both are sinners intent only on enriching themselves.
- Both turn on Christ to not just overthrow Him, but turn Him over to the destructive hands of the opposition. They both lead a combined hostile Gentile and apostate Jewish force.
- Both end up in their own place, the inevitable destination for every lifestyle of sin.
- Both require the revelation of Christ to disclose to His followers their true nature and identity.

The more we can learn about Judas, the more we will learn about this final figure. [Again, for a complete study on the subject, *Shadows of the Beast* by Jacob Prasch is highly recommended.]

Revelation is going to open the floodgates, so to speak, to allow us to revisit many figures and events already documented in God's written Word which will parallel the anti-king and/or his anti-kingdom, but with Judas we are provided a sort of foretaste of what is to come. While they will all greatly contribute to our biblical portrait of the final figure, none will be more important than Judas.

The Spirit of Antichrist

> 21*I have not written to you because you do not know the truth, but because you do know it, and because no lie is of the truth.* 22*Who is the liar but the one who denies that Jesus is the Christ? This is the antichrist, the one who denies the Father and the Son.* 23*Whoever denies the Son does not have the Father; the one who confesses the Son has the Father also.*
>
> — 1 John 2:21-23

The ultimate distortion of the truth which both antichrist precursors and the ultimate fulfillment practices are the lies at the center of their false teaching concerning the Father-Son relationship. Because Mormonism says Jesus is the spirit-brother of Satan, we know that it is antichrist; because Jehovah's Witnesses call Jesus "a god", we know that it is antichrist; because Islam reduces Jesus at best to just another prophet, we know that it is antichrist. As it has been pointed out by many, the present Dome of the Rock on the Temple Mount in Jerusalem bears a quote from the Quran which basically asserts, "God has no son"; it is antichrist. Today, when people like Kenneth Copeland claim Jesus only "died spiritually" on the cross and that anyone could have done it, we know that it is actually antichrist. It has and continues to come in similar forms from every corner of religion, some kind of compromise proposed when it comes to the deity of Christ. It is the ultimate, visible betrayal of an unsaved figure, movement or religion when a form of this is asserted in one fashion or another.

*[1]Beloved, do not believe every spirit, but test the spirits to see whether they are from God, because many false prophets have gone out into the world. [2]By this you know the Spirit of God: every spirit that confesses that Jesus Christ has come in the flesh is from God; [3]and **every spirit that does not confess Jesus is not from God; this is the spirit of the antichrist, of which you have heard that it is coming, and now it is already in the world**.*

— 1 John 4:1-3

For the first time in Scripture, John informs us that it is not just that many antichrists will foreshadow the final, ultimate one, but that there is "*the spirit of the antichrist*" already at work, a sort of counterfeit of the Holy Spirit.

It is ironic that in the secular world there is broad acceptance of what is termed the *Zeitgeist*, or "the spirit of the age". Although non-believers would describe this as a nexus of social trends, politics and the culture of the time all combining to create things they might call "The Roaring Twenties" or "The Renaissance", to a certain degree even the unsaved are sensitive to the working of the spirit of antichrist.

While the world is not fully aware, however, Christians are commanded ***not*** to "*believe every spirit, but test the spirits to see whether they are from God*". We are responsible for sorting through it all by applying the truth of God's Word to that which, by Scripture's definition, is not just abandoning the truth, but substituting something else in its place. It is worth noting that the church at Ephesus was commended personally by Jesus because, "***you put to test*** *those who call themselves apostles, and they are not, and you found them to be false*". (Rev. 2:2)

The doctrinal litmus test for revealing what qualifies as antichrist not only includes "*every spirit that does not confess Jesus is from God*", but those who claim Jesus did not really come in the flesh. This is an extension of what John previously taught where anything attempting to misrepresent the Father-Son relationship is antichrist. One of the earliest false teachings which seems to perpetually recycle itself throughout the whole of history is that Jesus did not actually come in the flesh, or at the least He transitioned in and out of it. But once again it is the embodiment of the overall problem of forsaking the truth, and the one supreme truth which ultimately defines and/or separates the two sides which matter is the truth when it comes to the Person and working of Christ. This is the "*mystery of lawlessness*" which Paul identified "*is already at work*". (2 Th. 2:7)

*[4]You are from God, little children, and have overcome them; because greater is He who is in you than he who is in the world. [5]They are from the world; therefore they speak as from the world, and the world listens to them. [6]We are from God; he who knows God listens to us; he who is not from God does not listen to us. **By this we know the spirit of truth and the spirit of error**.*

— 1 John 4:4-6

This issue of how the two opposite sides process and handle the truth is expressed here as "*the spirit of truth*" versus "*the spirit of error*". This actually sums up the primary issue when it comes to how human beings will navigate the eschaton. Each side will be divided according to what it does with the truth of God's Word.

The Error of the Literal

> *[7]For many deceivers have gone out into the world, those who do not acknowledge Jesus Christ as coming in the flesh. This is the deceiver and the antichrist.*
> — 2 John 7

The chief false teaching which can always be counted on to divulge the presence of something antichrist at work is a challenge to the deity and person of Christ. Again, it is the ultimate truth which is applied one way or the other for those who are being saved and those who are not.

It is telling when a teacher, author or scholar insists not only that the Church will completely escape contact with the Antichrist, but crosses the line so as to accuse anyone with an interest in him as looking for the coming of the Antichrist instead of the coming of Christ; Scripture clearly indicates we are to do both, as they each have their own "*parousia*". But if the Church is not going to encounter him, why are there so many warnings, so much information given about him, and repeated scenarios tying him to the activities of apostasy, deception and persecution of believers? The Antichrist, and anyone deluded by the working of the spirit of antichrist, by definition, have already successfully deceived their adherents; it is only the faithful in Christ who can successfully put this information to use so as to not just identify him, but properly react to him when he comes and perpetrates these things against them.

But perhaps those taking up such a position should carefully consider in particular what the Apostle John is plainly stating, that the many antichrists are ***already*** here, that the spirit of antichrist is ***already*** at work, and this justifies his accompanying warning to believers (the original audience of his Epistle) of the impending arrival of the final expected figure. John is telling us that if we do not properly deal with what is ***already*** at work, we are not going to be equipped to handle that which we are about to experience. Was the Apostle John deceived into looking for the coming of the Antichrist instead of the coming of Christ? Likewise, was the Apostle Paul confused in specifying that before the *Episunagoge* can take place, the Antichrist must be revealed? The spirit of antichrist has achieved its zenith whenever it can get someone to ignore the Antichrist in the first place.

A Change in Perspective

The Apostle John changes our perspective. When studying God's prophetic Word, and even the Olivet Discourse in particular, we might process it all as something for the future, but not necessarily relevant to our own time and place. We might believe everything written and willing to accept by faith it will all come about exactly as specified, but with the qualifier, "***When*** this happens, this is what it will be like ***then***". John brings the future into every generation's present by resetting the context, "*Children, **it is** the last hour*". (1 Jn. 2:18) This is precisely what has been asserted by other New Testament authors:

> *[11]Do this, knowing the time, that **it is already the hour** for you to awaken from sleep; for now salvation is nearer to us than when we believed.*
> — Romans 13:11

> *[7]**The end of all things is near**; therefore, be of sound judgment and sober spirit for the purpose of prayer.*
> — 1 Peter 4:7

> [1]*God, after He spoke long ago to the fathers in the prophets in many portions and in many ways,* [2]***<u>in these last days</u>*** *has spoken to us in His Son, whom He appointed heir of all things, through whom also He made the world.*
> — Hebrews 1:1-2

And whereas we might study all that Scripture has to offer concerning the ultimate anti-king to come, our expectations are adjusted to understand that not only are there already many antichrists presently working, but that the spirit of antichrist is ***always*** at work. Yes, the last generation of believers will have to deal with the final figure, but ***every*** generation of ***every*** age is actually having to deal with him in not just the prefigurements of the many counterfeits, but the evolving Zeitgeist when the spirit of antichrist attempts to carry out his agenda in every current social, cultural and political climate. All of the attributes documented in Daniel are not solely limited to the final figure, nor mere shadows in his forerunners, but constantly at work over and over again until the arrival of that last in the series.

But with the key New Testament revelations from Paul that the Antichrist works "*in accord with the activity of Satan*" (2 Th. 2:9), the reference to "*the man of lawlessness/son of perdition*" (2 Th. 2:3), and John's revelation, "*They went out from us, but they were not really of us*" (1 Jn. 2:19), the importance of Judas as the primary foreshadowment of the Antichrist comes to the foreground. This is actually something which every generation prepares for by discerning and dealing with the working of the spirit of antichrist and the many counterfeits so that the final manifestation will be rightly recognized and handled by the final generation to come.

The New Testament Before Revelation

That which the New Testament Scriptures adds to the topic of the anti-king/anti-kingdom may not seem like much until we look at it all at once such as in the following list. However, it can be seen that it mainly reinforces the main features of the final figure already scripturally established, and this in itself is a testimony by the fact that Christ and the New Testament writers let stand all that Daniel provided, Christ Himself even encouraging Daniel be studied for its relevance to His own teaching in the Olivet Discourse. The basic timeline established in Daniel and affirmed by Christ in the Olivet Discourse is again substantiated and will aid greatly when Revelation finally becomes available.

- A series of events in the character of "*birth pangs*" will precede him. (Mt. 24:4-8)
- The Church will experience a time of unprecedented deception, apostasy, and persecution immediately preceding his public revealing. (Mt. 24:9-14)
- There will be "*false Christs and false prophets*" (Mt. 24:24) and many who come in the name of Christ. (Mt. 24:5)
- "*...do not believe every spirit, but test the spirits to see whether they are from God, because many false prophets have gone out into the world.*" (1 Jn. 4:1)
- "*...many deceivers have gone out into the world, those who do not acknowledge Jesus Christ as coming in the flesh. This is the deceiver and the antichrist.*" (2 Jn. 7)
- "*...every spirit that does not confess Jesus i snot from God; this is the spirit of the antichrist, of which you have heard that it is coming, and now it is already in the world.*" (1 Jn. 4:3)
- "*...we know the spirit of truth and the spirit of error.*" (1 Jn. 4:6)

- "*...it is the last hour*", and "*antichrist is coming*". (1 Jn. 2:18a)
- "*...even now many antichrist have appeared; from this we know that it is the last hour.*" (1 Jn. 2:18b)
- "*They went out from us, but they were not really of us; for if they had been of us, they would have remained with us; but they went out, so that it would be shown that they are not of us.*" (1 Jn. 2:19)
- But we "*know*" who these are because, we "*have an anointing from the Holy One*". (1 Jn. 2:20)
- "*Who is the liar but the one who denies that Jesus is the Christ? This is the antichrist, the one who denies the Father and the Son*". (1 Jn. 2:22)
- The "*apostasy comes first*", and then "*the man of lawlessness is revealed, the son of destruction*". (2 Th. 2:3)
- Jerusalem will be surrounded by armies (Lk. 21:20), the Abomination of Desolation will take place, and those in Israel will flee. (Mt. 24:15-20)
- The anti-king "*opposes and exalts himself above every so-called god or object of worship*". (2 Th. 2:4)
- The anti-king proves this when "*he takes his seat in the temple of God, displaying himself as being God*". (2 Th. 2:4)
- Although "*the mystery of lawlessness is already at work*", the Abomination of Desolation takes place when "*he who now restrains...is taken out of the way*". (2 Th. 2:7)
- The anti-king's "*coming is in accord with the activity of Satan, with all power and signs and false wonders*". (2 Th. 2:9)
- This will be followed by the unprecedented worldwide phenomenon of "*great tribulation*" (Mt. 24:21) which, "*for the sake of the elect, those days will be cut short*". (Mt. 24:22)
- But for unbelievers, the satanically animated anti-king is coming "*with all deception of wickedness for those who perish*" upon whom "*God will send a deluding influence so that they will believe what is false*". (2 Th. 2:10-11)
- The biblical signs of the onset of "*the day of the Lord*" will immediately accompany the *Harpazo* of the Church. (Mt. 24:29-31)
- The *Harpazo* is both the resurrection of those asleep in the Lord and those alive at the time of this event. (1 Th. 4:15-17)
- Believers will not be overtaken by "*the day of the Lord*". (1 Th. 5:1-10)
- "*We know that we are of God, and that the whole world lies in the power of the evil one.*" (1 Jn. 4:19)

13 ❖ The Last Vision

No doubt we can now see the difference of approaching this last vision when first armed with the context of the visions and teachings which came before it. If we maintain as our priority for interpreting God's Word to first and foremost rely on God's Word itself, we see it in the illumination of the whole of God's already given Word and not as something set apart with its own authority. This is much more in the character of the 1st century eyes which first read Revelation. To be sure, it may be categorized as apocalyptic literature, but it is still integrated into the whole of God's Word and cannot be treated as standing apart from it.

The Prophet Daniel and the Apostle John, as the conduits of the first and last visions, are very similar bookends with much in common serving to bring the whole of God's prophetic Word into an integrated, final portrait. Each given portion was sufficient for that generation and time and yet is further illuminated by the next unveiling. But there are remarkable similarities in both the first and last visions:

- Daniel lives at a transition point in Israel's history and receives a divine vision providing God's entire plan not just for Israel, but for the world; John is the last "hinge" on the door in the Church's transition from the original Church to its future generations who receives a divine vision providing God's plan not just for the Church, but for the world.
- Daniel's visions begin with the revelation of an anti-king whose worldly attractiveness is comprised of various kingdoms, all of which will ultimately give way to the True King and His kingdom; John's vision reveals the anti-king's true spiritual character as a beast and his equally unattractive kingdom in its final hours before giving way to the True King and His kingdom.
- Daniel's visions are defined by the milestones and activities of the anti-king and anti-kingdom; John's vision is defined by the milestones and activities of the beast and his final kingdom.
- Daniel's visions begin with the literal, historical Babylon; John's vision ends with the recapitulation of "*Babylon the Great*".
- Both of their visions feature the battle which the anti-king wages against God's people, his battles with the kingdoms of the earth, and his ultimate battle with God.

These and many other comparisons which we could continue making show that there is a single, consistent, yet overall message provided in God's Word which cannot be properly understood by studying each book in isolation from each other. It is God's "Word"—***singular***, and it has been purposely rolled out in a progression properly fitted together. This is provided not just for the benefit of deriving the right result for a very deep and intricate plan, but to maintain something relevant for each generation and historical period along the way. It is a test of faith for every historical age, but the ultimate test of faith for the final one to come.

Just as an attempt to explain American culture and society in the 21st century without understanding the history of the United States leading up to it produces obviously flawed results, so is isolating portions of God's prophetic Word, or worse, treating the last to come as if it supersedes and alters all which came before. But we actually witness this all the time in the secular media when someone insists that a modern issue, such as the right to an abortion or for trans-gender bathrooms, is presented as something the founding fathers and framers of the Constitution intended from the very beginning. The last is used to reinterpret the first in a similar example of how the mishandling of God's Word takes place in the current environment.

The Combined, Global View

Each of the three presentations in Daniel, the Olivet Discourse and Revelation are not limited to the final week of years, but first provide a preface of events and conditions before concluding in Daniel's 70th Week. The text in each case does not always employ identical terms because each is based on a different perspective. In a very broad sense, think of how an eyewitness of the same thing who is in a helicopter would differ in their description from that of a pedestrian down on a street corner. The two points of view may share some commonalities, but just because some things are described with terms unique to their respective positions does not make what they witnessed two different events.

Just as the visions to Nebuchadnezzar (Dan.2) and then Daniel (Dan. 7) were two views of the same thing—first the worldly view of an attractive idol in the image of a man versus the beasts they truly are in God's estimation, Daniel's 70th Week is likewise revisited in a similar fashion for both the Olivet Discourse and Revelation. The terms employed are different but certainly bear a relationship so as to connect these three viewpoints together while maintaining their distinct perspective. This is because Daniel is the primary view provided for Israel; the Olivet Discourse is the primary view accorded to the Church. What appears at first as possibly being "different" is actually the result of a change of viewpoint.

Daniel provides a very long introductory period of specific world kingdoms in imitation of a final one to come, which is ultimately narrowed down to its activities in the 70th Week. From Israel's perspective, the milestones are the covenant and the Abomination of Desolation but with a greater emphasis on the latter half of that final week of years. From Israel's frame of reference, there is a gap between the 69th and 70th weeks which we know to correspond to the Church Age which Peter says ends with the onset of "*the day of the Lord*" (Acts 2:16-20) and per Paul concludes with the attainment of "*the fullness of the Gentiles*". (Rom. 11:25)

Christ and the New Testament writers speak of an overall organization of "*the present age*" (or "*this age*"), "*the end of the age*", and "*the age to come*". Current history will yield to a longer period of transition—"*the end of the age*", which is characterized as "*birth pangs*" of activity coming more frequently and powerfully together in concentric waves until, from the Church's perspective, it coalesces around the Abomination of Desolation in that final week of years. The

Church is much more involved in the first half of the 70th Week with its removal shortly after the overall halfway point.

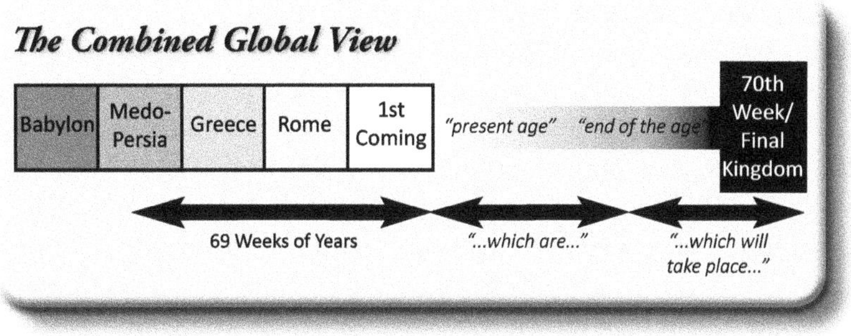

Revelation expresses its overall structure in Revelation 1:19 as:

- "*...these things which you have seen*" (Rev. 1)
- "*...the things which are*" (Rev. 2-3)
- "*...the things which will take place after these things*" (Rev. 4-22)

In Revelation's presentation, which combines the views of both Israel and the Church, the longer period leading up to the final week of years characterized as "*the things which are*" is played out in the letters to the seven churches, which are not just seven literal churches at the time Revelation was first published, but also characterize seven subsequent overlapping periods of Church history leading into Daniel's 70th Week. (Israel's perspective in Daniel is a much larger slice of history as Israel is around both before and after the Church, but the Church is only present from the Day of Pentecost until the Rapture.) Revelation 4 makes the distinction by designating, "*After these things*" so as to provide the transition from the longer, more general period to the finite conclusive sequence of the very end. In contrast to both Daniel and the Olivet Discourse, Revelation then provides more detail as to what comes after for everyone in the Millennial Kingdom, Final Judgment, and eternity to come.

Just as Judaism continued for a time in parallel to the Church while there was still a Temple before its removal from Israel into the Diaspora, a similar transition in reverse is experienced again during the final week of years. A third Tribulational Temple provides for a time this same kind of parallel working but culminating this time is the Church's removal and the flight of Israel when the betrayal of the covenant by way of the Abomination of Desolation takes place in that facility. In the First Coming Israel was removed spiritually, so to speak, in the Second Coming it is the Church who is removed literally. Israel's point of view provided in Daniel has a gap between the 69th and 70th weeks because of the Church Age, while the Church's view in the Olivet Discourse has a gap between "*great tribulation*" and the Millennial Reign because it is exempted from "*the day of the Lord*" in between.

The Same Focused View

Through Daniel is established the basic sequence of God's plan which revealed a series of prefiguring antichrist kings and kingdoms culminating in a final week of years with the ultimate Antichrist and his final kingdom. While the whole world will become involved and affected, it is primarily from the viewpoint of Israel which these things are first presented. Its beginning is defined by a covenant between the Antichrist and Israel, Jerusalem and its Temple become the focal point with the midway point's milestone of the Abomination of Desolation, and the latter half from that point on is given the most attention as his 3-1/2 year worldwide reign of destruction ends with his own shattering at the hands of the Messiah.

In the Olivet Discourse, and the supporting teachings of the New Testament writers, the same plan is presented from the viewpoint of the Church. For the Body of Christ, who never enters into a formal arrangement as does Israel, the beginning is a series of "*birth pangs*" which coalesce around the same midway milestone of the Abomination of Desolation. In the Church's case, however, their time under the formal reign of that final 3-1/2 years is cut short with its removal, and God's focus returns to Israel. The Olivet Discourse is really Daniel's 70th Week presented from the viewpoint of the Church, which explains why it skips "*the day of the Lord*"—that time devoted to the pouring out of God's wrath which characterizes most of the final 3-1/2 years, and picks up with the Millennial Kingdom. Everything which Jesus and Paul provide in their rendering of the final week of years is hyper-focused on the Church and those things which it will experience.

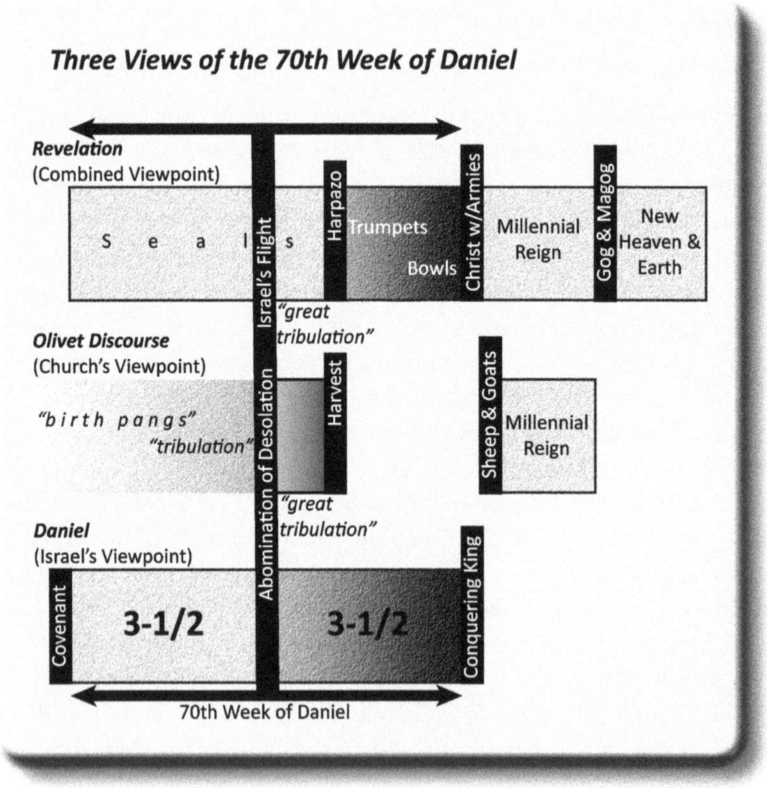

In Revelation, we are presented with this final sequence for ***both*** Israel and the Church. The opening text is highly concentrated on the Church until their removal between the 6th and 7th Seals. Just prior to this event a literal sealing of ethnic Jews devoted to Christ marks the transition in the remaining text back to Israel in the wake of the removal of "*the ones who come out of the great tribulation*". (Rev. 7:14) The lateral activities of the Antichrist as he rises to full power are provided in the Seals leading up to the Church's removal when Israel, realizing its betrayal at the hands of that final figure, flees at the midway point in parallel to what was described in the Olivet Discourse as a feature of the Abomination of Desolation.

Corollary Scriptures speak of this as a time when Israel's literal flight is also a spiritual flight to the Messiah. The Trumpet and Bowl judgments disclose what remains to be experienced by the kingdom of Antichrist until Christ's return and establishment of the Millennial Kingdom.

Daniel, the Olivet Discourse/New Testament, and Revelation are not three separate things, but one and the same presented from alternative viewpoints: Israel's, the Church's, then both. They have various intersecting points which merge into a greater, overall picture rather than stand on their own individually. Daniel is provided the answer of what will ultimately happen to Israel, the Olivet Discourse which is initiated by questions from a group of Apostles provides the answer of what will ultimately happen to the Church, and finally through the Apostle John is provided a supplement of what happens to everyone. But rather than being separate and unique from each other, they are actually a progressive revelation of the final working of God's plan.

Without first understanding the fundamental structure established in Daniel and affirmed in the Olivet Discourse, a proper understanding of Revelation is not possible. In fact, it is this author's contention that most of the time it is this tendency to handle them separately which produces such varied opinions when it comes to God's prophetic Word.

> *19So **we have the prophetic word made more sure**, to which you do well to pay attention as to a lamp shining in a dark place, until the day dawns and the morning star arises in your hearts. 20But know this first of all, that no prophecy of Scripture is a matter of one's own interpretation, 21for no prophecy was ever made by an act of human will, but men moved by the Holy Spirit spoke from God.*
> — 2 Peter 1:19-21

The Early Work of the Antichrist

While both Daniel and Revelation will be more heavily weighted to what takes place in the latter half of Daniel's 70th Week, both show the Antichrist working from the very beginning of the final week of years. In Daniel the metaphorical starter's pistol for the 70th Week is the Antichrist-initiated covenant with Israel which comes to a definitive end with the Abomination of Desolation at the halfway point.

> *27"And he will make a firm covenant with the many for one week, but in the middle of the week he will put a stop to sacrifice and grain offering; and on the wing of abominations will come one who makes desolate, even until a complete destruction, one that is decreed, is poured out on the one who makes desolate."*
> — Daniel 9:27

Related texts in Daniel will describe how this figure uses this strategy of making agreements with other nations as well, and when necessary, using outright force. Whether by deception and enticement or persecution and military force, the Antichrist, in the same manner employed by Imperial Rome, will bring everyone under his control as necessary. The greater focus is on the second half of the 70th Week beginning with the pinnacle public event of the Abomination of Desolation with much more detail of activities to follow, but he is nonetheless active in what appears to be the preparatory stage of his rise to power. This is actually the way in which the main activities are initiated in Revelation.

This is true of Christ in the First Coming. Although Scripture will be almost entirely devoted to His 3-1/2 year public ministry commencing with His baptism, there are still references to the first 30 years of His life. 14% of all the Old Testament prophecies about His First Coming were fulfilled in those decades leading up to his public ministry. There were visible signs at His birth not only with the what the Magi witnessed but the angelic appearance to the shepherds. Likewise the Antichrist is clearly documented as having appeared with the covenant at the very beginning, but it is the final 3-1/2 year public reign which is most emphasized.

The Pre-Counterfeit

> *[1]Then I saw when the Lamb broke one of the seven seals, and I heard one of the four living creatures saying as with a voice of thunder, "Come." [2]I looked, and behold, a white horse, and he who sat on it had a bow; and a crown was given to him, and he went out conquering and to conquer.*
> — Revelation 6:1-2

This beginning with a figure on a white horse is best understood when compared to Christ to come at the very close of the 70th Week:

> *[11]And I saw heaven opened, and behold, a white horse, and He who sat on it is called Faithful and True, and in righteousness He judges and wages war. [12]His eyes are a flame of fire, and on His head are many diadems; and He has a name written on Him which no one knows except Himself. [13]He is clothed with a robe dipped in blood, and His name is called The Word of God. [14]And the armies which are in heaven, clothed in fine linen, white and clean, were following Him on white horses. [15]From His mouth comes a sharp sword, so that with it He may strike down the nations, and He will rule them with a rod of iron; and He treads the wine press of the fierce wrath of God, the Almighty. [16]And on His robe and on His thigh He has a name written, "KING OF KINGS, AND LORD OF LORDS."*
> — Revelation 19:11-16

In modern English the prefix "anti" is attached to anything and everything which someone becomes opposed to, but its biblical usage is rooted in the original English rendering "in place of". This may be the most important aspect of his character which brings clarity to his true motives, that just as Satan wants to take the place of God, his protégé seeks in every way possible to take the place of Christ. In what can only be described as a pre-counterfeit of the way Christ will ultimately come with his armies on His white horse, the Antichrist attempts a preemptive entrance as a lookalike with a satanic agenda.

➤ *"a white horse"*	➤ *"a white horse"*
➤ *"had a bow"*	➤ *"From His mouth comes a sharp sword"*
➤ *"a crown was given to him"*	➤ *"on His head are many diadems"*
➤ *"he went out conquering and to conquer"*	➤ *"in righteousness He judges and wages war"*

Daniel not only documents the anti-king's political and military strategies of conquest, but repeatedly emphasizes his use of a false peace and prosperity which in the character of the Roman Empire was used to bring many nations and city-states under their rule. A false "Prince of Peace" kicks things off which seems to speak of his personal campaign to rise to power—"*he went out conquering and to conquer*".

Each of the kingdoms Daniel is told foreshadow the final one experienced a time of growing up in the shadows until a defining moment when they took complete control. Along the way smaller entities were consumed until each attained the size and scope to engulf the larger whole, known world of their time. Additional texts to come in Revelation will provide more detail as to how the anti-kingdom operates and comes to be which clearly reference time needed for its rise to prominence first through a confederation of ten kingdoms, and then in the course of further subduing three of them before arriving at the final configuration.

It Escalates

> 3*When He broke the second seal, I heard the second living creature saying, "Come."* 4*And another, a red horse, went out; and to him who sat on it, it was granted to take peace from the earth, and that men would slay one another; and a great sword was given to him.*
>
> — Revelation 6:3-4

The nature of the conflict in the Antichrist's initial foray is his personal campaign of "*conquering and to conquer*". This is an escalation of conflict assigned to a sort of follow-on frenzy, "*that* ***men*** *should slay one another*". The Seals perfectly mirror the "*birth pangs*" of the Olivet Discourse:

> 5*"For many will come in My name, saying, 'I am the Christ,' and will mislead many.* 6*You will be hearing of wars and rumors of wars. See that you are not frightened, for those things must take place, but that is not yet the end.* 7*For nation will rise against nation, and kingdom against kingdom, and in various places there will be famines and earthquakes.* 8*But all these things are merely the beginning of birth pangs.*
>
> — Matthew 24:5-8

Whereas each birth pang is an increasingly more powerful series of waves occurring ever more frequently, each seems to culminate in a corresponding Seal. Just as in an actual birth the previous pangs, although painful at the time, are nowhere near what is experienced in the course of the actual final event, so the Seal judgments are an ultimate fulfillment of the "*birth pangs*" in providing a final event unprecedented in their scope and degree of worldwide effect. We are told in Revelation 6:8 that the casualties from the Seal judgments alone will attain to at least "*a fourth of the earth*". If this occurred today, this would produce net global casualties in the neighborhood of 2 billion. Considering that the worst historical experience of loss in World War II was approximately 300 million, this speaks of the final event being 7 times that of the most powerful ever to come before it.

The Same Kind of Beginning

Although obviously providing much more text on the subject, Revelation provides in an expanded way the same basic, underlying structure of both Daniel and the Olivet Discourse. Although there is early mention of the activities of the Antichrist as he rises to prominence, the greater emphasis will be devoted to the latter half of Daniel's 70th Week when his achievements have attained full, worldwide stature. In the case of what is spoken of in Revelation, all the foreshadowing precursors which taught something of what it will ultimately be like give way to the reality of how unprecedented the final fulfillment truly is. There have been ***many*** wars, but nothing like that which he wages; there have been ***many*** antichrists, but nothing like this final one; there have been ***many*** earthly disturbances both manmade and in nature, but none like those unleashed in the culmination of the Seals. And just prior to his arrival, all previous persecutions of God's people combined will not equal the final one described in the Olivet Discourse which culminates in the 5th Seal.

Revelation is not an entirely new storyline, but a more detailed perspective of what has already been revealed. As a rough analogy, it is like visiting Washington, D.C. from a tour guide's overview, to attending a lecture on the founding fathers' intentions, to ultimately studying the architectural plans. Each successive level not only provides a different perspective and viewpoint, but employs an alternative yet corresponding vocabulary. Just because they each describe the Capitol Building with the differing verbiage of their particular point of view does not mean there must be three different or unique facilities. It is just that the terms and nomenclatures conform to their respective vistas. The tour guide provides a very general description, a study of the founders' intentions takes the discussion to a different level of detail in order to incorporate the philosophical viewpoint, but the descriptions from an architectural point of view become much more technical and detailed in ways not intrinsic to the previous perspectives. They can still be taken together as describing the same thing provided one recognizes where their respective vocabularies intersect.

Overall, Revelation provides a more detailed view first for the primary time of participation of the Church up through Revelation 7 with the first six Seals, and then with its removal (Rev. 7:9-17) provides more granular detail for Israel. Whereas Daniel is oriented toward God's people of the Old Covenant, and the Olivet Discourse toward God's people of the New Covenant, Revelation embraces both.

It may be helpful to notice that when it comes to God's progressive revelation, that it usually begins simplistically with the greatest detail supplied in the later rounds. The first vision of Daniel 2 was the simplest of an image of a man composed of various metals, but with each subsequent vision the focus not only narrowed but yielded increasingly specific details. Likewise, Revelation functions the same way provided we have established the foundation provided in all which came before the last book of the canon of Scripture.

14 ❖ The Three Woes

[13]Then I looked, and I heard an eagle flying in midheaven, saying with a loud voice, "Woe, woe, woe to those who dwell on the earth, because of the remaining blasts of the trumpet of the three angels who are about to sound!"
— Revelation 8:13

Once everyone saw Christ in the process of the execution of the Episunagoge between the 6th and 7th Seals in Revelation 7:9-17, things are no longer completely hidden from earthly view by taking place exclusively in the spiritual realm. From that point on, many things such as these are openly displayed in the earthly arena since the choice for Christ or Satan has essentially been completed. The prophetic veil—the "*apokalupsis*", is well on its way to being fully lifted. Likewise we are approaching a section of Revelation which serves as a sort of "flashback" to explain some of the things which have been taking place in parallel to the Seals and Trumpets which will continue laterally with the final sequence of the Bowls, and which mainly involve the anti-king and his anti-kingdom. In order to appreciate how this works, we need to understand the sequence of the three woes in providing a continuation of a sequential time line while setting up a parallel explanation of the rise and reign of the final figure and his domain. Although Revelation 13 may be devoted to the final beast, it must be understood within the proper overall context of the Scripture within which it is purposely positioned. There is much about the rise of the final figure in the preceding chapters, and a continuation of his kingdom's antics following.

The Preface of the Seals

For a more in-depth treatment of the correlation between the "*birth pangs*" of the Olivet Discourse and their culmination in the Seals of Revelation 6-7, the reader is again directed to the author's previous book, *And THEN The End Will Come*. But just because of the fact that the whole of the Seven Trumpets and Seven Bowls are actually entirely comprised of the very last 7th Seal, it is necessary to briefly revisit what has led up to the Trumpet judgments.

Since the Church's removal is specified between the 6th and 7th Seals in Revelation 7, we might believe that the contents of the chapters following the *Harpazo* means that the Church will be exempt from all that is still to come. While this may be true of the final sequential judgments of God's wrath as expressed in the Trumpets and Bowls, we will be shown how the antichrist and "*Babylon the Great*" have been present and working in parallel since the 1st Seal while the Church is still present.

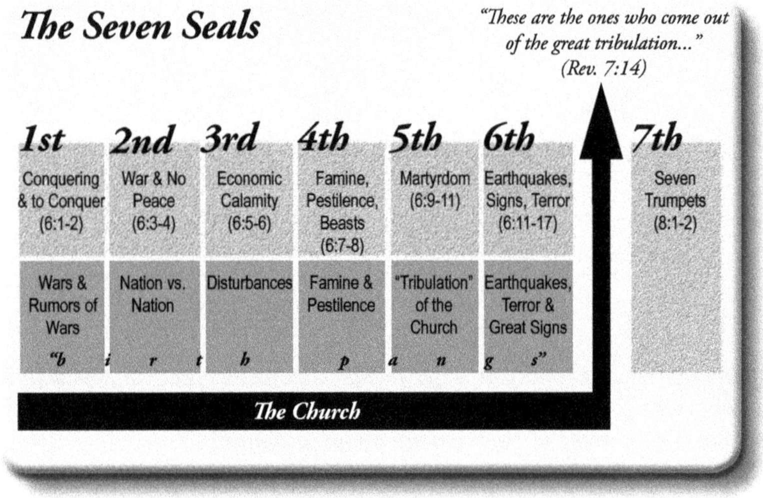

Each item Jesus identifies in the Olivet Discourse as a member of the "*birth pangs*" corresponds to an ultimate, final fulfillment in a counterpart Seal. Whereas the Seals are "judgments" which everyone must endure, the removal of the Church coincides with the escalation to God's "wrath" in the Trumpets and Bowls, which together comprise the entire 7th Seal. Believers and the Church are stipulated by God's Word to undergo judgment along with the rest of the world, but are specifically exempt from His wrath.

> [17]*For **it is time for judgment to begin with the household of God**; and if it begins with us first, what will be the outcome for those who do not obey the gospel of God?*
> — 1 Peter 4:17

> [8]*But God demonstrates His own love toward us, in that while we were yet sinners, Christ died for us.* [9]*Much more then, having now been justified by His blood, **we shall be saved from the wrath of God** through Him.*
> — Romans 5:8-9

This final time of the outpouring of God's wrath is prolifically spoken of in Scripture as "*the day of the Lord*". (Is. 13:6, 9; Eze. 13:5; 30:5; Joel 1:15; 3:1, 14; Amos 5:18, 20; Ob. 15; Zeph. 1:7, 14; 1 Co. 5:5; 1 Th. 5:2; 2 Th. 2:2) The signs of the 6th Seal and those of the corresponding "*birth pangs*" in the Olivet Discourse are referenced over and over again in Scripture as the accompanying signs which both inaugurate and characterize the final phase of the End Times known as "*the day of the Lord*".

So when we arrive at the Church's removal on the cusp of the 7th Seal, it would be natural to conclude that whatever comes after in the book of Revelation is not going to be experienced by the Church, that at most it is probably provided because this will be a time when God's focus returns to Israel. However, we know that it is the Antichrist who pre-counterfeits Christ in the very 1st Seal as the white horseman, which means he is obviously present and working from the very beginning in some capacity. But although the Church may not personally experience the contents of the Seven Trumpets and Seven Bowls, a textual mechanism is going to be employed within Revelation 9-11 to show how Revelation 12-18 provides the rise and working of the anti-king/anti-kingdom in parallel to the entire sequence of Revelation as expressed in the Seals, Trumpets and Bowls which ***is*** pertinent to the pre-Rapture Church.

The First Four Trumpets

7The first sounded, and there came hail and fire, mixed with blood, and they were thrown to the earth; and a third of the earth was burned up, and a third of the trees were burned up, and all the green grass was burned up. *— Rev. 8:7*	*8The second angel sounded, and something like a great mountain burning with fire was thrown into the sea; and a third of the sea became blood, 9and a third of the creatures which were in the sea and had life, died; and a third of the ships were destroyed.* *— Rev. 8:8-9*	*10The third angel sounded, and a great star fell from heaven, burning like a torch, and it fell on a third of the rivers and on the springs of waters. 11The name of the star is called Wormwood; and a third of the waters became wormwood, and many men died from the waters, because they were made bitter.* *— Rev. 8:10-11*	*12The fourth angel sounded, and a third of the sun and a third of the moon and a third of the stars were struck, so that a third of them would be darkened and the day would not shine for a third of it, and the night in the same way.* *— Rev. 8:12*

In a broad parallel to the ten plagues documented in the Exodus Narrative, these four trumpet judgments produce ten effects of their own:

- "*...a third of **the earth** was burned up...*" (v.7)
- "*...a third of **the trees** were burned up...*" (v.7)
- "*...all **the green grass** was burned up.*" (v.7)
- "*...a third of **the sea** became blood...*" (v.8)
- "*...a third of **creatures** which were in the sea and had life, died...*" (v.9)
- "*...a third of the **ships** were destroyed.*" (v.9)
- "*...a third of **the rivers and on the springs of waters**.*" (v.10)
- "*...a third of **the sun**...struck...*" (v.12)
- "*...a third of **the moon**...struck...*" (v.12)
- "*...a third of **the stars** were struck...*" (v.12)

Whereas the Seals were initiated in heaven out of direct sight and made visible with the representations of human and earthly agency in the guise of the Four Horsemen at the behest of the "*living beings*", the Trumpets are each announced by something coming down directly out of heaven or in the most dramatic of changes in the heavens themselves.

In the 1st and 2nd Trumpets, something is "*thrown*"—that is, "*ballo*" (Strong's #906), in the 3rd Trumpet something "*fell*"—that is, "*pipto*" (Strong's #4098), and in the 4th Trumpet was "*struck*"—that is, "*pleso*" (Strong's #4141). "*Ballo*", or to "throw" is the same thing God does to Satan when he is "***thrown** down to the earth*" (Rev. 12:13) and "***thrown** into the lake of fire*". (Rev. 20:14) "*Pipto*", or "to fall", is often used in the New Testament to describe a person or thing falling from a higher to lower place. "*Pleso*", or "struck", is most often used in the New Testament to invoke a plague or to afflict with disease, calamity or evil; all of which are connected to a direct, divine action. Although we know God certainly can use earthly things to act on His behalf, such as nuclear or technologically advanced weaponry, the verbs used in each instance specify that the source is still the hand of God.

But the last three Trumpets are called out in a special way that is different from the first four which is delineated by an interim, visible sign between the 4th and 5th Trumpets:

> [13]*Then I looked, and I heard an eagle flying in midheaven, saying with a loud voice, "Woe, woe, woe to those who dwell on the earth, because of* ***the remaining blasts of the trumpet of the three angels*** *who are about to sound!"*
> — Revelation 8:13

While these three "woes" are going to coincide with each of the Trumpets to follow in the sequence, they are also going to show that the Antichrist has not just been working in parallel to the Seals and Trumpets, but will continue to do so in the final sequence of the Bowls to come until the very end.

What is a "Woe"?

The pronouncement of each of the three "*woes*" ("*omai*", Strong's #3759) is best understood when looking at how Jesus used the term in the course of His earthly ministry. He pronounced "*Woe to you*" on the unrepentant cities of Chorazin, Bethsaida and Capernaum, (Mt. 11:20-24), declaring that the consequences for His "*woe*" would be experienced in "*the day of judgment*" because these places were where "*most of His miracles were done*", and yet "*they did not repent*". In other words, like that which takes place in Revelation, the signs are rejected, unbelief continues, and Jesus further specifies the ultimate consequence will be, "*You will descend to Hades*". (Mt. 11:23) These three woes issued by Christ against individual cities are replayed on a global scale in the eagle's woes announced to the entire world.

Jesus pronounces a series of eight woes against the scribes and Pharisees in Matthew 23:13-33, repeatedly accompanied with the charge of being hypocrites with corroborating proofs provided in each instance by their behavior. The inevitable consequences of their actions is summed up in the rhetorical question, "*You serpents, you brood of vipers, how will you escape the sentence of hell?*" (Mt. 23:33) (This episode is also recorded in Luke 11:37-54.)

But perhaps most telling of all is when Jesus pronounced a woe upon Judas:

> [21]*"For the Son of Man is to go just as it is written of Him; but* ***woe to that man*** *by whom the Son of Man is betrayed! It would have been good for that man if he had not been born."*
> —Mark 14:21

Jesus never employs a "woe" as a warning to repent or in the course of an offer for reconciliation, but solely to pronounce judgment where all that is left is God's wrath leading to the eternal destination of hell. These three woes in the midst of the Trumpets sequence is very strong textual evidence that what is taking place is God's wrath, which is why the Church has been removed previous to this, and why there is never any repentance on the part of the remaining "earth dwellers". In the same way Jesus pronounced woes on individual cities and persons, so these are divinely applied to the remaining world at large.

Three Milestones

At the conclusion of the text describing the 5th Trumpet of a demon horde which torments those without God's mark for five months (Rev. 9:1-11), the first "*woe*" is pronounced:

> [12]*The first woe is past; behold, two woes are still coming after these things.*
> — Revelation 9:12

At the conclusion of the 6th Seal of an enormous earthly army who "*would kill a third of mankind*" (Rev. 9:13-19), the text continues ***without*** pausing for one of the woes. It continues on through a heavenly interlude in Revelation 10 and then proceeds into Revelation 11 to return to earthly events in the activities of the Two Witnesses. It is only upon the completion of the Two Witnesses' mission when we are presented with the "*second woe*":

> [14]*The second woe is past; behold, the third woe is coming quickly.*
> — Revelation 11:14

The placement and timing of this second woe is very important because it is anchored to the death and resurrection of the Two Witnesses. (Rev. 11:11-13) Because each "woe" is assigned to each of the final three Trumpets, this means that the death and resurrection of the Two Witnesses is included as part of the 6th Trumpet.

These two figures are specified to operate for "*twelve hundred and sixty days*"—that is, one of the biblical references to 3-1/2 lunar years. By designating that their resurrection and rapture takes place between the 6th and 7th Trumpets by assigning it as part of the "*second woe*", this means they have been fully functioning in their public ministry in parallel to all that has been taking place for the preceding 3-1/2 years. Although they may have never been mentioned in Scripture until this point in the book of Revelation, they have nonetheless been active long prior in parallel to what has been taking place. Their public visibility would have spanned the preceding 3-1/2 lunar years before ending at this point.

FYI: This is also categorical textual proof refuting the notion put forth by so many that the Two Witnesses lead some kind of worldwide revival, or perhaps are spiritual guides of those who yet remain within ethnic Israel. This is completely incompatible with their function as a "*woe*"—that is, a curse, which ***is*** precisely compatible with what ***is*** stated about them, "*these two prophets* ***tormented*** *those who dwell on the earth*". (Rev. 11:10) It also refutes the presupposition that one of them must be the promised return of Elijah, because Jesus Himself stipulated, "*Elijah is coming and will* ***restore*** *all things*" (Mt. 17:11); again, a completely incompatible mission with that of the Two Witnesses. [For an in-depth treatment of this subject, see the author's previous book, *Elijah To Come*.]

This is especially important when it comes to our discussion of the Antichrist, because among other things, the Two Witnesses have come into conflict with the beast who has therefore been active in parallel to them:

> [7]*When they have finished their testimony, the beast that comes up out of the abyss will make war with them, and overcome them and kill them.*
> — Revelation 11:7

Each of the three woes is assigned by the eagle to the three remaining Trumpets, so the third is applied to the very next to come in the following verse, "*Then the seventh angel sounded*" (Rev. 11:15)—that is, the 7th Trumpet.

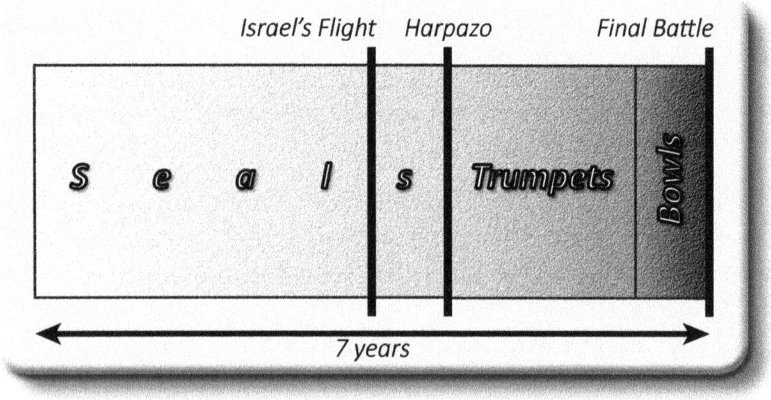

The more important point for us is that there is an obvious sequence in Revelation which follows the three sets of Seals, Trumpets and Bowls. Although they do not deviate from this order, it appears that they are not evenly spread out over Daniel's 70th Week. In fact, they seem to increase exponentially in the same way a snowball picks up speed as it progresses down the mountainside, with the Bowls taking place in the most compressed time span.

It is interesting to note that the introduction of the Two Witnesses is immediately prefaced by a reference to the Temple:

> *[1]Then there was given me a measuring rod like a staff; and someone said, "Get up and measure the temple of God and the altar, and those who worship in it. [2]Leave out the court which is outside the temple and do not measure it, for it has been given to the nations; and they will tread under foot the holy city for forty-two months.*
> — Revelation 11:1-2

In the Olivet Discourse, it is the Temple which is not just the focus for the anticipated Abomination of Desolation (Mt. 24:15), but is accompanied by "*Jerusalem surrounded by armies*". (Lk. 21:20) Daniel confirms that this event is both accompanied and effected with the assistance of the Antichrist's forces:

> *[31]"Forces from him will arise, desecrate the sanctuary fortress, and do away with the regular sacrifice. And they will set up the abomination of desolation.*
> — Daniel 11:31

In other words, there is a confluence at the Abomination of Desolation also involving armies descending on Jerusalem, the Antichrist publicly effecting his desecration with their participation, and the reaction of Israel by its flight into the wilderness which provides a solid, scriptural parallel attachment to that which is provided in Daniel, the Olivet Discourse, and Revelation to anchor them to the midway point of Daniel's 70th Week.

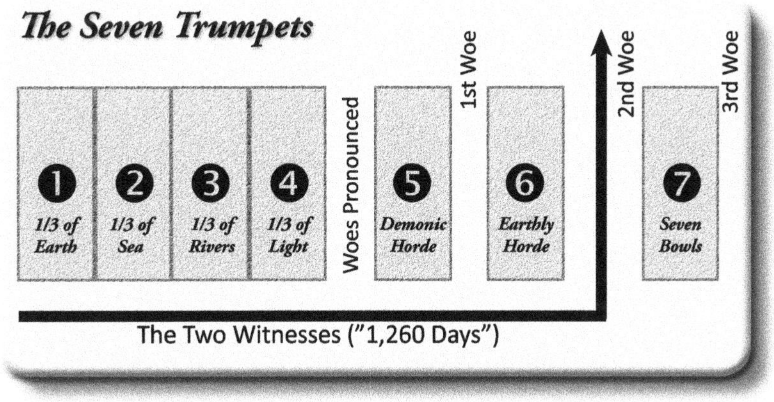

This textual mechanism of showing the parallel background activities of the Two Witnesses is going to temporarily give way to further corollary workings of Satan and Antichrist in Revelation 10-13 before returning to the overall time line with the Seven Bowls as the substance of the 7th Trumpet. We glimpsed the Antichrist from the outset in the 1st Seal as the white horseman, we have been shown that he has been at work during the course of the Trumpets by his interaction with the Two Witnesses, and now we will be provided his entire background working for the whole of Daniel's 70th Week in the next few chapters of Revelation before returning to the final countdown of the apocalypse in the Bowls.

15 ❖ Revelation 12: The Dragon

*...you saw the **feet and toes**...it will be a divided kingdom...(Dan. 2:41)*	*..a fourth beast... and it had **ten horns**... out of this kingdom **ten kings** will arise... (Dan. 7:7, 24)*	*...a great red dragon having **seven heads and ten horns**, and on his heads were **seven diadems**. (Rev. 12:3)*	*...a beast... having **ten horns and seven heads**, and on his horns were **ten diadems**... And the dragon gave him his power and his throne and great authority. (Rev. 13:1-2)*	*...a scarlet beast...having **seven heads and ten horns**. (Rev. 17:3)*

> *[9]And the great dragon was thrown down, the serpent of old **who is called the devil and Satan**, who deceives the whole world; he was thrown down to the earth, and his angels were thrown down with him.*
>
> — Revelation 12:9

> *[9]that is, the one whose coming is **in accord with the activity of Satan**, with all power and signs and false wonders,*
>
> — 2 Thessalonians 2:9

Never was it previously and plainly stated in Old Testament Scripture that the anti-king had a direct connection with Satan. Readers may have wisely surmised that someone so opposed to the things of God, God's people, and desiring to be deified was at the least influenced by, if not an outright agent of Satan, but the Old Testament text never explicitly stated such. Because we have lived our whole life with the entire Bible as it has ultimately been given, we read Daniel with the full knowledge that what is being described is nearly synonymous with Satan himself, but this only begins to enter into Christian thought with Paul's connection to "*the activity of Satan*" (2 Th. 2:8), and fully realized with Revelation 12. From the text to date, every scriptural and historical example of the anti-king was a lone, Gentile political figure obsessed with publicly deifying himself. A satanic connection was certainly inferred, but never word-for-word categorically stated. One of the functions of the many scriptural instances of the seven and the ten associated with a beast is to tell us to connect them together.

This later revelation of the true nature of the Antichrist is in keeping with the point made earlier about the textual structure of Revelation and its greater theme of the heavenly merging with the earthly. Satan has always been at work, but has Scripture has only shown him actually appearing, first before God in heaven in Job 1:6 and 2:1, and then before God accusing Joshua the high priest (Zech. 3:1-2), and of course before Christ in the Temptation Narrative. (Mt. 4:1-11; Mk. 1:12-13; Lk. 4:1-13) During the final week of years, together with the angels who rebelled with him, he is cast out of heaven and deposited on earth in line with the Last Days phenomenon of previously unseen heavenly figures and activities becoming visible and active in the earthly realm. Like the previous things cast down by God in the Trumpets, likewise thrown down are the heavenly rebellious. In other words, Scripture is specifically addressing the issue of Satan's involvement at the same time when God's Word is revealing a deterioration in the boundary between the spiritual and the natural. Whereas he was previously seen in heaven standing before God as an accuser, and temporarily before the Son of God as a tempter and deceiver, he becomes restricted to operating in the lowly domain of man before being sent on to his lowest, ultimate destination.

There were no chapter and verse markings in the original text, so many will go directly to chapter 13 without considering that it is actually in the middle of a much longer section extending from chapter 12 before it and on after into chapter 14. We will not be able to understand Revelation 13 without the proper context first provided in chapter 12 where we learn of the common relationship between several important things:

- The ten toes of the image in Daniel 2 representing the anti-kingdom;
- The beast with ten horns in Daniel 7 representing the anti-king/anti-kingdom;
- The dragon with seven heads and ten horns in Revelation 12 representing Satan;
- The beast with seven heads and ten horns in Revelation 13, representing Antichrist;
- The beast with seven heads and ten horns in Revelation 17, representing the anti-king/anti-kingdom;
- That they are all ***both*** Satan and Antichrist, ***both*** the anti-kingdom and its member kingdoms.

Together, these various uses of seven and ten as well as the depictions of a beast and a dragon are all intertwined with the same thing: Satan.

The Satanic Resume

We will find Scripture devoted to Satan, to the Antichrist, and to the anti-kingdom. Now we realize that they are almost interchangeable, and at the very least all address a common agenda, which is a major part of the reason the text so easily switches back and forth between a king and a kingdom. Essentially with Satan, the beasts of Revelation 13 and the spirit of antichrist we are presented with the ultimate counterfeit of the triune Godhead. This was Satan's goal from the very beginning.

The Ruler of Tyre

[1]The word of the LORD came again to me, saying, [2]"Son of man, say to the leader of Tyre, 'Thus says the Lord GOD,

"Because your heart is lifted up
And you have said, 'I am a god,
I sit in the seat of gods
In the heart of the seas';
Yet you are a man and not God,
Although you make your heart like the heart of God—
[3]Behold, you are wiser than Daniel;
There is no secret that is a match for you.
[4]By your wisdom and understanding
You have acquired riches for yourself
And have acquired gold and silver for your treasuries.
[5]By your great wisdom, by your trade
You have increased your riches
And your heart is lifted up because of your riches—

— Ezekiel 28:1-5

Ezekiel 28 uses the literal, historical figure of the "*leader of Tyre*" to provide an additional message and teaching about Satan's origins, character and ultimate destiny. From the outset is the primary characteristic found in every antichrist figure, both scriptural and historical, for self-deification. It is repeatedly visited in Daniel (Dan. 7:11, 25; 8:11, 25; 11:36-37), and highlighted by the Apostle Paul as someone "*who opposes and exalts himself above every so-called god or object of worship...displaying himself as being God*". (2 Th. 2:4) This is a characteristic affirmed by Isaiah as well, "'*I will ascend above the heights of the clouds; I will make myself like the Most High.*'" (Is. 14:14) This is especially evident in the statement, "*I sit in the seat of gods*", which is the literal thing he attempts in the course of the Abomination of Desolation which ties the various scriptural accounts together. Just as Christ initiated his 3-1/2 year ministry with a baptism witnessed not just by John the Baptist, but by the affirmation of God the Father and God the Holy Spirit, a satanic counterfeit inaugurates the final 3-1/2 years at the Abomination of Desolation with a fake representative of each.

To our growing list of traits and abilities of the anti-king, through Satan is attributed not just "*wisdom and understanding*", but even "*great wisdom*" beyond the ultimate human standard of Daniel. (Note that this still falls far short of achieving the same level of God's wisdom.) Likewise his earthly doppelgängers are so endowed. Perhaps by understanding his surpassing abilities in this area we can see why it takes the wisdom of Christ to recognize him and why he is so skilled at deception and intrigue.

Daniel also speaks of the anti-king's ability to use and multiply wealth both for himself and as an enticement of others (Dan. 11:24, 36, 39) in a parallel to the same attributed to Satan.

Present from the Beginning

[11]Again the word of the LORD came to me saying, [12]"Son of man, take up a lamentation over the king of Tyre and say to him, 'Thus says the Lord GOD,
"You had the seal of perfection,
Full of wisdom and perfect in beauty.
[13]You were in Eden, the garden of God;
Every precious stone was your covering:
The ruby, the topaz and the diamond;
The beryl, the onyx and the jasper;
The lapis lazuli, the turquoise and the emerald;
And the gold, the workmanship of your settings and sockets,
Was in you.
On the day that you were created
They were prepared.

— Ezekiel 28:11-13

The reference, "*You were in Eden, the garden of God*" reassures us of the greater figure who is being addressed in this passage. He was not created from the outset for what he became, but rather made his own choice. This might be worthy of a book in its own right, seeing how there is so much debate about God's will, with those even proposing that God made some for the express purpose of going to hell. Here we see that even with Satan that is not the case, and certainly goes a long way toward explaining Judas' free will as well. Just because God can see in advance the future outcome of someone's free will choices does not mean He willed it to happen that way.

It is interesting that Satan was such a beautiful being when first created, and the first image of him in Daniel 2, from an earthly point of view at least, is the ultimate eye candy. Although God through His Word ultimately reveals the beast that he has become in a reflection of how far afield he has strayed spiritually from his origins, he nonetheless resorts to that worldly image whenever possible.

> [13]*For such men are false apostles, deceitful workers, disguising themselves as apostles of Christ.* [14]*No wonder, for* ***even Satan disguises himself as an angel of light****.*
> — 2 Corinthians 11:13-14

This is one of the interesting departures from his obsessive-compulsive desire to counterfeit Christ, whose physical description is recorded in Isaiah:

> [2b]*He has no stately form or majesty*
> *That we should look upon Him,*
> *Nor appearance that we should be attracted to Him.*
> — Isaiah 53:2b

An immeasurable vanity apparently trumps his usual spurious propensity to imitate the Messiah. This is probably understandable in that he would never be able to conquer the world as a mild and gentle Lamb of God, so he instead opts to appear as the worldly ideal. Satan's ***always*** about the bling, but Scripture clearly reveals him for the beast he truly is.

Inherently Corrupt

> [14]*You were the anointed cherub who covers,*
> *And I placed you there.*
> *You were on the holy mountain of God;*
> *You walked in the midst of the stones of fire.*
> [15]*You were blameless in your ways*
> *From the day you were created*
> *Until unrighteousness was found in you.*
> [16]*By the abundance of your trade*
> *You were internally filled with violence,*
> *And you sinned;*
> *Therefore I have cast you as profane*
> *From the mountain of God.*
> *And I have destroyed you, O covering cherub,*
> *From the midst of the stones of fire.*
> [17]*Your heart was lifted up because of your beauty;*
> *You corrupted your wisdom by reason of your splendor.*
> *I cast you to the ground;*
> *I put you before kings,*
> *That they may see you.*
> — Ezekiel 28:14-17

There is a list of key character traits ascribed to Satan in this passage which, of course, mirror those found in the Antichrist and his forerunners:

- "*...unrighteousness was found in you*". (v.15)
- "*...internally filled with violence..*" (v.16)
- "*...you sinned...*" (v.16)
- "*...I have cast you as profane...*" (v.16)

But also revealed is how pride undermined both his heart and mind, showing that regardless of how the final figure will appear to the world, his beauty and wisdom are ultimately and very deeply flawed:

- "*...your heart was lifted up because of your beauty...*" (v.17)
- "*You corrupted your wisdom by reason of your splendor...*" (v.17)

One of the effects of Satan's being cast to earth for these final years is that his end is an earthly, public event in the same manner as the unceremonious end of his two beasts.

An Irreversible Spiral Down

12"How you have fallen from heaven,
O star of the morning, son of the dawn!
You have been cut down to the earth,
You who have weakened the nations!
13But you said in your heart,
'I will ascend to heaven;
I will raise my throne above the stars of God,
And I will sit on the mount of assembly
In the recesses of the north.
14I will ascend above the heights of the clouds;
I will make myself like the Most High.'
15Nevertheless you will be thrust down to Sheol,
To the recesses of the pit.
16Those who see you will gaze at you,
They will ponder over you, saying,
'Is this the man who made the earth tremble,
Who shook kingdoms,
17Who made the world like a wilderness
And overthrew its cities,
Who did not allow his prisoners to go home?'
— Isaiah 14:12-17

Through Isaiah the fundamental characteristics of self-deification are reinforced, but this time set against the background of his final destination/disposition. He is cast down from his original position, cast down to earth, and ultimately cast into the Lake of Fire to join his lookalikes. (Rev. 20:10) It may seem like a long time from our mortal, temporal perspective, but Satan has been irreversibly spiraling down further and further all along. It is the ultimate example of everything created with God's desire, "*not wishing for any to perish but for all to come to repentance*" (2 Pe. 3:9) and yet exercising free will so as to reap the consequences of their own choice:

> *4For in the case of those who have once been enlightened and have tasted of the heavenly gift and have been made partakers of the Holy Spirit, 5and have tasted the good word of God and the powers of the age to come, 6and then have fallen away, it is impossible to renew them again to repentance, since they again crucify to themselves the Son of God and put Him to open shame.*
> — Hebrews 6:4-6

Whenever Scripture speaks of Satan or someone acting in his character, such need to be studied in parallel with an application to not just the final anti-king, but the nature and roles of the anti-kingdom. Here in Revelation 12 the various prophetic passages sharing different aspects of the same imagery openly come together to expose the true source and agenda behind them all. The "*ten toes*" (Dan. 2:41), the "*fourth beast*" with "*ten horns*" (Dan.7:7, 24), the "*red dragon having seven heads and ten horns*" (Rev. 12:3), the "*beast having ten horns and seven heads*" with "*ten diadems*" (Rev. 13:1-2), and the "*scarlet beast...having seven heads and ten horns*" (Rev. 17:3) are all one and the same in Satan whether they refer to the individual anti-king or his entire anti-kingdom. Each is emphasizing different characteristics of the same thing.

Lessons from the Red Dragon

We know from what happened in the Garden of Eden that in the course of deceiving Eve, Satan took the literal form of a serpent, so it is no stretch for us to understand Scripture's metaphorical representation of him as a serpent carrying out his role of deception. However, Scripture has now made it clear that the metaphorical references to a dragon are still another picture of him which mirrors his role of persecution and open warfare. In Revelation 12:9, the text specifies he is, "*the great dragon...the serpent of old who is called the devil and Satan*", and in 12:13-17 alternates back and forth between calling him "*the dragon*" and "*the serpent*". So there is no guessing as to what these things mean. This is why we see the Antichrist repeatedly shown to first employ deception and apostasy before escalating to persecution; this is Satan's very nature as the serpent. But when he is engaged in open warfare or persecution he is portrayed as the dragon.

The fact that Scripture uses the figure of a dragon to portray Satan, whereas so many other metaphors and illustrations use either something mirrored in nature or at least resembling a composite of things found in creation, is an illustration in itself that Satan is not just a unique being, but definitely not a part of the natural order of things. He is not something regularly encountered. However, this does not make him equal to God, but ultimately reveals how his rejection of God has resulted in becoming the very opposite. There are no expressions of love, grace or mercy, not to mention the truth, to be found in this quintessential apostatizer. His rebellion has resulted in an ultimate state of lies, deception, violence and the very textbook example of self-deception compounded by narcissism.

A Basic Outline

The text of Revelation 12-13 is actually one continuous passage which begins with the dragon and shows he comes to work on earth through the two beasts. By making a basic outline of the passage we can see why we need to examine Revelation 12 before immersing ourselves in Revelation 13 which is a non-breaking continuation of the text.

12:1-2	"*A great sign appeared in heaven...*"
12:3-6	"*Then another sign appeared in heaven...*"
12:7-12	"*And there was war in heaven...*"
12:13-17	"*And when the dragon saw that he was thrown down to the earth...*"
13:1	"*And then the dragon stood on the sand of the seashore.*"

In keeping with the overall structure of the book of Revelation, something which originates in the heavenly realm produces consequences in the earthly arena. That which Satan pursued in heaven is exactly that which is continued on earth. Only now the physical realm personally experiences what had previously been mostly confined to the spiritual.

Two Great Signs

1A great sign appeared in heaven: a woman clothed with the sun, and the moon under her feet, and on her head a crown of twelve stars; 2and she was with child; and she cried out, being in labor and in pain to give birth.

3Then another sign appeared in heaven: and behold, a great red dragon having seven heads and ten horns, and on his heads were seven diadems. 4And his tail swept away a third of the stars of heaven and threw them to the earth. And the dragon stood before the woman who was about to give birth, so that when she gave birth he

might devour her child. [5]And she gave birth to a son, a male child, who is to rule all the nations with a rod of iron; and her child was caught up to God and to His throne. [6]Then the woman fled into the wilderness where she had a place prepared by God, so that there she would be nourished for one thousand two hundred and sixty days.
— Revelation 12:1-6

The woman with the crown of twelve stars is Israel, confirmed by supporting Scriptures describing Israel as a woman and mother. (Is. 54:5; Jer. 3:6-10) Whereas the stars in her crown represent the twelve founding patriarchs of each of Israel's tribes, the third of the stars which the dragon "*swept away*" from heaven to earth are the fallen angels who rebelled against God to side with Satan. This is going to help us connect what is going on here to what was provided through the Prophet Daniel, in this case:

[10]It grew up to the host of heaven and caused some of the host and some of the stars to fall to the earth, and it trampled them down.
— Daniel 8:10

The identity of the child as being Jesus the Messiah is clearly revealed by "*a son, a male child, who is to rule all the nations with a rod of iron; and her child was caught up to God and to His throne*". (Rev. 12:5) Ruling with a "*rod of iron*" is uniquely associated in Scripture with Christ alone. (Ps. 2:9; Rev. 2:27; 19:15) It was specified in God's prophetic Word that Israel as the woman would give birth to a child, the Messiah. (Mic. 5:2-3)

Through the seed line of Israel came the promised Messiah, and this is why Old Testament history has as one of its primary themes Satan's many attempts to either completely wipe out, or possibly pollute in some way, that lineage as his primary foray to prevent Jesus' coming. But having been repeatedly thwarted in those attempts to prevent Christ's birth, one of the preeminent events accompanying Jesus' infant arrival was Satan's attempt through Herod to literally kill Him as a baby. (Mt. 2:13-23) And even when Satan thought he finally succeeded by effecting His crucifixion, no one was more shocked and angry than Satan to witness the Resurrection when Christ was "*caught up to God and to His throne*". This is the meaning of what is presented here in the woman giving birth, the dragon attempting to devour the child, but the escape of her Child. The aspect of Israel's escape for 3-1/2 lunar years as something that is yet to be fulfilled shows how there is an ultimate fulfillment of these things yet to come while still affirming at least a partial fulfillment of these things in the First Coming.

This also provides a solid textual reason for our ability to understand that in the typology of Scripture, because they also acted in the same character, that Pharaoh, who attempted to kill all the Hebrew children to prevent their savior Moses from being born, and Herod who likewise attempted the same directly against Jesus Himself, are both types, or figures, of the Antichrist. Their own lives and actions teach something about the ultimate, final Antichrist to come because they mimic so many of the fundamental acts and behaviors of Antichrist, and their kingdoms likewise reflect the ultimate anti-kingdom in many ways.

But to show how God's prophetic Word must be carefully examined, especially when it comes to how it handles times and chronologies, take note how just between verses 4 and 5 there is a gap of at least 33 years spanning Jesus' birth and Resurrection. This is but a small lesson to make us aware that even within a sentence or two, God's Word sometimes alternates between different times or bridges enormous gaps very quickly. Our Western minds are conditioned to treat everything according to a linear organization of information to which the writers of the Bible do not always hold. Likewise, within this vignette is history not just covering the Old Testament and First Coming of Christ, but extending into what Jesus and the New Testament writers termed "*the end of the age*", the final transition to "*the age to come*".

In fact, it is important to note that it is these three figures—the woman, the child and the serpent/dragon, whom we find making their first appearance together at the very beginning of Scripture, are now resurfacing near the end to bring about a prophetic conclusion to the whole of God's Word:

> [15]*And I will put enmity*
> *Between you and the woman,*
> *And between your seed and her seed;*
> *He shall bruise you on the head,*
> *And you shall bruise him on the heel."*
>
> — Genesis 3:15

So there is not only the affirmation of no change in Satan's agenda when it comes to both the Messiah and His people, but in the very section of Scripture which is providing the most detail about the anti-king there is not one, but two references to the flight of Israel:

> [6]*Then* ***<u>the woman fled into the wilderness</u>*** *where she had a place prepared by God, so that there she would be nourished for one thousand two hundred and sixty days.*
>
> — Revelation 12:6

> [13]*And when the dragon saw that he was thrown down to the earth, he persecuted the woman who gave birth to the male child.* [14]*But the two wings of the great eagle were given to the woman, so that* ***<u>she could fly into the wilderness to her place</u>****, where she was nourished for a time and times and half a time, from the presence of the serpent.*
>
> — Revelation 12:13-14

Jesus associates this same activity as occurring when Jerusalem is surrounded and the Abomination of Desolation takes place:

> [20]*"But when you see Jerusalem surrounded by armies, then recognize that her desolation is near.* [21]*Then those who are in Judea must flee to the mountains, and those who are in the midst of the city must leave, and those who are in the country must not enter the city;*
>
> — Luke 21:20-21

In all likelihood this textual pause between the Trumpets and the Bowls revisiting events taking place in parallel is at this juncture connecting Revelation 12-13 with the Abomination of Desolation, but from the heavenly viewpoint. In other words, while we understand that the beast and his earthly armies will effect this desecration in a satanic act of self-deification, these chapters are showing what has happened in parallel in the heavenly realm to result in what takes place on earth.

It is worth noting that the only other figure in Scripture who was ***satanically*** possessed—that is, of course, Judas, was spoken of by Christ very early on in his ministry, "*and yet one of you is a devil*". (Jn. 6:70) Judas was around for quite awhile, acting ***in the character of*** Satan, but it was not until later when, "*Satan then entered into him*" (Jn. 13:27) and was finally ***possessed*** by Satan. It should not surprise us then that the Antichrist can be working as Satan's agent from the outset of the 70th Week of Daniel in negotiating the covenant with Israel which initiates the final week of years, as well as already seen in the 1st Seal, but not experiencing his actual possession by Satan until this midway milestone when Satan and his cohorts are ultimately and literally cast down to earth. That is when Judas led everyone in open oppostion to Chirst, and that is when Antichrist undertakes the same on a global scale. Nonetheless, it serves to provide a textual connection to the most repeated milestone of Daniel's 70th Week in the Abomination of Desolation.

War in Heaven

> 7 *And there was war in heaven, Michael and his angels waging war with the dragon. The dragon and his angels waged war,* 8 *and they were not strong enough, and there was no longer a place found for them in heaven.* 9 *And the great dragon was thrown down, the serpent of old who is called the devil and Satan, who deceives the whole world; he was thrown down to the earth, and his angels were thrown down with him.*
>
> — Revelation 12:7-9

This is not an event which occurred at some point in eternity past before the creation of the world, but something which takes place in parallel with the overall eschaton in what Jesus and the New Testament writers refer to broadly as "*the end of the age*". We know from Scripture, particularly as related in the book of Job, that Satan appears before God in heaven in an adversarial role:

> 6 *Now there was a day when the sons of God came to present themselves before the LORD, and Satan also came among them.* 7 *The LORD said to Satan, "From where do you come?" Then Satan answered the LORD and said, "From roaming about on the earth and walking around on it."*
>
> — Job 1:6-7

Until this heavenly war takes place, the "bad guys" not only have the ability to roam about the earth, but have access to heaven. In the example of Satan's role as accuser of Job can be seen what he attempts to effect against every believer of every age. As nearly every Bible dictionary tells us, the very name "*Satan*" (in Hebrew "*Satan*", Strong's #7854; in Greek "*Satanas*", Strong's #4567) actually means "Adversary". When his alternate title as "*Devil*" (Greek "*Diabolos*", Strong's #1228) is used, it is to direct attention to his even narrower related role of "slanderer, false accuser". Here in Revelation this is affirmed by being presented with the specific charges that he is not merely in the business of deception (v. 9), but is "*the accuser of our brethren*" (v.10)

This is something which is also specified again by Scripture in Zechariah 3, which may be particularly interesting in that it shows Satan actively pursuing his role as accuser against the High Priest Joshua, who is, along with Zerubbabel, the primary scriptural doppelgängers of the Two Witnesses just visited in Revelation 11:

> 1 *And the Lord showed me the great priest Joshua standing before the presence of the angel of the Lord, and the adversary stood on his right to resist him.*
>
> — Zechariah 3:1

But a time comes when Satan and his associates lose their access to heaven and are forced to carry out their spiritual conflict from the much lower, disadvantaged position of the earthly realm, and as with all wars, those in the vicinity of the action either find they must join sides or attempt to flee or they will become part of the collateral damage. Likewise this explains many aspects of Revelation and parallel Old Testament Scripture where the heavenly and earthly arenas are no longer strictly separated and activities begin to merge or crossover between them because the combatants have moved the site of the battle.

Perhaps it is too simplistic an explanation, but just as the Messiah had to literally come down and work on earth in order to fulfill all that God's prophetic Word spoke concerning Him, likewise the Second Coming must be literally fulfilled in the earthly realm. Even the Millennial Kingdom is a real and literal earth-based phenomenon and takes place down here before the ultimate transition to eternity. But even then, it is a New Heaven and a New Earth, one never soiled by the likes of Satan and his followers, which is transacted, not an elimination of sorts. From a certain point of view, an earthly realm is never abandoned, but merged with the eternal.

This event may also help to understand a number of End Times milestones which may all take place in close proximity to each other if not simultaneously for some. For instance, it may help to explain why Satan, through the Antichrist, is able for a time and to a point to successfully counterfeit Christ as a false savior and peacemaker, but then is openly revealed for who he truly is when he demands to be worshiped as God. This might be the point where Satan is cast down to earth to personally possess the Antichrist, and might also coincide with the 5th Seal of increased persecution as well as the flight of Israel when Jews and Christians alike react adversely to what is taking place. And since these milestones seem to inaugurate what Jesus calls "*a great tribulation*", a time of unprecedented spiritual darkness, we might appreciate the additional effect on all of this by the anticipated change in the Holy Spirit's working when He no longer restrains evil as at present. In other words, whereas just prior to the Abomination of Desolation the focus of his pressure and persecution was on the Church, with his public self-deification the pressure and persecution is placed on ***everyone*** in the whole world to worship him, regardless of their spiritual or political standing.

We can at least begin to better understand why Jesus stipulates that at such a nexus of every possible worst case scenario occurring on top of each other or in rapid succession that, "*for the sake of the elect those days will be cut short*", (Mt. 24:22) and His provision that this intense period of "*great tribulation*" will be "*such as has not occurred since the beginning of the world until now, nor ever will be*". (Mt. 24:21) The proverbial dominoes of Satan being cast down, the Abomination of Desolation, a supernatural increase in persecution, the pursuit and flight of Israel, as well as the Holy Spirit's cessation of restraining evil and going back to His Old Testament mode of working, might be successive triggers to the "*great tribulation*" which in itself signals the impending transition to "*the day of the Lord*".

The fact that the war in heaven is not undertaken by either the Godhead as a whole or by one of its Members, but is instead conducted by "*Michael and his angels*" should go a long way toward confirming doctrinally that Satan is not a being who is anywhere near equal to God, which seems to be a false belief held by far too many. As it turns out, Satan is not even equipped to handle the Archangel Michael. Satan may possess powers and abilities far beyond any human being's, but in the greater heavenly scheme of things he is just a former employee of God gone bad who wants to be like God so earnestly that he constantly imitates and counterfeits the Godhead. He is a limited heavenly being who will be overcome by another, not some kind of equal combatant with God as is so often portrayed in secular literature and film.

In what is a finalist to be an entry on every list ever assembled of the top five ironies of all time, note that Satan, who once boasted, "*I will make myself like the Most High*", (Is. 14:14) is defeated by Michael, whose name literally means, "Who is like God?" There may be additional ramifications to John's vision of all that is involved in this war in that Michael is also strongly associated in Scripture with literal Israel.

> [13]*"But the prince of the kingdom of Persia was withstanding me for twenty-one days; then behold, **Michael, one of the chief princes**, came to help me, for I had been left there with the kings of Persia.*
>
> — Daniel 10:13

> [1]*"Now at that time **Michael, the great prince who stands guard over the sons of your people**, will arise. And there will be a time of distress such as never occurred since there was a nation until that time; and at that time your people, everyone who is found written in the book, will be rescued.*
>
> — Daniel 12:1

Note how in these citations is a reference to warfare and another to "*a time of distress such as never occurred since there was a nation until that time*". That time seems to be the exact background for what is described in Revelation 12.

There are those who maintain that this all took place in the course of Christ's First Coming when upon the return of the seventy Jesus stated, "*I was watching Satan fall from heaven like lightning*". (Lk. 10:18) However, given the contexts of both Luke and Revelation, it is far more likely that Jesus is speaking prophetically, as the Godhead sometimes so refers to future events as if they have already taken place because they see things in the context of eternity. He clearly saw the connection between what was occurring then with how it would ultimately play out in the end, and this is no small connection to consider as we look at the next section of Revelation pertaining to this event. Jesus saw Satan falling as the ultimate result of the successful preaching of the Gospel by His disciples, and now having expanded to the entire Last Days Church are about to be credited for that exact, same thing when it comes to how they ultimately overcome Satan in John's vision. Luke 10 and Revelation 12 connect on both the literal and spiritual levels.

A Turning Point

> [10]*Then I heard a loud voice in heaven, saying,*
>
> *"Now the salvation, and the power, and the kingdom of our God and the authority of His Christ have come, for the accuser of our brethren has been thrown down, he who accuses them before our God day and night.*
>
> [11]*And they overcame him because of the blood of the Lamb and because of the word of their testimony, and they did not love their life even when faced with death.* [12]*For this reason, rejoice, O heavens and you who dwell in them. Woe to the earth and the sea, because the devil has come down to you, having great wrath, knowing that he has only a short time."*
>
> — Revelation 12:10-12

This is a turning point of finality specifically identified in heaven because what was at one time only clearly observable from a heavenly view has now been cast out of heaven and into the earthly realm as the last stop before falling even further into the Lake of Fire as the ultimate destination. There is quite a lot to ponder in trying to picture that as bad as things have been in this lowly realm in which we find ourselves, that Satan and his cohorts were not permanent residents, and yet a time comes when they are not only forced into a permanent change of address, but are fully self-aware they have lost and on the verge of the worst possible final relocation ever. All that awaits them is the final sequence of formalities spelled out by God's Word.

If it seems difficult to comprehend not only why someone goes on in the face of certain defeat, but actually becomes more outrageous and extreme than ever before, the answer is easily found in history's recent example of the Third Reich. If common sense had even a minimum chance of affecting the outcome, armistice agreements would have been reached long before any of the Allies undertook the total destruction of not just the Nazi regime but the land of Germany itself. But after so many years of what was nothing less than blind worship and devotion to their leader, even when they reached the self-realization very early on that they could not possibly win, they found themselves incapable of changing their ways. In a similar parallel to mankind's progressive reaction to all these things recorded in Revelation, they just keep getting more and more stubborn in the character of Pharaoh in the Exodus account, who no matter how many plagues he experienced actually kept getting worse and even more hardened of heart.

Juxtaposed against Satan's defeat at the hands of "*Michael and his angels*" in heaven is Satan's defeat by the Church on earth, which is attributed to three specific things in Revelation 12:11:

- "*...because of the blood of the Lamb...*"
- "*...because of the word of their testimony...*"
- "*...they did not love life even when faced with death.*"

In other words, Satan and company are ultimately defeated on every battlefield or realm regardless of its location, but in this case steadily downward from heaven to earth to the Lake of Fire, both literally and spiritually.

1st century Christian readers would have immediately recognized how all three items parallel what Christ specified in the Olivet Discourse, particularly emphasizing that the extreme conditions will provide believers the opportunity to not just preach the Word, but be visible witnesses of what the Word has accomplished within them, even to the point of death. Persecution and deception are the issues repeated far more than any other by Christ and the New Testament writers. But this is yet another indication that this part of John's vision is reviewing what takes place before the Church's removal and after the open appearance of the Antichrist and all that follows.

Yet another contrast is provided in giving the heavens a reason to rejoice at the same time all the earth is left to experience is biblical "*woe*"—or what is specifically described here as "*great wrath*". It is no coincidence that it is here specifically designated, "*Woe to the earth and the sea*" since the first two Bowl judgments to come will be literally poured out on the earth and the sea.

We have repeatedly visited the fact that whenever the English word "time" or "times" is offered by the translators that we should peek under the hood to see which actual Greek word is present, because it makes a difference. In this case, "*knowing that he has only a short* ***<u>time</u>***" is "*kairos*", which indicates a set limit that can be measured by the clock. This small detail affirms what is stated by both Christ and Daniel, that the most significant milestone of Daniel's 70th Week is the halfway point of the Abomination of Desolation, and there are specific time limits attached to this period which fall within the category of 3-1/2 lunar years. Satan is more aware of the time crunch than anyone, having just permanently arrived in this temporal realm. The intensity of what will take place from the Abomination of Desolation to the end of the 70th

Week is why Scripture provides far more attention to the last half of that final week of years when it is speaking of behaviors and activities of the final anti-king and his anti-kingdom. He is certainly around from the very beginning, but it is all at its worst when at the midway point, "*the devil has come down to you, having great wrath, knowing that he has only a short time*". (Rev. 12:12)

A Dramatic Rescue

> *13And when the dragon saw that he was thrown down to the earth, he persecuted the woman who gave birth to the male child. 14But the two wings of the great eagle were given to the woman, so that she could fly into the wilderness to her place, where she was nourished for a time and times and half a time, from the presence of the serpent.*
>
> — Revelation 12:13-14

The reference to an eagle's wings is not unique nor making its first appearance here in Scripture. The very first listing in our concordance provides its primary meaning:

> *4'You yourselves have seen what I did to the Egyptians, and how I bore you on eagles' wings, and brought you to Myself.*
>
> — Exodus 19:4

That which God did to rescue and protect Israel in the course of the Exodus Narrative is likened to "*eagles' wings*". But there is an important conditional purpose stated, "*and brought you **to Myself***". If we continue on in the same passage, it is explained that this rescue was intended to effect a special spiritual relationship between Israel and God:

> *5'Now then, if you will indeed obey My voice and keep My covenant, then you shall be My own possession among all the peoples, for all the earth is Mine; 6and you shall be to Me a kingdom of priests and a holy nation.' These are the words that you shall speak to the sons of Israel."*
>
> — Exodus 19:5-6

In other words, there is the repeated scriptural pattern not just relating God's protection of Israel in the course and even on the heels of great distress, but an accompanying explanation that such is working to restore the right relationship of faithfulness between God and His people so as to serve Him. (Dt. 32:11-12; Is. 40:31)

A Failed Attempt

> *15And the serpent poured water like a river out of his mouth after the woman, so that he might cause her to be swept away with the flood. 16But the earth helped the woman, and the earth opened its mouth and drank up the river which the dragon poured out of his mouth.*
>
> — Revelation 12:15-16

Because the scriptural usages of water so often represent the Gentile nations, especially a body of water which is so large as to appear overwhelming, the explanation of what is taking place here may have already been provided through David:

> *1"Had it not been the LORD who was on our side,"*
> *Let Israel now say,*
> *2"Had it not been the LORD who was on our side*

When men rose up against us,
[3]Then they would have swallowed us alive,
When their anger was kindled against us;
[4]Then the waters would have engulfed us,
The stream would have swept over our soul;
[5]Then the raging waters would have swept over our soul."
[6]Blessed be the LORD,
Who has not given us to be torn by their teeth.
[7]Our soul has escaped as a bird out of the snare of the trapper;
The snare is broken and we have escaped.
[8]Our help is in the name of the LORD,
Who made heaven and earth. (Psalm 124)
— Psalm 124

There is also an additional explanation provided through Isaiah:

[20]Come, my people, enter into your rooms
And close your doors behind you;
Hide for a little while
Until indignation runs its course.
[21]For behold, the LORD is about to come out from His place
To punish the inhabitants of the earth for their iniquity;
And the earth will reveal her bloodshed
And will no longer cover her slain.
— Isaiah 26:20-21

It is important to note that in this passage while Satan is dually referred to as "*the serpent*" and "*the dragon*", that the "*water like a river*"is said to pour out of the mouth of the serpent. In other words, not only does Satan as the dragon engage in persecution to literally destroy God's people, but as the serpent employs unprecedented deception to spiritually overwhelm and overtake God's people.

[17]So the dragon was enraged with the woman, and went off to make war with the rest of her children, who keep the commandments of God and hold to the testimony of Jesus.
— Revelation 12:17

So the flood of deception from the serpent having failed, the persecution of the dragon kicks in. The final detail of this event shows us that at this time the removal of the Church has not taken place, the only viable meaning of "*the rest of her children*" as followed up with a description of those already in a right and faithful relationship with Christ. This further confirms for us that we are in the midst of a "recap" of events in parallel with many if not all of that which came before in Revelation. This escalation of warfare directed specifically at the Church is more likely tied to the 5th Seal, just as the previous depiction of closely executed events as dominoes showed the 5th Seal of persecution to be among them. Christ specified in the Olivet Discourse that the final phase leading up to the Abomination of Desolation is a time of tribulation for the Church unprecedented in deception, apostasy and persecution. (Mt. 24:9-14)

The Satanic Agenda

There is a chilling contrast we can make which decidedly frames just how deep the relationship goes between Satan and his prodigies. In the case of Christ in the course of His own ministry, He categorically stated, "*the Son can do nothing of Himself, unless it is something He sees the Father doing*". (Jn. 5:19) The Antichrist is the spiritually darkest parallel to this, acting according to his father Satan to war against God, war against God's people, and bring every possible effort to bear both in the character of the serpent and the dragon.

As bad as things have been at any point in history, they pale with the wrath to come when Satan finally realizes just how short and finite his remaining time truly is, now having to spend time in a place where the clock works, unlike the eternal realm he came from. He will first and foremost attempt to take it out on Israel and the Church, but as we will discover in Revelation 17-18, this composite opposite of every characteristic of God will even turn on those who brought him to power. He is not actually building a kingdom of followers with whom he seeks to establish some kind of mutual loyalty or relationship, but desires to entice everyone's rebellion and fall beginning with those closest to God and see them destroyed. The Body of Christ is being built into Christ the Head for an eternal life in heaven; the body of Satan, as shown in the very first vision in Daniel 2, is shattered and ground to dust for an eternal death in hell.

16 ❖ Revelation 13: The Beast from the Sea

Having just studied all the obvious, overt references to the Antichrist in Scripture which would define 1st century understanding of this figure, we can immediately recognize those things which provide a parallel to what has already been given in God's Word and those unique to Revelation 13. The most obvious parallel is to Daniel in the use of the term "*beast*", but the most startling new revelation is the specification that there are actually ***two*** beasts.

Yes, we have lived all our life with the knowledge of the whole counsel of God's Word, so it is impossible for us to not have been reading any of the references to the Antichrist without murmuring to ourselves, "Yeah, but there's also the False Prophet". It would be surprising if this book's readers did not from time to time wonder why the author, to this very point, has so sparingly referred to a ***pair*** of beasts and the False Prophet specifically. It is a very important detail, especially in keeping with the prophetic progressive revelation of God, to understand that before Revelation 13, ***this fact was never known***.

For the many hundreds of years since the first vision in Daniel 2 up until John's vision on the Isle of Patmos, every scriptural and historical instance of the anti-king was always that of a lone, Gentile political ruler who commands a very large kingdom and at some point has himself deified. If we now look back at Nebuchadnezzar, Alexander, Epiphanes, and so forth, we do not have an obvious accompanying second figure in the character of the False Prophet. However, with this particular revelation, some other forerunners of the beasts are going to come to light, both historical and scriptural, and what was concealed but present all along will now be illuminated. We will shortly discuss the most important reason God chose to present the information in this manner, as the primary answer is divulged in this chapter's opening.

There are a number of similarities to previous scriptural references, such as their relationship to Satan portrayed as a dragon, and they are not just seeking political control but conquering hearts in order to be worshiped; this is actually what it truly means to "conquer the world". But while their goals and activities are complimentary, they are assigned distinct roles in order to carry these things out. It may be useful to first familiarize ourselves with Revelation 13 by looking side-by-side at what the passage offers for the beast from the sea versus the beast from the earth and make note of the similarities and differences, but in particular how distinct their roles are from each other:

The Beast from the Sea (13:1-10)	*The Beast from the Earth (13:11-18)*
[1]Then I saw a beast coming up out of the sea,	*[11]Then I saw another beast coming up out of the earth;*
having ten horns and seven heads, and on his horns were ten diadems, and on his heads were blasphemous names.	*and he had two horns like a lamb and he spoke as a dragon.*
[2]And the beast which I saw was like a leopard, and his feet were like those of a bear, and his mouth like the mouth of a lion.	
And the dragon gave him his power and his throne and great authority.	*[12]He exercises all the authority of the first beast in his presence.*
[3]I saw one of his heads as if it had been slain, and his fatal wound was healed. And the whole earth was amazed and followed after the beast 4they worshiped the dragon because he gave his authority to the beast; and they worshiped the beast, saying, "Who is like the beast, and who is able to wage war with him?"	*And he makes the earth and those who dwell in it to worship the first beast, whose fatal wound was healed.*
[5]There was given to him a mouth speaking arrogant words and blasphemies,	
and authority to act for forty-two months was given to him.	
[6]And he opened his mouth in blasphemies against God, to blaspheme His name and His tabernacle, that is, those who dwell in heaven.	
[7]It was also given to him to make war with the saints and to overcome them, and authority over every tribe and people and tongue and nation was given to him.	
[8]All who dwell on the earth will worship him, everyone whose name has not been written from the foundation of the world in the book of life of the Lamb who has been slain.	
	[13]He performs great signs, so that he even makes fire come down out of heaven to the earth in the presence of men.
	[14]And he deceives those who dwell on the earth because of the signs which it was given him to perform in the presence of the beast, telling those who dwell on the earth to make an image to the beast who had the wound of the sword and has come to life.

<table>
<tr><td></td><td>15 And it was given to him to give breath to the image of the beast, so that the image of the beast would even speak and cause as many as do not worship the image of the beast to be killed.</td></tr>
<tr><td></td><td>16 And he causes all, the small and the great, and the rich and the poor, and the free men and the slaves, to be given a mark on their right hand or on their forehead, 17 and he provides that no one will be able to buy or to sell, except the one who has the mark, either the name of the beast or the number of his name.</td></tr>
<tr><td colspan="2">18 Here is wisdom. Let him who has understanding calculate the number of the beast, for the number is that of a man; and his number is six hundred and sixty-six.</td></tr>
<tr><td colspan="2">9 If anyone has an ear, let him hear. 10 If anyone is destined for captivity, to captivity he goes; if anyone kills with the sword, with the sword he must be killed. Here is the perseverance and the faith of the saints.</td></tr>
</table>

Although it is universally accepted to refer to these two figures as the "*Antichrist*" and the "*False Prophet*", neither of those terms actually appear here. It is from John's Epistles that we are provided "*antichrist*" (1 Jn. 2:18, 22; 4:3; 2 Jn. 7) and it will not be until Revelation 19:20 that "*false prophet*" is categorically used. The first beast is the main figure who is attempting to counterfeit, or take the place of, Christ—that is, fulfilling the definition of "*antichrist*". The second beast is of the same spirit, but is actually a counterfeit of John the Baptist. This is clearly seen in the table above where their roles are not only so starkly different, but their physical descriptions as well. The bottom line truth of the text, however, is that it calls both of them "*beast*" and considers them coequally to be "Antichrist". But it is additionally obvious that one is more heavily weighted to the political side of the spectrum while the other to the religious, although there is enough crossover to see how they combine to use both ends in striving for a single, common goal, which is to worship and serve Satan the dragon.

It is worth noting that whenever someone offers that a particular person is the literal Antichrist, whether at any time in the whole of history or up to the present, that such is almost never accompanied by a proposed False Prophet even though Scripture is clear on this point. If someone were to bother documenting the long history of claims of those assigning a name to a literal fulfillment of the Antichrist, it would be very rare to find any proposed parallel speculations of someone accompanied by an equally identified False Prophet figure.

However, because the False Prophet is never mentioned in Scripture prior to this, it may be that, unlike John the Baptist, he is not a true forerunner working in advance of the Antichrist's arrival, but rather a visible advocate who takes his place when things turn from being mainly political to completely spiritual. Satan calls the first beat whose activites at first seem to parallel the rise of the ten kings which serve the earth up to him politically; the second beast is subsequently called by Satan in concert with the Abomination of Desolation when it all escalates to expose the real agenda. The False Prophet is only mentioned in the context of the last half of the 70th Week.

For 1st century readers, it is far more likely that one of the earliest scriptural and historical parallels they would likely associate with the events and figures in Revelation is what took place in the account of the Exodus. Pharaoh and his magicians who, to a point, could counterfeit the signs of Moses and Aaron would be seen as mirroring the Antichrist and False Prophet, the Two Witnesses as recapitulating the roles of Moses and Aaron, and the plagues themselves divided into three sections where everyone experienced the first third in the series, but after which God's people were exempted from that point on, just as it takes place between the Seals and the Trumpets. Other parallels in Scripture would be forthcoming after processing Revelation 13, but this is most likely the earliest "*pesher*" interpretation for the Early Church, a Jewish hermeneutic which sees two things in Scripture in a "this" is "that" comparison.

The first beast in Revelation, however, would be very familiar to them because he precisely aligns with what was established by Daniel and then left uncorrected and intact by Jesus in the Olivet Discourse. He is simultaneously the embodiment of a final, earthly kingdom and its leader who does not limit himself to openly opposing God, but seeks to be served and worshiped in place of Him. And, as a very important included detail, this first figure is seen "*coming up out of the sea*".

The Beast from the Sea

> 1 *And the dragon stood on the sand of the seashore. Then I saw a beast coming up out of the sea, having ten horns and seven heads, and on his horns were ten diadems, and on his heads were blasphemous names.*
> — Revelation 13:1

As stated previously, the two main pictures Scripture provides of Satan is a dragon when his primary work is persecution and a serpent when he is dedicated mainly to deception. So the identification of him here as "*the dragon*" speaks to this emphasis as he has been cast to earth and knows his time is short. Portraying him as standing on "*the sand of the seashore*" within the context of what follows is a way of stating that he is overseeing and animating the raising of these two figures to fulfill their roles on his behalf. Satan has been cast down to earth and works a counterfeit of the triune Godhead to first go after Israel and then the Church, as explained just prior in Revelation 12, and here it shows how he so operates on this level through these figures not just for that particular role, but in his pursuit of the whole world.

Although many have asserted that the beast is specifically coming up out of the Mediterranean so as to make a case for his identity, most usually attached to Rome, "*the sea*", or a great body of water, as already shown, is a regular Scriptural metaphor for the Gentile nations as a whole. This is specifying the ethnicity of this beast as Gentile. Until the New Testament associated Judas with the Antichrist, and John's revelation that antichrist figures "*went out from us*" (1 Jn. 2:19), every figure of the Antichrist presented in Scripture was an ethnic Gentile and it would appear that such is the case for this first one. In fact, this author dogmatically asserts that when the Early Church first read Revelation, this is one of the details which conformed to previous Scripture which affirmed for them the authenticity of its divine authorship. They knew from all previous instances of the horn/king/beast that he is a powerful Gentile ruler. This was historically fulfilled in the examples of Antiochus Epiphanes IV, General Pompey and Early Church speculation about the Roman emperors. Along with the well-established meaning of "*the sea*" as scripturally specific to the Gentile nations, early readers had absolutely no doubt that this plainly and unambiguously confirmed the Antichrist's Gentile ethnicity. The debate has been the bane of subsequent generations. But what about the Apostle John's revelation that this figure also comes in the character of Judas? Many are equally dogmatic in asserting that the Antichrist ***must*** be ethnically Jewish.

When John says he "*went out from **us***", he is referring to the Church, which is, by definition, blind to race and gender. "*Us*" is the Church, not Israel.

> [28]*There is neither Jew nor Greek, there is neither slave nor free man, there is neither male nor female; for you are all one in Christ Jesus.*
> — Galatians 3:28

Whereas descriptions to this point in Scripture have consistently presented the Antichrist as a Gentile political figure, an additional refining detail is being put forth that at some point in his life, in the character of Judas, he operates among our ranks so seamlessly that he will appear even to Christians to have been one of our own. But because by definition the Church is no longer ethnically segregated, ***anyone*** of ***any*** lineage is a candidate to do what Judas did. And as we have seen with Herod the Great and his descendants, the lack of being ethnically Jewish does not prevent someone from being accepted by the Jews themselves as Jewish.

Herod was ethnically Idumean—that is, from Edom, appointed over the Jews by the Romans. He was a Gentile accepted religiously as Jewish, Gentile by birth, and Roman by citizenship. He was able to travel back and forth, so to speak, between all three. Likewise, the final anti-king to come can be ethnically Gentile while having a resume as a convert to both Judaism and Christianity (and whatever other religion he deems necessary) to allow him the same kind of latitude exhibited in Herod the Great. Like Rome, he is all things to all men.

This back-and-forth today about the ethnicity of the Antichrist has a curious parallel to the First Coming, in that although Jesus was born in Bethlehem of Judea, he was raised in Nazareth of Galilee. Some assumed because of His known association with Galilee that He could not possibly be the Messiah. In other words, when it came to the actual Messiah, there was confusion for many concerning his true heritage, a detail which seems to be replayed in these two beasts today. But the way Scripture has been presented to this point, this was never originally given even a second thought by the Early Church, because Revelation so obviously confirmed that the Antichrist is ethnically Gentile and the False Prophet ethnically Jewish. Like Herod they may be able to subsequently make this identification more difficult as they incorporate subsequent multiple backgrounds, but like Herod they cannot change their original ethnicity, only influence how it will be received, and even misconstrued.

Ten Horns, Seven Heads, Ten Diadems

It may be subtle, but there are slight distinctions made in the descriptions of the Antichrist as a beast as presented in Daniel and Revelation:

[7]"After this I kept looking in the night visions, and behold, ***a fourth beast****...and it had* ***ten horns****. [8]While I was contemplating the horns, behold, another horn, a little one, came up among them, and* ***three of the first horns were pulled out by the roots*** *before it; and behold, this horn possessed eyes like the eyes of a man and a mouth uttering great boasts. (Daniel 7:7-8)*	*[3]Then another sign appeared in heaven: and behold,* ***a great red dragon*** *having* ***seven heads*** *and* ***ten horns****, and on his heads were* ***seven diadems****. (Rev. 12:3)*	*[1]And the dragon stood on the sand of the seashore. Then I saw* ***a beast*** *coming up out of the sea, having* ***ten horns*** *and* ***seven heads****, and on his horns were* ***ten diadems****, and on his heads were blasphemous names. (Rev.13:1)*

A common feature of each is the ten horns, which Daniel is plainly told means, "*out of this kingdom ten kings will arise*" and that the three horns which are pulled out is explained, "[he] *will subdue three kings*" (Dan. 7:20, 24) leaving seven, which appears to equate to the heads and horns of what is featured in Revelation 12-13. There is a common association of a "*seven*" and a "*ten*" in these visions which seems to be depicting different points along a common timeline where the "*ten*" begins the sequence at full strength but are visibly reduced at some point to a "*seven*", yet the legacy of the diadems are maintained throughout. In the very first vision in Daniel, the kingdom of the Antichrist is depicted as toes of "*iron mixed with common clay*" (Dan. 2:41), of which it is specifically stated, "*it will be a divided kingdom*", and along the way Scripture further provides three are subdued so that only seven remain by the end.

But whereas with Christ who, when He returns, we find "*on His head are many diadems; and He has a name written on Him which no one knows except Himself*," (Rev. 19:12) in a counterfeit contrast the diadems on the beast are limited in number and the names on each head are outwardly stipulated as being "*blasphemous*". Biblical blasphemy is a combination of slander, false witness, and an attempt to destroy someone's reputation in addition to just speaking evil of them. This kind of permanent marking on each of the beast's heads stands as a stark contrast to God's similar marking of the 144,000, and tells us something of the deeper meaning of the mark of the beast to come at the end of this chapter. To take the mark is being equated with assuming an overt stance against God by slandering and bearing false witness against Him. This fits with the fact that at the end of the 7th Bowl it is recorded, "*and men blasphemed God*"; (Rev. 16:21) their actions match their mark.

In Revelation 17:12-13 the horns are not only also explained as representing "*ten kings*", but further qualified, "*These have one purpose, and they give their power and authority to the beast*".

The Four Kingdoms Revisited

> *[2]And the beast which I saw was like a leopard, and his feet were like those of a bear, and his mouth like the mouth of a lion. And the dragon gave him his power and his throne and great authority.*
>
> — Revelation 13:2

In Daniel 7, four successive empires were associated with each figure, the lion being Babylon, the bear representing Media-Persia, the leopard as Greece, and a dreadful fourth beast embodying the kingdom of Antichrist first represented by Rome. John's description appears to provide their order in reverse of that given to Daniel as he looks backward from his position in the future, all those kingdoms having come as predicted except this final one. It speaks to the fact that the chief characteristics of these kingdoms are all ultimately assimilated into this present, final recapitulation of the Roman Empire on a much grander scale.

A very significant detail, however, which provides a deeper understanding of the greater spiritual goings on is that Satan "*gave him his power and his throne and great authority*" to show who and what is really being worshiped, served, and at work. What began in Revelation 12 is now fully realized in the two beasts for the final half of Daniel's 70th Week.

The Counterfeit Resurrection

> *3I saw one of his heads as if it had been slain, and his fatal wound was healed. And the whole earth was amazed and followed after the beast; 4they worshiped the dragon because he gave his authority to the beast; and they worshiped the beast, saying, "Who is like the beast, and who is able to wage war with him?"*
> — Revelation 13:3-4

This is the first of three instances in this chapter when specific mention is made of the first beast's wound. (Rev. 13:3, 12, 14) It is twice referred to as a "*fatal wound*", the underlying Greek clearly speaking of something which leads to death. The third reference builds on this meaning by stating it is "*the wound of the sword and has come to life*" to unmistakably define what is being described. In a continuation of Satan's attempt to counterfeit anything and everything authentic to the Messiah, it would appear that the first beast will counterfeit Christ's death and resurrection in some manner. Even if the beast literally dies and Satan effects a miracle to raise him from the dead, and as proved through Pharaoh's magicians, he can perform actual signs and wonders, it would still be a satanic counterfeit of what Christ actually experienced and accomplished.

Since the use of a literal "*sword*" in Scripture most often refers to an armed conflict, this is probably provided to indicate how this comes about in the course of a military action rather than by natural causes, assassination, subterfuge or the like. This is why, upon his miraculous recovery from a military-related death his followers go on to glowingly admire, "*and who is able to wage war with him?*" He appears to them to be militarily unconquerable and impervious to death.

This is also an interesting departure from the many things which Satan tries to copy from the First Coming. Just as Christ is physically described as meek and unassuming in appearance, Satan cannot successfully imitate that approach and instead appeals to the worldly notions of a leader by being handsome and charismatic. Likewise, he cannot imitate the humble sacrifice of Christ's crucifixion, but again in what is more likely to visually satiate the world, his counterfeit is effected in some kind of dramatic and public military setting. It would be roughly analogous to Custer appearing to rise from the dead after the massacre. There are some things which Satan and his marionettes cannot duplicate, so in such cases he opts for what is most appealing to the fleshly desires and notions of the earthbound. He will most likely claim, or let it be claimed on his behalf, that he made the ultimate sacrifice for the world in the course of this military-related forgery.

Notice that the reaction to all of this is that they are amazed, they follow after him, and as a result "*they worshiped the dragon…they worshiped the beast*". This is the real goal of this conflict, which is not really the possession of lands or resources, but control of the heart as defined by what each person worships. Satan openly betrayed this as his true, ultimate motive when in his third attempt to tempt Christ he "*showed Him all the kingdoms of the world and their glory; and he said to Him, 'All these things I will give You,* ***if You fall down and worship me.***'" (Mt. 4:8) The first beast may operate mainly in the political realm, but it is only to achieve this ultimate spiritual goal.

In Revelation 14:6-7, the first of three angelic messengers will warn the world to "***worship Him*** *who made the heaven and the earth*", and is followed by a third who warns, "***If anyone worships the beast*** *and his image, and receives a mark on his forehead or on his hand, he will also drink the wine of the wrath of God*". (Rev. 14:9-10) The issue of who and what we worship is the very thing which is at stake. And it is a repeated feature of not just the character of the two beasts, but the overall context of the book of Revelation.

In an ultimate counterfeit of the scriptural declarations, "*Who is like You?*" when referring to God, (Ex. 15:11; Ps. 35:10; 71:19; 89:8; 113:5) these worshipers enjoin a parallel satanic chorus, "*Who is like the beast?*" In every way possible, Satan strives to achieve what Isaiah revealed about him, "*I will make myself like the Most High*". (Is. 14:14)

An Habitual Blasphemer

> 5 *There was given to him a mouth speaking arrogant words and blasphemies, and authority to act for forty-two months was given to him.* 6 *And he opened his mouth in blasphemies against God, to blaspheme His name and His tabernacle, that is, those who dwell in heaven.*
>
> — Revelation 13:5-6

Three times in two verses we are presented with a reference to blasphemy, and such is specifically directed "*against God*", "*His name and His tabernacle*", and summarized as "*those who dwell in heaven*". Essentially, what Satan through the Antichrist does on earth by going into the Tribulational Temple and demanding to be worshiped—visibly blaspheming God, is overtly directed at all of their heavenly parallels.

As pointed out before, "42" is the biblical number of apostasy, arrived at by multiplying "6", the number of man", by "7", the number of completeness or perfection, to teach us it refers to man's corruption of the perfect. But during this time of the open reign of the Antichrist, notice that his chief, defining activity is to not merely rule the earth politically, but to openly turn every heart and mouth against the Godhead. By using "*forty-two months*" instead of one of the other parallel references to 3-1/2 lunar years, the spiritual aspect of apostasy is being emphasized in parallel with blasphemy as one of the chief spiritual definitions of the nature of his limited reign.

A Defining Difference

> 7 *It was also given to him to make war with the saints and to overcome them, and authority over every tribe and people and tongue and nation was given to him.* 8 *All who dwell on the earth will worship him,* ***everyone whose name has not been written from the foundation of the world in the book of life*** *of the Lamb who has been slain.*
>
> — Revelation 13:7-8

1st century readers would clearly understand from the qualifications provided in the Olivet Discourse that there was going to come an intense period of persecution and unprecedented spiritual darkness Jesus referred to as "*great tribulation*" when, in the character of His instructions to the church at Smyrna they were told, "*Be faithful until death*". (Rev. 2:10)

This is kicked off by the Abomination of Desolation followed closely by Israel's flight into the wilderness, and identified by Christ as so intense that "*for the sake of the elect those days will be cut short*" by the *Harpazo*.

But the purpose for which he exercises his authority is so that, "*All who dwell on the earth will worship him*", and the definition of an "earth-dweller" is someone not found in the book of life. This is the difference between those who worship "*the Lamb who **has** been slain*" and those who worship the beast with "*one of his heads **as if** it has been slain*". (Rev. 13:3) This is the qualifying separation between the members of God's kingdom and that of the Antichrist's and will be reiterated again before Revelation draws to a close:

> *8"The beast that you saw was, and is not, and is about to come up out of the abyss and go to destruction. And **those who dwell on the earth, whose name has not been written in the book of life from the foundation of the world**, will wonder when they see the beast, that he was and is not and will come.*
> — Revelation 17:8

An Overall, Transitional Message

> *9If anyone has an ear, let him hear. 10If anyone is destined for captivity, to captivity he goes; if anyone kills with the sword, with the sword he must be killed. Here is the perseverance and the faith of the saints.*
> — Revelation 13:9-10

There are those who employ the phrase, "the Rapture of the faithful" in their sermons, books or articles who are subsequently deluged with numerous harsh rebukes and even outright attacks for making the Rapture sound so exclusive and, in their antagonists' estimation, unforgiving. (Or highly partisan and inclusive, depending on how one looks at it.) Because the majority view is that it is a "secret" Rapture which takes place with absolutely no warning whatsoever, those adherents are outraged to hear that it is only "the faithful" who will be removed, expecting grace to kick in when this unexpected (in their view) event takes place. Because they think it happens as a complete surprise, they propose that whatever lifestyle of sin a born-again Christian is engaged in at that time will be forgiven so that they will not be left behind, and that everyone who goes to church will be taken in spite of their condition at the time it takes place. But that is not what we mean when calling it "the Rapture of the faithful" because we are looking at ***everything*** which Scripture says will have to be overcome before arriving at what is, in reality, going to be the most public, visible working of Christ to that point in history.

In order to participate in the Rapture, consider all the things which must be traversed both in the prolonged period of "*birth pangs*" leading into what Jesus calls "*tribulation*", and the ensuing more intense, albeit compressed, following period He calls "*great tribulation*". One must survive wars, rumors of wars, famine, pestilence, earthquakes and plagues as fellow Christians abandon their faith and not only apostatize, but openly turn against those who do not. We will not only be hounded by the courts and governments, but betrayed by family and friends and our previous church affiliations.

If we make it through all these things, which Scripture tells us will take a quarter of the earth's population, and we witness the surrounding of Jerusalem and the Abomination of Desolation, we will now navigate an unprecedented persecution and spiritual darkness never experienced in the whole of history, coming in tandem with a change in the way the Holy Spirit works, and with the full, open fury of Satan who has finally and literally been cast down to earth and knows he is down to his last 3-1/2 years. We know the physical casualties for Christians will be unprecedented because Jesus Himself states that if He did not supernaturally intervene to cut that time short, no believer would be left alive.

So consider who is actually left at the end of this process to experience the Rapture. By the fact of sheer physical attrition through all the wars, plagues and persecution, and the spiritual winnowing of the deceived and apostatized, the ***only*** kind of Christian who will be available for the Rapture is someone who is, by definition, "the faithful". Casual, nominal followers and followers in name only will have long left the ranks by the time the removal of the Church takes place. If they recognized any of the signs of His coming, but changed not their ways, as with all the examples in the Olivet Discourse, the Master will return and specifically exclude or remove them.

This is what this transitional admonition to believers in Revelation 13:9-10 is addressing, and why it is qualifying the need for perseverance and faith. As these judgments progress, it will be unavoidable that some of the casualties are going to be believers, and a major issue for them is whether they will remain faithful in spite of what takes place. It is going to be a "Rapture of the faithful" because after all which must be navigated in order to actually see that day, there will be no Christian remaining who is not the embodiment of what it means to be biblically faithful.

Characteristics of the First Beast

The first beast of Revelation 13 is physically described with nearly identical features of the beasts provided in Daniel so as to textually connect all of them together. The traits which are emphasized in this account confirm those provided previously:

- He is ethnically Gentile—"*coming up out of the sea*". (v.1)
- He is satanically sponsored—"*the dragon gave him his power and his throne and great authority*". (v.2)
- He counterfeits the resurrection—"*his fatal wound was healed*". (v.3)
- The world worships Satan through him. (v.4)
- The world thinks he is invincible—"*who is able to wage war with him?*" (v.4)
- He speaks "*arrogant words and blasphemies*". (v.5)
- He is given "*authority to act for forty-two months*". (v.5)
- He blasphemes "*God*", "*His name*", "*His tabernacle*", "*those who dwell in heaven*". (v.6)
- He will "*make war with the saints and to overcome them*".(v.7)
- He will have "*authority over every tribe and people and tongue and nation*". (v.7)
- All earth-dwellers—that is, "*everyone whose name has not been written...in the book of life*"—will worship him.

That which is provided can be considered a New Testament confirmation of all that was previously disclosed in the Old Testament, and is further proof that the partial historical fulfillments by the likes of Antiochus Epiphanes IV and others to follow were just that—partial historical fulfillments pointing to the ultimate and final one to come. The only new, additional detail provided is the counterfeit resurrection. An entirely new supplemental provision, however, is about to be provided in the feature of a false counterfeit of John the Baptist.

17 ❖ Revelation 13: The Beast from the Land

> [11]*Then I saw* ***another beast*** *coming up out of the earth; and he had two horns like a lamb and he spoke as a dragon.*
> — Revelation 13:11

> [20]*And* ***the beast*** *was seized,* ***and with him the false prophet*** *who performed the signs in his presence, by which he deceived those who had received the mark of the beast and those who worshiped his image; these two were thrown alive into the lake of fire which burns with brimstone.*
> — Revelation 19:20

Whereas the first beast arises from the Gentile nations metaphorically depicted as the sea, the second beast's "coming up out of the earth" is the corresponding image of someone coming out of Israel. And whereas Jesus as the authentic Messiah is repeatedly described as a Lamb, this counterfeit possesses "*two horns* ***like*** *a lamb and he spoke as a dragon*". Historically, Judaism has always experienced false messiahs within its own sphere, all of which have been ethnically Jewish, and have consistently rejected those of Gentile ethnicity, so it is not surprising that at least one of the two beasts comes from their own ranks in order to deceive them. There will be many nominal Christians who will buy into what they consider a badge of authority provided by a Jewish heritage as well.

Again, the lack of ethnic distinction in the Church does not prevent anyone from passing back and forth across its borders, (Gal. 3:28) so this figure will probably be able to claim some kind of standing within both camps. The fact that ethnically Jewish believers have been side-by-side members of the Church with their Gentile counterparts in every age of the Church provides an easy explanation of how someone can have a specific ethnicity and at the same time a Christian résumé. But it would not carry the weight within the Gentile Church-at-large necessary for acceptance by traditional adherents of Judaism, which is a big reason for this qualification. In the Apostle John's vernacular, for both Christianity and Judaism schooled in what the Scriptures say about the Antichrist, such a dual background would make him appear to both of them as going out "*from us, but they were not really of us*". (1 Jn. 2:19)

When one considers that Satan's primary goal is to deceive everyone into accepting him in place of Christ, it makes sense why each of these two figures rise respectively to represent every race and nation, as well as why they will need some kind of perceived qualifications connecting them to Christianity and Judaism, and most likely other religions as well. Every member of every race and religion who has already substituted something or someone else in place of Christ has already been successfully deceived and is therefore predisposed to accepting these two beasts; the greater difficulty is how to deceive the rest. And the warning issued by Christ and the New Testament writers more than any other is directed squarely at Christians to not be deceived, the one group who is supposed to know the difference. Or as the Apostle John stipulated, "*But you have an anointing from the Holy One, and **you all know***". (1 Jn. 2:20)

Whereas all other false religions such as Catholicism, Islam, Buddhism and so forth regularly cross racial and geographical boundaries so as to not exclude anyone, Judaism is tied both to the physical land of Israel and maintaining its lineage back to Abraham; they are not going to be deceived by someone who has no Jewish roots or ties, even if that figure dabbles for a time in Christianity. Deceiving Christians likewise requires some kind of perceived qualified formal association with the Church, regardless of ethnic origin, or that figure does not have a chance of success within that group either. This is why the landslide shift among so many denominations and organizations toward Ecumenism—everyone coming together under one roof, so to speak, is a chief sign of the End Times.

This aspect of possible "dual citizenship" within Christianity and Judaism may go a long way toward explaining why this second Antichrist figure is assigned the role of False Prophet, because both of these groups throughout history have proven themselves to be resistant to the pressures of political change in general. Unless they can be spiritually deceived, which has happened to factions within them from time to time, they will continue to operate in faith regardless of the political climate. Both have been dramatically persecuted and attacked and will either bear the circumstances or, very often, relocate to actually experience growth. The two beasts together are an embodiment of being all things to all men in order to deceive the most possible, but with the particular ability to reach into both the Christian and Jewish camps. And, when the time comes, they will be able to influence everyone so as to turn against "*the woman, and...her children*". (Rev. 12:17) An ethnically Jewish False Prophet would also appeal to those Christians who are friendly to Jews in the first place, but especially welcoming of their religious leaders.

This harkens back to a primary reason for the multiple visions presented in Daniel for the same thing but using alternative imagery. In the vision which was originally given to the earthly Gentile King Nebuchadnezzar, from his earthly viewpoint it appears as a beautiful and impressive image of various precious metals; in Daniel's visions, God provides His heavenly perspective to show the truth of their true identities and working as terrifying beasts. The multiple, overlapping visions reveal Satan working to reach across every boundary and into every camp regardless. Likewise, these two beasts possess something to recommend them to everyone whether they are a believer or not, and regardless of anyone's ethnic or religious origin; they strive to be all things to all mankind.

But with Satan standing on the shore to oversee the rise of these beasts, the more important issue which is being brought to our attention is to disclose the ultimate goal of this trio, which is to effect a complete counterfeit of the triune Godhead. Satan's goal is to provide a substitute for each of the Father, Son and Holy Spirit. This is the ultimate subversion of the truth.

An Exclusive Agent

> 12 *He exercises all the authority of the first beast in his presence. And he makes the earth and those who dwell in it to worship the first beast, whose fatal wound was healed.*
>
> — Revelation 13:12

In the opening image of this second beast as a counterfeit lamb, there is something missing: he has horns, but no crowns, which symbolize authority. This is remedied with the explanation that the authority he possesses comes exclusively through the first beast. We begin to clearly see why he is designated the False Prophet in that he does not act outside the first beast's presence in a visible example of his devotion and service to him, and that his chief function is to foster "*worship of the first beast*". This second reference to the first beast's "*fatal wound*" reinforces that what is being worshiped is not authentic but an eye-catching counterfeit in the same manner as the second beast. As a parallel counterfeit to John the Baptist, he points everyone to the counterfeit Christ. But whereas the authentic John confessed, "*He must increase, but I must decrease*" (Jn. 3:30), the counterfeit publicly works "*in his presence*".

A Master Manipulator

> [13]*He performs great signs, so that he even makes fire come down out of heaven to the earth in the presence of men.* [14]*And he deceives those who dwell on the earth because of the signs which it was given him to perform in the presence of the beast, telling those who dwell on the earth to make an image to the beast who had the wound of the sword and has come to life.*
>
> — Revelation 13:13-14

In a replay of the Exodus motif where Pharaoh's magicians, to a point, successfully counterfeited some of the signs performed by Moses and Aaron, the False Prophet mirrors at least one of the signs of the Two Witnesses in making "*fire come down out of heaven*". (Rev. 11:5) In other words, like Jannes and Jambres imitating Moses and Aaron, at least some of the signs which the Two Witnesses perform are duplicated by the False Prophet in an impressive public deception. That this is speaking of the performing of real miracles and therefore cannot be allegorized or spiritualized away is confirmed by the text's inclusion of the added detail that this takes place "*in the presence of men*". But the qualification, "*the signs which it was given him to perform*" reinforces that no one in Satan's camp is equal in power or ability to God's entire spectrum of authentic works. The things which the false can accomplish may be genuine signs and wonders, but they are limited in scope and always seem to mirror a smaller subset of the authentic. Like Jannes and Jambres, they can only duplicate things to a certain point.

These details further serve to confirm both Paul's teaching that the Antichrist is coming "*in accord with the activity of Satan, with all power and signs and false wonders*", (2 Th. 2:9) and Christ's Olivet Discourse stipulation, "*For false Christs and false prophets will arise and will show great signs and wonders, so as to mislead, if possible, even the elect*". (Mt. 24:24) But where the False Prophet is concerned, there is an accompanying restriction that he performs these things "*in the presence of the beast*" because his primary purpose is to deify and engender worship of the first beast. It is an interesting counterfeit of the authentic Messiah who once stated, "*Though you do not believe Me, believe the works so that you may know and understand that the Father is in Me, and I in the Father*" (Jn. 10:38), the False Prophet attempting a parallel deception by performing only in the presence of the first beast.

For those schooled in Israel's history and the Hebraic approach to studying Scriptures, two prominent associations most likely immediately come to mind when presented with the command to "*make an image to the beast*": Nebuchadnezzar and Antiochus Epiphanes IV.

In Nebuchadnezzar's God-given dream in Daniel 2, the king was portrayed as the topmost part of the impressive image as gold, trailed by subsequent kingdoms of diminishing metals covering less and less prestigious parts of the statue. But on his own accord in Daniel 3, he erects a whole image of himself made completely of gold and, in effect, self-deifies himself by ordering worship of the image. And, of course, what follows is the famous biblical account of Shadrach, Meshach and Abed-nego.

But historically, this also has parallels to the actions of Antiochus Epiphanes IV, who goes into the Temple and erects a statue of Zeus superimposing his own face on the image, and not only bans the reading of Scripture but all Temple practices so as to foster worship of his own example of self-deification in a forerunner of what to expect of the final Abomination of Desolation to come. Just as the two beasts represent both the Gentile nations and Israel, in the book of Daniel there are prominent examples of false images provided in both a Gentile and Jewish setting to draw upon. 1st century believers would see clear parallels to what to a certain point had already been experienced in both Israel's scriptural and historical narratives. This detail about the image dedicated to the beast would very comfortably fit with what they pictured of the Abomination of Desolation in keeping with what had already taken place.

But there is a very important detail in the text which seems to be rarely visited, "***telling*** *those who dwell on the earth to make an image to the beast*". Whereas Aaron once famously took it upon himself to supply the golden calf to those appealing to him for a false god (Ex. 32:1-4), the False Prophet places this burden on the earth dwellers. The image of the beast is something commonly acknowledged, but is actually only transacted by the second beast, not the first. It is important to note that the things which are assigned to the False Prophet are unique to him and not simply parallel activities or traits to the first beast. When the False Prophet bursts onto the scene, he is accompanied by activities assigned exclusively to him, and one of them is commissioning the first beast's followers to make this image.

A Supernatural Image of Worship

> *15And it was given to him to give breath to the image of the beast, so that the image of the beast would even speak and cause as many as do not worship the image of the beast to be killed.*
>
> — Revelation Rev. 13:15

The new aspect of all of this which 1st century Christians would have recognized as belonging exclusively to the final Abomination of Desolation is giving life to the image. But like both Nebuchadnezzar and Epiphanes IV, they would see the existing parallels that refusal to worship invokes a death sentence. The greater issue is not executing the ultimate "magic trick", but that the greater purpose behind all the signs and wonders is to regulate worship.

In modern times, before embracing the possibility of this taking place through the use of computers ("Siri, who is the god of this world?") or genetic engineering, due consideration needs to be given to the possibility that this is accomplished as the result of something actually coming to life. The world has been to Disneyland enough times to know the difference between something real and something animatronic. When we accept that there have been other beings such as an eagle who is seen active and living and speaking, it is not an outrageous leap of faith that the same thing can be effected upon an image. These figures counterfeit practically everything else, so why not a counterfeit creator? It would be a powerful addition to worshiping the beast recovered from his wound as having the perceived power over life and death.

When considering all the possibilities as to how something like this can come true, one of the distinct options which we should ***not*** automatically discard is a literal fulfillment. It is difficult to believe modern man, now so tech savvy in the majority of the world, can be fooled by a computer regardless of how well it mimics a person, and the context in which this is presented is that the False Prophet "*performs great signs…in the presence of men*". (Rev. 13:13) Like Jannes and Jambres, the signs which the False Prophet performs are authentic, albeit originating from a different source.

But once again the emphasis is overwhelmingly placed upon "*worship*". This irrecoverable act will later be associated with its eternal consequences when in hell they will experience "*the smoke of their torment goes up forever and ever; they have no rest day and night, those who worship the beast and his image*". (Rev. 14:11) All of this work and effort has the same goal for each of the members of this satanic trinity, to engender worship.

The Mark

> [16]*And he causes all, the small and the great, and the rich and the poor, and the free men and the slaves, to be given a mark on their right hand or on their forehead,* [17]*and he provides that no one will be able to buy or to sell, except the one who has the mark, either the name of the beast or the number of his name.*
>
> [18]*Here is wisdom. Let him who has understanding calculate the number of the beast, for the number is that of a man; and his number is six hundred and sixty-six.*
>
> — Revelation 13:16-18

We could probably pen an entire book on the subject of marking as provided in the whole of Scripture, and then another thousand volumes on all the speculation surrounding it. There is the marking of God's faithful in Ezekiel 9, his marking of the 144,000, the equivalent language assigned to what happens to Christians who are "marked", so to speak, with the Holy Spirit, and even the Mosaic Law which led to wearing phylacteries on the forehead and hand (Ex. 13:16) containing quotes from God's Word as examples on the "plus" side of the equation. On the opposite there is not just those taking the mark of the beast, but the Antichrist himself who is marked with blasphemous names on each of his heads, (Rev. 13:1) and we must not overlook the Roman mandated census in the Nativity Narrative which was actually "marking" the population for the purposes of financial control, which have obvious parallels to what is specified here as part of the mark of the beast.

There has been so much conjecture over this feature of the eschaton, which has become so famous that it is universally accepted by practically every secular corner of the world as well as nearly every religious venue regardless of origin, that we could spend the rest of our lives just listing and rebutting each and every variation. So we are going to make a good faith effort to limit our discussion to what may be the most important issues arising from an exegetical point of view—what can be gleaned from the ***text***?

That Satan would choose to do this is not actually something new to Scripture, but merely just another in a long line of attempts to counterfeit the authentic working of God. In the Old Testament covenant God's Word was to "*serve as a sign to you on your hand, and as a reminder on your forehead*", (Ex. 13:9, 16; Dt. 6:6-8; 11:18) the faithful in Ezekiel were marked on their forehead, (Eze. 9:4) and likewise in the New Testament the 144,000. (Rev. 7:3) In fact, one of the aspects concerning all who will live with God in eternity is that "*they will see His face, and His name will be on their foreheads*". (Rev. 22:4) It is to the utmost detriment for those who do not know that such marking is first and foremost a feature of a right relationship with God and are only aware of the satanic counterfeit. More concern needs to be exerted to obtain the mark of God so as to never need worry about the mark of the beast since, in all instances, it is no coincidence that all of the examples of God marking someone take place ***before*** those of the satanic counterfeits following them.

The common element which seems to most often get lost in the game show tussle over solving this puzzle is that the mark is actually an "either/or": "*the mark, **either** the name of the beast **or** the number of his name*". There is an unhealthy ignorance which comes with over-realizing just "*the **number** of his name*" to the exclusion of the actual "***name** of the beast*". Yes, ancient languages such as Greek and Hebrew for a time used their alphabets in place of separate ordinal numbers, assigning a number to each letter so that a mathematical equivalent is possible for any word in their language by adding up the sum of each letter. (This is called "Gematria".) But the text here specifies that this is only one way the mark will literally appear when applied; the other is for his whole name to be used. When it comes time to take the mark, it will not be offered in some manner which attempts to veil the Antichrist's true identity, but will provide the option of plainly and publicly using his name.

This may be a very important point because so many theories involve something "coded" so as to possibly deceive people into taking the mark against their will under surreptitious circumstances or by trickery. No, the plain and open alternative of being stamped with his literal name is addressing the key issue that although financial control is part of the equation, what this is primarily addressing is the issue of worship.

We know that 1st century readers unambiguously understood that to "*calculate the number of the beast*" meant to apply Gematria, where each letter's numerical value in a name is summed into an overall total, because almost immediately there are those who began the madness of calculating practically everyone's name. It did not merely begin with "Nero" nor end with "Henry Kissinger" or "Colonel Sanders", as there is no shortage of websites dedicated to this calculation. (The true craziness is when they do not stop with ancient Greek or Hebrew but employ it for languages which never engaged in this practice, such as English.) But there is no doubt that the Early Church received this as a reference to Gematria and it's been off to the "Bible codes" races ever since.

The keyword in all of this, however, which has most often escaped notice from the beginning to the present hour is "*wisdom*". The repeated biblical definition of "*wisdom*" is something which can only be possessed by Holy Spirit-filled believers in Christ.

> 20*Where is the wise man? Where is the scribe? Where is the debater of this age? **Has not God made foolish the wisdom of the world**?*
> —1 Corinthians 1:20

> 30*But by His doing you are in **Christ Jesus, who became to us wisdom from God**, and righteousness and sanctification, and redemption,*
> —1 Corinthians 1:30

That wisdom can only be possessed by believers is further reinforced by the additional qualifier, "*Let him who has understanding*", or as we have repeatedly quoted Daniel:

> 10*"Many will be purged, purified and refined, but the wicked will act wickedly; and **none of the wicked will understand, but those who have insight will understand**.*
> —Daniel 12:10

This is actually replaying the very first problem encountered in the first vision of Daniel 2, as explained in the *Introduction* to this book. No wisdom of the world can unlock the meaning. It will take the wisdom of God revealed to His servants in order to be understood.

When appropriate within the greater scheme of God's timing, there will come a milestone in the course of the eschaton when faithful, Holy Spirit-filled believers will successfully perform this calculation. In the meantime, there may be no more potent example of God allowing the wisdom of the world to display its true substance of foolishness than in the body of opinion and accompanying deliberation of "666".

A Beneficial Side-Effect

It is difficult to know how soon after the first readings of Revelation by the Church near the end of the 1st Century that Christians would leverage the revelation of "666" and the figures of each of the two beasts to understand previous portions of Scripture which, to that time, remained veiled. But because the Early Church was still very close to its Hebraic roots and way of handling Scripture, it is difficult to believe that it took very long. But in brief, there would be a number of references to "666" which would not redefine any previous point of knowledge or overall doctrine, but serve to provide affirmation to those challenged, "*If anyone has an ear, let him hear*" (Rev. 13:9). Some things previously concealed in the Old Testament...

- In the original Aramaic, "666" is the measurement of Nebuchadnezzar's false image (Dan. 3:1) drawing a textual connection to the image of Revelation 13.
- In the original Hebrew, this is the measurement of Goliath's size, armor and weaponry, (1 Sam. 17:4-7) a figure who was accompanied by a type of the False Prophet in his shield-carrier. Notice that David responds to Goliath's blasphemy of God in a replay of the character of the Antichrist who comes into conflict with the Son of David.
- Solomon was not only associated with receiving tribute of "*666 talents of gold*", (1 Ki. 10:14; 2 Ch. 9:13), but his throne consisted of six steps with six lions on each side. (1 Ki. 10:19-20). Along with his spiritual falling away, he very much looks like someone who "*went out from us*", (1 Jn. 2:19) someone with a complicated background traversing both ends of the spiritual spectrum.
- There would certainly be discussions about the entry in the post-Babylonian census, "*the sons of Adonikam, 666*". (Ezra 2:13)

Likewise when it was observed that the dragon pursues the child, obvious parallels to Herod the Great and his attempt to kill the Christ child (not to overlook both Herod's and the Antichrist's association with the Temple) would be observed. Many other figures in Scripture would now be seen which exhibited strong parallels to either one or both of the beasts not just in Nebuchadnezzar, Goliath and Solomon, but for others as well. None of these things replaced or redefined anything, but served to substantially add to what was already plainly stated in the overt text of Scripture. The details given concerning the Antichrist in Revelation actually unlock an even deeper understanding of what was originally established in the first place.

In point of fact, it is this author's opinion that the main recurring reason confusion and dissension is abundant when it comes to the topic of the Antichrist is that the aforementioned reversal of the chronology of Scripture is so often employed. For those who allow Revelation to be the starting point of interpretation and make all previous Scripture secondary and subordinate, effectively reversing the order in which God spoke on the topic, the range of results span from inconsistent to topsy-turvy. The primary order must be the same as demonstrated by Christ Himself, who in the Olivet Discourse first drew upon all that was established through Daniel. The book of Daniel, the Olivet Discourse, and the minimal additions of the Apostles Paul and John in their Epistles must be the starting basis for properly interpreting what is presented in

Revelation as the last in the sequence of what is revealed in God's Word. In turn, a retrospective revelation takes place uncovering elements of Scripture containing affirming parallels which are otherwise closed to the casual observer.

But there is another detail in the text which is largely overlooked when it comes to the mark, "*And **he** causes all...to be given a mark*". (Rev. 13:16) This is not something initiated or even maintained by the first beast, but one of the unique activities exclusively assigned to the False Prophet. The timing of the appearance of the False Prophet coincides with public campaign to worship the beast. This is the purpose of those things ascribed to the False Prophet alone in that he performs signs and wonders in the presence of the first beast, he commissions the earth dwellers to make the image he brings to life and commands to be worshiped, and he oversees the mark and its requirement of worship. These things which we often associated with the first figure we call the Antichrist are actually restricted to the domain of the False Prophet.

We have to consider the fact that until this point in the biblical text, where this nefarious pair is "*given...authority to act for forty-two months*" (Rev. 13:5) that they do not appear simultaneously nor is the False Prophet working from the very first appearance of the Antichrist. Satan calls the first beast from the sea, who we see active as the first horseman counterfeiting Christ in the 1st Seal near the beginning of Daniel's 70th Week. The dragon subsequently calls the second beast from the land, whose appearance seems to coincide with the midway point of the final week of years when the Abomination of Desolation takes place and the public self-deification of the first beast takes place. At that point the False Prophet would simultaneously launch the satanic campaign of worship through his signs and wonders, the commissioning of the image and giving it life, and the requirement of the mark, all of which are focused on worship. Whereas the Antichrist's activities were previously focused on the economic and geopolitical, it is all finally and openly revealed to actually be a spiritual agenda. This might go a long way in explaining why Israel will sign the covenant and so many nominal Christians will follow the first beast.

Summary

The understanding of the Antichrist prior to Revelation, which Jesus allowed to stand uncorrected in the Olivet Discourse, served as the baseline for what amounts to being expanded details which followed. The foundational description of a one-world Gentile political figure with tendencies toward self-deification was reinforced in the disclosure of a pair of figures in Revelation 13 because this is still the primary assignment of the first beast; the second beast defers and points to him. What emerged in the revelation of the second beast was the clarification that although politically powerful, the real issue at the core of their working is worship ultimately ascribed to Satan. The details pertaining to the Antichrist in Revelation serve to refine the overall picture so as to teach the greater spiritual issues at work rather than being tempted to focus solely on the geopolitical.

This satanic counterfeit of the Trinity, who will be able to cross not just ethnic but religious barriers, is specifically allotted "*authority to act for forty-two months*". (Rev. 13:5) As established in the Olivet Discourse, the emphasis is placed upon the last half of the 70th Week of Daniel initiated by the Abomination of Desolation; this is the same emphasis provided by Daniel as well, designating an overall "week of years" but focusing all the attention on the second half.

The specific assignment of this time limit is accompanied by descriptions of activities carried out by Satan through the two beasts which have more to do with their spiritual agenda to deceive and garner self-worship than anything else. The signs performed, the miraculous healing of the fatal wound, the introduction of a talking image—all of these things are qualified as either having to do with obtaining mankind's worship or leading them in open blasphemy against God. Having already documented their political agenda where the whole world is concerned, Revelation 13 focuses on their mutual religious intentions. Whereas Daniel is more oriented as a geopolitical road map emphasizing the succession of world kingdoms, Revelation is a very detailed exposé of how this is ultimately reflected in worship, and the decision of whether to worship Christ, or through Antichrist, Satan; it is a roadmap emphasizing the worship of the anti-king.

To complete the picture of what is truly taking place, there is the visible marking of the worshipers of the beast in yet another counterfeit of God's repeated examples of marking believers. It may be too simple to express this as the ultimate test of allegiance or a tool of persuasion by making economic slaves. The choice to be marked by God or marked by the beast is actually a life or death choice concerning worship.

Finally, consider the role that the Temple plays in all of these things, both the heavenly one repeatedly visited and referenced throughout Revelation and its earthly counterpart. In heaven, the throne of God is affixed within the Temple and it is from here that we do not merely observe God's authority and commandments being carried out, but repeated scenes of worship taking place. Satan is attempting to counterfeit this through the Antichrist by taking over the Tribulational Temple in order to rule and be worshiped himself albeit in the earthly realm. The reason there is such an emphasis on the last half of Daniel's 70th Week is that it is initiated by the Abomination of Desolation, and from that point forward Satan in every way is attempting to accomplish through the earthly Temple an imitation of what transpires in the heavenly. Just as the emphasis in heaven is worship, so is the aim of this satanic counterfeit on earth. And as will be seen in the following chapters of Revelation, in his quest for worship he will turn on his own surrogates.

We are not just looking for the first beast, but his accompanying False Prophet as well:

- The first beast comes as a counterfeit to Christ, the second as a counterfeit to John the Baptist.
- "*...coming up out of the earth...*" (v.11) He will be of Jewish ethnicity, even if his religious credentials span Christianity and beyond.
- "*...he had two horns like a lamb...*" (v.11) Like the first beast, he will attempt to look like Christ but be absent the corresponding crowns of authority.
- "*...he spoke as a dragon*". (v.11) He will also be animated by Satan.
- "*He exercises all the authority of the first beast in his presence.*" (v.12) In a counterfeit of John the Baptist, everything he does will be for the promotion of the first beast.
- "*...he makes the earth and those who dwell in it worship the first beast...*" (v.12) His true agenda is worship.
- "*He performs great signs, so that he even makes fire come down out of heaven to the earth in the presence of men*". (v.13) He will perform authentic signs, even counterfeiting, at least to a degree, those of the Two Witnesses.
- "*...he deceives those who dwell on the earth because of the signs which it was given him to perform in the presence of the beast...*" (v.14) Like the first beast and his primary instigator in Satan, he is a master deceiver.

- "*...telling those on the earth to make an image to the beast...*" (v.14) He will lead the earth-dwellers from mere worship into the deeper pit of idolatry.
- "*...it was given to him to give breath to the image of the beast, so that the image of the beast would even speak...*" He will take idolatry to a level never before witnessed.
- "*...cause as many as do not worship the image of the beast to be killed*". (v.15) He will replay the antics of those like Nebuchadnezzar and Antiochus Epiphanes IV whose penalty for failure to engage in idolatry involving their self-deification was death.
- "*...he causes all...to be given a mark on their right hand or on their forehead...*" (v.16) He will counterfeit God's marking.
- "*...provides that no one will be able to buy or to sell, except the one who has the mark...*" (v.17) He will leverage taking the mark by incorporating it into the economy.
- "*...the mark, either the name of the beast or the number of his name*". (v.17) It will not just be a number, but "*the name of the beast*" in a further surge both in false worship and idolatry.

This addition of the second beast provides the majority of the "new", not previously disclosed details concerning the Antichrist, and in particular the revelation of "666" opens up previous Scripture to provide more types and illustrations of these final figures. In particular, readers are going to want to study an example of the Antichrist and False Prophet which is recorded three times in the Old Testament in the time of King Hezekiah in the form of the King of Assyria as a figure of the Antichrist, and his emissary Rabshakeh as a figure of the False Prophet. (2 Ki. 18:13-19:37; 2 Ch. 32:1-31; Is. 36-37)

Their assigned ethnicities answer the critical question of how Satan's last foray will penetrate across groups who historically are at the least highly resistant to coming together voluntarily. Together with assumed claims of multiple religious affiliations, they combine to be all things to all men.

But because of his never previously being disclosed in Scripture until this designation of the final "*forty-two months*" of the final week of years, and the fact that each of his assignments are uniquely associated with worship of the first beast, it is not beyond a reasonable interpretation of the given text that this figure's appearance is delayed until the midway point—the Abomination of Desolation. Whereas the rise to power of the first beast can be mainly characterized as aimed at the economic and geopolitical, with that act of public self-deification coinciding with the halfway point it all becomes plainly and openly religious.

18 ❖ Revelation 17: Babylon the Great

Whereas the prior emphasis was on the anti-king, Revelation 17-18 provide a scriptural focus on the anti-kingdom. As touched on previously, the Antichrist is actually comprised of two beasts, the first one more oriented toward commanding a one-world political system, and the second the False Prophet who is focused on the one-world religious system which worships Satan through the first beast. Combined with the spirit of antichrist which is at work during every historical age, a counterfeit Trinity brings together on earth the final kingdom predicted by Daniel which attempts to control the whole world politically, economically and religiously.

Up until the progression of events associated with the eschaton, this has been a conflict mainly being played out in the spiritual realm. But a time comes in this process when Satan and his fallen angelic followers are permanently thrown out of heaven and down to earth where they openly make their last stand before ultimately being cast into their lowest final destination, the Lake of Fire. Revelation expresses this as a conflict between the kingdom of God and the kingdom of Antichrist, each kingdom defined by its citizenry. Whereas we might measure earthly kingdoms or nations by the amount of land they occupy or the natural resources they control or even the size of their military, in this case these things are secondary to the number of followers who are found to embrace it from the heart. The key indicator for the kingdom of God versus that of Satan has always been "worship"—do you worship the One True God, or through the many available alternatives, Satan?

Choosing Whom to Worship

As repeatedly pointed out in both the Old and New Testaments, the text is not exclusively fixated on the anti-king, but seamlessly alternates, sometimes even within the same sentence, between king and kingdom. Whom to follow and worship is specifically articulated by God through angelic agency in Revelation 14 when three consecutive messages are broadcast to the planet by angels "*flying in midheaven*"—that is, they visibly appear within mankind's sight in the atmosphere.

> 6*And I saw another angel flying in midheaven, having an eternal gospel to preach to those who live on the earth, and to every nation and tribe and tongue and people;* 7*and he said with a loud voice, "**Fear God**, and give Him glory, because the hour of His judgment has come; **worship Him** who made the heaven and the earth and sea and springs of waters."*
>
> — Revelation 14:6-7

The first announcement is the presentation of "*an eternal gospel*" accompanied with a call to "*Fear God...worship Him*". The positive alternative to worship the true King is first offered.

> *8And another angel, a second one, followed, saying, "**Fallen, fallen is Babylon the great**, she who has made all the nations drink of the wine of the passion of her immorality."*
>
> — Revelation 14:8

The second message is a pronouncement of God's judgment upon the anti-kingdom.

> *9Then another angel, a third one, followed them, saying with a loud voice, "**If anyone worships the beast and his image**, and receives a mark on his forehead or on his hand, 10**he also will drink of the wine of the wrath of God**, which is mixed in full strength in the cup of His anger; and he will be tormented with fire and brimstone in the presence of the holy angels and in the presence of the Lamb. 11And the smoke of their torment goes up forever and ever; **they have no rest day and night, those who worship the beast and his image, and whoever receives the mark of his name.**"*
>
> — Revelation 14:9-11

The third follows up with a pronouncement of judgment upon the anti-king and his followers, twice mentioning the determining criteria of "*worship*" of the beast. First the call to right worship, then the consequences for wrong worship.

The struggle between these two sides has been repeatedly brought up over and over again throughout the whole of Revelation. Even during the Church Age as represented by the letters to the seven churches, the issue of satanic activity is prominently documented. (Rev. 2:8, 13, 24; 3:9) This struggle began even before the creation of the earth, is currently being played out largely in the spiritual realms of both heaven and earth at present (Eph. 6:12), but a time comes when it is to be completely and totally resolved in this visible earthly venue before everything and everyone returns to living together with the Godhead in eternity. In the meantime, however, the chief activities of Satan through his Antichrist counterparts is to ultimately unify all the separate earthly kingdoms into a final one under his control, and in parallel to consolidate all the disparate religious factions into a one-world religion. This is why modern-day Christians pay so much attention to inter-faith movements such as when the pope extends invitations to normally competing faiths or assertions are made that all religions worship the same God. (The 500th anniversary of the Reformation this year was particularly disturbing in all the calls for ecumenical reunification.)

While it is easy for most of us to imagine the possibility of governments being conquered, coerced or signing on through negotiation to join a one-world government, it is much more difficult to envision how this could be accomplished across the world's religious landscape, given that even within the same religion there is often outright conflict between its own adherents. There may be a particular aspect of the Roman Empire which aids in explaining how this might be accomplished, which almost since its inception the Catholic Church employs and which we expect this final kingdom to emulate. One of the ways the Romans integrated nations with different religions was through the Roman Pantheon, where anyone's god could be added as long as their first allegiance was to the emperor. For a time this is what it will be like, where as long as the Antichrist is worshiped, every faith can participate.

In our time, every group who believes in some form of a Messiah is predicting theirs is about to return, albeit each having their own name for this figure, Christians and Jews included. It is not difficult to imagine the Antichrist coming as all things to all men and engaging in a process akin to a modern-day Pantheon inclusive of everyone's beliefs. It is also not difficult to see that such an endeavor is not strictly a religious enterprise but requires a parallel political compromise and process as well to succeed, and sometimes even outright military conflict, which goes hand-in-hand with financial control and incentives. The Romans were masters at employing both, and actually "conquered" more countries by negotiation than armed conflict, in each case adding yet another god to the Pantheon and increasing the number of the deified emperors' followers. Notice how the Seals open with the Antichrist pre-counterfeiting Christ on a white horse in a representation of false peace before assuming the overtly hostile role of the red horse employing outright force.

One of the reasons the False Prophet is not specifically mentioned in Scripture until the final half of Daniel's 70th Week when authority is given to these beasts (Rev. 13:5) may be that the first beast is active politically before the second engages the world religiously. This scenario would allow for the false peace and prosperity to take hold across all demographic boundaries. In other words, by conquering hearts and minds through avenues of the flesh both politically and economically so as to eliminate the political and social differences inherent in all societies, the ensuing campaign to abolish religious differences is accomplished much easier than if it began in that arena. The first success on a worldly level sets the stage for the subsequent success on the spiritual level. This may also help to explain the shock expressed over the economic loss of "Babylon the Great" when the Antichrist turns on and has her destroyed so as to be worshiped directly instead of through her. (Rev. 18:9-19) It also explains why she is riding on the back, leveraging the beast's political rise for her own spiritual rise.

However, whereas a modern-day Christian living in a Western democracy such as the United States views government as a three-legged stool equally comprised of the executive, legislative and judicial branches, the tripartite structure of the kingdom of the Antichrist is going to be political, religious, and economic. This is revealed in Revelation 17-18 as these three aspects are not only shown in greater detail, but in their respective reactions to what the beast does to the harlot.

For 1st century Christians absorbing all that Revelation has to contribute to what Scripture has already established eschatologically, they were living under this primary example of the Roman Empire and witnessed firsthand how it simultaneously used politics and religion to accomplish its goals to maintain its singular control. Especially with Roman emperors at the top of the system who deified themselves in the character of the final Antichrist to come, it was not difficult for early Christians to imagine that this would be just like the final earthly kingdom to come as expressed by both Daniel and the Apostle John. Especially because that first generation firmly believed Jesus was coming back in their lifetime—as every generation likewise does, they directly associated much of what John and Daniel provided with the literal Roman Empire and emperors under which they lived, even as parts of the Roman Empire lingered into the 5th Century. (Augustus Caesar became the first emperor in 31 BC and Romulus Augustulus was the last one deposed in 476 AD.) And as Peter specifically called Rome "*Babylon*" (1 Pe. 5:13), it is not difficult to see why they so often linked them together. That which early Christians were experiencing literally turns out to be a foreshadowing of the ultimate fulfillment to eventually come.

The Importance of Babylon

Having finished with each of the Bowl judgments, John is now provided a detailed account of what just took place with Satan's earthly institutions which have actually been active in one form or another ever since the Tower of Babel and Nimrod's establishment of the original Babylon on the plains of Shinar, again foreshadowing a literal, final institution which rises in the course of the eschaton as the central element of the kingdom of Antichrist. "*Babylon*" is one of those repeating elements throughout the whole of history, each iteration teaching something about the final one to come. Revelation takes another break from the chronological timeline to go back and explain what just happened to the institutions and followers of the Antichrist and False Prophet which have been plaguing the "*end of the age*" overall.

As an example of how important the issue and theme of Babylon is in Scripture, it is worth noting that most Christians do not even realize that this is the primary reason for the order of the books in the Old Testament. In a larger sense, the Old Testament uses the Babylonian Captivity as a major historical and spiritual hinge:

- There are twelve books of history. The first nine from Joshua through 2 Chronicles deal with Israel's history prior to the Babylonian Captivity; the last three (Ezra, Nehemiah, Esther) deal with Israel's Post-Babylonian return.
- There are five books authored by the four Major Prophets. The first two, Isaiah and Jeremiah, deal with Israel's history prior to the Babylonian Captivity; the last two, Daniel and Ezekiel, deal mainly with the Post-Babylonian era. The middle book, Lamentations, documents what took place during the fall to Babylon.
- There are twelve Minor Prophets. The first nine from Hosea through Zephaniah deal with Israel and Judah prior to the Babylonian Captivity; the final three (Haggai, Zechariah and Malachi) with the Post-Babylonian return.

The repeated issues of dealing with every historical iteration of Babylon up to and including the very last age of history is one of the most important re-visited themes of both biblical history and eschatology.

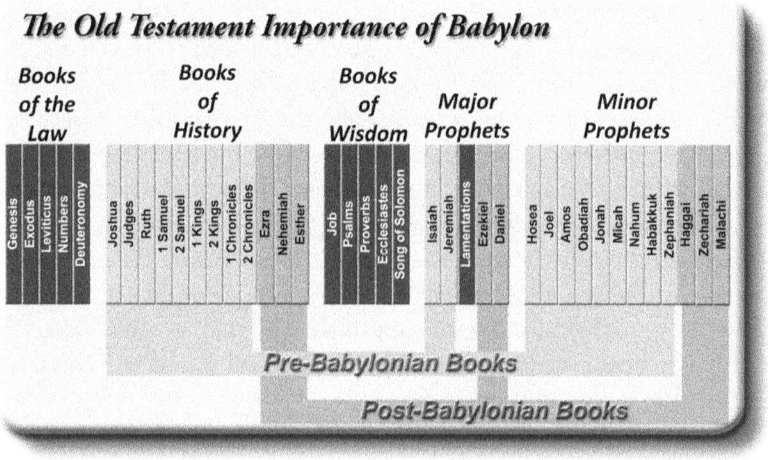

The Mother of Harlots

> *[1]Then one of the seven angels who had the seven bowls came and spoke with me, saying, "Come here, I will show you the judgment of the great harlot who sits on many waters, [2]with whom the kings of the earth committed acts of immorality, and those who dwell on the earth were made drunk with the wine of her immorality."*
>
> *[3]And he carried me away in the Spirit into a wilderness; and I saw a woman sitting on a scarlet beast, full of blasphemous names, having seven heads and ten horns. [4]The woman was clothed in purple and scarlet, and adorned with gold and precious stones and pearls, having in her hand a gold cup full of abominations and of the unclean things of her immorality, [5]and on her forehead a name was written, a mystery, "BABYLON THE GREAT, THE MOTHER OF HARLOTS AND OF THE ABOMINATIONS OF THE EARTH." [6]And I saw the woman drunk with the blood of the saints, and with the blood of the witnesses of Jesus. When I saw her, I wondered greatly.*
>
> *[7]And the angel said to me, "Why do you wonder? I will tell you the mystery of the woman and of the beast that carries her, which has the seven heads and the ten horns.*
>
> —Revelation 17:1-7

Two main characters are presented, "*the great harlot*" who sits on the beast and is named "*Babylon the Great*", and the beast carrying her which reverts to previous descriptions of him as a kingdom with "*seven heads and ten horns*".

Because Israel was the intended bride of Yahweh, one of the repeated themes throughout Scripture is the equating of marital faithfulness to spiritual faithfulness and marital adultery as a depiction of spiritual unfaithfulness. At times, when Israel's unfaithfulness achieved unprecedented depths, especially due to her forsaking God and in turn going after the false gods of the nations around them, He addressed them in the character of a harlot. This was because spiritually they went beyond merely being unfaithful to a single husband, spiritually selling themselves like a prostitute to a host of other false gods and religions. This is key to understanding the whole meaning of this woman being designated "*the mother of harlots and the abominations of the earth*" because this is not just describing merely being unfaithful to God, but the embodiment of the world religious system which spawns this adulterous spirituality in others and fosters the pursuit of anything and everything in place of the One True God.

In Alexander Hislop's seminal work, *The Two Babylons* [print and eBook versions available from Amazon.com], it is documented how the world's false religions, which had their beginning with Nimrod and the original iteration of Babylon which came through him after the Flood, were founded on what is commonly referred to as the mystery religions of Babylon. These were not only leveraged by most false religions to come throughout the entire world, but he shows how the core of this phenomenon made its way through modern Turkey ("*I know where you dwell, where Satan's throne is*"—that is, Pergamum in Revelation 2:13) and ultimately to Rome, in what was initially the previously discussed Pantheon, but ultimately incorporated by the Roman Catholic Church in their system of saints and such.

What appears to have begun with the Babylonian goddess Semiramis, and adopted into subsequent variants such as Venus, Fortuna or the Queen of Heaven (this is a particularly interesting example being that the Catholic Church has since assigned this name to their version of Mary), the point is that there has always been a major female figure at the forefront of these false religions and they have all carried with them this spirit of seduction. It is amazing how many similar characteristics they share, some of them even claiming to have performed a virgin birth to a son and many other things counterfeiting both Mary and Christ.

The important aspect for us to understand is that the greater representation of this woman has to do with the false religions of the world which spiritually seduce adherents away from a faithful relationship singularly dedicated to Christ in favor of going after anything and everything else in the character of a prostitute engaging many lovers. However, Scripture pinpoints the common source, assigning it specifically to Babylon the Great.

In Scripture, "good" women such as Ruth, Hannah, Sarah and the like typify a right and faithful spiritual relationship, whereas the "bad" ones such as Jezebel, Athaliah, Herodias and such not only typify spiritual unfaithfulness, but usually engage in active seduction so as to draw away as many as possible. In Revelation, it is a worthy study in itself to examine the four women presented:

- Jezebel (Rev. 2:20)—the very symbol of apostasy gaining a hold within the Church
- Israel (Rev. 12:1)
- The Harlot (Rev. 17)—the unfaithful world system
- The Bride of Christ, the Church (Rev. 19:7)

These teach about various aspects of spiritual faithfulness/unfaithfulness affecting everyone, Jew and Gentile alike, saved and unsaved alike. Apostasy within the Church or Israel proper is actually the result of succumbing to spiritual seduction, that to which the rest of the world has already capitulated.

In the closing chapters of Revelation, the comparison and contrast of two women is going to be specifically addressed, first here in chapter 17 with the harlot who rides the beast and the consequences she will suffer, but then in chapter 19 with the Bride of Christ and the benefits she will enjoy. The Bride is clothed in "*fine linen, bright and clean*" which characterize "*the righteous acts of the saints*" (Rev. 19:8); the harlot is "*clothed in purple and scarlet*" with all the accoutrements to make her appealing from a worldly point of view (Rev. 17:4), but her deeds are "*acts of immorality*" (Rev. 17:2), "*abominations*" and "*unclean things*" (Rev. 17:4), and the blood of the martyrs (Rev. 17:6). These are the ultimate, stark differences between spiritual faithfulness and unfaithfulness; the righteous are naturally pure and appealing from a heavenly perspective, whereas the unrighteous must make a show of their appearance in an attempt to look good to the world in an attempt to cover up their true nature.

The Beast Revisited

It is important to take into account that each of the main items or figures presented in Revelation 17:1-7 are more fully explained and even expanded upon in the whole of Revelation 17-18. Some of the common problems we will run into where competing interpretations are concerned is that quite often it is only a verse or two which is exposited to the exclusion of the further light which Scripture sheds when the whole of all the related texts are examined. Therefore we will study each within the whole context of these chapters.

> *8"The beast that you saw was, and is not, and is about to come up out of the abyss and go to destruction. And those who dwell on the earth, whose name has not been written in the book of life from the foundation of the world, will wonder when they see the beast, that he was and is not and will come. 9Here is the mind which has wisdom. The seven heads are seven mountains on which the woman sits, 10and they*

> *are seven kings; five have fallen, one is, the other has not yet come; and when he comes, he must remain a little while. [11]The beast which was and is not, is himself also an eighth and is one of the seven, and he goes to destruction. [12]The ten horns which you saw are ten kings who have not yet received a kingdom, but they receive authority as kings with the beast for one hour. [13]These have one purpose, and they give their power and authority to the beast. [14]These will wage war against the Lamb, and the Lamb will overcome them, because He is Lord of lords and King of kings, and those who are with Him are the called and chosen and faithful."*
>
> —Revelation 17:8-14

The angel first explains the meaning of the beast which was introduced in Revelation 13, but from Scripture has also been previously identified as a kingdom with seven heads and/or ten horns. (Dan. 7:7, 20, 24; Rev. 12:3; 13:1) The seeming entanglement of verbal tenses in describing him as "*was, and is not, and is about to come up out of the abyss and go to destruction*" is a confirmation that we have temporarily paused after the chronological completion of the Bowls to describe these specific things before returning to complete the sequence. "*Was, and is not*" means that the beast reigned on earth but has now been thrown into the Lake of Fire (Rev. 19:20-21), but the further designation "*and is about to come up out of the abyss and go to destruction*" points toward the final judgment and activities at the end of the thousand year Millennial Kingdom in Revelation 20:7-10 when Satan temporarily re-visits the planet before being permanently assigned to the Lake of Fire.

Being identified as "*scarlet*" (Rev. 17:3) connects the beast directly to Satan (Rev. 12:3) as well as the kingdom with seven heads and ten horns. (Rev. 12:3; 13:1) She rides to power on the back of the kings who come to power, all of whom "*have one purpose, and they given their power and authority to the beast*".

"Seven Heads", "Seven Mountains", "Seven Kings"

> *[9]"Here is the mind which has wisdom. The seven heads are seven mountains on which the woman sits, [10]and they are seven kings; five have fallen, one is, the other has not yet come; and when he comes, he must remain a little while. [11]The beast which was and is not, is himself also an eighth and is one of the seven, and he goes to destruction.*
>
> — Revelation 17:9-11

As part of the beast's kingdom, the heads are specifically identified as "*kings*", but as something the woman is sitting on they are alternatively defined as "*seven **mountains***".

Most expositors commonly refer to this as "seven hills" even though this contradicts the underlying Greek which actually specifies "*mountains*", which begs the question of how picky we should be as to whether or not we can freely substitute "hills". (We cannot.) Of the nearly twenty times the Greek "*oros*" is used in the New Testament (Strong's #3735), in only one case (Mt. 5:14) is it translated in the NASB into English as "*hill*"—in all other cases it is rendered as either "*mountain*" or "*mountains*".

The Bible does not employ synonyms in the same manner as secular literature, so the specific words inspired by the Holy Spirit matter. In fact, the word "*hill*"—in the Greek "*buonos*" (Strong's #1015), is actually used in passages where both "*mountain*" and "*hill*" are found in order to specify the difference; they are distinctly different words and not easily exchanged for one another as in the case of English. Many expositors insist on this translation because Rome is popularly known as "the city on seven hills" and they assert that the "*seven mountains*" are therefore the seven ***hills*** of Rome.

But the exegetical fact is that the text clearly specifies exactly what the "*mountains*" are: "*they are seven **kings***". It cannot possibly be the city of Rome. The confusion stems from not peeking ahead a bit to Revelation 17:18 where we are further told, "*The woman whom you saw **is the great city**, which reigns over the kings of the earth*". It is not the "*seven mountains*" which is a city, it is the ***woman*** who represents a city which is not only associated with a series of past ***kingdoms***, but the final one to come ruled by the Antichrist. The text is using the term "*mountains*" to differentiate these kingdoms as being the largest, most visible in history from all other smaller or less influential empires or nations. The seven kingdoms which have been raised in the End Times for the purpose of giving their authority to the Antichrist.

While it is true that Peter, while in Rome, called it "*Babylon*" during his time (1 Pe. 5:13), there are also references within Revelation which use the term "*the great city*" but specify that this label is referring to Jerusalem (Rev. 11:8; 16:19), as well as other Scriptures doing the same for both Nineveh (Jonah 1:2; 3:2; 4:11) and the literal city of Babylon (Rev. 18:10, 16, 18-19, 21). At present, Nineveh is an archaeological dig, and unless the original site of Babylon like Nineveh is reoccupied, this is more than likely a metaphor for whichever city it ultimately represents, which most expositors mistakenly attribute to Rome. This is because Daniel is told to expect a final kingdom in the character of a revived Roman Empire, and we have Rome identified as something which has taken on the character and attributes of Babylon as well.

With the consolidation of the mystery religions of Babylon having found their way to Rome, along with Peter's inspired identification of Rome with Babylon and Daniel's prophecies concerning a revived Roman Empire, it is difficult to make even a modest case that 1st century believers assigned Revelation 17-18 to anything else, but there are textual issues which still warrant every Bible student's prayerful consideration in order to seek confirmation of the final identity of this city from which the Antichrist will rule the final empire.

> [9]*"Here is the mind which has wisdom. The seven heads are seven mountains on which the woman sits,* [10]*and* ***they are seven kings; five have fallen, one is, the other has not yet come****; and when he comes, he must remain a little while.* [11]*The beast which was and is not, is himself also an eighth and is one of the seven, and he goes to destruction.*
>
> — Revelation 17:9-11

It is most often asserted that the five kingdoms which have fallen are Egypt, Assyria, Babylon, Persia and Greece, and that the "*one is*" in the present time from the Apostle John's perspective would be Rome, with the anticipated one to come being the kingdom of Antichrist recapitulating Rome. If such is the case, it would be difficult to make the case that Rome "*sat*" on all of these empires, not really rising to power until after Greece, whereas Jerusalem, also referred to in Scripture as "*the great city*", actually experienced them all.

In the first vision, however, it was stipulated that the stone which struck the statue "*becamse a great mountain and filled the whole earth*" (Dan. 2:35) in a representation of the Messiah's kingdom. A biblical "*mountain*" has been defined as a "kingdom" from the outset.

However, many seem to take little notice of the caveat, "*Here is the mind which has wisdom*", which is also stated when speaking of understanding the mark of the beast:

*[18]**Here is wisdom. Let him who has understanding calculate the number** of the beast, for the number is that of a man; and his number is six hundred and sixty-six.*
— Revelation 13:18

*[9]"**Here is the mind which has wisdom**. The seven heads are seven mountains on which the woman sits, [10]and they are seven kings; five have fallen, one is, the other has not yet come; and when he comes, he must remain a little while. [11]The beast which was and is not, is himself also an eighth and is one of the seven, and he goes to destruction.*
— Revelation 17:9-11

In other words, we have ***two*** things in Scripture which we are told are difficult to understand and which are going to require the wisdom of Christ to decipher. And just as pundits of the mark of the beast almost never mention the caveat that the mark is "***either*** *the name of the beast* ***or*** *the number of his name*", (Rev. 13:17), when it comes to the woman on the beast there is the common mix up of the meaning of the woman and the mountains. It is easy to throw out nearly all the proposed solutions for these two special items when they proceed to ignore the plain text to begin with.

"Ten Horns", "Ten Kings"

[12]"The ten horns which you saw are ten kings who have not yet received a kingdom, but they receive authority as kings with the beast for one hour. [13]These have one purpose, and they give their power and authority to the beast. [14]These will wage war against the Lamb, and the Lamb will overcome them, because He is Lord of lords and King of kings, and those who are with Him are the called and chosen and faithful."
— Revelation 17:12-14

In Nebuchadnezzar's opening vision (Dan. 2), the final kingdom associated with Rome is described as "*the feet and toes, partly of potter's clay and partly of iron*". (Dan. 2:40-43) What is interesting about these ten toes is that the text in Daniel 2:44 plainly calls them "*kings*" so that there is no doubt as to what they represent.

In Daniel's second personal vision (Dan. 7), the beast associated with the final kingdom of the Antichrist is described as having "*ten horns*", the meaning of which is clearly explained as, "*out of this kingdom* ***ten kings*** *will arise; and another will arise after them, and he will be different from the previous ones and will subdue three kings*". (Dan. 7:24) The first vision is actually speaking of an attempt by the final kingdom to bring ten kings together, while the second vision is addressing a sequence of ten kingdoms concluding in the last one. The "*ten toes*" and the "*ten horns*" are not the exact, same thing where these two visions are concerned. The first are "*kings*" of the final kingdom working in a false unity, the second are a sequence of "*kings*" leading to the final false one.

In Revelation 17, the "*ten horns*" are referring to "***ten kings*** *who have not yet received a kingdom, but they receive authority as kings with the beast for one hour*". So although they may be an additional description of the "*ten toes*" in Daniel's first vision, they are still not the same thing as what was presented in his second vision, which is a sequence of kingdoms leading up to the last one; these are not permanent fixtures in history, but will only come about at the end "*for one hour*", a metaphorical way of saying this is exclusively a unique feature of the eschaton or "*the end of the age*".

This may go a long way toward explaining all the fanciful conjecture and outright disagreement as to who or what is resurrecting the Roman Empire and the exact identity of these "*horns*" as "*kings*" because they do not actually exist yet. The ink on Revelation was hardly dry when even in the 1st century people published their preferred list of "ten", and were the first of many lists of "ten" to follow to this very hour, every one of which is most likely wrong. In the eschaton, just as there are extreme changes to the earth's geography and environment, there will likewise be corresponding fundamental changes to the political landscape as well. While we may be sensitive to present trends which are obviously setting the stage for all these End Times events and figures, we need to avoid prematurely declaring "this" or "that" an ultimate fulfillment taking place until we are quite sure Scripture is literally and fully being fulfilled.

There is another important caveat here, "*These have one purpose, and they give their power and authority to the beast*" because they are going to engage in open warfare not just with the followers of Christ, but Christ Himself.

This may help us to understand how unprecedented persecution is going to come about in the Last Days as well as worldwide financial control. Depending on the list, at present there are as many as 196 independent nations and an additional 50 or more "areas of geopolitical interest", all with their own governing structures and bodies of law. Imagine if they were all incorporated under the control of just ten leaders/governments all raised for the purpose of consolidating everything under the singular rule of the Antichrist. In the same sense that Israel had twelve tribes, the Antichrist will attempt to get by with just ten. (Which might be an imitation of replaying of the ten apostate tribes of Israel who formed their own northern nation along with a false religion in an early example of apostasy.) It is truly the world revisiting what it attempted to do under Nimrod with the original Tower of Babel and the first iteration of Babylon.

"Those Who Dwell on the Earth"

> *And those who dwell on the earth, whose name has not been written in the book of life from the foundation of the world, will wonder when they see the beast, that he was and is not and will come.*
>
> — Revelation 17:8b

But also identified as going to the same destruction as the beast is included, "*And those who dwell on the earth, whose name has not been written in the book of life from the foundation of the world*". Something which helps to explain why the unsaved will be so deeply attracted to this figure and willing to follow him is because they "*will wonder when they see the beast*".

The Greek word "*thaumazo*" (Strong's #2296) does not mean "*wonder*" in the sense that they are curious or even not quite sure and need to investigate further, but is alternatively translated in the New Testament as "*marveled*" (Mt. 8:10; 15:31; Jn. 7:21; 13:41), "*amazed*" (Mt. 8:27; 9:33; 21:20; 22:22; 27:14; Mk. 5:20; 15:5; Lk. 8:25; 11:14; 24:41; Acts 2:7; 4:13), "*awestruck*" (Mt. 9:8), and "*astonished*" (Mk. 6:51; Lk. 1:63; Jn. 7:15). When the text of Revelation 17:8 says they will "*wonder*", it is describing the kind of charismatic cult of personality to which followers are "awestruck" and "amazed" to the point that they "marvel". We have seen this kind of response in films not only of followers of Hitler in pre-war Germany, but time and again for those in cults dominated by an all-controlling personality.

But it is also important to point out that this is the same word used to express what John experienced when he witnessed the vision of the harlot on the beast in Revelation 17:6-7 when he says, "*When I saw her, I **wondered** greatly*", and the angel responds, "*Why do you **wonder**?*" In fact, John's initial response could be literally translated, "I wondered with a great wonder" to express the depth of astonishment and amazement he was experiencing upon seeing these figures. What we see taking place in the followers of cult figures is but a vague sample of the enthusiasm and emotion to come from followers of the beast.

Usually what appears to be a "new" false teaching making the rounds in the Church is found to be a repackaged variation of something very old which seems to cyclically return for nearly every generation and historic age of the Church. But recently something has arisen for which it is difficult to find historical precedent, which is the assertion that one can take the mark of the beast and still be saved. There is no use attempting to put forth a rational argument opposing this when the text of Scripture so plainly contradicts this completely from the outset; false teachers are just ignoring it to teach whatever they want to teach. It is deeply disconcerting that there might be Christians who have so distanced themselves from the regular reading and study of God's Word that they have, in effect, become the very "Foolish Virgins" (Mt. 25:1-13) Jesus warns against who simply accept something which is blatantly refuted by a simple reading of Scripture. But such are those who will "*wonder*" in amazement at the Antichrist and become his passionate followers.

In all likelihood, that which is happening at present cannot be outright separated from our nearness to the eschaton taking place—and an argument can be made that from a certain point of view it may have already begun. There is a rise in false teachings asserting that no matter what happens, one can still be saved. This is not only seen in recent assertions one can take the mark of the beast and still be saved, but in the insistence that there will be a revival among those disqualified from participating in the *Harpazo*. Satan is making a preemptive strike while there is still time to properly act so that many are being deceived into believing they will never actually be left behind, and if they are, will be afforded yet other opportunities to be "taken" which are not specified in Scripture.

"The Great Harlot"

> [9]*"Here is the mind which has wisdom. The seven heads are seven mountains on which the woman sits,*
>
> — Revelation 17:9

It is important to understand that the most common interpretation of this "*harlot*" is that she is limited to exclusively being made up of the apostate church and not the world in general. In actuality it is both and much more. First of all, in Revelation 17-18 we find references to her which are giving clues as to her identity:

- "*...sits on many waters...*" (v.1)
- "*...sitting on a scarlet beast...*" (v.3)
- "*...on her forehead is written, a mystery, "BABYLON THE GREAT, THE MOTHER OF HARLOTS AND OF THE ABOMINATIONS OF THE EARTH."* (v.5)
- "*The seven heads are seven mountains on which the woman sits...*" (v.9)
- "*...The waters...where the harlot sits, are people and multitudes and nations and tongues.*" (v.15)
- "*The woman...is the great city, which reigns over the kings of the earth.*" (v.18)

Whereas the beast is an individual who is also likened to a final, literal kingdom, the harlot is specifically identified as "*Babylon the Great*" and repeatedly called a "*city*" which represents the seat of power from which the two beasts of Revelation 13 reign politically, religiously and economically.

One of the most pertinent characteristics not to be rushed past here is that the "*many waters*" upon which she is said to sit in Revelation 17:1 is further explained in 17:15 as being "*people and multitudes and nations and tongues*". Great bodies of waters in Scripture consistently represent the nations of the world, and we have this plainly stated for us in these verses. In 17:18 it goes even further to show her not just reigning over the general population, but "*over the kings of the earth*" to define her as the beasts' political center of influence.

There are also references to her appearance so as to teach something about her greater character or the way in which she operates:

- "*...clothed in purple and scarlet, and adorned with gold and precious stones and pearls...*" (17:4)
- "*...having in her hand a gold cup full of abominations and of unclean things of her immorality.*" (17:4)
- "*She has become a dwelling place of demons and a prison of every unclean and hateful bird.*" (18:2)
- "*...her sins have piled up as high as heaven, and God has remembered her iniquities.*" (18:5)
- "*...she glorified herself and lived sensuously...*" (18:7)
- "*...she says in her heart, 'I SIT AS A QUEEN AND I AM NOT A WIDOW, and will never see mourning'.*" (18:7)
- "*...in her was found the blood of prophets and of saints and of all who have been slain on the earth.*" (18:24)

She makes herself appealing from an earthly point of view and even presents sin in an enticing earthly way in a "*gold cup full of abominations and of unclean things of her immorality*". (Rev. 17:4) Beside glorifying herself, the list of what she fosters in others leaves no doubt the source of her chief influence.

Then there are references to various groups associated with her often accompanied by a description of the behaviors she fosters in them:

- "*...with whom the kings of the earth committed acts of immorality...*" (17:2)
- "*...and those who dwell on the earth were made drunk with the wine of her immorality.*" (17:2)
- "*...The waters...where the harlot sits, are people and multitudes and nations and tongues.*" (17:15)
- "*For all the nations have drunk of the wine of the passion of her immorality...*" (18:3)
- "*...and the kings of the earth have committed acts of immorality with her...*" (18:3)
- "*...and the merchants of the earth have become rich by the wealth of her sensuality.*" (18:3)

The most common interpretation put forth for this harlot is that she is the apostate church, those expositors insisting that this is speaking only of those who have fallen away from the faith to explain John's amazement at seeing her and why she is described as a harlot. But this list of her willing participants in sin spans the ***entire*** population, both outright non-believers and apostatizers alike: "*kings of the earth*", "*those who dwell on the earth*", "*people and multitudes and nations and tongues*", "*the nations*", and "*the merchants of the earth*". This is a wide spectrum of people not strictly limited to apostates from within the Church proper, especially since three of the designations are specifically qualified with "***of the earth***".

There is also the text of Zechariah 5 to consider in the overall discussion, which among other things references a woman called "*Wickedness*" and the building of a "*temple for her in the land of Shinar; and when it is prepared, she will be set there on her own pedestal*". (Zech. 5:11) "*Shinar*" is another name for "*Babylon*", and here we again see the figure of an evil woman, false worship and the literal location of Babylon.

This might be best understood according to the sequence of Daniel's visions. The first one given by God to Nebuchadnezzar, the reigning earthly king at that time in Daniel 2, was from an earthly point of view. The statue looked impressive, particularly those features constructed of spectacular precious metals. But the vision God gave Daniel personally in Daniel 7 presented the same thing from a heavenly viewpoint. To Daniel they were shown in the character of how God viewed them as ugly and dangerous beasts. Daniel 2 is the viewpoint of the then-reigning king of the earth, Daniel 7 that of the eternal reigning King of Heaven. When the world sees the woman or the beast on which she rides, they are eye candy from that worldly vantage point; but the heavenly perspective reveals them for the beast and harlot which they truly are.

At any rate, the text does not allow for an interpretation that the harlot is restricted to being the apostate church because the descriptions of the kinds of people who follow her show her to be the embodiment of seduction to everyone who gives in to ***any*** individual attribute or combination of sensuality, immorality, sin, false worship, pursuit of wealth, persecution of the righteous and anything demonic if not outright satanic. In essence, the greater lesson here is that everyone not engaged in a personal relationship with Christ is prostituting themselves. Christ has the Bride of Christ, Satan has the harlot who rides the beast.

A Final Treachery

> [15]*And he said to me, "The waters which you saw where the harlot sits, are peoples and multitudes and nations and tongues.* [16]*And the ten horns which you saw, and the beast, these will hate the harlot and will make her desolate and naked, and will eat her flesh and will burn her up with fire.* [17]*For God has put it in their hearts to execute His purpose by having a common purpose, and by giving their kingdom to the beast, until the words of God will be fulfilled.* [18]*The woman whom you saw is the great city, which reigns over the kings of the earth."*
>
> — Revelation 17:15-18

In the Old Testament it is particularly true of the Assyrian and Babylonian Empires which God used as tools of judgment against Israel, that a time came when He in turn judged them for their own sin and steadfast refusal to turn to Him. Likewise a similar occurrence transpires for the harlot, upon whom the Antichrist and company turn and destroy.

It is noteworthy that there is a time of relative stability in this relationship before the Antichrist reveals his true, ultimate intentions toward her. In all likelihood, this follows the scenario of fostering a false peace while consolidating all things together under his rule until the Abomination of Desolation takes place, that event when the Antichrist openly demands to be worshiped. This might be indirect confirmation that the city the harlot represents is, indeed, Jerusalem, which at the time of the Abomination is also said to be surrounded by armies, and when ethnic Israel takes flight into the wilderness. But regardless of how the specific timing works, after some period of time during which the harlot is accepted and used by Satan through the beasts, he ultimately turns on her, too. The information being provided on Babylon may come in the closing chapters of Revelation, but the clear emphasis is on something which has been around for most if not all of the entire eschaton which is now suffering its final, predicted fate.

The greater spiritual issue which appears to be taking place is that a time comes when the Antichrist is no longer satisfied to be worshiped through the one-world system he has used to band together disparate nations and religions under one ruler. This is essentially what the Roman Pantheon accomplished, leveraging each individual nation's personality, culture, and power over its respective local population to work on its behalf to worship the emperor. In the final, revived Roman Empire of the Antichrist, however, this is not enough; he desires to be worshiped directly and without any further need of the harlot; he divorces his woman, so to speak.

Up until this point, it is very possible that the various religious leaders who have come under this common umbrella of worship, have maintained a religious filter to keep their particular ranks loyal to the beasts. In other words, they reinterpreted the beliefs and practices of their particular religion so as to make it appear as fulfilled in this final figure. In essence, the followers supplied by each religion are only possible because they are misled to believe that their particular religious construct can be interpreted as a fulfillment in the person of the anti-king and can transfer their practices and beliefs alongwith their loyalty. So a final step is involved where the facade of each religion, denomination, or affiliation is removed and everyone remaining truly becomes a part of one religion, one false faith. In a sense, it is a mechanism by which they "apostatize" from their individual false beliefs to embrace direct worship of Satan without any pretense.

This may make sense if we consider God's original plan for His people Israel. The tribes of Israel were originally intended to have no earthly king, but were to worship and be ruled by God directly. In an ultimate counterfeit, the kingdom of Antichrist duplicates this by getting rid of the "middle man" so to speak in order to be worshiped exclusively without the aid or inducement of anyone else. Whereas Israel still had an administrative structure of twelve tribes serving and worshiping Yahweh directly, the kingdom of Antichrist has ten kings performing this role on his behalf and can therefore be worshiped and served directly.

Such an event would also aid in explaining why the hardened of heart just keep getting harder and harder as the eschaton progresses, first merely rejecting God, but eventually openly blaspheming Him and finally willing to directly go to war with Him; they have gone from "wonder" to following to direct and personal worship to their own destruction.

But take note here that the harlot is overtly identified in the plain text of Scripture as "***<u>the great city</u>***, *which reigns over the kings of the earth*"—what will be the seat of power from which the Antichrist operates, and "*the waters*" is openly interpreted for us as the "*peoples and multitudes and nations and tongues*" which she will influence, a description of the Antichrist's one-world rule. As usual, Scripture is ***always*** the best interpreter of Scripture.

19 ❖ Revelation 18: "Fallen, Fallen is Babylon the Great!"

> [1]*After these things I saw another angel coming down from heaven, having great authority, and the earth was illumined with his glory.* [2]*And he cried out with a mighty voice, saying, "Fallen, fallen is Babylon the great! She has become a dwelling place of demons and a prison of every unclean spirit, and a prison of every unclean and hateful bird.* [3]*For all the nations have drunk of the wine of the passion of her immorality, and the kings of the earth have committed acts of immorality with her, and the merchants of the earth have become rich by the wealth of her sensuality."*
> — Revelation 18:1-3

There came a time when the original Babylonian Empire was described prophetically as coming to a permanent end in a similar fashion. The same prophetic ending for the historical instance is ultimately realized in the final "*Babylon the great*".

> [8]*Then the lookout called,*
> *"O Lord, I stand continually by day on the watchtower,*
> *And I am stationed every night at my guard post.*
> [9]*Now behold, here comes a troop of riders, horsemen in pairs."*
> *And one said, "**Fallen, fallen is Babylon**;*
> *And all the images of her gods are shattered on the ground."*
> — Isaiah 21:8-9

> [8]*Suddenly **Babylon has fallen** and been broken;*
> *Wail over her!*
> *Bring balm for her pain;*
> *Perhaps she may be healed.*
> [9]*We applied healing to Babylon, but she was not healed;*
> *Forsake her and let us each go to his own country,*
> *For her judgment has reached to heaven*
> *And towers up to the very skies.*
> — Jeremiah 51:8-9

And the second of the three angelic messages previously given warned of the inevitability of the final iteration of Babylon the Great's impending destruction and judgment:

> [8]*And another angel, a second one, followed, saying, "**Fallen, fallen is Babylon the great**, she who has made all the nations drink of the wine of the passion of her immorality."*
> — Revelation 14:8

Here that final condition and fulfillment of God's Word is reported as completed, which was said to take place in the course of the final Bowl judgment:

> [19]*The great city was split into three parts, and the cities of the nations fell. **Babylon the great was remembered before God**, to give her the cup of the wine of His fierce wrath.*
> — Revelation 16:19

But notice the symbiotic relationship between immorality, idolatry and greed, the main tools of seduction used to swell her ranks and for which each version is ultimately judged. These final hallmarks of the kingdom and work of Antichrist are present in the working of the spirit of antichrist during every historical age to this very hour.

It is worth noting within these verses that we are provided a list which defines the identity of this trilateral city, a world system and seat of power which occupies a position of influence over "*peoples and multitudes and nations and tongues*". (Rev. 17:15) It first begins with "*the nations*" who "*have drunk of the wine of the passion of her immorality*". The underlying Greek word "*porneuo*" (Strong's #4203), here translated as "*immorality*", actually describes someone who themselves acts and plays like a harlot committing fornication. This is not just associated in Scripture with idolatry, but the breaking of an existing relationship with God when someone worships idols. This was a specified charge which Christ brought against the church at Pergamum:

> [14]*'But I have a few things against you, because you have there some who hold the teaching of Balaam, who kept teaching Balak to put a stumbling block before the sons of Israel, **to eat things sacrificed to idols and to commit acts of immorality**.*
> [15]*So you also have some who in the same way hold the teaching of the Nicolaitans.*
> — Revelation 2:14-15

...as well as against Thyatira:

> [20]*'But I have this against you, that you tolerate the woman Jezebel, who calls herself a prophetess, and she teaches and leads My bond-servants astray so that **they commit acts of immorality and eat things sacrificed to idols**.*
> — Revelation 2:20

Just as Satan attempts in various ways to seduce even those among the ranks of God's people in this manner, it is here explained how successfully the woman "*Babylon the great*" has accomplished this seduction among the non-believing population. This connects the running commentary which is present throughout the whole of Revelation indicating that what is really taking place is the personal choice of whether to rightly worship Christ or, by counterfeit or corruption, to worship Satan.

But notice that next in the list in verse 3 it is added, "*and **the kings of the earth** have committed acts of immorality with her*". Earthly leadership has also prostituted themselves in the same manner, something which has been previously pointed out in John's vision and will be highlighted yet again:

> [1]*Then one of the seven angels who had the seven bowls came and spoke with me, saying, "Come here, I will show you the judgment of the great harlot who sits on many waters,* [2]***with whom the kings of the earth committed acts of immorality, and those who dwell on the earth were made drunk with the wine of her immorality****."*
> — Revelation 17:1-2

> [9]*"And* ***the kings of the earth, who committed acts of immorality and lived sensuously with her****, will weep and lament over her when they see the smoke of her burning,*
> — Revelation 18:9

Earthly leadership is seduced and engaging in the same behaviors not just associated with sexual sin, but idolatry—the substitution of something as god in place of the One True God, to the same degree as the general population over which they rule. The blind lead the blind and both fall into the ditch. (Mt. 15:14)

This can best be understood as replaying the golden calf incident (Ex. 32), where this behavior was not limited to just the general ranks of Israel, but taken up and endorsed by its leadership as represented by Aaron. He not only enabled the sensual behavior which involved the kind of false worship they pursued, but by a literal idol which he made and then declared to them, "*This is your god, O Israel*". (Ex. 32:4) The text says that their worship was not just to "*eat and drink*"—a sensuous behavior in its own right, but that they "*rose up to play*" (Ex. 32:6), a euphemism for incorporating deviant and public sexual practices into their so-called worship activities. This is what is being expressed in Revelation 17-18 for both the general population seduced by Babylon the Great and their leaders.

But notice a third group is listed, "*and the merchants of the earth have become rich by the wealth of her sensuality*". The charge is not merely acquiring wealth, but that they have attained financial gain from the same things by which the nations and the kings of the earth were seduced. Babylon the Great is the spirit of seduction who successfully corrupts with the tools of immorality, idolatry and sensuality so as to undermine the nations with "*the passion of her immorality*", leadership's "*acts of immorality with her*", and the means of "*the merchants of the earth*" to "*become rich by the wealth of her sensuality*". But in terms of determining the identity of the harlot, notice that all of the discussion has been in regards to the unsaved in the world.

This list is an important tool of accurate biblical exegesis so as to properly assess whether someone's assertion of the identity of the woman is correct or not. Some extract in isolation the single detail of Revelation 17:3 in order to talk about the woman who rides the beast without studying all the references to her in the whole of Revelation 17-18. They seem to overlook that she is not sitting on "seven hills" but on "*seven* ***mountains***" (Rev. 17:9) which are in turn scripturally identified as "*seven* ***kings***" (Rev. 17:10), that the "*waters*" she is likewise situated on is spelled out as the nations of the earth (Rev. 17:15), and even that she is unambiguously described as "***the great city,*** *which reigns over the kings of the earth*". (Rev. 17:18) Finally, we have this list of who is seduced and following her so that it is going to take all of these factors in concert together to resolve her identity, not just by highlighting and making a case for only a few of them. There seems to be a lot of guessing and theories which are not based on all the information these chapters provide, but by the aforementioned behavior of "proof texting"—that is, to isolate some of what Scripture says while excluding the rest to make a particular case.

Who is the Woman?

One of the most popular assertions is that this woman is the Catholic Church, an interpretation which would have been impossible for 1st century Christians to make since the founding of that institution was centuries ahead of them and completely divorced from their time. But even at present this case is insufficient because, among other things, it does not have, nor never had, the influence over the entire world's population, leadership and captains of industry that is described here. While at particular historic times it may have held an impressive kind of sway over the mainly European world in the West, or after its major split by Eastern Orthodoxy those portions it influenced in the East, it has never risen to the level of what is being described here in Scripture on a worldwide basis.

It is not unreasonable to see that the Roman Catholic Church will be a major player in facilitating the rise of the Antichrist, especially in its many continuing ecumenical efforts to bring all religions under one roof with its own agenda to consolidate them all under the pope. But like many things which are a type or shadow of the final prophetic fulfillment to come, it is an example of many of the prime qualities and behaviors of the harlot, but not the final harlot herself. It certainly acts like her, it is certainly a harlot in that same character, but is not the literal prophetic fulfillment of same. The Catholic Church on a smaller scale provides an example of what to expect from the final harlot to come much in the same way Hitler mimics the ultimate Antichrist to come and the way he will be followed and worshiped.

Another popular interpretation is that the harlot is the apostatized church. In order to adopt this conclusion, one must allegorize away the references to kings, nations, and especially merchants, not to mention being "*the great city*", and all the rest of the literal references to a geographic place conducting real-life activities. It is far more likely that this is just like in Daniel where there is a vision of the kingdoms of the world from a worldly point of view in Daniel 2 versus a heavenly perspective in Daniel 7. From the world's angle they are impressive and beautiful, but God sees them for what they are, ugly and dangerous beasts. Likewise in Revelation God shows us how He sees the Bride of Christ versus the woman of Satan, and she ain't winning no beauty contests.

Without a doubt, 1st century Christians' primary interpretation, especially because Daniel revealed that the final earthly kingdom would come in the character of the Roman Empire, was that these metaphors and literal character traits would be adopted, if not by the literal Rome of their time, by a "Rome to come", if you will. An answer which many have proposed to resolve the tensions within this issue is that the first beast rises out of a revived Roman Empire, but subsequently attempts to rule and be worshiped from Jerusalem, which Revelation 11:8 calls, "*the great city which mystically is called Sodom and Egypt*". This is typical in Scripture, where Jerusalem is not literally Sodom nor Egypt, but called such in order to make the case that Jerusalem is acting in the character of these two examples spiritually. Someone acting in the character of Babylon can therefore ***be*** Babylon regardless of its earth-given name, or its geographic location, which is what Peter meant when he called Rome "*Babylon*" in his day. (1 Pe. 5:13) As an example, Jesus says John the Baptist was the fulfillment of the prophecies that Elijah would come before the Messiah, but John was not literally Elijah but rather came "*in the spirit and power of Elijah*". (Lk. 1:17) A biblically qualified fulfillment of prophecy is someone or something which comes in the character of.

But like the issue of the mark of the beast, for which both of these are stipulated as needing the wisdom of Christ to understand at their proper time, it is more important for us to be ready to recognize a fulfillment which incorporates 100% of these factors stipulated by Scripture, and not engage in the cyclically futile attempts of fitting the metaphorical square peg into the round hole. This is speaking of something happening within the eschaton proper, not at any time in history in a vacuum without all the other signs and events of "*the end of the age*".

However, to show that there are alternatives outside the purview of the commentators' insisted solutions, we must consider the fact that every year for many, many years in our present time, an annual vote takes place within the United Nations due to the repeated official request of some of its members that its headquarters be permanently relocated and built on the site of the literal city of Babylon. There are those who would like to see it transformed from what is now basically an archaeological preserve to a literal, revived world capital, something which Saddam Hussein actually initiated, literally building on that site. Just like the fact that Scripture tends to provide precise definitions of the metaphors and symbols it uses so as to itself authoritatively explain what they mean, it is likewise possible, even at this late date, for literal fulfillments to come about in the Last Days which may not have been possible in previous historic periods.

Sins as High as Heaven

> 4*I heard another voice from heaven, saying, "Come out of her, my people, so that you will not participate in her sins and receive of her plagues;* 5*for her sins have piled up as high as heaven, and God has remembered her iniquities.* 6*Pay her back even as she has paid, and give back to her double according to her deeds; in the cup which she has mixed, mix twice as much for her.* 7*To the degree that she glorified herself and lived sensuously, to the same degree give her torment and mourning; for she says in her heart, 'I SIT as A QUEEN AND I AM NOT A WIDOW, and will never see mourning.'* 8*For this reason in one day her plagues will come, pestilence and mourning and famine, and she will be burned up with fire; for the Lord God who judges her is strong.*
>
> — Revelation 18:4-8

Just as the same issues demanding God's judgment existed for the historic iterations of Babylon as for the final Babylon the Great, so too the calls by God for His people to come out from her:

> 11***Depart, depart, go out from there,***
> *Touch nothing unclean;*
> *Go out of the midst of her, purify yourselves,*
> *You who carry the vessels of the LORD.*
>
> — Isaiah 52:11

> 6***FLEE FROM THE MIDST OF BABYLON,***
> *And each of you save his life!*
> *Do not be destroyed in her punishment,*
> *For this is the LORD's time of vengeance;*
> *He is going to render recompense to her.*
> 7*Babylon has been a golden cup in the hand of the LORD,*
> *Intoxicating all the earth.*
> *The nations have drunk of her wine;*
> *Therefore the nations are going mad.*
> 8*Suddenly Babylon has fallen and been broken;*
> *Wail over her! Bring balm for her pain;*

Perhaps she may be healed.
9We applied healing to Babylon, but she was not healed;
Forsake her and let us each go to his own country,
For her judgment has reached to heaven
And towers up to the very skies.
10The LORD has brought about our vindication;
Come and let us recount in Zion
The work of the LORD our God!
— Jeremiah 51:6-10

*45"**Come forth from her midst, My people,***
And each of you save yourselves
From the fierce anger of the LORD.
— Jeremiah 51:45

What may be of even more interest to present-day Christians is that the Apostle Paul employs this scriptural precedent in the course of his teaching not to bind oneself to an unbeliever so as to avoid participating in their sin or incorporating their false beliefs into one's own faith:

14Do not be bound together with unbelievers; for what partnership have righteousness and lawlessness, or what fellowship has light with darkness? 15Or what harmony has Christ with Belial, or what has a believer in common with an unbeliever? 16Or what agreement has the temple of God with idols? For we are the temple of the living God; just as God said,

"I WILL DWELL IN THEM AND WALK AMONG THEM;
AND I WILL BE THEIR GOD, AND THEY SHALL BE MY PEOPLE.
*17Therefore, **COME OUT FROM THEIR MIDST AND BE SEPARATE,**" says the Lord.*
"AND DO NOT TOUCH WHAT IS UNCLEAN;
And I will welcome you.
18And I will be a father to you,
And you shall be sons and daughters to Me,"
Says the Lord Almighty.
— 2 Corinthians 6:14-18

This is one of the greater doctrinal purposes behind both the Rapture of the Church and the flight of Israel in the course of eschaton, that His people in both cases be separated from Babylon the Great, not just to escape experiencing the judgments of God's wrath coming upon her, but even more importantly that they avoid her dangerous and damaging spiritual influence. Presented here is God's specific calling, "*Come out of her, my people, so **that you will not participate in her sins and receive of her plagues***". This is Paul's same warning to every believer of every generation:

11Do not participate in the unfruitful deeds of darkness, but instead even expose them;
— Ephesians 5:11

One of the basic biblical tenets for the Christian walk is to avoid sharing in the sins of others, as well as to forego relationships and situations which we already know in advance are going to do everything in their power to seduce us into joining with them in sin. As bad and sinful as we think this world has been up to the present hour, it is but a shallow foretaste of what is to come as the eschaton progresses from mere "*tribulation*" to that time of "*great tribulation*" when unprecedented apostasy, deception, temptation and sin is proffered by an earthbound Satan and company working furiously toward their own ends knowing that their time is short. Babylon the Great may start out as a conduit to amalgamate all political and religious activity into singular devotion to Satan through the Antichrist, but it will escalate into the embodiment of sin which corrupts the nations, its leaders, and even its merchants so as to undermine everyone and everything.

Note that there are two chief reasons God will "*give back to her double according to her deeds*" in that "*she glorified herself*" and "*lived sensuously*". In turn, the judgments for these behaviors is "*torment and mourning*", and when God brings it about, it will come about very quickly so that "*in one day her plagues will come*".

This is reminiscent of the fall of Babylon in Daniel's time (Dan. 5) when Belshazzar called Daniel to interpret God's message on the wall, and that event turned out to be taking place on the very last night as both the king and the Babylonian Empire who were overtaken by Darius and the Medo-Persian Empire the very next day. When a divine event comes to fruition, there may be signs leading up to it, but that which actually takes place can come about quite suddenly in and of itself.

This specification that the harlot "*will be burned up with fire*" is the second time that this feature of her destruction has been mentioned:

> [16]*"And the ten horns which you saw, and the beast, these will hate the harlot and will make her desolate and naked, and will eat her flesh* ***and will burn her up with fire****.* [17]*For God has put it in their hearts to execute His purpose by having a common purpose, and by giving their kingdom to the beast, until the words of God will be fulfilled.*
>
> — Revelation 17:16-17

This is yet another affirmation of the fact that this is a literal city, a literal geographical location, and not just a metaphor for something like either the Catholic Church or the apostate church. Those things may act in its character and teach something about it, but it is ultimately something quite literal. This nicely segues into the following verses when the kings and merchants of the earth lament the literal destruction of the harlot as well and witness the smoke from her rising. They are mourning something which they visibly experience, which is not possible if it were just representing something akin to the apostate church.

Whereas both the Antichrist figures and their followers are ultimately assigned to the Lake of Fire as their final spiritual destination, these verses, along with the following laments, speak of a fiery destruction taking place on earth much in the same way as what literally took place with Sodom and Gomorrah. That which takes place on earth is but a reflection of what will ultimately transpire in eternity. That which takes place on earth for these figures and their followers is actually just a foretaste of what they will forever experience in eternity.

The Laments of the Kings & the Merchants of the Earth

> [9]*"And the kings of the earth, who committed acts of immorality and lived sensuously with her, will weep and lament over her when they see the smoke of her burning,* [10]*standing at a distance because of the fear of her torment, saying, 'Woe, woe, the great city, Babylon, the strong city! For in one hour your judgment has come.'*
>
> — Revelation 18:9-10

First and again, what is taking place is obviously literal. The mourners themselves are physically present, "*standing at a distance because of the fear of her torment*" and "*they see the smoke of her burning*". As the text specifies, the harlot is an actual city, a literal place, which these eyewitnesses can observe experiencing God's judgment.

Second, however, notice that although they "*committed acts of immorality and lived sensuously with her*" that they recognize, "*For in one hour your judgment has come*". As specified in Revelation 17:16-18, the ten kings who are raised for the purpose of assigning their power to the beast "*will hate the harlot and will make her desolate and naked, and will eat her flesh and will burn her up with fire*"; but they subsequently experience not only deep regret, but permanent loss. They will turn on her because "*God has put it in their hearts to execute His purpose by having a common purpose*", and in spite of their personal reactions betray that ultimately they know by whom this judgment has come about.

> *11 "And **the merchants of the earth** weep and mourn over her, because no one buys their cargoes any more— 12 cargoes of gold and silver and precious stones and pearls and fine linen and purple and silk and scarlet, and every kind of citron wood and every article of ivory and every article made from very costly wood and bronze and iron and marble, 13 and cinnamon and spice and incense and perfume and frankincense and wine and olive oil and fine flour and wheat and cattle and sheep, and cargoes of horses and chariots and slaves and human lives. 14 The fruit you long for has gone from you, and all things that were luxurious and splendid have passed away from you and men will no longer find them. 15 The merchants of these things, who became rich from her, will stand at a distance because of the fear of her torment, weeping and mourning, 16 saying, 'Woe, woe, the great city, she who was clothed in fine linen and purple and scarlet, and adorned with gold and precious stones and pearls; 17 for in one hour such great wealth has been laid waste!'*
>
> *And every **shipmaster** and every **passenger** and **sailor**, and as many as make their living by the sea, stood at a distance, 18 and were crying out as they saw the smoke of her burning, saying, 'What city is like the great city?' 19 And they threw dust on their heads and were crying out, weeping and mourning, saying, 'Woe, woe, the great city, in which all who had ships at sea became rich by her wealth, for in one hour she has been laid waste!' 20 Rejoice over her, O heaven, and you saints and apostles and prophets, because God has pronounced judgment for you against her."*
>
> — Revelation 18:11-20

Again, a primary purpose for giving us this extensive list of merchandise which the harlot enabled to be sold by the merchants of the earth is to confirm for us that the harlot is a literal city and a literal place through which actual commerce is transacted and not a metaphor or symbol.

And the merchants, like the kings before them, "*stand at a distance because of the fear of her torment, weeping and mourning*", again affirming that this is a literal, geographic location which can be visibly observed as undergoing destruction. They likewise affirm, "*in one hour such great wealth has been laid waste*" to express the suddenness of what takes place.

But in a third affirmation of the literalness of this place, notice that in verses 18 and 19 they lament, "*What city is like **the great city**?*" and "*Woe, woe, **the great city***". This is further illustrated beginning in verse 17 when the testimony is included of "*every shipmaster and every passenger and sailor*" who "*saw the smoke of her burning*" and crying out, "*What city is like **the great city**?*" How many times does Scripture have to call something a "*city*" before we accept this as an actual city?

This inclusion of people literally assigned to ships does not mandate that "*the great city*" be literally located next to the ocean so as to exclude literal Jerusalem or Rome, neither of which are directly adjacent to the ocean. It can be exactly as it is in the case of Los Angeles, California, which is not situated directly on the oceanfront either and whose main port, if one looks at a map, is actually well south of the city proper. (They did very strange things with the city limits to place it in their jurisdiction.) But the port and supporting infrastructure is set up to bring much of what is exported and imported for the entire U.S. under the control of Los Angeles without literally occupying a footprint next to the ocean's shoreline where the city center is concerned, and it is amazing to consider that at present, if California were its own country, it would be the sixth largest economy in the world.

That being said, it is well worth considering that in Revelation 17-18, a great portion of the text is dedicated to elaborating on the economic impact of the harlot, so much so that it might be telling us something significant and literal about the final Babylon the Great to come. It definitely rules out such proposals as it being the Catholic Church or the apostate church or some kind of metaphor, and causes us to focus on a literal, geographic location which not only becomes the center of politics and religion, but worldwide commerce as well. Her demise goes hand-in-hand with a catastrophic economic destruction unparalleled in the whole of human history, and in this age of mass media has the possibility of being broadcast and witnessed by the world at large. However, every kingdom does not merely rule out of its chosen capital city, but makes it the center of the economy for the breadth of the world it controls.

It is outside the scope of this writing, but the avid Bible student may want to explore the lament over Tyre in Ezekiel 27 as it has a great many parallels to what is provided here, followed up in Ezekiel 28:1-19 where the King of Tyre is clearly associated with Satan and becomes a biblical type of the Antichrist:

> [1]*The word of the* LORD *came again to me, saying,* [2]*"Son of man, say to the leader of Tyre, 'Thus says the Lord* GOD,
>
> *"Because your heart is lifted up*
> *And you have said, 'I am a god,*
> *I sit in the seat of gods*
> *In the heart of the seas';*
> *Yet you are a man and not God,*
> *Although you make your heart like the heart of God—*
> [3]*Behold, you are wiser than Daniel;*
> *There is no secret that is a match for you.*
> [4]*By your wisdom and understanding*
> *You have acquired riches for yourself*
> *And have acquired gold and silver for your treasuries.*
> [5]*By your great wisdom, by your trade*
> *You have increased your riches*
> *And your heart is lifted up because of your riches—*
> — Ezekiel 28:1-5

The Saints

In Revelation 18:20 is a textual detail which needs to be highlighted. Among commentators there is much confusion over the meaning of the word "*saints*" in the book of Revelation, especially within that school of thought dogmatically asserting that it has a special definition only for the book of Revelation which is alone and separate from the rest of God's Word. This usually has to do with those who are making the case that the Church is removed simultaneous with the Apostle John's call to heaven in Revelation 4:1, and therefore chapters 4-19 basically have no application for the Church (in their view). But since they posit that the Church is removed from that point on, they need to explain why the text of Revelation keeps referring to "*saints*" (13 times in Rev. 8-20), a term used prior to Revelation ***at least 48 times*** in the New Testament to refer to the Church. One of the favored ways to redefine this term is to assert that John's vision is actually talking exclusively about a category they create called the "tribulation saints" and not all saints.

Basically these are those who, after the Church is removed, are said to come to Christ, and is a way for Pre-Tribulationists in particular to try to justify the Church's removal before the final seven year period and explain the great multitude which comes out between the 6th and 7th Seals in Revelation 7:9-17. Such assert that this multitude is not the Church, but rather the "tribulation saints", those who have come to faith in Christ after the Rapture, and those likewise martyred.

The first issue with this false notion is that most of the same expositors who passionately espouse this idea also subscribe to an interpretation of 2 Thessalonians 2:7 that simultaneous with the Church's removal, the Holy Spirit will leave earth and "go back" to heaven. Assuming we accept their interpretation (which we cannot since the Holy Spirit as a member of the Godhead is omnipresent), how will these "tribulation saints" get saved without the Holy Spirit? On the one hand they say the Church and the Holy Spirit will be removed, and then on the other they say those left behind will somehow get saved without the Holy Spirit. There is also the unresolved matter that they insist the Rapture fulfills God's promise that believers in Christ will not experience God's wrath, which is scripturally correct, but then create a new category who comes into existence who paradoxically have to experience it. And then of course, how to explain that these "tribulation saints" were removed between the 6th and 7th Seals but keep reappearing in the text after that event.

But the other thing is to carefully examine Revelation 18:20:

> [20]*"Rejoice over her, O heaven, and you saints and apostles and prophets, because God has pronounced judgment for you against her."*
>
> — Revelation 18:20

Notice that there is heaven above as a whole, and then it is specified "*saints and apostles and prophets*" to describe God's people below as a whole. This is the same way the rest of the New Testament designates all believers and does not provide for a new category of "*saint*" distinct from the rest. In fact, most conservative evangelical commentators, at least, will agree that there are "Old Testament saints" and "New Testament saints" who eventually become just "saints" united in the Person of Christ. This is what is being expressed here, the Word of God coming through the apostles and prophets and being received by all the saints as a whole without some kind of special designation for an additional, new group exclusive to Revelation.

The Angel & the Stone

> [21]*Then a strong angel took up a stone like a great millstone and threw it into the sea, saying, "**So will Babylon, the great city, be thrown down with violence**, and will not be found any longer.* [22]*And the sound of harpists and musicians and flute-players and trumpeters will not be heard in you any longer; and no craftsman of any craft*

> *will be found in you any longer; and the sound of a mill will not be heard in you any longer; [23]and the light of a lamp will not shine in you any longer; and the voice of the bridegroom and bride will not be heard in you any longer; for your merchants were the great men of the earth, because all the nations were deceived by your sorcery. [24]And in her was found the blood of prophets and of saints and of all who have been slain on the earth."*
>
> — Revelation 18:21-24

Twice before in Revelation John has documented the participation of a "*strong angel*", and although we are not informed if this is the same figure in each appearance or different ones, each time it is a direct involvement in the specific fulfillment of God's Word where Revelation is concerned:

- The first time is in the course of finding someone worthy to open the originally sealed scroll. (Rev. 5:2)
- The second time is after the 6th Trumpet when he comes down out of heaven bearing the *"little scroll*". (Rev. 10:1-3)
- And this third time when a stone symbolically representing the Word is cast into the sea in an expression of God's Word being completely fulfilled where Babylon is concerned as well as the Old Testament judgment for an abomination.

In this third appearance of such an angelic being at the end of all the judgments, this "*strong angel*" replays a similar event found near the very end of Jeremiah which is directly associated with the literal, historical Babylon of his time:

> *[60]So **Jeremiah wrote in a single scroll all the calamity which would come upon Babylon**, that is, all these words which have been written concerning Babylon. [61]Then Jeremiah said to Seraiah, "As soon as you come to Babylon, then see that you read all these words aloud, [62]and say, 'You, O LORD, have promised concerning this place to cut it off, so that there will be nothing dwelling in it, whether man or beast, but it will be a perpetual desolation.' [63]And **as soon as you finish reading this scroll, you will tie a stone to it and throw it into the middle of the Euphrates,** [64]**and say, 'Just so shall Babylon sink down and not rise again because of the calamity that I am going to bring upon her; and they will become exhausted**.'" Thus far are the words of Jeremiah.*
>
> — Jeremiah 51:60-64

But notice how there is now an even more extensive list of literal people: "*harpists*", "*musicians*", "*flute-players*", "*trumpeters*", "*craftsman*", "*bridegroom*", and "*bride*", all of which were literal residents of the harlot city. The sounds of music and the mill, the light of a lamp, and the voices of the bridegroom and bride, all of which will no longer be experienced in Babylon the Great are all ***literal*** things which cannot be easily allegorized or spiritualized away as symbols of something else. The text of Revelation 18 drills down to include lower levels of shared lamentation by people and things which cannot possibly be substituted for anything except their literal occurrence.

These things are also found to have taken place in the course of the historical Babylon of the Old Testament, and are yet another example of how prophecy is an increasingly stronger patterns leading up to a final, authoritative fulfillment:

> [8]*"Therefore thus says the* Lord *of hosts, 'Because you have not obeyed My words,* [9]*behold, I will send and take all the families of the north,' declares the* Lord*, 'and I will send to Nebuchadnezzar king of Babylon, My servant, and will bring them against this land and against its inhabitants and against all these nations round about; and I will utterly destroy them and make them a horror and a hissing, and an everlasting desolation.* [10]*Moreover,* ***I will take from them the voice of joy and the voice of gladness, the voice of the bridegroom and the voice of the bride, the sound of the millstones and the light of the lamp****.*
>
> — Jeremiah 25:8-10

Although too detailed for the current discussion, it is well worth studying Jeremiah 51 as a parallel to the fate of Babylon where God explains how the literal Babylon of Jeremiah's day will be judged for her sins and how that may speak to what is to take place in the final Babylon the Great yet to come.

It should be noted that two charges are added to the long list of specific behaviors for which the harlot will be judged, that "*all the nations were deceived by your sorcery*" and "*in her was found the blood of prophets and of saints and of all who have been slain on the earth*". (Rev. 18:24)

The Greek word "*pharmakeia*" (Strong's #5331) which is translated as "*sorcery*" embodies not just the occult and its practices of sorcery and witchcraft as we might understand it, but the use of illicit drugs by which practitioners invoked trances and what they called magical incantations. Occult practices are very much part and parcel of the kingdom of Antichrist, and it is one of the specific things mentioned from which his followers refuse to repent:

> [20]*The rest of mankind, who were not killed by these plagues, did not repent of the works of their hands, so as not to worship demons, and the idols of gold and of silver and of brass and of stone and of wood, which can neither see nor hear nor walk;* [21]***and they did not repent*** *of their murders nor* ***of their sorceries*** *nor of their immorality nor of their thefts.*
>
> — Revelation 9:20-21

But it is also something which the prophet Nahum associates with being a harlot when describing the similar sinful influence exerted by Nineveh over other peoples and nations:

> [4]*All because of the many harlotries of the harlot,*
> *The charming one, the mistress of sorceries,*
> *Who* ***sells nations by her harlotries***
> ***And families by her sorceries****.*
>
> — Nahum 3:4

Additionally it is not just "*the blood of prophets and of saints*" which is heaped upon the harlot figure of Babylon the Great, but "*of all who have been slain on the earth*", a group which encompasses all the deaths of non-believers as well. The harlot has been a conduit for both occult practices to kill mankind spiritually and the shedding of blood to likewise kill literally.

There is an interesting pattern in human history as recorded in Scripture which may help in explaining why the harlot is a literal city in that building a city has accompanied some of the worst spiritual milestones in the human timeline. Cain, notorious for being the first to shed blood, "*went out from the presence of the* Lord*...and he built a city*". (Gen. 4:16-17) Nimrod was not only responsible for the Tower of Babel, but embarked on quite a city building spree, (Gen. 10:8-12) and he was not only a hunter of men (as in spilling blood), but became the source of all false religion. There is a model of what Hitler planned to build in a shadow of what is to come, and this was a repeated feature of Roman emperors, Pharaohs, etc. The immorality, idolatry and apostasy of the final Babylon the Great as exemplified by the harlot riding the beast is but the final in a very long sequence of the same pattern replaying itself.

Summary

The chief activities of Satan through his protégés is to ultimately unify all the separate earthly kingdoms into a final one under his control, and in parallel to consolidate all the disparate religions under one ecumenical roof. However, a time comes when Satan is no longer satisfied to be worshiped through this one-world proxy, and desires to instead be worshiped directly without the aid of the harlot. This is a counterfeit of God's original plan concerning Israel where the tribes were to have no earthly king and instead worship and serve Him directly; Satan attempts to achieve this through the beast and his ten kingdoms after eliminating the harlot. He uses all his followers across the entire spectrum to turn on and destroy her, which ironically is actually carrying out God's will concerning her.

Whereas the beast is an individual who is also likened to a final, literal kingdom, the harlot is specifically identified as "*Babylon the great*" and repeatedly called a "*city*" which represents the seat of power from which the two beasts of Revelation 13 reign both politically and religiously. She is the world's center of commerce as well, and for a time the kingdom of the Antichrist is a three-legged stool each representing the government, religion and the economy. But when Satan turns everyone against the harlot, everyone is shocked to find that the economy was equally a casualty alongside the one-world religion that goes up in flames as well. All that is left is the final military conflict with Christ and His armies to come.

To understand how Satan could turn on such an important institution which helps bring the Antichrist and False Prophet to power, we can again turn to the example of Hitler, and in particular his handling of the Brown Shirts. They were critical in bringing him to power, but a time came when Hitler desired to be accountable to no one and to stand alone at the top, and as part of that process had them eliminated. Everyone from that point on, whether in his political party or as a member of the military or general population, swore their allegiance to him directly and personally.

In this case, however, it appears that there will not be a lot of time left between his turning on the harlot and his final comeuppance with Christ personally.

One of the chief sets of characteristics assigned to the final anti-kingdom is its use of "*the harlot*":

- She entices "*the kings of the earth*" by making them "*drunk with the wine of her immorality*". (Rev. 17:2)
- She is literally seen riding the "*scarlet beast*" so as to not be acting apart from either the anti-king or the anti-kingdom. (Rev. 17:3)
- Like the depiction in Daniel 2, she makes herself appealing by worldly standards, but is actually "*full of abominations and of the unclean things of her immorality*". (Rev. 17:4)
- The mark on ***her*** forehead is, "*Babylon the Great, the mother of harlots and of the abominations of the earth*". (Rev. 17:5)

- She also persecutes the God's people, being "*drunk with the blood of the saints, and with the blood of the witnesses of Jesus*" (Rev. 17:6), "*...in her was found the blood of prophets and of saints and of all who have been slain on the earth*". (Rev. 18:24)
- "*The waters...where the harlot sits, are peoples and multitudes and nations and tongues*" (Rev. 17:15)
- "*...the ten horns...will hate the harlot and will make her desolate and naked, and will eat her flesh and will burn her up with fire.*" (Rev. 17:16)
- "*The woman...is the great city, which reigns over the kings of the earth*". (Rev. 17:18)
- She will "*become a dwelling place of demons and a prison of every unclean spirit, and a prison of every unclean and hateful bird*". (Rev. 18:2)
- She has a global influence over "*the kings of the earth*", "*the merchants of the earth*", and "*all the nations*". Her chief tools are "*the wine of the passion of her immorality*" and "*the wealth of her sensuality*". (Rev. 18:3)
- "*...her sins have piled up as high a heaven...*" (Rev. 18:5)
- "*...she glorified herself and lived sensuously...*" (Rev. 18:7)

So we can see how closely her own qualities parallel those of the anti-king/anti-kingdom, making her the perfect companion, at least until she is "divorced" and disposed of so that none will stand between Satan and the earth dwellers worshiping him.

We additionally add to our list of features of the anti-kingdom, which at times will also apply to the anti-king:

- It is a recapitulation of past empires which acted like Rome in the Apostle John's day, but has a final, ultimate fulfillment yet to come: "*The beast that you saw, was, and is not, and is about to come up out of the abyss and go to destruction*". (Rev. 17:8)
- "*The seven heads are seven mountains on which the woman sits*". (Rev. 17:9)
- The seven mountains "*are seven kings; five have fallen, one is, the other has not yet come; and when he comes, he must remain a little while*". (Rev. 17:10)
- "*The beast which was and is not, is himself also an eighth and is one of the seven, and he goes to destruction.*" (Rev. 17:11)
- The "*ten horns*" will execute God's "*purpose...by giving their kingdom to the beast...*" (Rev. 17:17)

And to the anti-king personally is additionally attributed:

- Those who follow him are specifically identified as "*those who dwell on the earth*" and are distinguished literally because they "*will wonder when they see the beast*", and spiritually because their "*name has not been written in the book of life*". (Rev. 17:8)
- "*The ten horns...are ten kings which have not yet received a kingdom, but they receive authority as kings with the beast for one hour*". (Rev. 17:12)
- "*These have one purpose, and they give their power and authority to the beast*". (Rev. 17:13)

- *"These will wage war against the Lamb and the Lamb will overcome them..."* (Rev. 17:14)

A Final Thought

To be sure, there will be many who are "*antichrist*" in character, even to the point of attempting to counterfeit the Messiah themselves, coming both as individuals and organizations animated by the spirit of antichrist. While these are present during every historical age even up to the present, this wealth of scriptural information is intended to distinguish the last and final one in the series, set apart from all previous iterations. And of particular note are the features of the False Prophet and Babylon the Great.

In other words, the final "*beast from the sea*"—the main object of worship who is mostly oriented toward the political/military aspects does not appear nor operate in a complete vacuum independently on his own. His rise to prominence is supported by a worldwide kingdom formed from an alliance of ten kingdoms subjugating the world's lesser governments "*at the last hour*" for the purpose of giving "*their power and authority to the beast*". That which they accomplish politically is mirrored morally and economically by the parallel unprecedented efforts of the great harlot on his behalf.

To the third leg of the stool is added the activities of the second "*beast from land*"—the False Prophet, who under the umbrella of religion forges these activities of the kingdoms and the harlot together with his chief antics intended solely for the purpose of engendering worship of the first beast:

- He performs signs and wonders "*in the presence of men*" and "*in the presence of the beast*". (Rev. 13:13-14)
- He makes "*an image to the beast*" for the purpose of worship, enforcing the death penalty for all who do not comply. (Rev. 13:14-15)
- "*And he causes all...to be given a mark...and provides that no one will be able to buy or to sell except the one who has the mark...*" (Rev. 13:16-17)

The False Prophet bridges the activities of the Antichrist, their kingdom, and the harlot so as to focus it all back upon the ultimate goal of being worshiped in place of the One True God.

Ultimately, just as it was revealed in the very first vision of Daniel 2, so it is ultimately verified in the very last vision given John, that neither the anti-king, nor his kingdom, harlot nor even counterfeit John the Baptist, be left standing, but will be completely obliterated. But in the mean time, for those with the wisdom of Christ who look for the scriptural fulfillment of these things, a powerful set of textual standards has been supplied, provided that we are not solely over focusing on just one figure or one aspect. He is both a king and a kingdom, supported by kings, the greatest of all harlots, and the False Prophet.

As it turns out, it is much more than just a single, lone figure, and it is a mistake to just be looking for this figure by himself. There is a duality to the milieu out of which he will arise in a military/political unification of the earth under a final confederation of ten kingdoms which will ultimately subordinate themselves into the final anti-kingdom, and a worldwide religious merging facilitated by the sensuality and immorality of the harlot. The sort of "glue" who melds the political, economic and religious into the final product dedicated to worshiping the Antichrist is the equally antichrist False Prophet. In looking for the final figure, we are actually looking for these things in parallel with him. Without all of these present, regardless of how evil a figure and his supporting organization acts, they are still just a forerunner of the final one to come.

20 ❖ The Total Scriptural Picture

With the last disclosures of the final book of the canon of Scripture, we can see that there are many figures, both biblical and historical, who teach about the final anti-king to come. Prior to the New Testament writings, adherents of God's given Word to that point would have recognized Nebuchadnezzar and Antiochus Epiphanes IV as the primary examples of the final figure anitcipated. And the historical actions of the Roman General Pompey, who entered the Holy of Holies in the Temple, would have joined the collective picture as well. But with the additional details provided in the New Testament, especially through the book of Revelation, many other figures in Scripture would have been revealed which were actually residing in the text all along, but concealed until revealed by the illumination of the New Testament.

As stated previously, there are two very important works already published on the topic of the Antichrist which the reader is highly encouraged to obtain. Because they both go into much more detail where each of the scriptural and historical types of the Antichrist are concerned, the same exhaustive ground will not be revisited here. But any serious study of this topic really does require the additional reading of *Shadows of the Beast* by Jacob Prasch (www.moriel.org) and *Antichrist* by A. W. Pink (available online on many websites or in print from Amazon).

This book purposely focuses on the aspect not heavily covered in those works having to do with the corresponding anti-kingdom. But as Proverbs provides, "*in abundance of counselors there is victory*" (Prov. 11:14; 24:6), and this is offered to support the necessary concept that there are "many voices, but one Spirit". In other words, no one is in sole possession of the truth as we are merely interpreters of what has been presented, so multiple voices on the subject are not just desirous and helpful, but really quite necessary. In the age of the Holy Spirit and the easy access to His Word, the One Voice speaks through many.

The examples of this final figure are so plentiful because he ***is*** so difficult to figure out. It takes a combination of a large number of examples from both the texts of history and Scripture to even begin to formulate a usable portrait of the final figure. This can be seen from the extensive list to follow gleaned from all that we have examined. But while each preceding type will effectively illustrate particular traits of the anti-king, they really are but shadows of the ultimate realization to come. And it is important to keep in mind that the only reason we understand those aspects which make them a candidate as a forerunner of the anti-king in the first place is because of the plain text of Scripture providing the parameters. In other words, it is God's Word which has revealed these figures in the character of the anti-king, not the other way around. They do not illuminate or add to God's Word, but are rather ***exposed*** because of what God's Word has first established as axiomatic.

Different Aspects of the Same Thing

It is important to establish why Scripture regularly employs different names for the same thing. Unlike human writers, the Holy Spirit does not infuse colorful alternative synonyms to make the reading interesting. Across both Testaments, across all the books, and regardless of the type of literature unique to each, the individual words, because they ***are*** the very Words of God, are very consistent in the original languages. Human writers know it is a literary sin to repeatedly use the same word or phrase, especially in close proximity to each other:

> "My **really big** nose experienced a **really big** itch which resulted in a **really big** sneeze ejecting a **really big** booger".

My English teacher would give me a much better grade if I instead submitted:

> "My **Pinocchio-like** proboscis, experiencing an **irresistible and exasperating** itch, eventually produced a **herculean eruption** catapulting into planetary orbit a **capacious** booger".

Scripture does not rotate the words just to keep the reader interested, but will keep using the exact, same word in the exact, same way because God's Word is the eternal, unalterable truth. "*Sin*", "*transgression*" and "*iniquity*", for instance, are related, but are never substituted for each other because they are unique Greek and Hebrew words consistently describing a different, specific condition within an overall spectrum. The Holy Spirit did not get "tired" of using "*sin*" and therefore mixed in "*transgression*" or "*iniquity*" to make the reading interesting like secular literature. This is why we can perform word studies across the whole Bible for the express purpose of seeing how "*sin*" (falling short of the standard) is different from "*transgression*" (rebelling from the standard).

There are instances where Scripture does, indeed, use different descriptors for the same thing, but this is always done for the express purpose of emphasizing a different aspect or characteristic of the same thing. In other words, it is a teaching device. A prolific example found in Scripture is when God calls the nation "*Jacob*" rather than "*Israel*". The historical figure of Jacob is a picture of someone before they meet Christ. In other words, prior to Jacob's all-night struggle wrestling with the angel of the Lord (Gen. 32:24-32), he is the picture of a sinner, completely operating in the flesh according to the world's ways; after he comes face to face with God, he is not just changed, but even given a new name, a representation of what we might call a "new creature in Christ". (2 Co. 5:17) When God calls them "*Jacob*", it collectively refers to the nation in a sinful, backslidden state, as opposed to "*Israel*" figuratively speaking of spiritually transformed people acting the way they should. These are not synonyms, but a teaching device in God's Word emphasizing something of a spiritual nature.

There are other examples of this such as when the city is called "*Jerusalem*" in referring to a fallen, earthly institution, as opposed to "*Zion*" as its perfect, heavenly counterpart. It has even been observed that the order of His name is important in this respect, "*Jesus Christ*" emphasizing His earthly ministry, "*Christ Jesus*" speaking to His heavenly, eternal working. Scripture employs multiple terms for the same person, place or thing in order to specifically highlight a different detail—usually a ***spiritual*** detail. Again, it is an important teaching device.

Perhaps this is best understood in all the various names for God or Christ. Each is employed to focus on a specific character trait so as to give mortal minds as much understanding as they are capable of when it comes to comprehending someone not just immortal, but eternal. These descriptors in turn point us to figures in the text who act "in the character of" Christ, whose lives provide examples of these things in action such as the Patriarchs and particularly Joseph and David. Knowing the character traits of Christ provides a powerful parallel of the kinsman-redeemer in the book of Ruth and even of Esther and Mordecai in their roles to save Israel. What we call "typology" identifies a person, place or thing which typifies, or strongly focuses on, a particular characteristic overtly specified in Scripture.

For us mere mortals, it takes a lifetime of prayer, obedience and study to even begin to fully grasp the limited picture provided of the Godhead, but the figures of Satan and his beasts are complex and daunting as well. They have also been assigned multiple terms in order to teach respective characteristics, albeit the worst and most negative in the spectrum. When we consider them all together in the list at the end of this chapter, however, it especially becomes apparent that Scripture-studying believers are well-educated on the topic.

In our examination of Scripture, the anti-king has been variously described as "*king*", "*beast*", "*horn*", "*leader*", "*false Christ*", and "*antichrist*". He has even been assigned specific monikers such as "*the king of the north*" and acting in the character of various figures such as Nebuchadnezzar, Alexander the Great, and because of the fulfillments to a point of Daniel 11, Antiochus Epiphanes IV in the Inter-Testamental Period. His unique relationship with Satan, where in Revelation 12 for all practical purposes it is shown that they are one and the same, also causes us to cross over and apply those variously assigned designations and supporting traits as well. As the anti-kingdom, he has been ascribed as a statue, various beasts, and even possessing multiple heads and crowns. Specific empires beginning and ending with Babylon are applied to this model, and in particular we are shown the importance of both the Roman and Seleucid Empires in the fundamental character of the final kingdom to come. A very complicated picture is subdivided in this manner in order to ultimately teach about the whole.

It may not be so difficult to understand why Scripture employs this mechanism because the final anti-king and anti-kingdom is far greater than the sum of all its predecessors' parts. Each of the forerunners of the final figure and/or institution are but dim shadows of the final ones to come, so each characteristic is contributed from a corresponding example in Scripture and/or history. As evil, destructive, and over-the-top bad each previous type of the Antichrist has been, the final combined fulfillment is many multiplied times worse.

The "Man" and the "Son"

*3Let no one in any way deceive you, for it will not come unless the apostasy comes first, and **the man of lawlessness** is revealed, **the son of destruction**, 4who opposes and exalts himself above every so-called god or object of worship, so that he takes his seat in the temple of God, displaying himself as being God...8Then that **lawless one** will be revealed whom the Lord will slay with the breath of His mouth and bring to an end by the appearance of His coming; 9that is, the one **whose coming is in accord with the activity of Satan**, with all power and signs and false wonders,*

— 2 Thessalonians 2:3-4, 8-9

In the case of the final figure to come, there are additional unique designations provided for this very purpose: the "*man of lawlessness*" (2 The. 2:3-8) and the "*son of destruction*" (2 Th. 2:3; Jn. 17:12).

In some translations, "*lawlessness*" is translated as "*sin*", but the underlying Greek word is "*anomia*" (Strong's #459)—that is, "*lawlessness*". In the New Testament this is not used to mean there is an absence of law and order, but is specifically describing the violation of God's ***written*** Law. From God's perspective, if we are not obedient to ***His*** Law, we are not obedient to ***any*** law. This is a powerful illustration of how opposite the counterfeit king is from the authentic King. Whereas Christ is the very Word of God (Jn. 1:1), and therefore no one operating in the character of Christ can do so in isolation from God's Word, the Antichrist is "*the man of lawlessness*" who operates completely apart from the Word.

This is a term Christ used to describe as an irrecoverable condition, that even if one does things in His name or believes they are carrying out God's work but fail to be obedient to the whole Word of God in the process, they will be just as rejected as "*the man of lawlessness*" himself:

> *22 "Many will say to Me on that day, 'Lord, Lord, did we not prophesy in Your name, and in Your name cast out demons, and in Your name perform many miracles?' 23 And then I will declare to them, 'I never knew you;* ***DEPART FROM ME, YOU WHO PRACTICE LAWLESSNESS****.'*
>
> — Matthew 7:22-23

"*Lawlessness*" is a condition associated with those sent to hell:

> *41 "The Son of Man will send forth His angels, and they will gather out of His kingdom all stumbling blocks, and* ***those who commit lawlessness****, 42 and will throw them into the furnace of fire; in that place there will be weeping and gnashing of teeth.*
>
> — Matthew 13:41-42

Paul uses it to describe the very condition of our previous unsaved nature from which we are supposed to be changed, something addressed at the very center of the purpose of the work of sanctification in each believer's life:

> *19 I am speaking in human terms because of the weakness of your flesh. For just as you presented your members as* ***slaves*** *to impurity and* ***to lawlessness, resulting in further lawlessness****, so now present your members as slaves to righteousness, resulting in sanctification.*
>
> — Romans 6:19

We can see why the King James Version translators chose "*man of* ***sin***" because they understood what the context of "*anomia*" in the Greek New Testament was addressing:

> *4 Everyone who practices sin also practices lawlessness; and* ***sin is lawlessness****.*
>
> — 1 John 3:4

The second designation of "*the son of destruction*" is particularly interesting because the underlying Greek word "*apoleia*" (Strong's #684) is used in reference to Judas, the Antichrist and false believers. This particular term has been described as referring to one's state, after death, when one's exclusion from salvation becomes a realized fact, that point wherein it is consciously understood what might have been which instead is completely lost and ruined.

In the case of Judas, it speaks of what happens to him personally, which is why the translators chose the alternative rendering of "*perdition*":

> [12]*"While I was with them, I was keeping them in Your name which You have given Me; and I guarded them and not one of them perished but **<u>the son of perdition</u>**, so that the Scripture would be fulfilled.*
> — John 17:12

But this term is clearly also applied to the final anti-king as well:

> [3]*Let no one in any way deceive you, for it will not come unless the apostasy comes first, and the man of lawlessness is revealed, **<u>the son of destruction</u>**, [4]who opposes and exalts himself above every so-called god or object of worship, so that he takes his seat in the temple of God, **<u>displaying himself as being God</u>**.*
> — 2 Thessalonians 2:3-4

This is the exact, same word assigned to the ultimate fate of this figure:

> [8]*"The beast that you saw was, and is not, and is about to come up out of the abyss and **<u>go to destruction</u>**. And those who dwell on the earth, whose name has not been written in the book of life from the foundation of the world, will wonder when they see the beast, that he was and is not and will come...[11]"The beast which was and is not, is himself also an eighth and is one of the seven, and he **<u>goes to destruction</u>**.*
> — Revelation 17:8, 11

Peter additionally ascribes this as the ultimate consequences for false teachers and false prophets (2 Pe. 2:1-3), "*ungodly men*" (2 Pe. 3:7), and those who distort the teachings of the Apostle Paul. (2 Pe. 3:15-16) Jesus specifically associates this term with hell as well:

> [13]*"Enter through the narrow gate; for the gate is wide and the way is broad that **<u>leads to destruction</u>**, and there are many who enter through it.*
> — Matthew 7:13

As touched on previously, this is a chief characteristic of the Antichrist in that he brings destruction to everyone and everything possible, carrying with it the irony that it all leads to his own destruction. In the very first vision of Daniel 2, it was stipulated from the outset that the Messiah would ultimately crush and put an end to both the anti-king and his anti-kingdom. (Dan. 2:44) The final scriptural glimpse provided is being "*thrown alive into the lake of fire*". (Rev. 19:20)

The Primary New Testament Anti-King

But the fact that both the Antichrist and Judas are referred to as "*the son of perdition*" causes Judas to be thrust further into the foreground of the final overall portrait when considered in the light of the revelatory remarks provided by the Apostle John:

> [18]*Children, it is the last hour; and just as you heard that antichrist is coming, even now **<u>many antichrists have appeared</u>**; from this we know that it is the last hour. [19]**<u>They went out from us, but they were not really of us</u>**; for if they had been of us, they would have remained with us; but they went out, so that it would be shown*

> *that they all are not of us. [20]But you have an anointing from the Holy One, and you all know.*
>
> — 1 John 2:18-20

Judas is called by the same name as the Antichrist, they are the only two figures in Scripture who are ***satanically*** possessed, and Judas was someone who was not just a believer at one point, but one of the inner circle of Apostles. He was definitely someone who "*went out from us*". Even though very early in His ministry Christ specified the ulterior character of his presence (Jn. 6:70-71), it was not until Jesus revealed him at the Last Supper that he was publicly identified. (Jn. 13:26) Especially when considered with the other characteristics and actions of Judas, we can see that he is the primary New Testament type of the Antichrist:

- He "*was counted among us and received his share in this ministry*" (Acts 1:17) according to the Apostles.
- He "*is a devil*". (Jn. 6:70)
- Satan is at work through Judas. (Jn. 13:2)
- He is not just influenced by, but possessed by Satan. (Lk. 22:3; Jn. 13:2, 27)
- He is a betrayer of Christ. (Mt. 10:4; 26:14-15; Mk. 3:19; 14:10; Lk. 6:16; 22:3-4)
- He is a thief. (Jn. 12:6)
- Whereas the Apostles address Christ as "*Lord*", Judas only goes so far as to acknowledge Jesus as "*Rabbi*", the same kind of acknowledgment strangers and enemies often use of Christ in the course of denying His divinity. (Mt. 26:22-25)
- Jesus indicated that Judas is not spiritually "*clean*" in spite of an outward washing. (Jn. 13:10-11)
- Judas' literal time of departure—"*and it was night*", (Jn. 13:30) is representative of the greater environment of his spiritual working.
- He is a "*guide to those who arrested Jesus*" (Acts 1:16) and led both Gentile and Jew against Christ. (Mt. 26:47-50; Mk. 14:43-46; Lk. 22:47-53; Jn. 18:2-12)
- Judas leads a combined force against Christ in a time of great apostasy as characterized by His abandonment in the Garden of Gethsemane by the other disciples. (Mt. 26:56; Mk. 15:50)

It is evident that so many of these points directly relate to characteristics of the anti-king provided in Scripture so as to further confirm the textual connection between this pair. Therefore to study Judas is to study the final figure to come. And in particular, we can see that this figure is going to have a Christian "pedigree" which is going to deceive many. Regardless of ethnicity, ***both*** beasts can employ this background and replay these attributes, but will be much more powerful and greatly multiplied in the first beast to come.

The Primary New Testament Anti-Kingdom

Scripture is often found to be so fluid in going back and forth between a king and a kingdom that the distinctions between them are not just sometimes blurred, but actually shared. After all, by definition a kingdom or government carries out the will of its leader so that what he desires is undertaken by others as members of that regime. But just as "*the son of perdition*" textually connects Judas and the Antichrist, so does Revelation 12 afford an equally strong connection to Herod the Great, but not just as a king, but equally as a kingdom.

> [4]*And his tail swept away a third of the stars of heaven and threw them to the earth. And the dragon stood before the woman who was about to give birth,* ***so that when she gave birth he might devour her child****.*
>
> — Revelation 12:4

> [16]*Then when Herod saw that he had been tricked by the magi,* ***he became very enraged, and sent and slew all the male children*** *who were in Bethlehem and all its vicinity, from two years old and under, according to the time which he had determined from the magi.*
>
> — Matthew 2:16

This common feature of attempting to kill the Christ-child is particularly compelling when it is additionally considered how Satan as "*a great red dragon having seven heads and ten horns*" is not just inextricably connected to the kingdom and person of Antichrist, but is replayed in Herod the Great's life as well. Just as we are repeatedly told that three of "*the ten*" are purposely removed by the beast to provide a final "*seven*", so this is literally found in the legacy of Herod the Great. He had ten sons, three of whom he murdered while the other seven all served as respective kings at one time or another.

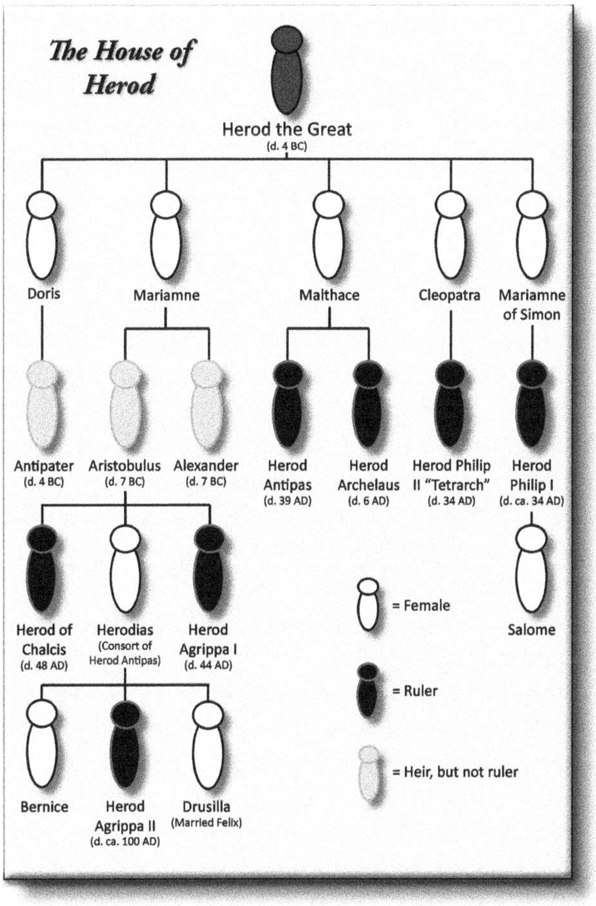

In other words, like the beast with ten heads, Herod the Great had ten sons, but just as the beast overthrew three of them, so Herod "removed" three of his sons. And like the dragon/beast, he tries to have the Child killed.

But one of the most prominent features of Herod the Great was his acceptance across nearly all ethnic, political and religious divides. He was not actually Jewish, but Idumean—that is, originating from Edom and yet also holding Roman citizenship—a Gentile. So in this figure we have someone who is a Gentile political ruler, accepted religiously as a Jew, but also as a Roman. He is essentially all things to all people. Like Antiochus Epiphanes IV, he very much favored Greek culture and also attempted to Hellenize Israel, although at a much more gradual pace.

Beside being appointed by Rome, he maintained power with the aid of a military mainly composed of foreign soldiers and embarked on a building campaign that appealed both to the local population and his masters in Rome. One of his major building projects was the restoration of the Temple. However, his reign was characterized by a paranoia which resulted in the murder of his own sons based on what amounted to rumors of their ill intentions, and various other murders and violent acts are attributed to him throughout his reign as well. Many of the Antichrist's characteristics can be seen in him personally and the kingdom through which he ruled.

But the aspect of the Temple might be of particular interest where Herod the Great is concerned, as there may be a parallel in his rebuilding of the Temple and the association of the final figure with the third Tribulational Temple yet to come. It puzzles this author that Herod's endeavors in this regard are universally described as a "restoration", as the Temple constructed in the time of Joshua and Zerubbabel, more commonly referred to as the "Second Temple", was completely replaced. And it would seem that because he undertook this project for the practitioners of Judaism, he was able to also construct numerous temples to pagan gods throughout the land as well, so he negotiated compromises among verious factions.

Herod's Temple was not a replica of Solomon's Temple, nor did it adhere exactingly to biblical requirements alone. The architecture in general was more elaborately Greek so as to compete with other great structures of the period throughout the Mediterranean world, and its overall perimeter was greatly expanded upon to approximately 35 acres. The core footprint of the main facility was retained, but replaced even down to its foundation stones and largely covered with a gold veneer. The expanded area around it was divided into four courts: the most outer being the Court of the Gentiles, then the Court of Women, the Court of Israel, and finally the Court of Priests. There were various adornments not originally specified in Scripture, but a particular departure was assigning the two cherubim inside the respective male and female gender, a new rabinnic tradition insisting this represented God's love for Israel His bride. It was a strange variant of idolatry which was not just tolerated, but accepted.

The Temple is a stated fixture in Revelation 11, side-by-side with the account of the Two Witnesses who come into constant conflict with the Antichrist, and it is no coincidence that the Two Witnesses and Joshua and Zerubbabel are both co-identified as "*the two olive trees*". (Zech. 4:1-14; Rev. 11:4) Joshua and Zerubbabel come into conflict with those in the land who wanted to join in the building of the Temple. Similarly, Revelation 11, which is mainly dedicated to the topic of the Two Witnesses, begins with a command to take measurements of the Temple, and in Zechariah 4:9-10 is mentioned "*the plumb line in the hand of Zerubbabel*". Just as there were issues involving the Temple upon the return from the Babylonian Captivity in Joshua and Zerubbabel's days, something seems to have been replayed at Christ's First

Coming in Herod's Temple which will ultimately be present in the Second Coming involving the Third Tribulational Temple in which the Abomination of Desolation will be committed.

Herod the Great and the continuing spiritual battles which would ensue with other Herodian rulers descended from him all share common scriptural traits of the anti-king and anti-kingdom. From time to time Jesus had to deal with a group specified as the Herodians, who were often seen conspiring with the Pharisees. (Mt. 22:1; Mk. 3:6; 12:12-13) They essentially represent those whose religious agenda is satiated through secular political endeavors, a sort of precursor to what we might today call a "social gospel" at best.

Other Types to Study

There are many other personalities in whom we find the scriptural attributes of either the anti-king or anti-kingdom present. The aforementioned books, along with the reader's personal study, will greatly aid in understanding the ultimate fulfillment to come.

Biblical Types

- Absalom
- The Assyrian
- Goliath
- Haman
- Herod the Great
- The House of Herod
- Ishbi-benob
- Judas
- Julius Augustus
- King of Assyria
- King of Babylon
- King of Tyre
- Lahmi
- The Man of Sixes
- Nebuchadnezzar
- Nimrod
- The Pharaohs
- Saph
- Sennacherib
- Sethur
- Solomon
- Soter
- Ziklag

Historical Types

- Mahmoud Ahmadinejad
- Idi Amin
- Napoleon Bonaparte
- Nicolae Ceausescu
- Charlemagne
- Constantine the Great
- Antiochus Epiphanes IV
- Wallace Farad
- Adolph Hitler
- Saddam Hussein
- Kim Jon Il
- Jim Jones
- David Koresh
- Vladimir Lenin
- Charles Manson
- Mao Tse Tung
- Mohammed
- Benito Mussolini
- Gamal Nasser
- The Pharaohs
- Roman General Pompey
- The Popes
- Pol Pot
- The Roman Emperors
- Xavier Solano
- Joseph Stalin

Jewish Types

- Simon Bar Kochba
- Judas of Galilee
- Shabbatai Zvi
- Jacob Frank
- Menachem Schneerson

There are very likely potential additions to each of these lists, but what should be clear is the tremendous amount of information and real-life illustrations which have been supplied when it comes to this final figure and his kingdom. The previously endorsed books go into much more detail where many of these figures are concerned and would at least double the current length of this book to properly provide that which they have already so thoroughly covered.

The Anti-King

The list of scripturally-given characteristics and activities directly associated with the first beast is incredibly extensive. Many of these will obviously be shared traits with his anti-kingdom and found present in both the False Prophet and the harlot, Babylon the Great:

He is a Beast

- ❑ *"…a fourth beast, dreadful and extremely strong…"* (Dan. 7:7)
- ❑ *"…it had large iron teeth."* (Dan. 7:7)
- ❑ *"...a beast coming up out of the sea..."* (Rev. 13:1)
- ❑ *"...like a leopard, and his feet were like those of a bear, and his mouth like the mouth of a lion".* (Rev. 13:2)
- ❑ *"The beast...was, and is not, and is about to come up out of the abyss and go to destruction."* (Rev. 17:8)
- ❑ *"The beast which was and is not, is himself also an eight and is one of the seven..."* (Rev. 17:11)

He is a Horn

- ❑ *"…another horn…possessed eyes like the eyes of a man and a mouth uttering great boasts".* (Dan. 7:8)
- ❑ *"...larger in appearance than its associates."* (Dan. 7:20)
- ❑ *"...will arise after them* [the ten horns]*...will be different from the previous ones..."* (Dan. 7:24)
- ❑ *"…a rather small horn which grew exceedingly great toward the south, toward the east, and toward the Beautiful Land."* (Dan. 8:9)

He is a King

- ❑ *"...a king will arise..."* (Dan. 8:23)
- ❑ *"It devoured and crushed and trampled down the remainder with its feet…"* (Dan. 7:7)
- ❑ *"…The fourth beast will be a fourth kingdom on the earth…"* (Dan. 7:23)

- ❑ *"...different from all the other kingdoms and will devour the whole earth and tread it down and crush it."* (Dan. 7:23)
- ❑ *"The seven heads are seven mountains on which the woman sits, and they are seven kings; five have fallen, one is, the other has not yet come; and when he comes, he must remain a little while."* (Rev. 17:9-10)

He is Given a Set Time Limit

- ❑ *"...authority to act for forty-two months was given to him."* (Rev. 13: 5)

He is Satanically Animated

- ❑ *"...the dragon gave him his power and his throne and great authority..."* (Rev. 13: 2)

He is a Conqueror

- ❑ *"...another* [horn] *will arise after them, and he will be different from the previous ones and will subdue three kings."* (Dan. 7:24)
- ❑ *"His power will be mighty, but not by his own power..."* (Dan. 8:24)
- ❑ *"...he will destroy to an extraordinary degree..."* (Dan. 8:24)
- ❑ *"He will destroy mighty men and the holy people."* (Dan. 8:24)
- ❑ The conflicts with the King of the South will replayed again. (Dan. 11:40)
- ❑ *"He will enter the Beautiful Land, and many countries will fall, but these will be rescued out of his hand: Edom, Moab and the foremost of the sons of Ammon."* (Dan. 11:41)
- ❑ *"...he will stretch out his hand against other countries, and the land of Egypt will not escape."* (Dan. 11:42)
- ❑ *"...he will gain control over all the precious things of Egypt..."* (Dan. 11:43)
- ❑ *"...Libyans and Ethiopians will follow at his heels."* (Dan. 11:43)
- ❑ *"...rumors from the East and from the North will disturb him, and he will go forth with great wrath to destroy and annihilate many."* (Dan. 11:44)
- ❑ *"...authority over every tribe and people and tongue and nation was given to him."* (Rev. 13:7)

He is s Despicable Person, Yet Successful

- ❑ *"...he will...prosper and perform his will..."* (Dan. 8:24)
- ❑ *"...a despicable person will arise..."* (Dan. 11:21)
- ❑ *"...he will prosper until the indignation is finished..."* (Dan. 11:36)

He is Self-Promoting & Self-Deifying

- ❑ *"...the sound of the boastful words which the horn was speaking..."* (Dan. 7:11)
- ❑ *"He will speak out against the Most High..."* (Dan. 7:25)
- ❑ *"...he will intend to make alterations in times and in law..."* (Dan. 7:25)
- ❑ *"It even magnified itself to be equal with the Commander of the host..."* (Dan. 8:11)

- ❑ *"…he will magnify himself in his heart…"* (Dan. 8:25)
- ❑ *"…the king will do as he pleases…"* (Dan. 11:36)
- ❑ *"…he will exalt and magnify himself above every god…"* (Dan. 11:36)
- ❑ "…[he] *will speak monstrous things against the God of gods…"* (Dan. 11:36)
- ❑ *"He will show no regard for the gods of his fathers…"* (Dan. 11:37)
- ❑ *"…nor will he show regard for any other god…"* (Dan. 11:37)
- ❑ *"…he will magnify himself above them all [any other god],"* (Dan. 11:37)
- ❑ "*…who opposes and exalts himself above every so-called god or object of worship…*" (2 Th. 2:4)

He is Personally & Spiritually Disturbed

- ❑ "[He will show no regard] *for the desire of women…"* (Dan. 11:37)
- ❑ *"…he will honor a god of fortresses, a god whom his fathers did not know; he will honor him with gold, silver, costly stones and treasures."* (Dan. 11:38)
- ❑ *"He will take action against the strongest of fortresses with the help of a foreign god…"* (Dan. 11:39)
- ❑ "*…the man of lawlessness is revealed, the son of destruction…*" (2 Th. 2:3)

He is a Master of Deception

- ❑ *"…it will fling truth to the ground and perform its will and prosper."* (Dan. 8:12)
- ❑ *"…Insolent and skilled in intrigue."* (Dan. 8:23)
- ❑ *"…through his shrewdness he will cause deceit to succeed by his influence…"* (Dan. 8:25)
- ❑ *"After an alliance is made with him he will practice deception…"* (Dan. 11:23)
- ❑ *"..he will accomplish what his fathers never did, nor his ancestors…"* (Dan. 11:24)
- ❑ *"…he will devise his schemes against strongholds…"* (Dan. 11:24)
- ❑ "*…coming…with all the deception of wickedness for those who perish…*" (2 Th. 2:10)
- ❑ "*…not really of us…*" (1 Jn. 2:19)

He Performs Signs & Wonders

- ❑ *"…whose coming is in accord with the activity of Satan, with all power and signs and false wonders…"* (2 Th. 2:9)
- ❑ *"I saw one of his heads as if it had been slain, and his fatal wound was healed."* (Rev. 13:3)

He is Worshiped

- ❑ *"…they worshiped the dragon because he gave his authority to the beast; and they worshiped the beast…"* (Rev. 13:4)
- ❑ *"All who dwell on the earth will worship him…"* (Rev. 13:8)
- ❑ *"…those who dwell on the earth…will wonder when they see the beast…"* (Rev. 17:8)

He is an Agent of Apostasy

- ❑ *"...he will come back and show regard for those who forsake the holy covenant."* (Dan. 11:30)
- ❑ *"By smooth words he will turn to godlessness those who act wickedly toward the covenant..."* (Dan. 11:32)
- ❑ *"...they* [the people who know their God] *will be granted a little help, and many will join with them in hypocrisy."* (Dan. 11:34)
- ❑ *"...the apostasy comes first..."* (2 Th. 2:2)

He Persecutes God's People by Open Warfare

- ❑ *"...that horn was waging war with the saints and overpowering them..."* (Dan. 7:21)
- ❑ *"...He will...wear down the saints of the Highest One..."* (Dan. 7:25)
- ❑ *"...they will be given into his hand for a time, times, and half a time."* (Dan. 7:25)
- ❑ *"...it would be for a time, times, and half a time; and as soon as they finish shattering the power of the holy people, all these events will be completed."* (Dan. 12:7)
- ❑ *"The overflowing forces will be flooded away before him and shattered, and also the prince of the covenant."* (Dan. 11:22)
- ❑ *"...he will go up and gain power with a small force of people."* (Dan. 11:23)
- ❑ *"...he persecuted the woman who gave birth to the male child".* (Rev. 12:13)
- ❑ *"...enraged with the woman, went off to make war with the rest of her children, who keep the commandments of God and hold to the testimony of Jesus".* (Rev. 12:17)
- ❑ *"It was also given to him to make war with the saints and to over come them..."* (Rev. 13:7)

He Takes Down Heavenly Beings as Well as People

- ❑ *"It* [horn] *grew up to the host of heaven and caused some of the host and some of the stars to fall to the earth, and it trampled them down."* (Dan. 8:10)

He Makes & Breaks a Treaty

- ❑ *"...he will make a firm covenant with the many for one week, but in the middle of the week he will put a stop to sacrifice and grain offering..."* (Dan. 9:27)
- ❑ *"After an alliance is made with him he will practice deception..."* (Dan. 11:23)

He Commits the Abomination of Desolation

- ❑ *"...it removed the regular sacrifice from Him..."* (Dan. 8:11)
- ❑ *"...the place of His sanctuary was thrown down."* (Dan. 8:11)
- ❑ *"...on account of transgression the host will be given over to the horn along with the regular sacrifice..."* (Dan. 8:12)
- ❑ *"...'How long will the vision about the regular sacrifice apply, while the transgression causes horror, so as to allow both the holy place and the host to be trampled?'...'For 2,300 evenings and mornings, then the holy place will be properly restored."* (Dan. 8:13-14)

- ❑ *"…on the wing of abominations will come one who makes desolate, even until a complete destruction, one that is decreed, is poured out on the one who makes desolate."* (Dan. 9:27)
- ❑ *"From the time that the regular sacrifice is abolished and the abomination of desolation is set up, there will be 1,290 days. How blessed is he who keeps waiting and attains to the 1,335 days!"* (Dan. 12:11-12)
- ❑ *"Forces from him will arise, desecrate the sanctuary fortress, and do away with the regular sacrifice."* (Dan. 11:31)
- ❑ *"…they will set up the abomination of desolation."* (Dan. 11:31)
- ❑ *"...he takes his seat in the temple of God, displaying himself as being God".* (2 Th. 2:4)

He Acts Against the Godhead

- ❑ *"He will even oppose the Prince of princes…"* (Dan. 8:25)
- ❑ *"…his heart will be set against the holy covenant, and he will take action and then return to his own land."* (Dan. 11:28)
- ❑ *"…he will be disheartened and will return and become enraged at the holy covenant and take action…"* (Dan. 11:30)
- ❑ "*...denies that Jesus is the Christ...*" (1 Jn. 2:22)
- ❑ "*...denies the Father and the Son*". (1 Jn. 2:22)
- ❑ "*...does not confess Jesus...*" (1 Jn. 4:3)
- ❑ "*...do not acknowledge Jesus Christ as coming in the flesh*". (2 Jn. 7)
- ❑ "*There was given to him a mouth speaking arrogant words and blasphemies...*" (Rev. 13:5)
- ❑ "*...he opened his mouth in blasphemies against God, to blaspheme His name and His tabernacle, that is, those who dwell in heaven.*" (Rev. 13:6)

He Takes Up Residence in Israel

- ❑ *"He will pitch the tents of his royal pavilion between the seas and the beautiful Holy Mountain…"* (Dan. 11:45)

His End Will Come

- ❑ *"…the beast was slain…"* (Dan. 7:11)
- ❑ *"…its body was destroyed and given to the burning fire."* (Dan. 7:11)
- ❑ *"…until the Ancient of Days came and judgment was passed in favor of the saints of the High One…"* (Dan. 7:22)
- ❑ *"…and the time arrived when the saints took possession of the kingdom."* (Dan. 7:22)
- ❑ *"But the court will sit for judgment, and his dominion will be taken away, annihilated and destroyed forever."* (Dan. 7:26)
- ❑ *"Then the sovereignty, the dominion and the greatness of all the kingdoms under the whole heaven will be given to the people of the saints of the Highest One…"* (Dan. 7:27)
- ❑ *"…he will be broken without human agency."* (Dan. 8:25)

- ❑ *"…he will come this end, and no one will help him."* (Dan. 11:45)
- ❑ *"...having great wrath, knowing that he has only a short time".* (Rev. 12:12)
- ❑ *"...is about to come up out of the abyss and go to destruction."* (Rev. 17:8)
- ❑ *"...he goes to destruction."* (Rev. 17:11)

The Second Beast: The False Prophet

Again, it is worth noting that although this figure shares the first beast's satanic DNA, he has a specific role and to him alone are assigned some of the most notable features of the anti-king/anti-kingdom:

- ❑ "*…coming up out of the earth…*" (Rev. 13:11)
- ❑ "*...he had two horns like lamb...*" (Rev. 13:11)
- ❑ "*...he spoke as a dragon.*" (Rev. 13:11)
- ❑ "*He exercises all the authority of the first beast in his presence*". (Rev. 13:12)
- ❑ "*...he makes the earth and those dwell in it worship the first beast...*" (Rev. 13:12)
- ❑ "*He performs great signs, so that he even makes fire come down out of heaven to the earth in the presence of men.*" (Rev. 13:13)
- ❑ "*...he deceives those who dwell on the earth to make an image to the beast...*" (Rev. 13:14)
- ❑ "*...it was given to him to give breath to the image of the beast, so that the image of the beast would even speak...*" (Rev. 13:15)
- ❑ "*...cause as many as do not worship the image of the beast to be killed.*" (Rev. 13:15)
- ❑ "*...causes all, the small and the great, and the rich and the poor, and the free men and the slaves, to be given a mark on their right hand or on their forehead...*" (Rev. 13:17)
- ❑ "*...provides that no one will be able to buy or to sell, except the one who has the mark...*" (Rev. 13:17)

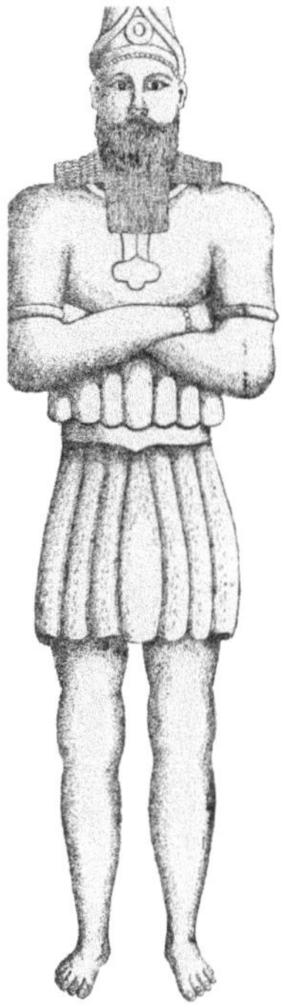

The Anti-Kingdom

Many of the aforementioned traits obviously apply here as well, and vice versa:

It is Satan Cast Down to Earth

- ❑ *"…he was thrown down to the earth, and his angels were thrown down with him…"* (Rev. 12:9)

It Will be a Powerful, Yet Divided, Kingdom

- ❑ *"…a fourth kingdom as strong as iron…"* (Dan. 2:40)
- ❑ *"…feet and toes, partly of potter's clay and partly of iron…"* (Dan. 2:41)
- ❑ *"…it will be a divided kingdom…"* (Dan. 2:41)
- ❑ "*...it will have the toughness of iron...*" (Dan. 2:41)

- ❑ *"…some of the kingdom will be strong and part of it will be brittle.."* (Dan. 2:42)
- ❑ *"…it had ten horns."* (Dan. 7:7)
- ❑ *"...different from all the other kingdoms..."* (Dan. 7:23)
- ❑ *"...will devour the whole earth and tread it down and crush it."* (Dan. 7:23)
- ❑ *"...three of the first horns wee pulled out by the roots before it..."* (Dan. 7:28)
- ❑ *"…ten horns…ten kings…"* (Dan. 7:24)
- ❑ *"...a great red dragon having seven heads and ten horns, and on his heads were seven diadems*". (Rev. 12:4)
- ❑ *"...a beast coming up out of the sea, having ten horns and seven heads, and on his horns were ten diadems, and on his heads were blasphemous names*". (Rev. 13:1)
- ❑ *"...a scarlet beast, full of blasphemous names, having seven heads and ten horns."* (Rev. 17:3)
- ❑ *"The ten horns...are ten kings who have not yet received a kingdom, but they receive authority as kings with the beast for one hour."* (Rev. 17:12)
- ❑ *"These* [the ten horns/kings] *have one purpose, and they give their power and authority to the beast."* (Rev. 17:13)

It Will Turn on the Harlot Babylon

- ❑ *"The ten horns...and the beast, these will hate the harlot and make her desolate and naked, and will eat her flesh and will burn her up with fire."* (Rev. 17:16)

It is an Improper Mixture

- ❑ *"…the iron mixed with clay, they will combine with one another in the seed of men, but they will not adhere to one another…"* (Dan. 2:43)

It Brings a Temporary False Peace & Prosperity

- ❑ *"…he will destroy many while they are at ease."* (Dan. 8:25)
- ❑ *"…he will come in a time of tranquility and seize the kingdom by intrigue."* (Dan. 11:21)
- ❑ *"In a time of tranquility he will enter the richest parts of the realm…"* (Dan. 11:24)
- ❑ *"…he will distribute plunder, booty and possessions among them…"* (Dan. 11:24)
- ❑ *"…he will give great honor to those who acknowledge him and will cause them to rule over the many, and will parcel out the land for a price."* (Dan. 11:39)

A Tool of God's Will

- ❑ *"For God has put it in their hearts to execute His purpose by having a common purpose, and by giving their kingdom to the beast, until the words of God will be fulfilled"* (Rev. 17:17)

Babylon the Great

The one-world, ecumenical religious structure which will rise in parallel with the anti-king/anti-kingdom will be an important feature propelling the first beast toward the achievement of his geopolitical and economic agenda, but with the arrival of the False Prophet in concert with his public outing at the Abomination of Desolation, he turns everyone against her in an effort to be directly worshiped rather than approached through her. Movement in the religious environs is just as important to keep track of as in the political.

- ❑ "*...the great harlot...*" (Rev. 17:1)
- ❑ "*...sits on many waters...*" (Rev. 17:1)
- ❑ "*...The waters...where the harlot sits, are peoples and multitudes and nations and tongues.*" (Rev. 17:15)
- ❑ *...with whom the kings of the earth committed acts of immorality...*" (Rev. 17:2)
- ❑ "*...those who dwell on the earth were made drunk with the wine of her immorality.*" (Rev. 17:2)
- ❑ "*...sitting on a scarlet beast, full of blasphemous names, having seven heads and ten horns.*" (Rev. 17:3)
- ❑ "*...clothed in purple and scarlet, and adorned with gold and precious stones and pearls...*" (Rev. 17:4)
- ❑ "*...in her hand a gold cup full of abominations and of the unclean things of her immorality...*" (Rev. 17:4)
- ❑ "*...on her forehead a name was written, a mystery, 'BABYLON THE GREAT, THE MOTHER OF HARLOTS AND THE ABOMINATIONS OF THE EARTH'.*" (Rev. 17:5)
- ❑ "*...drunk with the blood of the saints, and with the blood of the witnesses of Jesus.*" (Rev. 17:6)
- ❑ "*The seven heads are seven mountains on which the woman sits, and they are seven kings...*" (Rev. 17:9-10)
- ❑ "*The woman...is the great city, which reigns over the kings of the earth.*" (Rev. 17:18)
- ❑ "*...in one day her plagues will come, pestilence and mourning and famine, and she will be burned up with fire...*" (Rev. 18:8)
- ❑ "*...the kings of the earth...will weep over her when they see the smoke of her burning.*" (Rev. 18:9)
- ❑ "*...the merchants of the earth weep and mourn over her, because no one buys their cargoes any more...*" (Rev. 18:11)
- ❑ "*...every shipmaster and every passenger and sailor, and as many as make their living by the sea...were crying out as they saw the smoke of her burning...*" (Rev. 18:17-18)
- ❑ "*...in her was found the blood of prophets and of saints and of all who have been slain on the earth.*" (Rev. 18:24)

A Closing Thought

When I look at the previous 8 pages presenting such an extensive list culled from Scripture, it truly brings to light the deception that is currently propagated, (1) that it is not necessary for the Church to concern themselves with this because they will never meet the Antichrist, and (2) that to study this is to forsake "looking for Jesus" and somehow substituting "looking for the Antichrist". In truth, this book did not even enfold the entire subject, but merely attempted to address a perceived gap in the already extensive writings of *Shadows of the Beast* by Jacob Prasch and *Antichrist* by A. W. Pink. If this doesn't apply to the Church, aside from the fact that Christ Himself along with with the Apostles Paul and John specifically state otherwise, why does God's Word contain so much on the subject?

But for those of us who understand to the contrary, this study should have underscored a very valuable tool of identification where the Antichrist is concerned, that this is not exclusively about an individual. He is not just coming as a king, but a kingdom, and he is accompanied not just by a counterfeit John the Baptist in the False Prophet, but a counterfeit Body of Christ in the harlot "Babylon the Great".

Probably mostly due to secular media, but also long-time errors perpetuated by Christian academia, the topic of the Antichrist has over-focused on a single individual, attributing to him many things which are actually authored by the accompanying figures and institutions of the ten kings combining into a single kingdom, the harlot religious system which initially propels him, and his personal director of worship in the False Prophet. We seem to have been slow in adopting the plain text of God's Word where these figures are concerned, and instead of anticipating how they support and work with each other, have set much of it aside in favor of an artificial portrait which has surreptitiously cropped key elements and contributors from the crucial picture. We need to regularly revisit that initial image of the first vision in Daniel 2 to remind us that he is both a king and a kingdom, and to enjoin the whole counsel of God's Word to keep all of the elements in proper balance.

Perhaps what is most paradoxical to this author is that when it comes to God's prophetic Word, this is not turning out to be a test ***of*** faith, but a test ***for*** faith. The general consensus, at least at present in the Western Church, is that "no one knows for sure", so we are supposed to collegiately accommodate any and all interpretations, because, "anyone could be right". This is actually a direct contradiction of God's Word on the subject. In fact, when it comes to Scripture, are there any other doctrines, teachings or references which "no one knows for sure"? That ***anyone*** could be right about? Possibly the key deception of our time is this very notion when it comes to anything touching the prophetic portions of God's Word.

The Prophet Daniel absolutely stipulated this to the contrary:

> 10"*Many will be purged, purified and refined, but the wicked will act wickedly; and* ***none of the wicked will understand****, but* ***those who have insight will understand****.*
> — Daniel 12:10

It is not intellectual ability or even a supernatural gift from God which Daniel espouses, but the issue of spiritual faithfulness. Those who practice the Word are those who are capable of understanding ***all*** of His Word.

Likewise, the Apostle Peter stipulates the absence of confusion or mystery in this arena:

> [19]*So **we have the prophetic word made more sure**, to which you do well to pay attention as to **a lamp shining in a dark place**, until the day dawns and the morning star arises in your hearts.* [20]*But know this first of all, that no prophecy of Scripture is a matter of one's own interpretation,* [21]*for no prophecy was ever made by an act of human will, but men moved by the Holy Spirit spoke from God.*
>
> — 2 Peter 1:19-21

While the pundits attempt to include any and every viewpoint regardless in the name of "no one knows for sure", God's Word says directly to the contrary that even when it comes to "*the prophetic word*", that we are "*made **more** sure*".

Yes, it is true that there is a single milestone contained within the overall eschaton which Jesus stipulated no one can know, that being the day and hour of the *Harpazo*. (Mt. 24:36) But it's as if like a toddler with a temper tantrum we stomp all around the room crying, "Well, if we can't know that ***one*** thing, then I guess we can't know ***any***thing", and carry that notion into all which is plainly revealed. Jesus stipulated that Holy Spirit-filled, Bible believing and practicing Christians will not just recognize these things, but their place in the overall sequence:

> [32]*"Now learn the parable from the fig tree: when its branch has already become tender and puts forth its leaves, you know that summer is near;* [33]*so, you too, **when you see all these things, recognize that He is near, right at the door**.* [34]*Truly I say to you, this generation will not pass away until all these things take place.* [35]*Heaven and earth will pass away, but My words will not pass away.*
>
> — Matthew 24:32-35

But even more so when it comes to the specific topic of the Antichrist, we do not have to wait until we see the actual mark, nor actually the image talking, nor even witness all of the many parallel proofs of the final figure's identity. The Apostle John addresses this categorically, that Holy Spirit-filled Christians are able to specifically recognize antichrist antics:

> [18]*Children, it is the last hour; and just as you heard that **antichrist is coming**, even now many antichrists have appeared; from this we know that it is the last hour.* [19]*They went out from us, but they were not really of us; for if they had been of us, they would have remained with us; but they went out, so that it would be shown that they all are not of us.* [20]***But you have an anointing from the Holy One, and you all know.*** [21]*I have not written to you because you do not know the truth, but because **you do know it**, and because no lie is of the truth.* [22]*Who is the liar but the one who denies that Jesus is the Christ? This is the antichrist, the one who denies the Father and the Son.* [23]*Whoever denies the Son does not have the Father; the one who confesses the Son has the Father also.* [24]*As for you, let that abide in you which you heard from the beginning. If what you heard from the beginning abides in you, you also will abide in the Son and in the Father.*
>
> — 1 John 2:18-24

Attached to the very first scriptural instance where the anti-king is finally called "*antichrist*", an accompanying scriptural caveat stipulates that those who have the Holy Spirit "***all know***".

When we look back at the previous 8 page summary of all the scriptural attributes associated with the final Antichrist and company, we can understand these to be textual affirmations of the promises made through God's Word by the Apostles and Christ Himself that there most certainly ***will*** be those who know for sure. Not the world, the academically trained elite, or even intellectually advantaged, but the faithful practitioners of God's Word. Such "*who have insight will understand*", "*have the prophetic word made more sure*", "*recognize that He is near*", and ultimately "*know*" the final anti-king and anti-kingdom because of "*an anointing from the Holy One*". Until then...

> [14]*Therefore, beloved, since you look for these things, be diligent to be found by Him in peace, spotless and blameless,*
> — 2 Peter 3:14

21 ❖ Roles & Goals

This book has attempted to raise awareness that it is not the sole figure of the Antichrist which must be exclusively considered, but that which equally accompanies him. It is not just the first beast as the primary object of power and worship, but the second beast—the False Prophet, who will champion the transition from someone who begins as a purely political figure to a self-proclaimed deity. It is not just about the final satanic pair, but the institutions which propel and support them, one mainly political as a conglomeration of ten overarching dictatorships, the other the ultimate harlot of spiritual seduction bringing all things religious under one unified roof in concert with that anti-kingdom.

Far too many books and movies have featured scenarios which fixate on the one beast with almost no mention of the roles or even the presence of these necessary parallel supporting resources. While it can be understood that such have deceived non-believers, or the nominal Christians who rarely visit their Bibles and are therefore susceptible to deception, God's Word has provided Holy-Spirit, Bible-believing practitioner's of His Word with a very deep template of what to look for, not just in the way of nefarious individuals designated as the Antichrist and False Prophet, but in how they will be accompanied by an unprecedented change in the political landscape by the ten kings who, "*have one purpose, and they give their power and authority to the beast*" (Rev. 17:13), and a parallel spiritual paradigm shift orchestrated by "*the great harlot*" designated "*Babylon the Great*". In other words, we are looking for ***both*** a king and kingdom, and not just individuals but the accompanying institutions which consolidate all things both political and religious under them. It's not just a pair of guys but a pair of organizations as well. We need to be looking for all of these things as they rise into view.

At present, the global partisan differences render it very difficult to envision a scenario where all the nations of the world are first consolidated under ten super kingdoms, much less subsequently being voluntarily enfolded under a single leader. (Right now, we can't even get all the Republicans on the same page.) Likewise, the strife not just between incompatible religious beliefs, much less the infighting among those claiming to belong to the same sect or denomination, do not provide a foreseeable avenue where we can envision them all coming together. But without both of these accompanying albeit unprecedented occurrences, there can be no appearance of the Antichrist and False Prophet; their agenda is dependent on them.

> [8]*"But all these things are merely the beginning of birth pangs.*
> — Matthew 24:8

Jesus does not begin with a warning to look for an individual person, but for a change in the whole environment. The things which Jesus cites which will be increasingly and cyclically worse in the character of "*birth pangs*" corresponding to ultimate, final fulfillments in each of the Seal judgments. By the 4th Seal alone, an unprecedented scale of death and destruction will be experienced by "*a fourth of the earth, to kill with sword and with famine and with pestilence and by the wild beasts of the earth*". (Rev. 6:8) If this were to take place today, total casualties would approach 2 billion. To put this in perspective, World War II caused a combined military and civilian loss of approximately 300 million. What is to come is seven times worse than anything previously experienced in just the first round! It is in an environment of unprecedented chaos, loss and catastrophe in which the Antichrist begins to work, and by which these supporting institutions take shape.

> *"...[7]it had ten horns. [8]While I was contemplating the horns, behold, another horn... came up among them..."*
> —Daniel 7:7-8

Just as the "*birth pangs*" build until they are ultimately realized in the Seals, so the anti-kingdom begins to take shape, eventually producing the necessary public platform for the first beast's arrival. A dramatic change in the political landscape is going to provide the proper stage for this final figure, and will most likely form prior to his biblical fulfillment of the white horseman in the 1st Seal.

All of the Antichrist figures prior to the giving of Revelation were all lone, Gentile political rulers, such as Nebuchadnezzar, Antiochus Epiphanes IV, or individual Roman emperors. This is how the Antichrist is initially depicted as the first horseman of the 1st Seal, "*conquering and to conquer*". (Rev. 6:2) That which he is able to do, as well as the worldwide consolidation of all things political under the ten kings, is occurring against this backdrop of catastrophic loss at every natural and manmade level on a scale the world is incapable of knowing how to deal with. Its "coping mechanism" when faced with the dominoes of war, famine, pestilence, global disturbances and economic turmoil in such intense and quick succession will be to turn to those who can provide ***any*** kind of remedy whatsoever. The environment of the "*birth pangs*" culminating in the Seals is the great facilitator of desperation that not only brings the normally politically incompatible together, but the religious as well.

But then imagine that a rising figure who has had success both negotiating opponents into his fold and overcoming them militarily, appears to be killed in battle, but miraculously rises from the dead. ("*...as if it had been slain, and his fatal wound was healed...*" Rev. 13:3) Things take an unprecedented turn as "*the whole earth was amazed and followed after the beast*", and do not just rally around him politically, but "*they worshiped the beast saying, 'Who is like the beast, and who is able to wage war with him?*'" (Rev. 13:3-4) The unification of religious factions which had previously largely done so because of political and economic expediency begins to accelerate in tandem with the political following because of this supernatural counterfeit of a resurrection in the course of a military conflict. For everyone on planet earth, at this point it all begins to turn into a greater spiritual issue.

To accelerate the consolidation of his support, he employs the same rallying lie that Hitler used, only this time instead of blaming the Jews, this figure blames the Christians. A worldwide persecution results which not only reduces the Church's ranks through martyrdom, but the greatest falling away—that is, apostasy, ever experienced by those unwilling to endure such for their faith. As with all persecution of the Church, however, "*the gospel of the kingdom shall be preached in the whole world as a testimony to all the nations*". (Mt. 24:14) While there are no guarantees of how it will be received, the Church nonetheless accomplishes what Christ originally instructed them to do at His Ascension. (Acts 1:8)

This all takes shape in the shadow of the Abomination of Desolation about to take place, but is further multiplied by a change in the working of the Holy Spirit so that He no longer restrains. (2 Th. 2:6-10) The Holy Spirit, in anticipation of what is about to come, reverts to working in the Old Testament manner on an individual basis. And what is coming, of course, is Satan being cast out of heaven and down to the earth (Rev. 12:3-4) simultaneous or in close proximity to the Antichrist going into the Temple and publicly deifying himself in the course of the Abomination of Desolation.

This is the fixed milestone which Jesus cites, the exact midway point of Daniel's 70th Week. Here the False Prophet comes into play, who for the final half of the final week of years oversees worldwide worship of the first beast when he:

- "*...exercises all the authority of the first beast in his presence.*" (Rev. 13:12)
- "*...deceives those who dwell on the earth because of the signs which it was given him to perform in the presence of the beast...*" (Rev. 13:14)
- "*...telling those who dwell on the earth to make an image to the beast*", giving it life and ordering all to worship it. (Rev. 13:14-15)
- And "*causes all...to be given a mark*" without which "*no one will be able to buy or to sell*". (Rev. 13:16-17)

Previously, the Antichrist had support from some, perhaps even many, political factions in his own campaigns and the rise of the ten rulers who would ultimately consolidate under him, but now ***everyone*** must absolutely submit spiritually. Likewise and until this point, the harlot's various religious factions were operating in the character of the Roman Pantheon, where all religious practices could be continued "as is" as long as the emperor was acknowledged above them all. With the advent of the Abomination of Desolation and meteoric rise of the False Prophet, there is no longer any accommodation for other gods or practices, but the demand to be directly and exclusively worshiped.

> 37 *"He will show no regard for the gods of his fathers or for the desire of women, nor will he show regard for any other god; for he will magnify himself above them all.*
> — Daniel 11:37

This is why Jesus specified that with the Abomination of Desolation, "***then*** *there will be a* ***great*** *tribulation, such as has not occurred since the beginning of the world until now, nor ever will be.*" (Mt. 24:21) The satanic agenda is now completely out in the open—***everyone*** must worship the beast; ***no one*** is allowed to any longer maintain their past political or religious associations. ***Everyone*** must give themselves over entirely to Satan through the worship of the beast. There has never been a darker period in the whole of history, one where every single human, regardless of ethnicity, politics or religious persuasion is automatically under a death sentence should they refuse to engage in worship of the beast.

> 22 *"Unless those days had been cut short,* ***no life would have been saved****; but for the sake of the elect those days will be cut short.*
> — Matthew 24:22

And yet for those left behind, the impossibly severe will continue to an even impossibly further extreme when Babylon the Great is brought down in an appointed destruction by "*the son of destruction*" which will ultimately lead to their combined destruction at the end of his "*forty-two months*". His leading all to turn on and destroy the harlot is the prelude to leading them all to their ultimate destruction upon the return of the Messiah. Even the Antichrist and False Prophet themselves will suffer the consequences. (Rev. 19:11-21)

While it is true that faithful Christians are to know and therefore reject following the Antichrist, and they are to know and reject the enticements of the False Prophet to engage in false worship of Satan through the first beast, they are equally required to recognize the primary institutions which will propel him to power in the parallel realms of both the political and religious. We have been informed in advance not just to anticipate the appearance of a counterfeit Messiah with an accompanying counterfeit John the Baptist, but the rise of a counterfeit kingdom as well, all of which is supported by the rise of the harlot of ultimate spiritual seduction.

There is an overlapping sequence bringing these four together, but not necessarily all at the very same time, and each having specified roles and goals.

> [25]*'He will speak out against the Most High and wear down the saints of the Highest One...*
>
> — Daniel 7:25a

> [9]*"Then **<u>they will deliver you</u>** to tribulation, and will kill you, and you will be hated by all nations because of My name. [10]At that time many will fall away and will betray one another and hate one another. [11]Many false prophets will arise and will mislead many. [12]Because lawlessness is increased, most people's love will grow cold. [13]But the one who endures to the end, he will be saved. [14]This gospel of the kingdom shall be preached in the whole world as a testimony to all the nations, **<u>and then the end will come</u>**.*
>
> — Matthew 24:9-14

For believers, the most imposing obstacles of apostasy, deception and persecution will have to be endured even before the onset of the whole world's "*great tribulation*". The Church will finally complete its commission to "*be My witnesses...to the remotest part of the earth*", (Acts 1:8) although the text provides no guarantee of the degree of responsiveness this final surge of worldwide testimony will experience. Christ provides the dual caveat and promise, "*But the one who endures to the end, he will be saved*".

> [9]*Then another angel, a third one, followed them, saying with a loud voice, "If anyone worships the beast and his image, and receives a mark on his forehead or on his hand, [10]he also will drink of the wine of the wrath of God, which is mixed in full strength in the cup of His anger; and he will be tormented with fire and brimstone in the presence of the holy angels and in the presence of the Lamb. [11]And the smoke of their torment goes up forever and ever; they have no rest day and night, those who worship the beast and his image, and whoever receives the mark of his name." [12]**<u>Here is the perseverance of the saints who keep the commandments of God and their faith in Jesus.</u>** [13]And I heard a voice from heaven, saying, "Write, 'Blessed are the dead who die in the Lord from now on!'" "Yes," says the Spirit, "so that they may rest from their labors, for their deeds follow with them."*
>
> — Revelation 14:9-13

When Revelation revisits the sequence leading up to the Church's removal, there is first a call to endure this time of transition when the Antichrist and False Prophet force everyone to make a spiritual commitment. This time of extreme spiritual testing and persecution, marked by the possible consequences of martyrdom for many, is stipulated ***before*** the text continues with the follow-on milestone of the harvest of the faithful:

> *[14]Then I looked, and behold, a white cloud, and sitting on the cloud was one like a son of man, having a golden crown on His head and a sharp sickle in His hand. [15]And another angel came out of the temple, crying out with a loud voice to Him who sat on the cloud, "Put in your sickle and reap, for the hour to reap has come, because the harvest of the earth is ripe." [16]Then He who sat on the cloud swung His sickle over the earth, and the earth was reaped.*
>
> — Revelation 14:14-16

Just as the visions in Daniel 2 and 7 are the same thing but from an earthly vs. a heavenly perspective, so the same occurs with this event in the New Testament. This is the heavenly perspective of the *Harpazo* of the Church showing the viewpoint of Christ in the cloud looking down. The same event is depicted in reverse in the Olivet Discourse from the earthly point of view where those on earth looking up see Him in the clouds:

> *[30]"And then the sign of the Son of Man will appear in the sky, and then all the tribes of the earth will mourn, and they will see the* SON OF MAN COMING ON THE CLOUDS OF THE SKY *with power and great glory. [31]And He will send forth His angels with* A GREAT TRUMPET *and* THEY WILL GATHER TOGETHER *His elect from the four winds, from one end of the sky to the other.*
>
> — Matthew 24:30-31

The point is that both the Olivet Discourse and Revelation affirm that while the Church will not endure the concluding phase of the 70th Week when nothing is left except the wrath of God's judgment, we will nonetheless enter into that final week of years to experience the common judgments to be endured by the whole world which characterize the first part. ***Everyone*** will deal with the Antichrist, False Prophet, and the institutions propelling them in a test of faith to see who "*worships the beast and his image, and receives a mark on his forehead or on his hand*" (Rev. 14:9) as a prelude to whether they will be part of the first harvest taken unto Christ, or remain for the second harvest:

> *[17]And another angel came out of the temple which is in heaven, and he also had a sharp sickle. [18]Then another angel, the one who has power over fire, came out from the altar; and he called with a loud voice to him who had the sharp sickle, saying, "Put in your sharp sickle and gather the clusters from the vine of the earth, because her grapes are ripe." [19]So the angel swung his sickle to the earth and gathered the clusters from the vine of the earth, and threw them into the great wine press of the wrath of God. [20]And the wine press was trodden outside the city, and blood came out from the wine press, up to the horses' bridles, for a distance of two hundred miles.*
>
> — Revelation 14:17-20

Finally, it would appear that there are incompatible dogmatic assertions about particular aspects of these things. There are those who insist the anti-king must be Jewish, others holding he is exclusively Gentile, and even a relatively recent rise in assertions he is specifically Islamic. Likewise, are seemingly contradictory positions on the anti-kingdom being a recapitulation of the Roman Empire while others are looking for a literal rebirth of Babylon. It just may be that not all of these and other such passionate positions are entirely wrong, but each attaining at least to a partial truth when it comes to the ultimate answer.

The problem seems to be that the Western mind sees nearly everything in an either/or, black-or-white context where "it" has to be "this" and therefore excludes "that". What is actually needed, which the Middle Eastern cultures to whom the Bible was originally written are much more amenable, is to hold things in equal tension with each other rather than allow them to cancel each other out. This is necessary because while the traits of past figures and kingdoms will certainly be present in the final iterations, those last in the series will be as different and unique from all the rest precisely ***because*** they are such a complicated amalgamation of all their precursors. But to be sure, there are certain models which Scripture is telling us to place closer to, if not completely at, the top of the list as the primary influence.

The Antichrist is both Gentile—the beast from the sea, and Jewish—the beast from the land, but that does not preclude them from possessing parallel religious or political backgrounds in the character of Herod. In fact, the primary scriptural type for the first beast is Antiochus Epiphanes IV, who to a point fulfilled all that was predicted for "*the king of the North*", but then left a large body of those prophecies for the final "*king of the North*" to come. As the ruler of the Seleucid Empire from what is today dominated by various factions of Islam, that the first beast could also have an Islamic background is not out of the question. But like Herod who was accepted and seamlessly moved back and forth between Edom, Israel and Rome, so will these figures be able to be all things to all men regardless of their ethnicity.

The anti-kingdom is the part of the greater picture which recapitulates Rome. Being a beast which is equally antichrist and satanic, it will share character traits from the many other scriptural and historical types, but as illustrated in the very first vision in Daniel 2, its primary model is the Roman approach to domination through negotiation first, warfare if necessary. Its inherent institution of the Pantheon, where it easily accommodates any and every god and religion makes it an ideal steed on whose back the harlot woman of Satan will be able to leverage her own parallel rise to power.

Likewise the woman who is actually called "*Babylon the great*" is chiefly operating in the character of Babylon, the source all the world's false religions. While the others will share some of the same traits of Babylon's rulers and structure, it is the false religious system which most emulates Babylon on whom the beast will eventually turn. Satan's instigation of all the counterfeit alternatives was never intended to be rewarded for their loyalty or to be built into a united body in the manner of the Body of Christ. Satan ultimately divorces his woman. He wants what was originally intended for Israel, who was to have no earthly king but all serve and worship the Heavenly King directly. Whereas Yahweh has the twelve tribes, Satan has the ten kingdoms.

Ultimately these things are a recapitulation of the Tower of Babel where everyone is brought together, both politically and spiritually, under a single banner of rebellion against God. This time, however, the rebellion is not merely spiritual, but absolutely literal.

The real wild card in the deck is the False Prophet, whose sole function on several fronts is to foster worship of Satan through the first beast. His appearance signals the transition from what was disguised as a political revolution to its true agenda as the ultimate spiritual paradigm shift. Everyone, no matter their religious belief or political affiliation, is exempt from a death sentence for failing to worship the a beast, his image, and to take his mark. With his appearance, the harlot's days are numbered because the first beast will no longer tolerate receiving worship by proxy through her.

All of this combines to show that many are right for the aspect they are passionately espousing, but ultimately wrong for allowing it to dominate the discussion and even diminish or completely negate other equally important aspects of these personalities and institutions. They ***are*** Rome ***and*** Babylon, Gentile ***and*** Jew, Herod ***and*** Epiphanes. And, of course, much more. They are all things to all people, and particularly where the Church is concerned, they are Judas, because, "*They went out from us, but they were not really of us*". (1 Jn. 2:19) The deep complications of all these past influences coming together in these final fulfillments is why the wisdom of Christ is required to successfully navigate everything which is intended to be revealed in advance, and those things which we need to recognize when they occur.

The Last Days Christian is provided a lot of information in advance because so much is at stake.

> [20]*He who testifies to these things says, "Yes, I am coming quickly." Amen. Come, Lord Jesus.*
>
> — Revelation 22:20

Appendix A: When Change Is Expressly Forbidden

The following commentary was originally published on the Walk with the Word site in 2013. This is a much more detailed explanation of the serious issue ultimately involving 2 Thessalonians 2:1-12.

> *"**You shall not add to the word** which I am commanding you, **nor take away from it**, that you may keep the commandments of the LORD your God which I command you. (Deuteronomy 4:20)*
>
> *"Whatever I command you, you shall be careful to do; **you shall not add to nor take away from it**. (Deuteronomy 12:32)*
>
> ***Do not add to His words***
> *Or He will reprove you, and you will be proved a liar. (Proverbs 30:6)*
>
> *Now these things, brethren, I have figuratively applied to myself and Apollos for your sakes, so that in us you may learn **not to exceed what is written**, so that no one of you will become arrogant in behalf of one against the other. (1 Corinthians 4:6)*
>
> *I testify to everyone who hears the words of the prophecy of this book: **if anyone adds to them, God will add to him the plagues which are written in this book; and if anyone takes away from the words of the book of this prophecy, God will take away his part from the tree of life and from the holy city**, which are written in this book. (Revelation 22:18-19)*

There are those who try to tell us that the warning at the end of the Book of Revelation applies exclusively to revisions attempted to only that book of the Bible and not the rest, but as with all things biblical, our understanding of any principle of the Lord comes from the whole of Scripture and not by lifting out and highlighting just a single reference. Moses, Solomon and Paul, at various points of history, provide the foundation for what is finalized in the last verses of the Bible on behalf of the whole of Scripture, that God's entire Word is closed canon and provides no option for human editing, be it in any form of redaction or embellishment. And yet something has taken place within the walls of the Church since the turn of the new millennium for which I can find no previous historic parallel in the name of Evangelicism: openly changing God's Word in spite of the express mandate otherwise.

›me of the most popular leaders within Christianity have altered God's Word in ways that no Christian cult, no rival religion, nor any enemy of the cross I know of has dared to do. If such distortions of God's Word had been engaged in by the usual suspects working against the true Church, I would characterize it as some kind of desperate attempt to fabricate their lie to give it an outward appearance of authority. But how does one explain this coming about at the hands and from the mouths of those whom most of the present-day Church's membership recognize as their own?

Most of us get why the Mormons had to write an additional book, or the Jehovah's Witnesses create their own translation, or Islam provides the Quran and Hindus the Bhagavad Gita; cults and false religions ultimately substitute something else in place of Scripture in order to say something that is ultimately contrary to the closed, authoritative Word of God. But when those recognized as members of mainstream Christianity corrupt and misrepresent the very Word of God itself? It disturbs me so deeply I am struggling to find the words to fully express how profoundly I am shaken, so this is much longer than the usual commentary. But I am equally convinced these prominent individuals, accepted inside the mainstream Church, are doing it for the same reason, to inject something into Christianity which God's Word in its uncorrupted presentation does not actually justify.

A Cut-and-Paste Hermeneutic

The first time this was brought to my attention was several years ago in Rick Warren's teaching concerning what he sees as a distraction to Christians by biblical prophecy specifically, and the End Times in general. In *The Purpose Driven Life*, Warren did something which I had never even heard of anyone doing before, but is outrageous just by the fact that he so boldly tries to get this past us as if no one would notice:

> Today there's a growing interest in the second coming of Christ and the end of the world. When will it happen? Just before Jesus ascended to heaven the disciples asked him the same question, and his response was quite revealing.
>
> He said, "It is not for you to know the times or dates the Father has set by his own authority. But you will receive power when the Holy Spirit comes on you; and you will be my witnesses in Jerusalem, and in all Judea and Samaria, and to the ends of the earth."
>
> When the disciples wanted to talk about prophecy, Jesus quickly switched the conversation to evangelism. He wanted them to concentrate on their mission to the world. He said in essence, "The details of my return are none of your business. What is your business is the mission I have given you. Focus on that!" (The Purpose Driven Life, pages 285-286)

Warren uses the question asked of Jesus by the Apostles in Matthew 24:3 and employs his word processor to cut-and-paste it together with the answer He gave to a completely different question posed in Acts 1:6-7! The net result of this "cut-and-paste" hermeneutic is to nullify Christ's instructions for Believers to pay close attention to the prophetic signs of the Last Days. Warren switches things around to misrepresent Scripture in the most egregious manner possible, representing the exact opposite of what Christ teaches about His return.

At the beginning of the Olivet Discourse, the Apostles ask Jesus to tell them what will be the sign of His second coming:

> *As He was sitting on the Mount of Olives, the disciples came to Him privately, saying, "Tell us, when will these things happen, and what will be the sign of Your coming, and of the end of the age?" And Jesus answered and said to them, "See to it that no one misleads you. (Matthew 24:3-4)*

Notice that Jesus not only answers their question, but goes into such length and detail that it takes Matthew two whole chapters to record it all. (Mt. 24-25) In this End Times discourse, Jesus warns at least four times that anyone ***NOT*** looking for these things is a high-risk candidate for being deceived. (Mt. 24:4, 11, 24-25, 42-51)

But this is not to be confused with a second and completely different question posed by the Apostles just prior to His Ascension into heaven in Acts 1:

> *So when they had come together, they were asking Him, saying, "Lord, is it at this time You are restoring the kingdom to Israel?" He said to them, "It is not for you to know times or epochs which the Father has fixed by His own authority; (Acts 1:6-7)*

This is a very "Hebraic" question posed by His Jewish Apostles, who are not asking, "*What will be the sign of Your coming, and of the end of the age?*" as they asked in Matthew 24:3, but inquiring if this is the time when He would establish the Millennial Kingdom as they knew the Messiah must do in order to fulfill all the prophecies about the Messiah in the whole of God's Word which specifically pertain "*to Israel*". This is not like the previous question about Christ's second coming, but a completely new and different question about when He would fulfill the messianic prophecies concerning Israel and His Millennial Kingdom. Jesus does not say here that their question is incorrect, but that it is not the subject of their focus for their present work assignment in this current age. They must first carry out the work of the Suffering Servant who came to die for sin for that work to qualify entrance into the Millennial Kingdom to be ushered in at His second coming.

Rick Warren takes the question posed in Matthew 24:3 about Christ's return, cuts it out, and presumptuously pastes it to Jesus' reply, belonging to an entirely different question in Acts 1:7, and presents us with something which Jesus never actually said. In fact, this translocation of two bits of Scripture into something of Warren's own creation actually contradicts what Jesus taught about His return:

> When the disciples wanted to talk about prophecy, Jesus quickly switched the conversation to evangelism. He wanted them to concentrate on their mission in the world. He said in essence, "The details of my return are none of your business. What is your business is the mission I have given you. Focus on that!" (The Purpose Driven Life, page 285)

Taken to Warren's logical conclusion, I suppose the right thing to do would be to publish Bibles without any of the prophetic passages, which are apparently none of our business. Do you have any idea how much of the Bible Warren is telling us to ignore? Shall we publish Bibles without the Olivet Discourse in Matthew 24-25, Mark 13 and Luke 21? Jesus told us not just to simply be aware of these things, but cautioned against our being deceived by not paying attention to them! Who are you going to listen to, Warren or Christ?

I submit that this is one of the many definitive proofs that what Rick Warren has to offer is patently false, because like any other false religion or cult, he has to introduce something to replace God's Word in order to justify his false teachings. A prominent Utah-based group attempts with *The Book of Mormon* to replace the authority of God's Word in the same manner as Warren with his *Purpose Driven* books in all their variations.

Ever since this was first brought to my attention, I have held this to be the most egregious abuse of Scripture I have ever witnessed or even heard of. I am not aware of anyone else who simply spliced together different snippets of Scripture to not only fabricate a biblical justification for their own teaching, but in so doing to actually nullify a direct instruction from Christ Himself. Usually a false teacher simply lifts part of a Scripture out in isolation from the rest of the text in an attempt to trick us into believing God's Word says something it in fact does not. As stated before, however, not even a Mormon or Jehovah's Witness or Muslim has dared employing Warren's "cut-and-paste hermeneutic" which can be so easily exposed for its dishonesty, because at least they would be embarrassed to have their academic integrity exposed and ridiculed. But I recently discovered yet another prominent figure doing this exact, same thing and, in reality, far worse.

When It Becomes a Double Switch-A-Roo

Tim LaHaye, most noted for *The Left Behind* fictional series on the Rapture and the End Times, is an editor and contributor for *The Popular Handbook on the Rapture*. In chapter 10, "The Wrath to Come is Not for Believers", he replicates Warren's cut-and-paste technique in almost the same way by likewise quoting the first part of one question but pasting in the answer from an entirely different, second question.

In 1 Thessalonians 4 the question posed to Paul by that church was what happens to those who die in Christ before the Rapture takes place:

> *But we do not want you to be uninformed, brethren, about those who are asleep, so that you will not grieve as do the rest who have no hope. For if we believe that Jesus died and rose again, even so God will bring with Him those who have fallen asleep in Jesus. (1 Thessalonians 4:13-14)*

Later in 2 Thessalonians 3, an entirely different issue at a much later date is addressed by Paul in an entirely different letter when outside agitators were coming into the church and preaching that the day of the Lord had already come:

> *Now we request you, brethren, with regard to the coming of our Lord Jesus Christ and our gathering together to Him, that you not be quickly shaken from your composure or be disturbed either by a spirit or a message or a letter as if from us, to the effect that the day of the Lord has come. Let no one in any way deceive you, for it will not come unless the apostasy comes first, and the man of lawlessness is revealed, the son of destruction, who opposes and exalts himself above every so-called god or object of worship, so that he takes his seat in the temple of God, displaying himself as being God. (2 Thessalonians 2:1-4)*

But LaHaye states on page 133 of the book:

> "During the first century, believers living in the city of Thessalonica were concerned that they may have missed the rapture and were about to enter the Tribulation."

And then follows up with Paul's answer to their real question of what happens to Believers who pass away in the Lord:

For this we say to you by the word of the Lord, that we who are alive and remain until the coming of the Lord, will not precede those who have fallen asleep. For the Lord Himself will descend from heaven with a shout, with the voice of the archangel and with the trumpet of God, and the dead in Christ will rise first. Then we who are alive and remain will be caught up together with them in the clouds to meet the Lord in the air, and so we shall always be with the Lord. Therefore comfort one another with these words.

— 1 Thessalonians 4:15-18

This was Paul's answer to their question in the preceding two verses about those who have "*fallen asleep in Jesus*". LaHaye not only pastes an answer from a different question in place of the original, but notice how he even takes it a step further than Warren by performing a ***double*** switch-a-roo by altering the question itself!

In 2 Thessalonians they did not express to Paul a fear that they "were about to enter the ***Tribulation***"—a very specific term LaHaye capitalizes to unmistakably mean that final seven year period leading into the Millennial Reign of Christ—their question was about the arrival of "*the day of the Lord*". Even if we buy into the assumption that these two things represent the same, exact thing, Scripture never uses them interchangeably. There is Scripture devoted to "*the day of the Lord*" and Scripture assigned to the "Tribulation", so let's at least demonstrate the academic honesty to use the term the actual passage of Scripture is using. (More on why LaHaye is purposely doing this in a moment—it's not an accident.) But LaHaye does not stop at duplicating Warren's cut-and-paste behavior and takes it to a whole new level.

Promoting a Single Eschatology

I often qualify my belief in the "inerrant Word of God" with the caveat, "in the original languages". Translators can make mistakes, the discovery of additional ancient documents can refine our understanding of words in those original languages, so our trust is not solely limited to the English renderings but in the infallibility of the original manuscripts in the original languages. After all, just compare the English of the 1611 King James Version to the English of the 1995 New American Standard Bible. The underlying manuscripts in the original Greek, Hebrew and Aramaic did not change, but four centuries of English history, culture and geopolitical influences have certainly and dramatically altered the English language. (Try explaining in today's English what, "Suffer the little children to come unto Me" from the KJV means.) But we have the assurance that regardless of any language into which the Holy Scriptures are translated, and no matter how much change a given culture undergoes, the original manuscripts written in their originally given languages are an absolute that transcends man's transitory nature and the way his vocabulary tends to reinvent itself over time.

But what happens when someone alters ***NOT*** the English translation, but the original? Rick Warren effected a cut-and-paste of the English—how would you feel about someone reaching in to cut-and-paste the original Greek words? A renowned, self-proclaimed Evangelical leader playing games with the English translation is egregious in itself beyond words, so I am not sure how to articulate the actions of an equally famous and important Christian figure reaching down to manipulate Scripture by cut-and-pasting one Greek word over another in the original, inerrant text so he can get his own message across.

The general editors for *The Popular Handbook on the Rapture* are listed as Tim LaHaye, Thomas Ice and Ed Hindson. Fourteen well-known, mostly multi-degreed and prominent scholars and leaders of present-day Christianity contributed the contents of the book's twenty-one chapters. While the title might lead one to believe the reader is going to be provided an academic treatment of all the particulars characterizing each of the various main eschatologies and their differing viewpoints on the Rapture, the truth is that this is not a "handbook" in the sense of documenting everything pertaining to the Rapture, but an extremely one-sided presentation of just the Pre-Tribulational view alone. Given that LaHaye and Ice co-founded the "Pre-Trib Research Center", a group of academics who annually meet to exclusively promote Pre-Tribulationism, and the fact that the contributors to this book are all members of or closely aligned with that organization, it should not surprise anyone that this book, in spite of its title, is really only devoted to espousing one eschatology. Granted, this may be an example of poor scholarship, but it is certainly neither a sin nor what is at the heart of the matter in question.

Just in case someone does not actually know this, one of the bedrock platforms of Pre-Tribulationism is that the Rapture of the Church will take place at some point before the final seven year period of history known as the "Tribulation" begins. It is their fervent belief that the Church will not enter into nor experience any part of what takes place in Revelation 6-18 covering God's judgments expressed as seven seals, seven trumpets and seven bowls.

Various classic arguments have been raised in support of this from within the circles of Pre-Tribulationism, the first being the assumption that this final seven year Tribulational period, and something prolifically spoken of throughout Scripture called "*the day of the Lord*", are the exact same thing. This actually is an important, key issue which must be scripturally discerned because "*the day of the Lord*" is not a literal twenty-four hour period, but describing a period when the full wrath of God's final judgment is poured out on the earth in a prelude to Final Judgment. Since Scripture repeatedly and specifically states that Believers will never suffer God's wrath, which is repeatedly associated with "*the day of the Lord*" in Scripture, most everyone agrees that the greater theological purpose of the Rapture is to remove the Church in fulfillment of God's promise we will not experience His wrath. Even Pre-Tribulationism so stipulates this doctrinal qualification for the Rapture.

It's this specific point, however, that because non-Pre-Tribulationists disagree as to what constitutes "*the day of the Lord*", for why we have major differences of opinion as to when the Rapture will actually take place. For Pre-Tribulationists, "*the day of the Lord*" and the seven year Tribulation are the exact, same thing, so this is one of the foundational reasons why they believe the Rapture must take place at some point prior to the opening of the first seal in Revelation 6. (This sheds some light on the previous discussion of the importance of noting when Tim LaHaye deftly substitutes "Tribulation" when the text explicitly states "*the day of the Lord*". He assumes they're one and the same thing and wants us to accept that as well.)

There are also a couple of additional supporting reasons proposed by most Pre-Tribulationists, such as the Church being mentioned so prominently in the first three chapters of Revelation and the word for "church" seeming to disappear with John's being taken into heaven in Revelation 4:1, the presence of twenty-four elders in heaven in Revelation 5, twelve of whom they believe to represent the Church already in heaven with Christ, and the way that in the Last Days God returns to working through Israel to fulfill all the as-yet-unfulfilled prophecies and promises exclusively pertaining to them.

There are an untold number of books, websites and papers devoted to decades of debate over these points in particular and many related ancillary issues. Personally, for most of my Christian life I have managed to live with these issues and tried to not allow what I characterized as "differences of opinion" to be a source of division. No one will ever convince me, even now, that what one believes about the Rapture gets them sent to heaven or hell; it is simply not foundational to one's salvation. And I will state what I will expressly elaborate upon again later on, that the primary issue here is ***NOT*** the timing of the Rapture, but the right handling of the Word of God!

The Sequence Becomes the Issue

But regardless of the weight of each of these particular aspects of End Times prophecy, what is perhaps the most potent point of scriptural tension when Pre-Tribulationism comes under attack by its opponents is what Paul has to say in 2 Thessalonians:

> *Now we request you, brethren, with regard to the coming of our Lord Jesus Christ and our gathering together to Him, that you not be quickly shaken from your composure or be disturbed either by a spirit or a message or a letter as if from us, to the effect that the day of the Lord has come. Let no one in any way deceive you, for it will not come unless the apostasy comes first, and the man of lawlessness is revealed, the son of destruction,*
>
> — 2 Thessalonians 2:1-3

Apparently some false teachers visited Thessalonica in Paul's day who asserted "that the day of the Lord has come", and because of Paul's previous teaching, the Thessalonians knew there was a specific sequence preceding that event. Taken on its face as the text here provides, Paul warned against the deception that "the day of the Lord has come" outside of the proper sequence "*unless the apostasy comes first*", after which "*the man of lawlessness* [the Antichrist] *is revealed*", and only afterward could "*the day of the Lord*" be experienced. Why is this such a huge scriptural point highlighted by the opponents to Pre-Tribulationism?

Go back to what we discussed as to their belief that "*the day of the Lord*" and "***The*** Tribulation" are the same thing and that the Church, in their view, has to be extracted before this all takes place. The problem is that a great spiritual falling away—"*apostasy*", and the visible arrival and working of the Antichrist, are things spoken of inside that part of the Book of Revelation when Pre-Tribulationists say the Church will already be removed. Taken at face value, Paul's sequence of events directly conflicts with the assertions of Pre-Tribulationism which states we will not be here to witness the arrival of the Antichrist or to experience the full effects of the apostasy preceding him. They are presented with the problem of how to justify their own sequence of events because they agree that the Antichrist will not be revealed until within the seven year Tribulation, but which they assert will be missed in its entirety by the Church, and the apparent contradiction of Paul's teaching that the Church will still be here to witness the arrival of the Antichrist just prior to the onset of "*the day of the Lord*" from which all agree the Church will be exempted.

The "problem" for Pre-Tribulationism is in the original Greek text, the word "*apostasia*" which the NASB here translates as "*apostasy*". Even more pointed, the original text states it as "***ho*** *apostasia*", which is why it is rendered as "***the*** *apostasy*". It is not just a general apostasy that could refer to people who fall away spiritually at any and every period of history, but "***the*** *apostasy*" to specify a particular and unique time of spiritual falling away like no other which Scripture teaches will characterize the Last Days.

So to justify the Pre-Tribulationists' proposed sequence of events, they must reconcile why Paul teaches something plainly contradicting it. How do they do that? Well, in Tim LaHaye's and company's case, he first effects his double switch-a-roo with the English translation as previously discussed, but then takes it further to cut-and-paste the original text! But as a prelude to what he is about to do with the Greek, LaHaye performs a another switch-a-roo with the English which only Rick Warren could appreciate.

A Switch-A-Roo within a Switch-A-Roo

In *The Popular Handbook on the Rapture*, Tim LaHaye personally authors chapter 13, "'Departing' Rather than 'Falling Away' in 2 Thessalonians 2:3". The title nicely summarizes what is going to be presented, and the following quote come from that chapter.

> Consider how the difference in the translation of a single Greek word can affect a person's conclusion about the timing of the rapture.

The Pretrib Rapture	**The Mid- or Post-trib Rapture**
Let no one deceive you by any means; for that Day will not come unless the ***departing*** comes first, and the man of sin is revealed, the son of perdition (2 Thessalonians 2:3)	Let no one deceive you by any means; for that Day will not come unless the ***falling away*** comes first, and the man of sin is revealed, the son of perdition (2 Thessalonians 2:3)

The quotation of 2 Thessalonians 2:3 on the right-hand side is exactly as it appears in the New King James Version. What a difference the translation of a single word makes? Yes, that may be true, but let's understand from the outset that it is Tim LaHaye who superimposes "departing" in the left column over the NKJV's translators' provision of "*falling away*" for the underlying Greek word "*apostasia*". In this chapter of the book devoted to this one and only issue, which is one of the longest chapters in the whole book, LaHaye tries to make the case that "*ho apostasia*" is not actually referring to "*the falling away*" from the faith spiritually, but is instead referring to the literal "departing" of those remaining faithful—the Rapture of the Church! His very detailed and circuitous arguments are designed to get us to believe that this word means something decidedly opposite of its plain, basic meaning, and he begins by superimposing his own translation over that provided by the NKJV.

In fact, we cannot find an English Bible translation beginning with the KJV published more than 400 years ago up to this present day, when so many are available as never before, which translates "*apostasia*" in this verse as "departing". More than four centuries of English translations, lexicons and Bible dictionaries offer a range of definitions which all seem to conform to some variation of the unfaithful "*falling away*" spiritually, but the faithful "departing" in the Rapture is nowhere to be found in any of them. In the twenty-three English translations in my Bible software package I found five which translated "*apostasia*" as "*the apostasy*", six as "*the falling away*", (the Amplified uses both), ten which offer "*the rebellion*" and one each choosing "the turning away from God" and "*until people rise up against God*". LaHaye even admits there are no Bible translations from the 1611 KJV onward which employ "departing" in this verse, but that does not inhibit him from doing so himself. Yes, a single word can make a difference, Mr. LaHaye, especially when you are the making the substitution!

Just in case, I checked with the seemingly myriad of Bible dictionaries, concordances and lexicons within my software (and the old fashioned printed books still gracing my bookshelves) which provide English definitions of each respective Greek word. I thought that perhaps there were Greek-to-English resources which might agree with LaHaye's assertion. The range of what I found never even came close to describing the Rapture of the faithful, but provided a breadth of renderings all conforming to a description of the unfaithful falling away from the faith: "rebellion", "abandonment", "breach of faith", "apostasy", "revolt", "desertion" and "defection". Just as none of the English Bibles in use for the past 400 years provide a hint of justifying LaHaye's one word difference, neither do any of the supporting Greek-to-English resources.

LaHaye even provides the caveat that normally the Greek word "*apostasia*" refers to a spiritual falling away, but then offers that this is the one exception.

> We who believe the rapture will take place before the Tribulation readily admit there are at least three Bible passages that predict there will be a global apostasy on the earth when Jesus raptures the church. But this is not one of them! (Page 158) [His emphasis.]

Of course, even in the English language, the context of "the departing" could mean exactly the same thing as "*the falling away*" if they are construed to be both referring to a spiritual "departing", but that is not LaHaye's position in the least. He insists that instead of referring to a spiritual "*falling away*", it actually refers to the Rapture—"to mean 'departing' (as in the physical departing) rather than 'falling away' or 'rebellion'". (Page 159) Whereas he agrees that "*apostasia*" refers to a spiritual falling away of the unfaithful everywhere else it appears in Scripture, in this one instance alone he proposes it suddenly means "the Rapture of the faithful". Instead of the unfaithful "departing" from the faith, it is assigned an entirely opposite meaning of the faithful "departing" this planet! Just like Warren, LaHaye turns Scripture inside out, claiming a meaning that is the exact opposite of what it plainly teaches!

Historical Proof-Texting

If we cannot find an English Bible affirming LaHaye's substitution, nor any Greek lexicon or dictionary agreeing with that rendering, then how could he possibly justify this assertion? According to him, it can only be explained if we go back to English translations created before the 1611 Kings James Version.

Yes, there were seven major English versions pre-dating the KJV: the Wycliffe Bible (1384), Tyndale Bible (1526), Coverdale Bible (1535), Cranmer Bible (1539), Breeches Bible (1576), Beza Bible (1583) and Geneva Bible (1608). These oldest of the English translations rendered "*ho apostasia*" as "the departing".

Of course, this begs the question, when these pre-KJV translations used "departing", did they do so because they knew the true meaning of "*apostasia*" was the faithful Church "departing" from the earth in the Rapture as LaHaye represents? Or were they simply using it in the then-present day English vernacular to mean the unfaithful spiritually "departing" from the faith? In other words, even if someone chose "departing", did they do so in order to describe the Rapture, or were they still actually describing "*falling away*" spiritually?

Just as Rick Warren so brazenly and publicly proclaimed a cut-and-paste misrepresentation which he seems to have thought no one would check on, so it might appear LaHaye has likewise done in desperately reaching back to pre-KJV English translations. This is a variant of bad exegesis I call "historical proof-texting" where one searches for an obscure exception from antiquity and then insists it must be substituted in place of everything else published since. But the fact is that not all of the ancient sources LaHaye quotes actually support his argument!

First of all, the Wycliffe Bible which he quotes does not say "the departing" but "*the dissension*"! In fact, it adds a note to help explain what "*the dissension*" means by adding the qualifier, "departing away"! I guess "departing" is technically in the mix, but certainly cannot possibly allude to the Rapture of the faithful—it agrees with all the modern translations.

Likewise the *Tyndale Concise Bible Commentary* in relation to LaHaye's naming of the Tyndale Bible explains that although the term may literally be translated "departure", they concede it "may refer to a departure of doctrine". Not exactly a ringing endorsement for LaHaye's assertion, is it?

The Geneva Bible literally translates it as, "*except there come a departing first*", which it then goes on to state, "Note 1: A wonderful departing of the most part from the faith" and "Note 2: He sheweth them that the day of the Lord shal not come, til the departing from the faith come first". (Pardon the original English spelling, but this is the exact quote.) This is the third resource LaHaye himself cites which not only does not support his assertion, but actually contradicts it!

But that was the Geneva Bible as published in 1560. When it was edited, revised and published in its 1599 form, still 12 years before the KJV (which LaHaye and company blame as the source for the mistranslation of "*apostasia*" by every English Bible going forward), the Geneva Bible translators ***DROPPED*** "departing" and published the updated version with "*falling away*"!

> *Let no man deceive you by any means: 3 for [that day shall not come], except there come a falling away first, and that man of sin be revealed, the son of perdition; (2 Th. 2:3) - 1599 Geneva Study Bible*

I am no Bible savant or gifted researcher with powers beyond the ordinary. I did not go to obscure, alternative resources unavailable to the average seeker or spend months earnestly scratching and clawing to discover these facts. I uncovered all of this in the course of a very basic, cursory search of the references which Tim LaHaye himself cites! Did he bother to determine what these translators meant when they selected "departing", or was he so fixated on assigning his own meaning to the verse that he never bothered to check? Can someone be so arrogant and prideful that they cite sources knowing they not only do not support their assertion but actually contradict it? Or are they so deceived themselves that they never bother doing the most fundamental research required of a first-year college student and assume no one else will either? (Both are equally disturbing.)

Not Just the English, But the Greek

If you've stuck with me this long, I cannot sufficiently express my appreciation, but this does not end here—in fact, it gets worse, because only a small part of LaHaye's chapter tries to justify this double switch-a-roo with the English definition; the majority of space is devoted to the even more egregious action of replacing "*apostasia*" with a substitute Greek word. He not only does a cut-and-paste with the English, but extends it to the original Greek text itself.

Of course, I have avoided the whole issue, which would involve an equally lengthy discussion to this already long dissertation, that the Greek word from which "rapture" is derived is actually "*harpazo*" (Strong's #726), which literally means a violent snatching away. In the Septuagint it is used to describe ripping a wing from a bird or a leg from an animal at the dinner table or by a hunter, a fairly vivid picture of what it means to be "violently snatched away". "Rapture" has been commonly used because Jerome, in the Latin Vulgate, translated the Greek "*harpazo*" into the Latin "*rapturo*" which we then Anglicized into "rapture". But the underlying Greek word is actually "*harpazo*" when speaking of the Rapture, nothing even remotely resembling "*apostasia*". Most of LaHaye's argument after misrepresenting the English, however, involves misrepresenting the Greek.

In a very detailed explanation on pages 160-169, LaHaye is in agreement with the other scholars he cites that "*apostasia*" must be replaced in this instance with its root, "*aphistemi*" (Strong's #868), a word that is indeed sometimes used in Scripture to describe a physical departing, such as in Acts 12:10.

> *When they had passed the first and second guard, they came to the iron gate that leads into the city, which opened for them by itself; and they went out and went along one street, and immediately the angel* ***departed*** *from him. (Acts 12:10)*

Yes, the Greek word "*aphistemi*" is often literally translated to mean someone "departing"—physically leaving a place, but we aren't allowed to just switch Greek words in the original text to suit us! We don't decide on our own to replace "*apostasia*" with "*aphistemi*" any more than we would arbitrarily switch them the other way around. LaHaye and the very same Bible scholars who are so closely aligned with him, as a core aspect of their teaching, often walk us through even the most subtle variations of a Greek word's usage, placing an importance on even a modest change in case, possession, or the most sensitive context. And yet in this one-and-only case we are to accept replacing the whole, original Greek word with an entirely different Greek word? If they caught anyone else doing this with any other verse in Scripture, they would be the first and loudest to denounce it themselves!

One of the real ironies here is that by doing just a basic, cursory search on the word "*aphistemi*" itself. By doing so we discover that even this alternative is not always interpreted as being something drastically different from "*apostasia*":

> *"After this man, Judas of Galilee rose up in the days of the census and* ***drew away*** *some people after him; he too perished, and all those who followed him were scattered. (Acts 5:37)*

Sometimes this word chosen by LaHaye to replace "*apostasia*"—a spiritual falling away, is actually used to also describe the exact, same spiritual "falling away" in other Scriptures as in…

> *Take care, brethren, that there not be in any one of you an evil, unbelieving heart that* ***falls away from the living God****. (Hebrews 3:12)*

> *But the Spirit explicitly says that in later times some will* ***fall away from the faith****, paying attention to deceitful spirits and doctrines of demons, (1 Timothy 4:1)*

Do you really think that the underlying Greek word "*aphistemi*" used in both of these verses is referring to anything other than a spiritual "departing"? Even the substitute Greek word LaHaye and company want to use as a cut-and-paste substitute is found in the original text to be often used to mean the exact, same thing they are attempting not just to simply replace, but to reverse what it plainly says!

This occurs twice in the Septuagint when Jewish scholars translated the Hebrew Old Testament into Greek. They actually chose "*aphistemi*" to describe a spiritual "departing":

> *"For they will t**urn your sons away from following Me** to serve other gods; then the anger of the LORD will be kindled against you and He will quickly destroy you. (Deuteronomy 7:4)*

> *"So you shall stone him to death because he has sought **to seduce you from the LORD your God** who brought you out from the land of Egypt, out of the house of slavery. (Deuteronomy 13:10)*

Just as the English resources LaHaye cites not only do not support his assertion, but actually and directly refute them, so works against him this attempt to cut-and-paste the Greek. We are not only supposed to accept his word that the English resources he cites don't say what they really say but something else entirely, so we are also expected to blindly accept his personal superimposition over the original Greek which again turns out to actually work against him. His switch-a-roo of the English backfires, his second switch-a-roo to pre-KJV Bibles backfires, and his third switch-a-roo of the Greek backfires. Does the phrase, "Three strikes and you're out" mean anything here?

Different Individuals but a Common Goal

As I stated at the outset, when someone inside or outside of the Church provide something additional to supplant the closed canon of God's Word such as the Book of Mormon, the Quran, their own special version of the Bible, or to cut-and-paste their way to a new conclusion, it is always to justify something that cannot be accomplished with the plain text as provided. In the cases of both Warren and LaHaye (and company), it is important to note that their common target is God's prophetic Word. In Warren's case it is to entice us to ignore prophecy and all things related to the End Times all together; in LaHaye's case it is to promote an eschatology which has provided the basis for the sale of tens of millions of books fictionalizing the End Times which cannot be supported by the plain and simple reading of Scripture.

Christ and the Apostles repeatedly warn that in the Last Days the Church will itself become the target of deception where the End Times are concerned. These warnings about false Christs, false prophets and false teaching have surprisingly little reference to cults such as Mormonism and outright false religions such as Islam; the common denominator to them all are repeated descriptions of attacks that will come from within the Church itself.

I readily admit there is a significant difference between Rick Warren and Tim LaHaye. In the course of reading some of Warren's *Purpose Driven* books, I was disturbed by not only never finding a clear, biblical presentation of the basic Gospel message of salvation, but alternative presentations which did not merely dilute the message, but more often redefined it into something else altogether. It is not surprising Warren wants us to ignore God's prophetic Word when, from the outset, he is obscuring even the most fundamental scriptural presentation of the basic Gospel of salvation.

In Tim LaHaye's writings, however, we repeatedly find the sound presentation of the Gospel of salvation. I don't doubt anyone who testifies that they came to know Christ through one of his books, because when it comes to presenting the scriptural message of salvation in

Christ, his preaching is flawless. The presentation of the Gospel is present in spite of a flawed choice of eschatology. This is probably why I was even more disturbed by what LaHaye has done than similar actions by Warren. But the hard truth we must face here is that just because someone's soteriology is right (the fancy seminary term for the doctrine of salvation), it does not automatically confer legitimacy to their eschatology (End Times theology).

No matter how many books someone sells or how large the attraction to their ministry, their teachings cannot be justified by undermining the ultimate foundation of God's Word upon which the true Body of Christ rests. This is not merely a case of not being able to rightly handle God's Word, but extending way beyond in an attempt to manipulate and change Scripture in order to present something that cannot be justified by the plain, given text. The fact that this common behavior is easily proved in the two men who have, in the past 15 or so years, sold more of their books to Christians than almost everyone else in Christendom combined should bring upon us great sorrow and spiritual remorse.

Because these activities took place in the course of their teachings related to the Rapture and/or eschatology, I have been forced to discuss these topics, but as stated previously, this is ***NOT*** the fundamental, core issue of what is wrong. Perhaps the Rapture will take place exactly when Pre-Tribulationism anticipates, but I refuse to believe that any position can be justified by attempting to alter the biblical text to make it appear so. Even more importantly, the ends never, ***ever*** justify the means as a matter of biblical principle. We cannot slice and dice God's Word as we see fit regardless of our intentions and no matter how well we might present the basic Gospel message in the process. We are called to a much higher standard.

> *"Do not think that I came to abolish the Law or the Prophets; I did not come to abolish but to fulfill. For truly I say to you, until heaven and earth pass away, not the smallest letter or stroke shall pass from the Law until all is accomplished. Whoever then annuls one of the least of these commandments, and teaches others to do the same, shall be called least in the kingdom of heaven; but whoever keeps and teaches them, he shall be called great in the kingdom of heaven. For I say to you that unless your righteousness surpasses that of the scribes and Pharisees, you will not enter the kingdom of heaven. (Matthew 5:17-20)*

Index

Scripture References

Genesis
1:5 • 37, 96
1:8 • 37, 96
3:15 • 184
4:16-17 • 240
10:8-12 • 240
19:11 • 111
21:2 • 85
22:17 • 36
26:4 • 36
32:1-4 • 208
32:24-32 • 246
34:18 • 85
37:9 • 36
37:34 • 70

Exodus
13:9, 16 • 209
13:16 • 209
15:11 • 200
19:4 • 189
19:5-6 • 189
23:15 • 85
32:1 • 36
32:4 • 231
32:6 • 231

Numbers
33 • 100

Deuteronomy
1:10 • 36
4:2 • 111
4:20 • 273
6:6-8 • 209
7:4 • 284
8:3 • x
11:18 • 209
12:32 • 273
13:10 • 284
19:15 • 110
27-28 • 47
32:11-12 • 189

Judges
12:1-7 • 100

1 Samuel
17:4-7 • 211

2 Samuel
24:15 • 85

1 Kings
10:14 • 211
10:19-20 • 211

2 Kings
2:23-25 • 100
10:12-14 • 100
17:13-15 • 47
18:11-12 • 47
18:13-19:37 • 214

2 Chronicles
9:13 • 211
32:1-31 • 214

Ezra
1:1-2 • 55
2:13 • 211
4:6 • 76
4:7 • 76
4:24 • 76
6:1-3a • 55
6:7 • 56
7:14-18 • 56
10:6 • 70

Nehemiah
1:1-4 • 56
1:4 • 70
1:11 • 56
2:7-8 • 57

Esther
9:20-21 • 99

Job
1:6 • 178
1:6-7 • 185
1:6-9 • 73
2:1 • 178
2:1-3 • 73
19:26 • 107

Psalms
2:9 • 183
17:15 • 107
35:10 • 200
71:19 • 200
89:8 • 200
113:5 • 200
124 • 190

Proverbs
11:14 • 245
24:6 • 245
30:6 • 111, 273

Isaiah
2:2 • 5
7:8-9 • 17
10:25 • 29
13:6, 9 • 170
14:12-14 • 36
14:12-17 • 181
14:14 • 179, 186, 200
17:12-13 • 14
21:8-9 • 229
26:19 • 107
26:20-21 • 190
36-37 • 214
40:31 • 189
52:11 • 233
53:2b • 180
54:5 • 183
66:22-24 • 107

Jeremiah
3:6-10 • 183
4:7 • 16
25:8-10 • 240
29:10 • 52
30:7 • 106, 107
49:14 • 16
49:22 • 16
50:17 • 16
50:44 • 16
51:6-10 • 234
51:8-9 • 229
51:45 • 234
51:60-64 • 239

Lamentations
2:6 • 29
4:19 • 16

Ezekiel
1:27 • 71
7:12 • 70
9 • 209
9:4 • 209
13:5 • 170
17:3 • 16
28:1-5 • 179, 237
28:1-19 • 237
28:11-13 • 179
28:14-17 • 180
30:5 • 170
38-39 • 33, 61, 87, 102, 104
39:9 • 61

Daniel
1:3-4, 6 • ix
1:08 • ix
1:12-16 • x
1:17-20 • x
2:1-3 • vi
2:4-7:28 • 27
2:4-11 • vi
2:12-16 • vii
2:17-18 • 43
2:17-19a • vii
2:19-23 • 43
2:20-23 • vii
2:26-30 • viii
2:27-28 • 5
2:31-35 • 3
2:32, 39 • 31
2:34-35 • 18, 118
2:35 • , 12, 11
2:36-38 • 6, 16
2:38 • 17
2:39 • 7, 16, 17
2:40 • 18, 125, 259, 261
2:40-43 • 7, 223
2:41 • 125, 177, 181, 198, 259
2:42 • 125, 260
2:43 • 125, 260
2:44 • 18, 223, 249
2:44-45 • 10, 23, 118
3 • 145
3:1 • 211
3:18 • 43
5:30-31 • 7
6:10-11 • 43
7:1 • 13
7:2 • 14
7:3 • 15
7:4 • 16
7:5 • 16, 31
7:6 • 17, 32
7:7 • 19, 25, 121, 125, 221, 254, 260
7:7-8 • 18, 198, 266
7:7, 24 • 177, 181

7:8 • 121, 254
7:9-11 • 23
7:11 • 122, 124, 145, 147, 179, 255, 258
7:12 • 24
7:13-14 • 24
7:17 • 14, 15
7:18 • 15
7:19 • 25
7:19-22 • 18
7:20 • 20, 25, 26, 121, 221, 254
7:20, 24 • 198
7:21 • 26, 123, 257
7:22 • 124, 147, 258
7:23 • 18, 19, 122, 125, 254, 260
7:24 • 20, 25, 121, 122, 125, 147, 221, 223, 254, 255, 260
7:24-26 • 20
7:25 • 25, 26, 62, 91, 95, 122, 123, 135, 145, 179, 255, 257
7:25a • 268
7:26 • 23, 26, 124, 258
7:26-27 • 25, 147
7:27 • 24, 125, 258
7:28 • 125, 260
8:1 • 27
8:1-2 • 27
8:3 • 16
8:3-4 • 31
8:5-8 • 32
8:9 • 121, 254
8:9-14 • 34
8:10 • 35, 123, 257
8:11 • 122, 124, 145, 179, 255, 257
8:12 • 123, 124, 147, 256, 257
8:13-14 • 54, 95, 124, 257
8:14 • 37
8:15-19 • 29
8:17 • 38
8:19 • 85
8:20 • 16, 31
8:21-22 • 17, 32
8:21-26 • 34
8:22 • 33
8:23 • 36, 122, 123, 147, 254, 255, 256
8:24 • 36, 40, 122, 147, 255
8:25 • 36, 37, 40, 122, 123, 124, 125, 145, 147, 179, 256, 258, 260
8:26 • 38
9:1-3 • 44
9:2 • 5, 51
9:3 • 45
9:4-6 • 46
9:7-8 • 46
9:9-12 • 47
9:13-14 • 48
9:15-17 • 48
9:18-19 • 49
9:20-22 • 43
9:20-23 • 50
9:22-23 • 51
9:24 • 53
9:24-27 • 49, 52
9:25 • 58
9:26 • 57, 135
9:26-27 • 59
9:27 • 22, 58, 62, 86, 88, 96, 124, 134, 165, 257, 258
9:27b • 60
10:1 • 69
10:1-11:1 • 70
10:2 • 72
10:2-3 • 70
10:4-9 • 71
10:10-14 • 72
10:12 • 44
10:13 • 187
10:14 • 67
10:15-21 • 73
11:1 • 74
11:2-12:3 • 70
11:2-34 • 74
11:21 • 86, 122, 125, 255, 260
11:22 • 123, 257
11:22-24 • 86
11:23 • 123, 256, 257
11:23-24 • 147
11:24 • 123, 125, 179, 256, 260
11:25-28 • 87
11:27 • 85
11:28 • 124, 258
11:29 • 85
11:30 • 123, 124, 257, 258
11:30-31 • 88
11:30-34 • 147
11:31 • 34, 124, 135, 174, 258
11:32 • 123, 257
11:32-35 • 89
11:34 • 123, 257
11:35 • 81, 85, 93
11:35-39 • 100
11:35-45 • 76
11:36 • 30, 90, 122, 179, 255
11:36-37 • 21, 145, 179
11:36, 45b • 93
11:37 • 122, 123, 256, 256
11:38 • 123, 256
11:39 • 123, 125, 179, 256, 260
11:40 • 122, 255
11:40-44 • 147
11:40-45 • 102
11:41 • 106, 122, 255
11:42 • 122, 255
11:43 • 122, 255
11:44 • 122, 255
11:45 • 124, 147, 258
12:1 • 105, 187
12:2 • 107
12:3 • xi, 44, 50, 108
12:4 • 108
12:4-13 • 70
12:5-7 • 109
12:6 • 112
12:6-7 • 98, 135
12:7 • 71, 91, 123, 257
12:8-9 • 110
12:10 • xi, 44, 50, 81, 111, 147, 210, 262
12:11 • 62
12:11-12 • 98, 124, 135, 258
12:11-13 • 112
12:12 • 116

Joel
1:6 • 16
1:15 • 170
3:1, 14 • 170

Amos
5:18-20 • 70
5:18, 20 • 170

Obadiah
15 • 170

Jonah
1:2 • 222
3:2 • 222
4:11 • 222

Micah
4:1 • 5
5:2-3 • 183
7:9 • 29

Nahum
3:4 • 240

Habakkuk
1:8 • 16
2:3 • 85

Zephaniah
1:7, 14 • 170
1:14-15 • 30

Zechariah
3:1 • 185
3:1-2 • 178
4:1-14 • 252
4:9-10 • 252
5:11 • 227
12:2-3 • 104
13:8-9 • 107

Matthew
2:1-8 • 138
2:13-23 • 183
2:16 • 251
4:1-11 • 178
4:8 • 200
4:16-17 • 110
5:14 • 221
5:17-20 • 285
7:2 • 31
7:13 • 153, 249
7:22-23 • 248
8:10 • 224
8:27 • 224
9:8 • 224
9:33 • 224
10:4 • 250
11:20-24 • 172
11:23 • 172
13:14-30 • 45
13:24-30, 36-43 • 68
13:39-40, 43 • 138
13:41-42 • 248
15:14 • 231
15:31 • 224
16:11-12 • 63
17:11 • 173
21:20 • 224
21:42-44 • 6, 118
22:1 • 253
22:22 • 224
23:13-33 • 172
23:33 • 172
23:39 • 57
24:3 • 138, 274, 275
24:3-4 • 275
24:3-8 • 62

24:4 • 275
24:4-5 • 154
24:4-8 • 136, 159
24:5 • 159
24:5-8 • 167
24:5, 11 • 121
24:6 • 59
24:8 • 265
24:9-10 • 89
24:9-14 • 22, 62, 136, 159, 190, 268
24:11 • 275
24:14 • 136, 267
24:15 • vi, 35, 62, 119, 151, 174
24:15-16 • 60, 63, 97, 136
24:15-18 • 88
24:15-20 • 136, 160
24:21 • 106, 160, 186, 267
24:21-22 • 63, 90
24:21-23 • 136
24:22 • 90, 137, 160, 186, 267
24:24 • 159, 207
24:24-25 • 275
24-25 • 275
24:25 • 155
24:29 • 137
24:29-31 • 63, 106, 160
24:30 • 24, 137
24:30-31 • 269
24:31 • 137, 146
24:32-33 • 144
24:32-35 • 263
24:36 • viii, 263
24:37 • 112
24:42-51 • 275
24:45 • 115
24:45-46 • x
24:45-51 • 44
25:1-13 • 44, 138, 225
25:13 • 144
26:6 • 24
26:14-15 • 250
26:22-25 • 250
26:47-50 • 250
26:56 • 250
27:14 • 224
28:20 • 138

Mark
1:12-13 • 178
3:6 • 253
3:19 • 250
5:20 • 224
6:51 • 224
12:12-13 • 253
13:2 • 24
13:14 • 35, 62
14:6 • 24
14:10 • 250
14:21 • 172
14:43-46 • 250
15:5 • 224
15:50 • 250

Luke
1:5-20 • 95
1:17 • 232
1:63 • 224
2:36 • 22, 62, 134
3:2-3 • 106
3:17 • 118
4:1-13 • 178
6:16 • 250
8:25 • 224
10:18 • 187
11:14 • 224
11:37-54 • 172
17:26 • 112
17:28 • 112
18:8 • 113
21:11 • 136
21:18-19 • 90
21:20 • 59, 136, 160, 174
21:20-21 • 184
21:20-22 • 88
21:24 • 89
21:25-26 • 15
21:26 • 59
22:3 • 250
22:3-4 • 250
22:47-53 • 250
24:41 • 224
24:44-45 • 131

John
1:1 • v, 72, 248
1:7 • 110
3:30 • 207
4:1-2 • 106
5:19 • 191
5:28-29 • 107
5:31-32 • 110
6:70 • 155, 184, 250
6:70-71 • 250
7:15 • 224
7:21 • 224
7:70-71 • 155
10:22 • 28, 37, 82
10:38 • 207
12:4-6 • 155
12:6 • 250
13:2 • 250
13:10-11 • 250
13:24-30 • 155
13:26 • 250
13:27 • 184, 250
13:30 • 155, 250
13:41 • 224
14:15 • x
15:10 • x
16:7-11 • 147
17:12 • 153, 248, 249
18:2-12 • 250
20:20-23 • 131

Acts
1:6-7 • 94, 274, 275
1:6-8 • 117
1:7 • 275
1:8 • 63, 130, 267, 268
1:9-11 • 138
1:16 • 250
1:17 • 250
1:24-25 • 153
2:7 • 224
2:16-20 • 162
4:13 • 224
5 • 151
5:36-37 • 121
5:37 • 283
9:1-7 • 72
10 • 130
12:10 • 283
15:12 • 72
17 • 141
17:10-11 • 132
17:10-12 • 120
18:2 • 28

Romans
5:8-9 • 170
6:19 • 248
9-11 • 53
11:25 • 162
12:2 • ix

1 Corinthians
1:18-29 • v
1:20 • 210
1:24, 30 • v
1:30 • ii, 108, 210
4:6 • 111, 273
5:5 • 170

2 Corinthians
5:17 • 246
6:14-18 • 234
11:13-14 • 180

Galatians
3:28 • 197, 205

Ephesians
4:11-16 • 11
4:14 • 12
5:11 • 234
6:12 • 73, 216

Philippians
1:28 • 153
2:9-11 • 11

Colossians
3:16 • ii, 108

1 Thessalonians
4:13-14 • 142, 276
4:15-17 • 114, 143, 160
4:15-18 • 277
4:17 • 24
5:1-2 • 144
5:1-10 • 160
5:2 • 170
5:3-7 • 144
5:8-10 • 144

2 Thessalonians
2:1 • 146
2:1-2 • 145
2:1-4 • 114, 276
2:1-12 • 142, 273
2:2 • 170, 257
2:2-3 • 21
2:3 • 19, 54, 93, 146, 152, 160, 255, 256, 280
2:3-4 • 35, 62, 249
2:3-4, 8-9 • 247
2:3-5 • 145
2:3-8 • 248
2:4 • 154, 160, 179, 256, 258
2:4b • 114
2:6-7 • 146, 154
2:6-10 • 267
2:7 • 157, 160, 238
2:8 • 177
2:8-10 • 53, 115, 147
2:9 • 160, 207, 256
2:10 • 256
2:10-11 • 160
2:11-12 • 147

1 Timothy
1:10 • 113
4:1 • 283
6:14 • 113

2 Timothy
4:1 • 113

4:8 • 114

Titus
2:11-14 • 113
2:12 • 116
2:14 • 116

Hebrews
1:1-2 • 109, 110
3:12 • 283
6:4-6 • 181
11:39 • 69

1 Peter
1:20 • 110
1:20-21a • 109
3:20 • 112
4:17 • 170
5:13 • 217, 222, 232

2 Peter
1:19-21 • viii, 165, 263
2:1-3 • 249
3:7 • 249
3:9 • 181
3:14-18 • 115
3:15-16 • 249
3:15b-18 • 142

1 John
2:1 • 11
2:2 • 11
2:18 • 121, 154, 160, 195
2:18-20 • 250
2:18-24 • 263
2:19 • 155, 160, 196, 205, 211, 256
2:19-20 • 155
2:20 • 155, 160
2:21 • 155
2:21-23 • 156
2:22 • 160, 195, 258
3:4 • 152, 248
4:1 • 159
4:1-3 • 157
4:3 • , 159, 258, 11
4:4-6 • 157
4:6 • 159
4:19 • 160

2 John
7 • , 158, 159, 258, 11

Revelation
1 • 71
1:12-20 • 71
1:19 • 163
2:2 • 157
2:7 • 90
2:8 • 216
2:10 • 200
2:11 • 90
2:13 • 216, 219
2:14-15 • 230
2:17 • 90
2:20 • 220, 230
2:24 • 216
2:26 • 90
2:27 • 183
3:5 • 90
3:9 • 216
3:12 • 90
3:21 • 90
4:1 • 238, 278
4-5 • 13
4-19 • 238
5 • 278
5:2 • 239
6:1-2 • 86, 97, 166
6:2 • 266
6:3-4 • 167
6:8 • 167, 266
6-18 • 278
7:3 • 209
7:8 • 20
7:9-11 • 223
7:9-17 • 168, 169, 238
7:13-14 • 71
7:14 • 164
8:7 • 171
8:8-9 • 171
8:10-11 • 171
8:12 • 171
8:13 • 169, 172
8-20 • 238
9:1-11 • 173
9:12 • 173
9:13-19 • 173
9:20-21 • 111, 240
10:1-3 • 239
10-13 • 175
11:1-2 • 89, 174
11:2 • 98, 100, 135
11:3 • 98, 99, 135
11:4 • 252
11:5 • 207
11:7 • 135, 173
11:8 • 222, 232
11:10 • 173
11:11-13 • 173
11:14 • 173
11:15 • 173
12:1 • 220
12:3 • 20, 177, 198, 221
12:3-4 • 267
12:4 • 35, 258, 260
12:5 • 183
12:6 • 98, 99, 135, 184
12:7 • 20
12:7-9 • 105, 185
12:7-12 • 35
12:9 • 177, 182, 259, 261
12:9, 12 • 30
12:10-12 • 187
12:11 • 188
12:12 • 189, 259
12-13 • 198
12:13 • 171, 257
12:13-14 • 136, 184, 189
12:13-17 • 182
12:15-16 • 189
12:17 • 190, 206, 257
12:18 • 20
13:1 • 20, 25, 196, 198, 209, 221, 258, 260
13:1-2 • 17, 177, 181
13:1-10 • 194
13:2 • 198, 254
13:3 • 199, 201, 256, 266
13:3-4 • 199, 266
13:4 • 256
13:4-7 • 98, 100
13: 5 • 255
13:5 • 25, 91, 136, 212, 217, 258
13:5-6 • 21, 25, 200
13:5-7 • 99
13:6 • 258
13:7 • 19, 25, 255, 257
13:7-8 • 200
13:8 • 74, 256
13:9-10 • 201, 202
13:11 • 205, 259, 261
13:11-18 • 194
13:12 • 199, 206, 259, 267
13:13 • 209, 259
13:13-14 • 207, 243
13:14 • 199, 259, 267
13:14-15 • 243, 267
13:15 • 208, 259
13:16-17 • 243, 267
13:16-18 • 209
13:17 • 223, 259
13:18 • i, ii, xi, , 223
14:6-7 • 200, 215
14:8 • 216, 230
14:9 • 269
14:9-10 • 200
14:9-11 • 216
14:9-13 • 268
14:11 • 209
14:14-15 • 24
14:14-16 • 269
14:17-20 • 269
15:1 • 60
16:9-11, 21 • 111
16:18 • 96
16:19 • 222, 230
16:21 • 198
17 • 220
17:1 • 71, 226, 261
17:1-2 • 231
17:1-7 • 219, 220
17:2 • 220, 241, 261
17:3 • 20, 25, 177, 181, 221, 231, 241, 260, 261
17:4 • 220, 226, 241, 261
17:5 • 241, 261
17:6 • 220, 242, 261
17:6-7 • 224
17:8 • 74, 201, 224, 242, 254, 258, 259
17:8, 11 • 249
17:8-14 • 221
17:9 • 20, 225, 231, 242
17:9-10 • xi, 255, 261
17:9-11 • ii, 221, 222
17:10 • 231, 242
17:11 • 242, 254, 259
17:11-12, 17 • 21
17:12 • 20, 25, 242, 260
17:12-13 • 8, 102, 198
17:12-14 • 223
17:13 • 242, 260, 265
17:14 • 243
17:15 • 14, 226, 230, 231, 242, 261
17:15-18 • 227
17:16 • 20, 25, 242, 260
17:16-17 • , 12
17:16-18 • 236
17:17 • 242, 260
17-18 • 85, 90, 191
17:18 • 222, 226, 231, 242, 261
18:1-3 • 229
18:2 • 242
18:3 • 242
18:4-8 • 233
18:5 • 242
18:7 • 242
18:8 • 261
18:9 • 231, 261
18:9-10 • 235
18:9-19 • 217

18:10 • 222
18:11 • 261
18:11-20 • 236
18:16 • 222
18:17-18 • 261
18:18-19 • 222
18:20 • 237, 238
18:21 • 222
18:21-24 • 239
18:24 • 240, 242, 261
19:7 • 220
19:8 • 220
19:11-16 • 86, 143, 166
19:11-21 • 21, 115, 268
19:12 • 198
19:15 • 183
19:19-20 • 25
19:20 • 38, 195, 205, 249
19:20-21 • 24, 221
20:4-6 • 108
20:7-10 • 221
20:10 • 181
20:11-15 • 24
20:14 • 171
21:7 • 90
21:9 • 71
22:4 • 209
22:6-7 • 72, 110
22:10 • 109, 110
22:11 • 111
22:16 • 72
22:18-19 • 273
22:20 • 271

General References

1 & 2 Maccabees • 82
"1,260 days" • 98, 99, 116
"1,290 days" • 99, 116
"1,335 days" • 99, 116
2 Maccabees 9:5-10 • 38
15th of Adar • 99
"42" • 200
"42 months" • 98, 99
69th and 70th week(s) • 117, 162, 163
70 ad • 4, 28, 35, 129, 130
70th Week of Daniel • 21, 22, 61, 62, 63, 88, 95, 97, 100, 105, 112, 134, 135, 136, 137, 143, 146, 148, 162, 163, 164, 165, 166, 167, 174, 175, 184, 185, 188, 198, 199, 212, 213, 217, 267, 269
95 ad • 130
144,000, the • 198, 209
666 • ii, 95, 211, 214

A

Aaron • 196, 207, 208, 231
Abomination of Desolation • 4, 30, 32, 34, 35, 53, 54, 60, 62, 63, 81, 88, 89, 90, 92, 94, 96, 97, 106, 112, 114, 115, 119, 120, 124, 132, 135, 137, 138, 145, 146, 148, 152, 156, 160, 162, 163, 164, 165, 174, 179, 184, 185, 186, 188, 190, 195, 200, 201, 208, 212, 213, 214, 267, 261, 266, 267, 257
Abraham • 72, 85, 206
Absalom • 25, 253
Adam • 54
Adar • 99
Adonikam • 211
adown (Heb. #113) = lord, or sir • 74
Africa • 87, 89
"age to come, the" • 162, 181, 184
Ahaseurus • 76
Ahmadinejad, Mahmoud • 253
Al-Aqsa Mosque • 35
Alexander • 193
Alexander's Empire • 75
Alexander the Great • 7, 9, 17, 32, 33, 35, 75, 76, 247
Alexandria • 83, 84
Amazon.com • 219
Amin, Idi • 253
Ammon • 106
Amplified Bible, The • 280
"And THEN The End Will Come" by D. E. Isom • 22, 30, 61, 132, 138, 169
Anna • 134
anomia (Gr. #458) = lawlessness • 152, 248
"Antichrist" by A. W. Pink • 245, 262
antichristos (Gr. #500) = antichrist • 132, 11
Antiochus Epiphanes IV • 4, 21, 25, 34, 35, 36, 37, 38, 39, 41, 53, 73, 74, 79, 81, 82, 83, 84, 85, 87, 90, 91, 92, 95, 96, 101, 102, 118, 119, 120, 132, 145, 154, 193, 196, 203, 207, 208, 214, 245, 247, 252, 253, 266, 270, 271
Antiochus III • 77, 78, 79
Antiochus II Theos • 76
Antipater • 17
aphistemi (Gr. #868) = departing • 115, 283, 284
Apocrypha • 28, 82
apokalupsis (Gr. #602) = revelation or unveiling • 109, 114, 139, 169
apoleia (Gr. #684) = desruction or perdition • 153, 248
Apollonius • 84
apostasia (Gr. #646) = apostasy • 115, 279, 280, 281, 282, 283
apostasy • 36, 40, 114, 141
apostate church • 235, 237
Arabian Peninsula • 87
Armageddon • 87
Armenia • 31
Artaxerxes • 56, 76
Ascension • 95, 109, 110, 119, 138, 267, 275
Asia Minor • 17, 31
Assyria • 222
Assyria, King of • 25, 214, 253
Assyrian Empire • 16, 31, 104, 227
Assyrian, The • 253
Athaliah • 220
Attalus • 82
Augustus Caesar • 217
Augustus, Julius • 253
avon (Heb. #5771) = iniquity • 54

B

Babylon • 7, 9, 14, 16, 17, 18, 24, 25, 31, 33, 37, 39, 71, 102, 103, 198, 217, 218, 219, 220, 222, 224, 225, 227, 228, 229, 230, 231, 232, 233, 234, 235, 237, 238, 239, 240, 241, 243, 247, 253, 260, 261, 265, 268, 270, 271
Babylonian Captivity • 3, 4, 52, 69, 71, 130, 218, 252
Babylonian Empire • 15, 104, 117, 227, 229, 235
Babylon, King of • 13, 16, 25, 253
Babylon the Great • ii, 9, 33, 58, 102, 161, 170, 215, 219, 220, 225, 229, 231, 268, 233, 234, 235, 237, 239, 240, 241, 243, 254, 262, 265, 267, 270
ballo (Gr. $906) = thrown • 171
Bar Kochba Revolt • 28
Belshazzar • 69, 235
Berea • 141
Berean(s) • 120, 134
Berenice • 76, 77
Bethlehem • 197
Bethsaida • 172
Beza Bible • 281
Bhagavad Gita • 274
Bible codes • 210
"birth pangs" • 94, 97, 112, 152, 159, 162, 164, 167, 169, 170, 201, 266
Bithynia • 76
"blessed hope, the" • 113, 114, 116
Blood Moons • xi
Bonaparte, Napoleon • 25, 81, 253
book of life • 74, 194, 200, 201, 202

Book of Mormon, The • 276
Bowls, The • 165, 169, 170, 171, 172, 174, 175, 184, 188, 218
7th Bowl • 198
Breeches Bible • 281
Bride of Christ • 220, 227
Brown Shirts • 241
Buddhism • 206
buonos (Gr. #1015) = hill • 221
Byzantine Empire • 39

C

Cain • 240
Cambyses • 76
Camp David Accords • 58
Capernaum • 172
Carson, D. A. • 61
Cassander • 17, 33, 76
Catholic Church • 232, 235, 237
Catholicism • 104, 206
Ceausescu, Nicolae • 253
Charlemagne • 253
chatta-ah (Heb. #2403) = sin • 54
Chorazin • 172
Christophany • 71
chronos (Gr. #5550) = a sequence of events • 94, 95, 97, 100, 112
Claudius • 28
Cleopatra • 78, 79, 82
Clinton administration • 58
Conquering King • 60
Constantine the Great • 35, 253
Constitution, U. S. • 162
Copeland, Kenneth • 156
Cornelius • 130
Court of Israel • 252
Court of Priests • 252
Court of the Gentiles • 252
Court of Women • 252
Coverdale Bible • 281
Cranmer Bible • 281
Creation Narrative • 37, 96
Custer, General • 199
cut-and-paste • 274, 276, 277, 280, 282, 283, 284
Cyprus • 84
Cyrus • 27, 55, 56, 69

D

Damoxenus • 78
dara'own (Heb. #1860) = contempt • 107
Darius • 43, 44, 55, 56, 74, 76, 235
Darius Hystaspes • 76
David • 211
"day of the Lord, the" • 30, 63, 85, 114, 115, 137, 138, 144, 145, 146, 160, 162, 163, 164, 170, 186, 276, 277, 278, 279, 282
Demetrius • 79
Deutero-Daniel • 67
Deutero-Isaiah • 67
diabolos (Gr. #1227) = slanderer, false accuser • 185
Diaspora • 28, 152, 163
"Didache, The" • 148, 149
Disneyland • 208
Dome of the Rock • 156
Dominionism • 10, 53

E

Eastern Orthodoxy • 232
Ecumenism • 206
Edom • 106, 197, 252, 255, 270
Egypt • 16, 17, 31, 33, 36, 48, 76, 77, 78, 82, 83, 84, 87, 222, 232
Egyptian Empire • 104
Eleusis • 84
Elijah • 100, 173, 232
"Elijah To Come" by D. E. Isom • 173
Elisha • 100
Elymais • 79
"end of the age, the" • 138, 141, 143, 162, 184, 185, 218, 223, 233
Ephesus • 157
Epimanes • 82
epiphaneia (Gr. #2015) = to appear, or manifest • 113, 115
episunagoge (Gr. #1997) = gathering • 146, 169
Eropus • 78
Etch A Sketch • 134
Ethiopia • 31, 87
Eumenes • 82
Euphrates River • 77
European Union • 88
Evangelicism • 273
Eve • 54, 182
Exodus, the (from Egypt) • 48, 71, 188, 189, 195, 207
Ezra, the Scribe • 56, 69

F

Fall, The • 54
False Prophet • 15, 17, 19, 24, 30, 38, 57, 103, 193, 195, 196, 197, 206, 207, 209, 211, 213, 214, 215, 217, 218
Farad, Wallace • 253
Feast of Dedication, the • 28, 37, 82, 92
Feast of Unleavened Bread • 71
Final Judgment • 163, 278
Flood, The • 219
Fortuna • 219
"forty-two months" • 22, 91, 200, 212, 268
Frank, Jacob • 254
"fullness of the Gentiles, the" • 162

G

Gabriel • 29, 38, 43, 50, 95
Galilee, the land of • 197
Gamaliel • 151
Garden of Eden • 54, 182
Garden of Gethsemane • 250
Gaza • 77
Gematria • 210
Geneva Bible • 281, 282
Germany • 188
Gog and Magog • 61, 87, 102, 104
golden calf • 208, 231
Goliath • 211, 253
Google • 96
"great tribulation" • 22, 30, 63, 155, 160, 163, 186, 200, 201, 235, 268
Greece • 7, 9, 17, 18, 24, 31, 32, 73, 33, 39, 74, 76, 79, 103, 222, 33, 222
Greek Empire • 15, 17, 24, 27, 33, 34, 104, 117

H

Hadrian, Emperor • 35
Haman • 253
HaMaschiah ben David • 60
HaMaschiash ben Jozef • 60
Hannah • 220
Hanukkah • 28, 37, 82
hapax legomenon (Lat.) • 96
"Harpazo" by Jacob Prasch • 142
harpazo (Gr. #726) = to snatch violently away • 94, 143, 144, 145, 146, 147, 149, 160, 169, 201, 225, 263, 269, 283
Hasmonean Period • 82, 132
Heliodorus • 79
Hellenization • 9
Herodian(s) • 84, 119
Herodias • 220
Herod the Great • 19, 21, 25, 138, 183, 197, 211, 251, 252, 253, 254, 270, 271
Hezekiah • 214
Hindson, Ed • 277
Hindus • 274
Hislop, Alexander • 219
historical proof-texting • 282
Hitler, Adolph • 25, 81, 86, 232, 240, 241, 253

Holy of Holies • 35, 119, 245
House of Herod • 253
Hussein, Saddam
Saddam • 253

I

Ice, Thomas • 277
Idumean • 197, 252
Il, Kim Jon • 253
India • 17
inter-faith • 216
Inter-Testamental Period • 21, 28, 82, 132, 247
Ionia • 33
Iran • 33, 87, 89
Iraq • 33, 102
Ishbi-benob • 253
Islam • 87, 104, 156, 206, 270, 284,
Islamic • 269, 270
Israel
land of • 31, 33, 35
Northern Kingdom of • 32

J

Jannes and Jambres • 207, 208, 209
Jehovah's Witnesses • 96, 156, 274
Jehu • 100
Jephthah • 100
Jerome • 283
Jerusalem • 28, 46, 47, 48, 51, 52, 53, 55, 56, 57, 58, 59, 64, 78, 79, 83, 84, 88, 89, 99, 104, 130, 135, 136, 138, 156, 163, 184, 222, 227, 232, 237, 246
Jezebel • 220
John the Baptist • 95, 105, 106, 110, 179, 195, 203, 207, 213, 232, 243, 262, 268
Jones, Jim • 253
Jordan River • 78
Josephus • 28, 82
Joshua, the high priest • 178, 185, 252
Joshua, the Patriarch • 47
Judas Iscariot • 151, 153, 155, 156, 159, 172, 180, 184, 185, 196, 197, 248, 249, 250, 251, 253, 254
Judas Maccabeus • 37
Judas of Galilee • 151, 254
Judea • 78, 79, 82, 84, 88, 97, 105, 136, 154, 197
Jupiter • 4, 35, 79, 84

K

kairos (Gr. #2540) = somethng timed • 94, 95, 97, 99, 100, 112, 188
Kingdom Now Theology • 10, 53
King James Version • 277, 280
"king of the North, the" • 120, 270
Kissinger, Henry • 210
Kittim • 84, 88, 92
Koresh, David • 253

L

LaHaye, Tim • 276, 277, 278, 280, 281, 282, 283, 284, 285
Lahmi • 253
Lake of Fire • 24, 38, 153, 154, 181, 187, 188, 220, 221, 12
Laodice • 76, 77
Last Supper • 155, 250
"Late, Great Planet Earth, The" by Hal Lindsey • iii, 103
Latin Vulgate • 143, 283
leap month • 99
leaven • 63
"Left Behind" by Tim LaHaye & Jerry B. Jenkins • 276
Lenin, Vladimir • 253
Levant • 79, 104
Libya • 87
Lindsey, Hal • iii, 103
Los Angeles • 237
Lot • 112
Lucius Scipio Asiaticus • 78
Lydia • 16, 31, 33
Lysimachus • 17, 33, 76

M

Maccabean Revolt • 28, 34, 119
Maccabean(s) • 84
Maccabees • 82, 84, 90
Maccabees, Books of • 28, 36
Macedonia • 17, 33, 76
Magi • 138, 166
Magnesia • 78
Manifest Sons of Destiny • 53
"man of lawlessness, the" • 93, 145, 147, 152, 159, 247, 248, 249, 256
"man of sin" • 54, 248
Man of Sixes • 253
Manson, Carles • 253
mark of the Beast • v
Mary, the mother of Jesus • 219, 220
Media • 16, 31
Media-Persia • 198
Medo-Persia • 7, 9, 14, 16, 18, 24, 103
Medo-Persian Empire • 7, 15, 16, 17, 24, 27, 31, 32, 33, 104, 117, 235
Memphis • 83
Menelaus • 84, 90
Menocles • 78
Michael • 72, 73, 74, 105, 185, 186, 187, 188
Middle East • 17, 77, 87, 88, 89, 104
Mid-Tribulationism • 61
Millennial Kingdom/Reign • 4, 24, 25, 39, 53, 60, 73, 94, 138, 163, 164, 165, 221, 275, 277
Millerites • 95
Moab • 106
Mohammed • 253
Moriel Ministries (www.Moriel.org) • i
Mormonism • 156, 284
Mormons • 274
Moses • 183, 196, 207, 273
Mt. Ebal • 47
Mt. Gerizim • 47
Muslim • 276
Mussolini, Benito • 253
"mystery of iniquity" • 154
"mystery of lawlessness" • 154, 157
mystery religions • 219, 222

N

Nasser, Gamal • 253
Nativity Narrative • 137, 209
Nazareth • 197
Nebuchadnezzar • vi, viii, ix, x, 14, 16, 18, 29, 31, 39, 43, 69, 75, 81, 102, 119, 120, 145, 162, 193, 206, 207, 208, 211, 214, 245, 247, 253, 266
Nehemiah, the Cup Bearer • 56
Nero • 210
New American Standard Bible • 277
New Earth • 186
New Heaven • 186
New King James Version • 280
Nile River • 84
Nimrod • 218, 240, 253
Nineveh • 222, 240
Noah • 112, 144

O

Olivet Discourse • vi, viii, 22, 24, 25, 35, 44, 45, 46, 59, 62, 64, 94, 97, 105, 106, 112, 114, 115, 132, 133, 134, 136, 137, 138, 141, 144, 146, 151, 152, 154, 155, 158, 159, 162, 163, 164, 165, 167, 168, 169, 170, 174, 196, 200, 202, 207, 211, 212, 269, 274, 275
Olso Accords • 58
omai (Gr. #3759) - woes • 172

"one Messiah, two comings" • 118
orge (Gr. #3709) = wrath • 30
oros (Gr. #3735) = mountains • 221

P

Palestine • 17
Paneas • 78
Pantheon • 216, 217, 219, 228, 267
Pan-Tribulationism • 61
Parable of the Faithful vs. Evil Slave • 44
Parable of the Talents • 45
Parable of the Tares • 68
Parable of the Ten Virgins • 44
parousia (Gr. #3953) = the coming • 143, 144, 145, 147
Passover • 71, 155
Patmos, the Isle of • 129, 151, 193
Paul • 141, 142, 143, 144, 145, 146, 273, 276, 277, 279, 280
Pelusium • 83, 84
Pentecost, the Day of • 120, 129, 130, 132, 148, 152, 163
Pergamos • 82
Pergamum • 219, 230
Persia • 14, 16, 18, 24, 31, 32, 39, 72, 73, 74, 76, 77, 78, 222
pesha (Heb. #6588) = transgression • 54
pesher • 196
Pharaoh • 183, 188, 195, 199
Pharaohs, the • 253
Pharisees • 172, 253
pharmakeia (Gr. #5331) = sorcery • 240
Philip the king of Macedon • 78
Phrygia • 33
phylacteries • 209
Pink, A. W. • 245, 262
pipto (Gr. $4098) = fell • 171
pleso (Strong's #4141) = struck • 171
Pompey, Roman General • 4, 35, 119, 120, 132, 196, 245, 253
Popes, the • 253
Popilius Loenas • 84
"Popular Handbook on the Rapture, The" Edited by Tim LaHaye, Thomas Ice & Ed Hindson • 276, 277, 280
porneuo (Gr. #4203) = immorality • 230
Post-Babylonian Return • 218
Post-Tribulationism • 61
Pot, Pol • 253
Prasch, Jacob (Moriel Ministries) • i, 61, 99, 113, 245, 262
"pre-counterfeiting" • 133
"present age, the" • 162
Pre-Trib Research Center, The • 278
Pre-Tribulational • 278
Pre-Tribulationism • 61, 113, 278, 279, 285
Pre-Tribulationist(s) • 238, 278, 279, 280
Pre-Wrath • 61
"progressive revelation of God, the" • 133, 134, 193
Promised Land • 47, 48, 71
Ptolemaic Empire • 32, 33, 87, 104, 118
Ptolemy • 33
Ptolemy III Euergetes • 77
Ptolemy II Philadelphus • 76
Ptolemy I Soter • 17, 76
Ptolemy IV Philopater • 77
Ptolemy V Epiphanes • 78
Ptolemy VI Philometor • 82, 83
Purim • 99
"Purpose Driven Life, The" by Rick Warren • 274, 275

Q

qodesh qadashim (Heb.) = most holy place • 54
Queen of Heaven • 219
Quran • 156, 284,

R

Rabshakeh • 214
Raphia • 77, 78
Rapture • viii, 61, 112, 113, 114, 115, 116
rapturo (Lat.) = used for the Greek "harpazo" • 283
rapturo (Lat.) = used for the Greek "harpazo" • 143
Reformation, The • 216
Replacementism • 10, 53
Replacementist(s) • 10
Roman Catholic Church • 216, 219
Roman Emperors, the • 25, 253, 266
Roman Empire • 7, 8, 9, 10, 24, 15, 19, 20, 39, 42, 117, 102, 117, 119, 166, 199, 198, 217, 222, 223, 227, 228, 232, 247, 12
Roman Empire, Eastern • 39
Roman Empire, Western • 39
Rome • 8, 9, 19, 28, 39, 78, 79, 84, 86, 88, 102, 103, 104, 118, 165, 196, 197, 198, 217, 219, 221, 222, 223, 232, 237, 242, 252, 270, 271
Romulus Augustulus • 217
Russia • 33, 87, 89
Ruth, the woman • 220

S

Sabbath • 36
Saddam Hussein • 233
Samaria • 130
Sanhedrin • 58
Saph • 253
Sarah • 85, 220
Satan • 19, 21, 30, 35, 36, 39, 81, 86, 87, 88, 93, 105, 106, 112, 114, 115, 135, 147, 148, 156, 159, 160, 169, 171, 175, 177, 178, 179, 180, 181, 182, 183, 184, 185, 186, 187, 188, 190, 191, 193, 195, 196, 199, 200, 201, 202, 205, 206, 207, 209, 212, 213, 215, 216, 218, 219, 221, 225, 226, 227, 228, 230, 232, 235, 237, 241, 242, 267, 247, 250, 256, 259, 266, 267, 268, 270, 214
Satanas (Gr. #4567) = Satan • 185
Satan (Heb. #7854) - Satan • 185
Schneerson, Menachem • 254
Scopas • 78
Scribes • 172
Scythia • 31
Seals, The • 164, 167, 168, 172, 196, 217
  1st Seal • 86, 97, 170, 175, 184, 266
  4th Seal • 266
  5th Seal • 168, 186, 190
  6th & 7th • 164
  6th and 7th Seals • 169, 238
  6th Seal • 170, 173
  7th Seal • 169, 170
Second Temple Period • 117
Seleucid • 102, 103, 104
Seleucid Dynasty • 34
Seleucid Empire/Kingdom • 32, 33, 35, 39, 87, 88, 103, 104, 118, 247, 270
Seleucus • 33
Seleucus I • 76
Seleucus II Callinicus • 77
Seleucus III Ceraunus • 77
Seleucus I Nicator • 17, 76

Seleucus IV Philopater • 79
Semiramis • 219
Sennacherib • 253
Septuagint • ii, 13, 30, 94, 283, 284
serpent and the dragon, the • 86
Sethur • 253
seven churches, the • 216
"seven hills" • 231
"seven kings" • 231
"seven mountains" • 231
Seventh-day Adventists • 96
seventy, the • 187
seventy weeks • 52, 53, 54, 55, 64, 65
seven weeks and sixty-two weeks • 52, 55
"seven years" • 134
"Shadows of the Beast" by Jacob Prasch • i, 113, 156, 245, 262
Shadrach, Meshach & Abed-nego • 208
Shinar • 218, 227
Simon Bar Kochba • 152, 254
Siri • 208
Smyrna • 200
Sodom • 232, 235
Sodom and Gomorrah • 110, 235
Solano, Xavier • 253
Solomon • 211, 253, 273
"son of destruction, the" • 145, 153, 247, 248, 249, 256
"son of perdition, the" • ii, 19, 153, 156, 159, 249, 250
Soter • 253
soteriology • 285
spirit of antichrist, the • 151, 154, 157, 158, 159,
Stalin • 25, 86
Stalin, Joseph • 253
Suffering Servant • 60, 275
Syria • 17, 31, 33, 76, 77, 78, 83, 102

T

Talmud • 98
Tanakh • 120
Taurus • 79
Temple
Herod's Temple • 252, 253
Millennial Temple • 96
Solomon's Temple • 252
Tribulational Temple • 58, 96, 163, 200, 213, 252, 253
Temple Institute, The • 58
Temple Mount • 58, 156
"textual reversal" • 133
thaumazo (Gr. #2296) = wonder, amazed, awestruck, astonished, marveled • 224
"The Great Tribulation" • 137
therion (Gr. #2342) = unclean beasts • ii, 13
Thessalonica • 141, 146
"The Tribulation" • 22, 61, 62, 63, 114, 133, 134, 137, 279
Theudas • 151
Third Reich • 188
thlipsis (Gr. #2347) = tribulation • 22
Thrace • 17, 33, 76
three woes • 169, 172
Thyatira • 230
"time of Jacob's distress, the" • 106
"times of the Gentiles, the" • 88
"time, times, and half a time" • 22, 91
Titus, Roman General • 35
Torah • 36, 37, 85
Tower of Babel • 218, 224, 240, 270
"tribulation" • 63, 201, 235
"tribulation saints" • 238
Triumphal Entry • 57
Triumphalism • 10, 53
Trumpets, The • 165, 169, 170, 171, 172, 173, 174, 175, 184, 196
1st Trumpet • 171
2nd Trumpet • 171
3rd Trumpet • 171
4th Trumpet • 171, 172
5th Trumpet • 172
6th and 7th Trumpets • 173
7th Trumpet • 173, 175
Tung, Mao Tse • 253
Turkey • 33, 87, 89, 219
"twelve hundred and sixty days" • 173
twenty-four elders • 278
"Two Babylons, The" by Alexander Hislop • 219
"two olive trees" • 252
Two Witnesses • 99, 109, 110, 135, 173, 174, 175, 185, 196, 207, 213, 252
Tyndale Bible • 281, 282
Tyndale Concise Bible Commentary • 282
Tyre, King of • 25, 237, 253

U

United Nations • 79, 104, 233
United States • 162, 217

V

Venus • 219

W

Walk with the Word (www.WalkWithTheWord.org) • 273
Warren, Rick • 274, 275, 276, 277, 280, 281, 282, 284, 285
Washington, D.C. • 168
World War II • 266
Wycliffe Bible • 281, 282

X

Xerxes • 76

Y

YouTube • 143

Z

za'am (Heb. #2195) = indignation • 30
Zacharias • 95
Zealot • 119
Zeitgeist (Ger.) = spirit of the age • 157, 159
Zerubbabel • 185, 252
Zeus • 34, 208
Ziklag • 253
Zion • 246
zoa (Gr. #2225) - singular for "zoon", or clean animals • ii, 13
zoon (Gr. #2226) = clean beasts • 13
Zvi, Shabbati • 254

Lightning Source UK Ltd.
Milton Keynes UK
UKHW030634200420
361941UK00007B/309